# Schools for an Information Age

# SCHOOLS FOR AN INFORMATION AGE

## Reconstructing Foundations for Learning and Teaching

BYRD L. JONES
ROBERT W. MALOY

PRAEGER

**Westport, Connecticut**
**London**

**Library of Congress Cataloging-in-Publication Data**

Jones, Byrd L.
    Schools for an information age : reconstructing foundations for
learning and teaching / Byrd L. Jones, Robert W. Maloy.
        p.    cm.
    Includes bibliographical references and index.
    ISBN 0–275–95395–5 (alk. paper). — ISBN 0–275–95396–3 (pb : alk.
paper)
    1. Education—United States—Aims and objectives. 2. Educational
change—United States. 3. Constructivism (Education)—United
States. 4. Educational technology—United States. 5. Educational
equality—United States. 6. Pluralism (Social sciences)—United
States. I. Maloy, Robert W. II. Title.
LA217.2.J65        1996
370'.0973—dc20     95–34417

British Library Cataloguing in Publication Data is available.

Library of Congress Catalog Card Number: 95–34417
ISBN:  0–275–95395–5
       0–275–95396–3 (pbk.)

First published in 1996

Praeger Publishers, 88 Post Road West, Westport, CT 06881
An imprint of Greenwood Publishing Group, Inc.

Printed in the United States of America

The paper used in this book complies with the
Permanent Paper Standard issued by the National
Information Standards Organization (Z39.48–1984).

10 9 8 7 6 5 4 3 2 1

# Contents

# Illustrations

# Preface

This book invites prospective and experienced educators to envision new schools for an emerging information age. The future is being forged every day by the ways students and teachers make sense of their experiences in classrooms. Learning is a developmental process of practicing skills and competencies in ever-widening spheres of endeavor that shape cognitive frameworks, individual aspirations, and community norms. By exploring what education is and might become, we can expand the range of plausible possibilities for ourselves, for schools, and for a global society.

Although thinking about education tempts us to dream of new futures, no institution seems so difficult to reconceptualize and change as schools. Students sense that idle curiosity, unconventional views, and many personal goals fall outside the formal curriculum. Teachers feel isolated, overburdened in their classrooms, and unable to effect meaningful curricular improvements. Many parents and voters also feel uncertain and powerless to improve prospects for today's children. Everyone experiences schooling from their own perspective and somehow copes with its dominant institutional culture, but few share their ideas in open and supportive discussions.

Most studies forecast educational needs for the 21st century based on plausible technological and economic trends; we seek, instead, to engage readers in discussions about desirable and feasible possibilities. We hope to broaden the range of perceived choices by juxtaposing voices of educators with summaries of current knowledge about schools, information technologies, economic and social organizations, political possibilities, and emerging trends. At the same time, we seek to strengthen democracy as a process for decisionmaking and as a commitment to equality. A resulting critical dialog about oppressive experiences can empower students and teachers to reframe educational goals around a curriculum of caring about others.

## CONSTRUCTIVIST APPROACHES

Exploring future schools benefits from a constructivist perspective that considers how people make sense of the world in light of their sensory experiences and familiar vocabularies. Learning, as understood by constructivists, entails reconciling conflicting interpretations through reflection and then reestablishing an interpretive framework. For instance, more than 20 years ago the authors taught classes of predominantly White students and later advanced to racially and culturally diverse classrooms. We soon recognized that familiar ideas conveyed sharply mixed messages. For one author, these contradictions became obvious when repeating a commonplace that American history exemplified freedom and equality—to a mostly Black audience. After reflection, it seemed clear that Eurocentric and middle-class perspectives had become embedded in a well-structured and seldom-questioned curriculum that poorly served a multicultural classroom.

Because meanings are socially constructed through daily interactions, people hold multiple accounts of reality, and understandings evolve through communication. Constructivism applies in at least three contexts. First, it refers to sequential stages of cognitive development as explicated by Jean Piaget and others who have built on his insights. Young children establish a sense of self, acquire language, categorize features of an external world, and understand formal operations or relationships by age 16. Second, adult learning entails a reconstruction of cognitive frameworks or embedded perspectives when puzzling anomalies or contradictions arise. Ordinarily, adults define themselves, maintain relations with others, function as productive citizens, and express values using a shared language and context to act effectively. Maturation as well as changing conditions may bring fresh puzzles, reflections and reinterpretations about oneself as well as relationships to others, work and social values.

Third, because human meanings and frameworks are socially constructed through dialog, groups share ideas and images in ways that stabilize many beliefs. Widely shared assumptions about important relationships are left unsaid. People "fill in" around the words, drawing from cognitive frameworks (or coherent beliefs) about the way the world works. In turn, those categories shape what is singled out from a multitude of sensory inputs. Accordingly, the meaning-making activities of people constitute families, organizations and cultures. Symbols such as the flag or family evoke common responses among those who feel included in White, middle-class American society.

Implicit in these three uses of constructivism lies a possibility for a social revolution—a set of interrelated changes that affect the way people commonly think and talk about their lives. For instance, the Social Security Act of 1935 allowed older Americans to view themselves as less dependent on their children. More recently, the Civil Rights

Movement from *Brown v. Topeka* to the Voting Rights Act of 1965 revised norms for treating African Americans in texts, schools and society. Presently, the end of the Cold War sharply reduces demands for military-industrial research and weapons manufacturing, but its implications for how citizens view peaceful trade, bureaucratic secrecy, and national goals are still unknown.

In one paragraph, our hypothesis is that a narrative that made sense of industrial progress has fractured. No longer does it appear unquestionable that academic achievement brings higher income and a satisfying life. Abundance no longer seems assured by science and technology coordinated by hierarchical organizations in democratic nation-states. Yet emerging information technologies make it possible for everyone to know enough to work together with fewer rules or commands. Various critiques by ecologists, feminists, and Afrocentric or Asian philosophers have weakened a presumption of assured progress under capitalist democracy, but no alternative has gained force that combines material well-being with America's democratic ideology of equality.

This book rests on our belief that information technologies will generate new ways for people to make sense of their lives. Schools that taught children to compete for consumer goods may now be asked to help them to enjoy aesthetic creativity, to build connections, and to cooperate voluntarily. Forward-looking educators have started to teach cooperation rather than competition, multicultural perspectives rather than a "Western" heritage, a holistic view rather than fragmented subunits, aesthetic creativity rather than mass consumerism. Teachers seek to liberate students from industrial-era mindsets by addressing issues of class, race and gender hierarchies.

## THE ORGANIZATION OF THE BOOK

Schools are places of natural tension between past and future. By plan and practice, teachers seek to transmit to the young that accumulated knowledge needed to function as productive citizens. Students want to learn what will enable them to fulfill their personal aspirations within a context of realistic prospects. In historical perspective, an aging instructional force now faces students whose aspirations and prospects differ from those of their own youth. In social terms, more children live in poverty and find their lives blighted by class, race and gender inequalities without expectations for economic growth. Indeed, the quality of life has declined for four out of five households over the past 20 years—a reality especially affecting those with children in public schools. That disjunction may increase frustrations with, and within, schools. Or it may hold the seeds for a transformation as new teachers replace a retiring staff and directly address concerns about self-identity and injustices within a multicultural society.

We have sought to raise issues for discussion, to offer starting points for further investigation, to introduce key perspectives, and to identify important concepts—all while connecting the material in this book to the everyday pressures and concerns facing students and teachers in schools today. They find themselves partly in the past and partly in the future without a coherent framework. They focus on one or another issue depending on the immediate context. We see them struggling in "contested terrain," caught uneasily between industrial-era and information-age ways of making sense of schools and society:

|                                        |       |                                          |
|---------------------------------------:|:-----:|:-----------------------------------------|
| an industrial economy                  | <—>   | a postindustrial economy;                |
| hierarchical prospects for jobs         | <—>   | aspirations for a meaningful life;       |
| supervision in hierarchical structures  | <—>   | cooperative decisionmaking;              |
| behaviorism in an objective world       | <—>   | social construction of meanings;         |
| schooling to reproduce categories       | <—>   | exploring new roles and values;          |
| learning in academic frameworks         | <—>   | transdisciplinary approaches;            |
| authoritative adult knowledge           | <—>   | jointly constructed understandings;      |
| replicating class, race and gender      | <—>   | crossing cultural boundaries; and        |
| corporate domination of democracy       | <—>   | democratic discourse and social justice. |

School structures still embody the assumptions and beliefs of the left column while students and emerging information-age organizations are attracted to those in the right column. Teachers find themselves uncomfortably in between, trying to mediate or reconcile approaches that are contradictory. Meanwhile, access to information is substantially eased by new technologies so that everyone needs a general idea about what others do; knowledge work (storing, processing and distributing numbers, words and symbols) is better coordinated through cooperative groups than through hierarchies of command based on bureaucratic systems. With global interdependence, people need to communicate across cultural as well as class, race and gender boundaries. Finally, living and working together require diverse interactions among democratic groups, each attending to relevant levels of decisions within a consensus about fairness or equity.

The first chapter introduces socially constructed meaning systems by presenting wide-ranging perspectives of social scientists, societal elites, and frontline educators about current prospects for schools and society. Chapter 2 summarizes alternative accounts of industrial-era schooling—one from a progressive viewpoint and the other focusing on class conflicts. Each explains some outcomes and directs attention to characteristic dilemmas that might account for unequal education and resistance among students. Chapter 3 examines dysfunctional tensions endemic in teachers' roles and school structures, especially contradictions between learning as liberation and teaching as control by adults.

Chapters 4 through 6 present contemporary analyses and historical accounts of household production, organizational dynamics, and democratic dilemmas. Schools serve both public and private interests that may coincide or conflict, depending on one's situation and prospects. First, we examine meanings of work, information, and well-being in postindustrial societies. Academic learning connects to paid employment and household well-being—and vice versa. Next, we probe how hierarchical organizational structures that coordinate interactions among things and people now hinder working together effectively. In an interdependent economy, legal rights and economic fairness increasingly depend on political institutions and social justice, as discussed in Chapter 6.

The final four chapters advance possibilities for participatory learning communities in light of the dilemmas inherent in current curricular goals and practices. Chapter 7 examines how class, race, ethnicity, and gender categories help sustain oppression and offers suggestions for opening dialog across existing cultural and intellectual boundaries. Chapter 8 explores some consequences for thinking about transmitting information through structured disciplines in light of ecological and feminist critiques of science and technology. We urge a more self-aware approach to knowledge and its humane purposes. In Chapter 9, we suggest various ways for households, schools, workplaces, and governments to collaborate in supporting lifelong learning around productive activities. A concluding chapter sketches out promising directions to empower students' choices that support personal and social values in an emerging information age.

## GUIDE TO FEATURES

We conducted open-ended informal interviews with 16 teachers and administrators who were involved with school improvement efforts. Their words and feedback from students in our classes introduce key issues that concern frontline educators. These voices are sometimes contradictory, and their proposals are often incomplete; yet they provide a "reality check" for abstract ideas and analyses. Their words are in italics and without other attribution as to their source.

We quote extensively from a few prominent scholars to demonstrate how they wrestled with puzzling interpretations of events or cultural beliefs. When multiple passages appear within a paragraph, an in-text reference following the first quotation lists the pages in order of their appearance. Italics within quotations are from the text unless otherwise noted. When paraphrasing, we seek to convey thoughts within that analyst's interpretive framework. Our normative beliefs are set forth at the end of Chapter 1. If there is a bias in the quoted passages, it lies in two directions. First, we describe in some detail nonmainstream views because most of us are relatively unfamiliar with postmodernist perspectives. Second, we emphasize statements by mainstream commentators that reflect their awareness of learning as a sense-making process.

Although linear arguments of objective causes leading to effects are familiar, they entrap us in industrial-era metaphors and assumptions. Because a new vocabulary is still under construction, we present key ideas in a spiral format:

- *Socially constructed realities* are defined in the Preface and the first chapter; Chapter 3 presents both Piagetian cognitive stages and adult development; and Chapters 7 and 8 apply constructivism to multiculturalism and science.

- *Class, race and gender*, as introduced in Chapter 2, contradict a school's goal of equal opportunity and a teacher's desire to help others. We incorporate those concerns into a positive definition of *democratic processes* through dialog around *social justice* in Chapters 7, 9, and 10.

- *Cognition, information and knowledge* are raised as issues in Chapter 1 and then treated more fully in Chapters 3, 4, and 7 through 10. In particular, Chapter 8 focuses on science and technology as hierarchical, patriarchal frameworks for conveying information in ways that enhance top-down authority.

- *Institutions*, both public and private, raise puzzles about *stability and change*. Chapter 2 presents historical perspectives on schools, while group dynamics in schools are described in Chapter 3. Their role in hierarchical organizations is elaborated on as characteristic of competitive, industrial societies in Chapter 5. In Chapter 6, democratic dilemmas reveal hierarchical, patriarchal power relationships embedded in institutional patterns. Then, Chapter 9 describes how future organizations may use low-cost information to enhance democratic participation and productivity.

Constructivism invites this self-consciousness about levels of interpretive description because they always rest on a presumed context more or less shared by authors and readers.

In each chapter, we invite readers' reactions to key issues by setting off some questions or exercises within boxes. At the end of chapters, we list some accessible readings to supplement those summarized or cited in the text. The positive transformations in schools and society presented in the last two chapters should be read neither as our predictions nor preferences. We advance current curricular and structural reforms to move from critiques of the past toward reconstructions of social meanings for learning, teaching, working, raising children, creating, planning, governing, and enjoying life in the future.

Our implicit focus throughout is on powerful economic and political organizations in the United States in the 1990s. Consequently, many generalizations apply less accurately to poor Americans and not at all to many people in the rest of the world. Cross-national comparisons guard against a narrow perspective but would enormously complicate an already difficult discussion. Because the limits to industrial production are visible precisely where techniques are most advanced, leading nations have incentives, resources and power to redirect personal and collective purposes in ways that sustain well-being.

# Acknowledgments

We appreciate help and support from colleagues and friends who read the manuscript and offered comments and criticisms: Ann E. Allegra, Lori Bartlett, Jodi L. Bornstein, Tina L. Browne, Marie-France Cambronne, Richard J. Clark, Moira Collins, Jennifer Cook, Christopher J. Dede, Peter Demereth, Julianne Eagan, Edwin Eckel, Sharon A. Edwards, Alan Elms, Leigh Fairchild, John C. Fischetti, Angela K. Frusciante, Manuel Frau-Ramos, Atron A. Gentry, Joy Goldsmith, Jeannie M. Jones, Celina Kapoor, Monica Nascimento, Alexander Nguyen, Martha A. Potyrala, Susan D. Savill, Irving E. Seidman, Charlotte M. Steen, and Robert L. Woodbury.

For participating in the interviews, we thank many friends and former students who have struggled with us to make sense of schools and the processes of implementing significant change. Finally, we dedicate this book to all those who welcome an opportunity to work toward better schools.

# Schools for an Information Age

# 1

# Thinking about Future Schools

"I touch the future. I teach." Teacher and astronaut Christa McAuliffe's words highlight the excitement and mystery involved in helping young people develop and take their place as productive citizens. Exploration also involves risk, as the tragic explosion of the Challenger space shuttle reminds us. A quick listing of what has changed since 1900—or since 1950—suggests the hazards of forecasting. Nevertheless, everyone who anticipates living in the 21st century has to learn and adapt based on someone's projection. Ordinarily people proceed as though trends will continue so their tomorrows will be familiar, but better. Charged with instructing the young, teachers mostly act on that basis. They build a curriculum informed by industrial-era understandings about how people interact, earn a living, participate in organizations, and respond to community values.

Discussing educational purposes requires heroic generalizations or value-laden terms: "as long as we care about schools they will touch our deepest emotions about ourselves, our children, our past, and our future" (Lazerson, McLaughlin, McPherson, & Bailey, 1986, p. xiii).

Schools must be both equal and excellent. Equality in education is predicated on the belief that in a democracy all citizens are entitled to the skills necessary for thoughtful and active citizenship. Excellence in education comes from a commitment to learning, ranging from the basic skills of literacy and problem solving, to creative and critical thinking, to the desire to expand still further one's knowledge and skills.

Equity, efficiency and excellence sound like positive goals; however, their specific applications depend on unexpressed assumptions about what lies ahead.

How can we make sense of schools whose outcomes match neither their public mission statements nor the exciting possibilities opened by information technologies in an ever-changing world? Teachers describe their role as preparing independent and responsible adults, but they organize classroom activities to minimize student autonomy. Although critical thinking about words and numbers is projected as a key competence for knowledge workers, most grading still rewards docility. Required courses in history and English emphasize a Eurocentric heritage, ignoring multicultural perspectives and global interdependence. Policymakers mandate minimum educational standards, yet norm-referenced achievement tests label half of the students as below average. Value statements about democracy and equality are contradicted by pervasive class, race and gender discrimination.

Aware of these dynamics, the authors describe people's accounts of schools and society as "multiple realities." The term suggests the diversity of perspectives and interests of different parties to events, the range of historical and social accounts offered in a multicultural society, the fragmentation of beliefs in a postmodern world, and an epistemological base for understanding human learning as socially constructed. Although the discipline of writing a book entails a focus on an imagined audience and then presenting a coherent, sequential argument or thesis, multiple realities suggest a kaleidoscope that rearranges partial accounts into new cognitive patterns.

One way of approaching this text is to start with a common theme that schools should prepare productive citizens for a future society. That often-reiterated mission statement rests on a number of seldom-questioned assumptions. First, teachers can transmit a body of knowledge to the young. Second, educators know what skills, competencies and experiences will be useful two decades from now at work, at home, and in one's public roles as a citizen. Third, individual learners necessarily adapt to technological, organizational and political conditions. Although we have learned much from critical thinkers who raise troubling questions about functionalist purposes of schooling, we generally accept the idea that schools should, as a minimum, prepare children for a healthy, comfortable and satisfying life.

We differ, however, in several aspects with what seems the mainstream interpretation of that mission.

- We suggest that the meanings students make of the curriculum usually diverge from the "lesson plan" information and beliefs that educators intend to transfer to others.
- We argue that an end to industrialism entails a transformation in the skills, competencies and experiences that will be needed for a productive life.
- We believe that economic growth no longer needs to be the primary goal for schools or society and that an equitable distribution of resources can assure abundance for everyone.

- For students to learn to act on personal and social values, they must reconstruct technological and political frameworks.

- Finally, we emphasize making choices about desirable future societies and exploring what sorts of knowledge will be useful in that new world rather than outlining a reform agenda for schools based on someone's projection.

This chapter raises a number of puzzles or contradictory beliefs about how schools can best serve future societies. Many teachers and citizens advocate educational reforms; yet everyone seems frustrated by the glacial pace of change. People who are concerned about current disruptions in families, work, productivity, and international relations find little agreement about how to prepare children as productive citizens. Few students participate in that debate—nor are their concerns at its center. By introducing multiple voices, we seek insights into how people think about schools. Some contradictory explanations are dialectically opposed, while others present alternative frameworks for interpreting events. We proceed in a spirit of inquiry, seeking to encompass multiple views in a context of social transformation.

We begin with a variety of voices from political and economic elites, educational commentators, and progressive teachers to illustrate a range of plausible futures and how personal experiences constrain projections. Then, we present evidence of a transformation in what people do, how organizations function, what social purposes are important, and how Americans discuss them in a postindustrial world. Next, we introduce an epistemological framework—variously labeled "constructivism" or "phenomenological sociology"—that shows how personal and cultural knowledge is socially constructed and reconstructed. Then, we introduce some ways that usable information, or what seems worth teaching, is shaped by both past experiences and future purposes. Finally, we identify normative stances that guide our questions and interpretations.

## PROJECTING FUTURES

According to a classic definition, all educators are futurists—"one who makes other people's futures more real to them" (quoted in Dede, 1990, p. 85:1). During a social transformation, however, conventional wisdom based on old maps and current trends is misleading at best. As critical theorist Henry Giroux (1988, pp. 9–10) commented, "our very survival depends on the degree to which the principles of communality, human struggle, and social justice aimed at improving the privileges of all groups eventually prevail." After reflecting on postmodern conditions, O. B. Hardison, Jr., depicted a terrifying paradox: "We are

hurtling toward an unknown and unimaginable future that we
ourselves are creating" (*Fortune*, 1990, p. 158).

An appealing method for arriving at some consensus about educational challenges during a revolutionary period is to consult a panel of
experts. Presumably, people who have examined current conditions
within a coherent disciplinary framework or from a leadership position
have greater insights and perspective on what will develop. But asking
economists about employment trends or senators about health care
entails the problem that each role has its own blinders. Students,
parents and teachers seldom share their dreams or wrestle dissonant
ideas into coherent accounts. Typically, there are silences when addressing organizational or political powers. Their voices, nonetheless, reveal
recurring themes in their stories. By paying particular attention to
their dreams for better schools, we hope to gain insights from their
frustrations and expectations.

## Elite Viewpoints

We start with a convenient panel of experts who speculated on
emerging trends—but were not asked to explain their implications for
schools. For its 60th Anniversary issue, *Fortune* magazine asked
executives and policymakers to comment on futures within their areas
of immediate concern and acknowledged expertise: management,
science, finance, economics, media and marketing, global issues, and
societal trends. The 126 individuals interviewed included 7 women and
4 male African Americans with the remainder overwhelmingly older
White men. Apparently the editors regarded those elites as more
insightful than ordinary citizens.

Because they have enjoyed success, however, leaders easily confused
autobiographical lessons with social progress. Most took for granted
technological advances, a Judeo-Christian heritage, and consumerism.
In one case, Citicorp's chief executive officer explained how the Third
World reacted to scenes of refrigerators in movies: "people living in a
mud hut see this and say, 'My God, there's something else out there'"
(*Fortune*, 1990, pp. 64, 68). Many White males foresaw demographic
changes, new roles for women, less structured workplaces, revolutionary impacts of computers, and global markets but could not
viscerally place themselves within those developments.

Typically, business leaders projected immediate organizational
imperatives. Charles Lazarus of Toys "R" Us offered a recipe: "You just
listen to the customers and then act on what they tell you" (*Fortune*,
1990, pp. 42, 32, 33, 31). According to Reuben Marx of Colgate-
Palmolive, "partnerships of all kinds will be the thrust of the Nineties
and beyond: increasingly strategic interdependencies between companies, governments, people." Steve Jobs, the "whiz kid" of Apple and
NeXT computers, advised that "hiring the right people is only the

beginning—you have to build an open corporation." H. Ross Perot described his travels to Asia and Europe as "looking at tomorrow," whereas in U.S. cities, "I see decay and neglect and I feel like I'm looking at yesterday."

Scientists extrapolated from research and technological break-throughs as though further developments necessarily followed: New generations of computers would transfigure everyday life as software made huge databases accessible to everyone through wireless communication of voice, text and images. Scientists anticipated superconductivity, sending people to Mars, curing cancer, engineering genes, a vaccine for AIDS, and treatments for drug addiction. Others warned about the greenhouse effect, nuclear power to replace nonrenewable resources, dioxin from pulp and paper, and solid-waste disposal. Awaiting further miraculous discoveries, a physicist confidently asserted that "we're in what you may call a pause in which we need more information from the laboratory to make our next conceptual jumps" (*Fortune*, 1990, p. 80).

Media and marketing specialists foresaw that overseas expansion of soft drinks, professional sports, and advertising entailed global communications. An editor expected to extend magazines through "television, videocassettes, laser discs, fax newsletters, teaching devices, whatever" (*Fortune*, 1990, pp. 120, 68, 121). A computer and video game manufacturer heralded interactive television, while a Japanese software specialist predicted the "integration of digital, audio, and video technology with the PC" within a decade. An entrepreneur imagined advanced versions of Epcot Center and Channel One for schools that immerse students in "walk-through" or "location-based" virtual realities. Imagine an electronic Walden Pond to inspire future Thoreaus!

Political and public policy leaders—sounding like veterans from past battles—cited inequities based on race, gender, age, urban location, or illness. An early supporter of Head Start noted, "women could fill two-thirds of these [new] jobs—but only if they can find reliable child care" (*Fortune*, 1990, pp. 148, 149, 158). Former President Jimmy Carter anticipated social benefits from arms limitations. Bill Clinton, then governor of Arkansas, advocated "comprehensive educational institutions that will be community colleges, vocational schools, specific industry training centers, and adult literacy centers all in one." A big-city mayor urged programs to bring welfare recipients "back into the economic mainstream and give them a stake in society." Academic experts summarized conclusions from their latest research, but they sounded disparate themes—warning about firms lacking the size and scope to compete internationally, growing inequalities, or foreign ownership of U.S. factories.

One of the most successful chief executive officers of the 1980s, General Electric's John F. Welch, Jr., believed "competition will be

relentless"; "globalization is now no longer an objective but an imperative, as markets open and geographic barriers become increasingly
blurred and even irrelevant"; and marketable innovations "will be
accelerating ever faster." He warned against sure-fire recipes: "Simply
doing more of what worked in the Eighties—the restructuring, the
delayering, the mechanical, top-down measures that we took—will be
too incremental. . . . The winners of the Nineties will be those who can
develop a culture that allows them to move faster, communicate more
clearly, and involve everyone in a focused effort to serve ever more
demanding customers" (*Fortune*, 1990, p. 30).

As *Fortune*'s commentators demonstrated, projecting extensions of
what is in vogue offers unclear guidance for educational planning.
Based on the space allotted to news stories, Naisbitt and Aburdene
(1989) forecast ten trends for the 1990s: a global economic boom, a
renaissance in the arts, free market socialism, global lifestyles and
cultural nationalism, privatization of the welfare state, power flowing to
Pacific Rim nations, women as leaders, biological discoveries, religious
revival, and a triumph of individualism. Such inclusive lists contradict
themselves: Do Japanese firms exemplify innovative management or
conforming workers? Iranian students wearing tee shirts and blue jeans
during anti-American protests illustrate cultural fundamentalism and
international styles, but not leadership by women. Fads are confusingly
mixed with fundamental shifts in social structures.

Elites presume their successful experiences apply to the whole
society. Their accounts are individualistic, optimistic, fragmented,
technology driven, and materialistic. These idiosyncratic views offer few
prospects for interdisciplinary, long-term, global perspectives. Asked to
project a future in 20 minutes or less, commentators seldom delve into
their taken-for-granted assumptions about what is important or possible. Implicitly, most Americans assume that science leads to
technology, which drives the economy. In turn, it shapes politics, the
government and other institutions, which influence social values.
Powerful people seldom ask how subordinates make sense of their
situation or how to build political consensus or alliances. Presumably,
the curriculum should adapt to the knowledge required to function in a
postindustrial economy.

### Educational Reformers

Beginning with the publication of *A Nation at Risk,* mainstream
policy recommendations called for more courses and homework, tough
tests and strict graduation requirements. The members of the National
Commission on Excellence in Education (1983, pp. 5, 7) concluded: "Our
nation is at risk. Our once unchallenged preeminence in commerce, industry, science, and technological innovation is being overtaken by competitors throughout the world." Japanese automobile companies, South

Korean steel mills, and German machine manufacturers "signify a redistribution of trained capability throughout the globe. Knowledge, learning, information, and skilled intelligence are the new raw materials of international commerce and are spreading throughout the world as vigorously as miracle drugs, synthetic fertilizers, and blue jeans did earlier."

Education was blamed for America's shortcomings—"*the average graduate* of our schools and colleges today is not as well-educated as the average graduate of 25 or 35 years ago" (National Commission on Excellence in Education, 1983, pp. 11, 18, 13). Schools should require more mathematics, biology, chemistry, physics, and geography. "Secondary school curricula have been homogenized, diluted, and diffused to the point that they no longer have a central purpose." The National Commission proposed an attitude change: "We should expect schools to have genuinely high standards rather than minimum ones, and parents to support and encourage their children to make the most of their talents and abilities." Such rhetoric fed a back-to-basics movement as part of a conservative political agenda.

Most educational experts start from a diagnostic-prescriptive framework, first identifying what is wrong and then proposing solutions. John Goodlad's (1984, pp. 358–359) comprehensive empirical study of over 1,000 classrooms exemplified this approach. He linked two observations: "the pedagogical variability and creativity required to engage the young in challenging encounters with knowledge tended to decline with upward progression through the schools" and so did "the academic self-concepts of many students." Youth paid more attention to peers and their own identity than to academic learning. "The result is a disjuncture between what powerfully preoccupies adolescents and what secondary school teachers perceive their job to be." Consequently, teachers should pay more attention to their students' concerns— although school structures and schedules often enforce an impersonal, adult-controlled curriculum.

Whereas Goodlad focused on classrooms and the disjuncture between a mandated curriculum and students' search for identity and self-expression, other reformers responded to alienating schools in metropolitan districts by calling for a renewed sense of community. For example, Mario D. Fantini (1986, p. 227) predicted that "modernization will link school and various community environments into a coordinated and comprehensive system of human learning." Information technologies should connect a variety of communities in new networks "between people and their institutions—a combining of efforts to achieve common goals." Democratic community, he hoped, would

---

reconcile excellence in learning with social equity; and computers might reconnect schools to other institutions in a democratic society.

Many educators assume that schools could catch up with a changing world by adopting the latest innovations. Pioneers envision "model" classrooms. Tom Snyder, a creator of exemplary educational software, gently asked for "an old-fashioned phone" in every classroom (in Bruder, 1990, pp. 27, 30, 24, 27). Ideally, he urged, every teacher would have a copy machine, a computer, networking capability, a large monitor, a modem, and a low-cost word processor for each student. An educator urged a "move away from large group instruction to more small and individualized instruction, in which the teacher is a facilitator and works with students." Computers should be "tools for students to create and share their own information." By "video recording, digitizing of sound and editing," youth might "produce their own documentaries and research papers" at media stations. A teacher dreamed that "kids could sit in my classroom and could interact 'face-to-face' with kids all over the world" as well as use "remote imaging . . . to reach beyond the earth's boundaries."

Parents, as well as educators, find it hard to insist on normative values in a society that stresses consuming for pleasure. Founder and president of the Children's Defense Fund, Marian Wright Edelman (1992, p. 60) sounded almost old-fashioned in recommending ongoing learning: *"Don't ever stop learning and improving your mind* or you're going to get left behind. The world is changing like a kaleidoscope right before our eyes. College pays and is a fine investment. It doubles your chance of getting a job over a high school graduate. But don't think you can park there or relegate your mind's and soul's growth to what you have learned or will learn at school." Recurring adult development suggests a curriculum that is forever incomplete.

When all the projections are combined, they add up to confusion—or multiple realities. For instance, Benjamin (1989, p. 9) identified 14 predictions for schools (ranked by frequency of mention in futurists' literature): active learning, higher cognitive skills, service learning, past-present-future focus, lifelong learning, whole-person education, coping with diversity, general education, transdisciplinary education, personalized learning, process approach, education for communication, early childhood education, and smaller organizational structures. Popular trends, however, soon sound vague and clichéd.

---

What projections do you agree with, and what implications do they hold for a school curriculum? What assumptions underlie your views? For example, if computers are as common in homes as televisions today, how will teachers and cultural values adjust?

Projecting a "technological, overloaded with information, independent, global, change-driven" society, futurists urge a curriculum that
enables everyone "to think critically, uncover bias and propaganda,
reason, question, inquire, use the scientific process, remain intellectually flexible, think about complex systems, think holistically, think
abstractly, be creative, and view and read critically." Oddly, Benjamin
mentioned computers as neither problem nor solution.

Many educational reformers have struggled through so many
promising innovations without noticeable improvement that they have
grown pessimistic about all curricular proposals. A psychologist with a
profound understanding of group dynamics, Seymour Sarason (1983,
pp. 180–181) concluded "that at its root the problem of our schools is not
moral, political, economic, or technical. Rather, the problem flows from
the hold that custom and tradition have on our thinking, a hold that
prevents us from recognizing that the axiom that education best takes
place in schools may be invalid." He acknowledged that some people had
benefited from schooling but doubted "that schools have ever been able
to nurture the need and desire of children to explore and master their
environment and establish self-worth."

## VOICES OF FRONTLINE EDUCATORS

Normally, teacher preparation programs require a course in social,
historical and philosophical foundations of education, but few explicitly
examine probable or desirable futures. When we challenged students in
a teacher preparation course to describe curricular goals for 2010, they
reiterated then-popular ideas. Small groups had difficulty reconceptu-
alizing a curriculum to serve new purposes. Although these prospective
teachers had grappled with how cultural beliefs impact on schools, this
exercise asked them to envision the future being implanted by current
classroom patterns. Apparently assuming that science and technology
impelled change, they resisted crediting schools as positive driving
forces. If curriculum enables individuals to adjust to technological
advances, then schools always will be lagging institutions.

These prospective teachers infused then-current educational agendas with a moralistic tone. They listed "better communication skills,"
promoting self-esteem, techniques for negotiation or conflict mediation,
respect for others, ethics and social values, multicultural awareness,
leadership, interdisciplinary approaches, and "never present one side of
an issue" (italicized text is from student papers or our interviews). To
reduce alienation in contemporary life, a group proposed that
"production will increase when people enjoy their work. People must be
given choices—options—empowered." No one addressed how organizational structures and perceived opportunities for a meaningful adult
role mediate a sense of oppression or liberation.

Another group started with then-popular curricular ideas. Their list included process writing, attention to health (including sexuality) as a matter of lifestyle choices, cooperative learning, multicultural texts, hands-on activities for science and technology, social studies as inquiry into policy issues, and linking work-school experiences through outside partnerships. Implicitly, their school-based strategies connected with diagnoses of social concerns. For instance, a need to break down cultural barriers supported the inclusion of multiple texts and a whole language approach to writing. Those who perceived the irrelevance of textbook assignments urged experiential activities.

Some students treated the question as potentially well-structured. They set out to describe society in 2010, but quickly questioned each descriptor. With the breaching of the Berlin Wall then in the news, they agreed that only change itself was predictable. The instructor suggested that some causes and outcomes have high probability: Current trajectories in science and technology bring both benefits and fresh problems; large corporations efficiently manage complex, multistage activities but are ecologically wasteful; and formal education for humans between the ages of 3 and 20 stabilizes society by reproducing cultural norms. These prospective teachers then proposed courses covering global awareness; literacy (including technology); environmentalism; learning to change; *"open-minded respect for others and for yourself; cooperation, participation and understanding of purpose"*; and physical fitness. Last, they suggested periodic recertification of occupational competencies, including pedagogy.

These able students sought to make the future "manageable" by identifying plausible "technical" responses. If rapid change were the problem, then add a course about social adaptation and require periodic retesting of adults. As products of relatively privileged educational backgrounds, they knew little of the frustrations of poverty or racial discrimination. They did not ask what subordinate groups might want to learn. For instance, working-class families might resent schools that reproduce blue collar status for their children *and* those that promote humanistic values. Like most undergraduates today, these prospective teachers praised mutual respect and multicultural perspectives without specifying how they fit into existing curriculum or testing practices.

After compiling a list of key themes based on our classes and readings, we summarized our thoughts about a future curriculum in a paper first drafted in 1989 (Jones & Maloy, 1993). We shared this essay with students and colleagues, who found it intriguing but wanted more direct prescriptions of competencies needed in the 21st century. Then, we identified beginning and experienced teachers whose engagement in professional development suggested an interest in expanding their influence over school practices. A balanced group of eight females and eight males, seven of whom were currently in administrative roles, made time to talk with us. The group included three African Americans, two Latinos, and one Asian, as well as those with math, science or vocational experiences. In two interviews, we followed standard ethnographic procedures for recording and categorizing responses. Their words introduce key themes that will be taken up in subsequent chapters.

## Beginning Teachers

New teachers shared their enthusiasm but worried about how they might fit into a school with its history and cultural patterns. A prospective teacher felt awed by her influence over a child's development: *"You've helped in making that shape, but you are also responsible, like artists are responsible, for whatever piece they make; and I don't want to take that responsibility yet, though it's a beautiful responsibility."* A social studies major argued, *"History is also the study of the human condition . . . studying the past as the window to the future."* They saw social forces impinging on them: *"We really do need to break down those classroom walls and make the world a classroom and everyone who is a member of that world, a teacher."*

An intern in an urban vocational school recognized the limited choices open to her and to her students, yet she optimistically conveyed her dreams and her successes:

*If we could develop more community choices/options for coming back to school, then people would tend to be more willing to come back to school later in life.*

*The second thing is in school itself, we are far too structured and we limit ourselves by bells, by desks, by walls. You sit in your desk, I, the teacher, am going to impart my knowledge to you! You are going to scribble it in your notebook and Friday we are going to have a test on all of this material, and don't you try and bring in any information from your outside life . . . . Don't bring history into my English class, don't bring math into my English class— this is just English. And what do we learn in English? My students are constantly telling me, "Ms. B___, this isn't English; Ms. B___, this doesn't seem like English class." Because it is not a short story, it's not a poem, it's not a play and it is not a novel, so it is not English. We can't use the newspaper, they get upset with me—this isn't English. We can't read something about science because it is not English. They, themselves, have been trained to put everything into its own little categories. . . .*

*We have to stop giving off such a clear presentation of what is success. We give such a clear definition to students: "This is success. If you do A, B, C, D and E or 1, 2, 3, 4 and 5, I will give you an A in this class and you will succeed." What we are saying is, do it my way and you get an A. Students get in the habit of doing exactly what their teacher/presenter, whatever, is telling them to do so they never evaluate what is success for themselves or what it is they want. They are never forced to create the formula—just follow the recipe. Teachers need to find ways to let students work in a more interactive, integrated way so that they can come up with their own recipes and then present them to other people. That is the only way they are going to work effectively in an information society. . . .*

*This is what I get excited about—cooperative learning. We shouldn't maintain this hierarchy in which elementary school students never meet the middle school students; middle school the high school; high school the college. We need to break down the barriers, we need to form partnerships . . . . We need more high school students helping the middle school students with their math. We need more community and business people participating in the schools. . . . They need to see schools and education as a whole, as an integrated part of society. . . .*

*We need to make teaching a profession so that when people are in high school or freshmen in college they say, "I am going to be a teacher" the same way that they say "I am going to be a lawyer" or "I am going to be a doctor."*

An African American who had taught for six years in an elementary school serving a low-income Black neighborhood reflected on the difficulties and sacrifices required to achieve equality in a diverse society:

*Basically what I see now is that we are losing a lot of [academic] bases in mathematics and other things. In the early years, children are missing out, they are not writing. The children are losing out. We need to take a step back and fill in those things. There is violence, drugs and other things. Children are not on grade level. In the early years something is missing. Maybe we need a more creative approach to teaching—not so much on the technical level, but more hands on. Less use of textbooks. Get down on the floor. Take kids out to the environment, things of that nature. . . .*

*Well, of course, technology is changing with computers. We have to have our children prepared for that. Business and jobs are moving in that direction. People are losing their jobs. Jobs will be taken over by robots. Our students will have to be good with math and science, work with computers and calculators. . . .*

*Well the problem that I have seen is that children were grouped according to ability and children were losing out because you had a group of slow children together and then you had the high achievers. Then, we moved to a program called cooperative learning where low, middle, and high achievers are mixed together, which I have found to be highly effective. . . . The children are learning from one another and that way the children are having successful experiences. Children need as much success as they can. The more successful they are the happier they are with school. . . .*

*Also, we have the issue of racial isolation. A mixture to me is better because I have been in both. . . . So I had a chance to see some of everything. Whereas the children here in this particular area they only see one side. It would be better if it were more mixed. . . . We need more good strong Black teachers, as well as White teachers, who care and want to make a difference. . . .*

*Children only do what you expect from them. So we have to give them an extra push. . . . We have to give them materials. In this situation I have to spend so much money on materials; but I am willing to do that because I care. They do not have things. I have to go out and buy things so that they have the same chance.*

*And gender. Yes. Sometimes there is a distinction between males and females in certain areas. Boys do better in science or math when they could do just as well in reading. And girls can be good mathematicians. We have to push our girls more to do math and science. . . .*

*Of course, I would like to see a society where persons are judged by who they are rather than by the color of their skin. Then I would like a school system that is more integrated than it is; where we were getting an equal amount of money to buy materials and have the resources that we need to prepare our children; and communities that are more mixed. Then of course I want to see that my children are prepared so that when they go to a job, they can do it and make a good impression.*

*Schools should be run in a different way. I think teachers should have more input into how schools are run. Many times people are more impressed with the plan book than by what is going on in the classroom. . . . There should not be just one person making decisions. It's not wrong to have input or make changes. There should be more input. But then again with cooperative learning our students will have more experiences in making decisions. . . .*

*Obviously, I would want a society where there is no crime—where you are paid in equal amounts to do the same job as anyone else, where we could get equal promotions. We should start in kindergarten making kids aware of drugs and so forth. But we have waited too late, because kids know more now than they used to. . . . We cannot wait until they are in fifth or sixth grade or in high school.*

## Experienced Teachers

Veteran educators in our interviews discussed reforms against a backdrop of their immediate frustrations—because they believe schools can do better. They talked animatedly about new lessons or reform initiatives. Their voices conveyed enthusiasm when describing cooperative learning or multidisciplinary units. We heard delight when a reading specialist discussed the gains that vocational students made when they wrote freely in their journals. When site-based management was introduced, she noted that *"the teachers in our school come alive now that they have some power."* A building principal noted that her teachers wanted to *"restructure and reorganize and revitalize schools"* if there was public support: *"We know what kids need to learn and we know in a lot of ways how to provide those experiences for children but I think we have not figured out yet how to provide the resources for that to happen."*

Teachers found mathematics, science and technology particularly troubling in terms of their ability to deliver instruction relevant to future needs.

*The traditional modes of teaching both math and science need to be reworked. The whole idea of how we group kids and who has access to higher level math and science have to reworked. One of the things that we know that schools have traditionally done is to be gatekeepers. That is, an X amount of people be let in*

*and many more people be kept out. And as schools are struggling with the
ability grouping issue, until we get that resolved, the numbers of people who
need to be prepared in higher level math and science is a depressed number and
that is another piece that breaks down along racial lines. And that is a lot of
hard work ahead.*

In her thinking, *"the time for the introduction to computer education is
in kindergarten and that the need for schools to be constantly right there
on the edge in terms of feeding kids the latest software, use of Logo in the
classroom, certainly basic word processing, data banks."*

A vocational teacher urged better staff development to cope with a
range of students—60% on free lunch, 80% from single-parent homes:

*We are barely able to get in our graduation requirements. A lot of our students
who are in the voc-trade areas, we have to waive summer graduation requirements because they can't fit everything in. For example, with the shop areas,
they cannot spend half a day in shop and the other half a day which is only 3
periods, fitting in the 2 years of math, science, 4 years of English. . . . We would
have to look at a 11 month structure or go a longer day. But I think that if we
were to do either one of those things, we would have to think about the impact
on our working students who need that financial money to take care of things
at home.*

*We also have to take a look at teacher needs and most of the teachers I know
work two jobs also. We would take a look at their financial needs. The way
things are going statewide/citywide—last Friday we heard of a 6 million
dollar cut in our budget. We are looking at losing teachers and programs; and
they just cut our whole summer school out. That wipes out not only
opportunities for our students, which is certainly what education is all about,
but also teacher's pay.*

Asked about curriculum and staffing, a middle school administrator
again drew on his recent experiences with restructuring to team
teaching:

*Each cluster has two teams: one math-science, one language arts-social studies.
All four teachers on the cluster team teach two subject areas. These children are
divided up into clusters where there are between 80 and 100 students (closer to
80) that are assigned to the cluster team so that the teachers have a very
intimate ongoing knowledge about the children and they make group decisions
about how they will run their cluster, what are the parameters in terms of all
kinds of things—discipline, how you are going to spend the resources. . . .*

*We have talked a lot in education about the notion of teacher empowerment
and I think that until we really give teachers the decisionmaking authority that
they need, and then obviously hold them accountable for those kinds of
decisions, that things aren't going to happen as long as we maintain a real
hierarchical kind of organizational structure.*

*In terms of curriculum, I think there is a far greater need for children to
spend less time focusing on the memorization of facts and giving back those*

*facts, than giving them the tools to go beyond just the knowledge level. And give
them the tools that they need to be able to synthesize and analyze and evaluate
and generally just make good decisions in problem-solving kinds of contexts.
. . . Certainly we need to provide them also with the basic skills of reading,
writing and math. . . . We need to be moving much further along in terms of
having them work through problems to solutions and helping them to learn
also how to work in a team, how to work with other people, which means
certainly going away from homogeneous grouping and looking at instructional
techniques such as cooperative learning and helping kids to learn how to work
in a group and make team decisions. . . .*

A high school administrator sought to envision a way to change a
veteran staff that visibly resisted new challenges from culturally
diverse students: *"We were just evaluated here this week by the New
England Association and they came out with some interesting observations aside from the repairs in the building and that sort of thing. They
talked about the importance of opening up lines of communication, the
obligation of the staff and the administration to do that sort of thing,
and they talked about the need for more extracurricular activities."* She
proposed alternatives within the building: Schools *"are too large, they
are too impersonal."* The covert warfare between teachers and students
might fade *"if we could increase the comfort level of students, and with
teachers if we can get them to do things differently so that students feel
comfortable with them."*

An instructional coordinator pondered whether schools in the past
had simpler purposes: *"We used to educate farmers to be farmers, factory
workers to be factory workers, teachers to be teachers, men to be men,
women to be women."* The future demands *"renaissance people. You can't
be productive in the information age if you don't know how to talk to a
diverse population, use a computer, understand a world view instead of
a parochial view, write, speak."* A district administrator warned against
thinking small: *"We are talking about restructuring our schools, . . . we
are talking about teacher empowerment, we are talking about changing
the curriculum—different methodologies, cooperative learning. That is
tinkering. And I have always felt that the educational bureaucracy is
like a huge dinosaur."*

> **Questions to ponder: Why do newcomers and outsiders so often
> bring fresh insights to institutional patterns and values? If students
> fail to question the value and appropriateness of education, who
> will? How can teachers support that dialog?**

A sense of conflict with dominant regularities in schools is clear
among teachers; every interview records some initiatives blocked by
a presumption that the status quo makes sense. Busy in their

classrooms and offices, educators seldom share their hopes for better schools. When teachers strive to engage or empower learners, they find their students, as well as parents, puzzled over unfamiliar roles. Or they discover that powerful political or economic interests in their communities block new resources—especially when aimed at a fairer curriculum. At the same time, words pour forth from educators when invited to consider what would improve teaching, demonstrating their interest in flexible, autonomous professional roles.

Like all commonsense ideologies, these accounts reveal more than their surface meanings through their choices of problems and solutions, their contradictions and silences: "Asking a person to produce his or her assumptions about reality is equivalent to asking a person to produce a map of his or her conscious and unconscious mind and to show the interactions between them—no small or simple task!" (Mitroff, 1983, p. 170). Although we may miss some nuances, we believe that constructing new realities requires a keen ear for partially expressed views, underlying tensions, and silences around proposals that threaten the privileges of the powerful and the comfortable.

Like earlier voices from elites in the *Fortune* interviews, educators sound positive when discussing familiar territory where they exercise some control, but they lack an encompassing map—or a framework that builds connections to other occupations, disciplines and cultures. Only when knowledge becomes conscious of historical developments, social situations, and cognitive understandings for making sense of daily life can it encompass multiple realities. Leaders and experts bring important perspectives as well as more coherent paradigms to the discussion, but too often their attempts to understand events are treated as cut-and-dried prescriptions. Their insights must be linked to the experiential knowledge of classroom teachers and students in order to revise the "job description" of learners and educators.

## A POSTINDUSTRIAL TRANSITION

The words of frontline teachers and administrators convey ambiguous messages about how to cope with young learners within current curricular and organizational arrangements. Youth appear wrapped up in material acquisitions, but they also want a decent future—one that is ecologically safe and open to diversity with disputes settled without war or force. An initial idealism among many teachers erodes as they struggle to manage a class, get students ready for state-mandated tests, and establish personal rapport. Interactions in classrooms and corridors are increasingly dysfunctional, primarily because students face a growing gap between their personal aspirations and their economic prospects. We start to explain this puzzle with a stark contrast between two centuries of industrial growth and economic stagnation today for large parts of the population.

Longstanding patterns of learning, working and interacting with people and machines no longer sustain growing production. Starting early in the 19th century, industrialization drove economic, political and social development in the United States for 150 years. Production shifted from households to factories, from self-sufficiency based on the land to interdependence based on markets, from self-directed labor to hierarchical organizations. Capital equipment complemented specialized labor, and management coordinated them in rationalized sequences through bureaucratic information systems. Externally, firms adjusted to each other by competing in open markets—hiring workers as well as resources and then selling their products or services. As long as economic growth made competition for the rewards of education, work and saving into a positive-sum game, most individuals benefited from conforming to capitalist institutions.

## Economic Stagnation

Prolonged gains in industrial productivity incorporated growth into the United States' economic, political and social systems. Expansion counterbalanced a variety of problems associated with industrial hierarchies of income and control. High wages compensated workers for their segmented, subordinate and alienating roles. Science and technology yielded ever more goods and services to support growing populations. Cities attracted immigrants into ethnic and racial neighborhoods. Communication flows were supported by the rise of public schools, low-cost printing, bureaucratic systems, and stable organizational functions. Teachers prepared students for available jobs; owners arranged production around those competencies. Progress seemingly flowed from capitalist and democratic institutions.

Despite remarkable economic growth, that system was not without internal contradictions. Capitalists coordinated specialized roles for labor and equipment over space and time in hierarchical organizations that divided people into stable social structures—notably workers, owners, and a growing middle class of technicians, professionals and managers. Segmented individuals then interacted in familiar ways based on their distinct roles as students, producers, consumers, or citizens. Americans presumed that their material success validated their ideology and viewed other nations as undeveloped or undemocratic. As work shifted from households to markets, changing family roles revealed patriarchal dominance. Moreover, ecological disaster loomed if everyone depleted nonrenewable resources and polluted the environment in the way Americans did.

Though still a revolutionary force in much of the world, industrialism no longer drives change in the United States. Note the following evidence:

- Since 1973, labor productivity has stagnated while other countries have gained on, or surpassed, the U.S. standard of living.
- Technicians, professionals and managers outnumber blue-collar workers in an economy where industry contributes about 35% to total domestic output and services add 62%.
- Investment in human capital through formal schooling, on-the-job learning, and informal education at home and in communities exceeds investment in physical plant and equipment.
- Specialization of labor and information segments occupations and hinders communication—the stock-in-trade of knowledge workers.
- Mass production based on assembling standardized parts cannot respond flexibly to diverse and shifting consumer demands for technological goods.
- Workers resist hierarchical supervision with differential access to information, while citizens resent impersonal bureaucratic procedures and regulations.

Recent scientific, technological and organizational advances have undermined key beliefs in industrial societies—notably, that technology driven by competitive firms brings human progress and that nation-states are natural economic and social units. First, people's identity is not contained within their role as functional workers or consumers, and they seek to express diverse cultural values. Second, technology itself appears as a threat to global ecology. Third, competition among individuals, firms and nations hinders concerted action to protect workers and the environment. Finally, managerial supervision is inefficient when coordinating knowledgeable people working with high-tech machines. These shifts have generated puzzling contradictions and multiple attempts to make sense of emerging roles for individuals in a complex world.

While exploring new directions, however, society necessarily builds on capital accumulations, sequential production, science and technology, bureaucratic organizations, and images of individuals acting purposefully in local settings. Presumably, industrial productivity and technological advances (flowing from research and development) will continue to reduce the costs of manufacturing and of market transactions. Computer-controlled machines will fabricate goods and keep records—achieving the efficiency of mass production with the flexibility of customized crafts and the responsiveness of personal interactions. Yet information technologies also may facilitate oversight and control over students, workers and citizens. Whatever future is created will determine what kind of knowledge will benefit the young.

## Industrial Legacies

For almost a century, American schools have maintained durable organizational patterns and a culture based on adults transmitting knowledge—or cultural capital—to the young. Large institutions represent major investments in familiar ways of handling crucial social processes. For instance, common school experiences bring predictability to interpersonal interactions. Over time, patterns harden into unchallenged routines, and few can envision alternative approaches to long-standing social systems and their regularities. Teacher control and competitively rank-ordered test scores have marked schools for so long that few dare dream of equitable and cooperative practices.

Historically, schools socialized most students for supervision by others in a time-scheduled environment. "The training of young people in the old economy resembled the system of high-volume, standardized production," as social analyst Robert Reich (1988, p. 21) noted:

Responsibility was exercised by a very few, at the top. The majority of students were pushed, as if on an assembly line, through a preestablished sequence of steps. Each step involved particular routines and practices. Teachers—the production workers—had little discretion over what they had to do to each batch that passed through; students passively received whatever was doled out. Inspectors tried to weed out the defects, sometimes returning them to an earlier step for reworking.

Teachers did not encourage most students to express opinions, ask questions, or try out new approaches and values. Only a few were invited to think critically and to act independently.

In a postindustrial society, schools "must motivate teachers and students alike to love learning" (Reich, 1988, pp. 21, 25). An innovative and adaptive workforce should learn "numeracy, literacy, responsibility, and collaboration." Teacher empowerment and school-based management would "push responsibility downward toward teachers and students; invite continuous, incremental innovation at all levels; foster collaboration among parents, teachers, principals, community groups, and the private sector; and encourage flexibility." Reich urged that "we invest substantially in one another."

After examining working conditions in schools, Susan Moore Johnson (1990, p. 335 [italics omitted]) recommended that educators "abandon industrial models of schooling that prize standardization or promote narrow measures of productivity; they must redirect their attention to improving teaching and learning for inquiry and higher-order thinking." Once teachers move beyond reading, writing and arithmetic, however, they often disagree about what should be included in the curriculum. Do numeracy and literacy require computers to calculate, to check spelling, and to maintain records of attendance and achievement? Or should educators stress why accurate calculation or communication matter? Critical approaches with multiple answers based on personal understandings do not readily translate into lectures and tests.

Once competition is viewed as a zero-sum game where winners are matched by losers, then rank-ordered hierarchies often generate selfish behaviors that reduce the group's effectiveness. The paradox entails a fallacy of composition: What is true for one person in a group may not be true for everyone as a whole. For instance, a single fan at a soccer match rises to see more of the playing field; but if others do the same, the now-standing audience has not improved its view. Because any one person can study harder, work longer, and thereby get ahead relative to the average does not mean that everyone following that example would change overall ranks or averages. In many cases, competition reinforces negative behaviors. The first person to stand can see more of the playing field, but the first person to sit in a crowd sees someone's back.

In our interviews, a curriculum coordinator recalled almost quitting his college work twice because he felt inadequate. In his school, he noted the negative effects of competition: *"It is a turn-off because every student is unique in his own way and he has good qualities."* Teachers *"should concentrate on those positive attributes of people and moving those along."* Competition for limited rewards motivates some individuals to greater effort but leads others to give up. Under cutthroat competition for grades, students may mislead classmates about assignments or engage in cheating to get an A. Although almost everyone would benefit from a clean, safe and secure learning environment, some students aggressively act out their frustrations. Their lack of cooperation alters and distorts all communication between teachers and students.

The fallacy of composition suggests why preparing productive citizens seems such an unchallengeable educational goal. Most youth compete for jobs by acquiring skills to produce goods and services for markets; and they enhance their employability by obeying laws, conforming to social norms, and supporting dominant ideologies. Individuals who seek social justice believe they must first gain academic and work credentials; but when everyone competes for power, it is diluted for most and concentrated in the hands of those on top. According to a recent poll, almost half of high school seniors agreed that they could "do very little to change the way the world is today." Presumably, good citizens work hard, vote, pay taxes, and die if necessary to protect national sovereignty; but they do not question the visible contradictions between rhetoric about democratic freedoms with equal justice and the barriers to their actualization faced by those who lack education and income.

### Dilemmas for Teachers

Most Americans are familiar with industrial-age schools and thus lack an outside perspective to observe afresh or to reflect on their taken-for-granted functions. In a classic study, *The Culture of the School and the Problem of Change*, Sarason (1982, pp. 26, 28) discussed obstacles to innovation. He identified prevailing school regularities and embedded beliefs as normal responses to a structural pattern that "governs roles and interrelationships within that setting." He concluded:

We remain imprisoned in conceptions that are based on assumptions that never get verbalized and, therefore, challenged. Today we may support this effort at educational change, tomorrow that one, or we may do both at the same time, but when we see that the more things seem to change the more they seem to remain the same, we direct blame outward because we cannot entertain the possibility that we, and those we blame, have basically the same conception of what schools are and should be.

The experiences and prospects of youngsters shape their aspirations and visions of a better future. If worker docility facilitates efficient coordination, then teacher dominance in classrooms prepares youth for employment. If emerging business firms seek self-starters who work well with colleagues, then independent study and cooperative projects will prepare youth for new roles. If nuclear war is probable, then basic survival skills, international diplomacy, and military discipline hold priority over Shakespeare and matrix algebra. If democracy rests on cultural coherence, then schools should underscore patriotic myths rather than multicultural approaches. Either choice entails political struggles over class, race and gender in the implementation of equity, yet students are told that tests are fair and grades are reliable measures of their intelligence. Only a compelling vision can inspire teachers and students to work together to make schools equitable.

---

**Twenty years ago, we were excited by a revolutionary fervor in a school of education (University of Massachusetts at Amherst). Its catalog raised questions about why children aged 5 to 16 are made to sit in classes for 6 hours a day, 5 days a week, 40 weeks a year.**
- **Is this the best way for children to spend those important years?**
- **What do children learn in schools?**
- **How do they learn it?**
- **Is what happens in schools good for children?**
- **Should they spend less time in schools?**
- **What is a school, anyway?**

---

Human development entails interacting with others in widening circles of power, which may account for a persistent ambivalence in teaching-learning relationships. As Urie Bronfenbrenner (1979, pp.

288, 289) noted, "the developing person, upon entering into new settings, participates in new roles, activities, and patterns of interrelationships." Thus, "activity is at once the source, the process, and the outcome of development." Children establish mental categories and relationships through their explorations. Yet teachers are typically regarded as the source of knowledge and authority. They are urged to base curricular objectives on their learners' backgrounds, contemporary issues, educational philosophies, cognitive psychology, and subject area expertise in order to help each child reach her or his potential. Even if teachers had time to bring all that knowledge to bear on each classroom interaction, it would leave little space for a student's questions or personal concerns.

To understand a society in transition, consider how schools should prepare productive citizens for the year 2020. When viewpoints shift from what exists to what *might be created*, even familiar images such as a teacher with a class of 20 some students become problematic. Television, now viewed as mainly entertainment supporting consumerism, could serve as a powerful educative force. In John Dewey's (1929, p. 265) terms, social values build on personal experiences, and those "judgments . . . should regulate the formation of our desires, affections and enjoyments." Unexamined experiences leave people subject to "prejudice, the pressure of immediate circumstance, self-interest and class-interest, traditional customs, institutions of accidental historic origin."

As teachers build their visions on personal histories as individuals engaged in complex professional roles, they seldom discuss what might have "happened" differently. For example, an achievement test reveals differences in what students failed to learn from among the tested objectives. It cannot reveal that some students drew quite different lessons—such as, my teacher does not expect girls to learn geometry. Americans live in a country that is affluent, educated, technologically advanced, democratically governed, and well-stocked with information sources. But we have little basis for imagining a society with cooperation among occupational groups or with racial and gender equality. Educators want pleasant places that empower students and staff, but they lack models for reconstructing existing schools.

## SOCIALLY CONSTRUCTED MEANINGS

Does thinking about the future make a difference? Can educators envision alternatives to competitive hierarchies that might engage alienated students? The challenge is to reframe old ideas into fresh relationships that open different possibilities. This entails connecting personal, group, and system-wide explanations in ways that incorporate both stability and change. To begin this process, we adopt a constructivist perspective, drawing on insights from Alfred Schutz's essays on phenomenological sociology written in the 1940s and 1950s (collected

and republished in 1962 and 1971). He described how individuals construct personal meaning systems through interactions with others.
They assign words and meanings to sensory inputs and then act on
those understandings in ways that enable them to communicate with
others.

That new framework for understanding cognitive development is
usually labeled constructivism and may be paraphrased roughly as
follows: *Meanings are socially constructed through interactions with
others. As children develop, what they experience is shaped by the
categories and relationships embedded in everyday language, activities
and values exhibited in their family, neighborhood and larger society.
New learning occurs when anomalous events raise questions about one's
taken-for-granted beliefs. Consequently, communications or interactions
should be interpreted in light of the history and social situation of both
speaker and listener as well as their personal and community
aspirations.*

Phenomenologists and constructivists continually ask: "How do we
know what we know?" Thoughtful observers often explain varied interpretations of events as personal perspectives on a generally objective
and knowable world; constructivism shifts the emphasis from the
natural world to the mental processes of interpreting sensory inputs.
What we see, hear, touch, smell and taste is fitted into categories and
relationships that are given a "name" and thus come to seem real. Facts
are contingent on one's perspective and setting; reasoning is personal
and developmental; language and cultural values both constrain and
enable communication of ideas. For example, visitors to an open-space
classroom may observe noisy disorder, whereas the teacher sees
students actively engaged in learning.

Constructivists depict accumulated knowledge as a compilation of
experiences as personally understood. Reality then is multiple—not
unitary, fixed or known-in-advance truths, accessible to all social actors.
That insight transforms the crucial question: How do people manage to
communicate at all? Following Schutz, phenomenological sociologists
ask how subjective interpretations become consistent enough for
language and text. They look at how more or less fixed meanings are
constructed through communication during ordinary interactions. In
that way, constructivism incorporates radically individual meanings,
social constructions of shared understandings for interpreting experiences, and taken-for-granted frameworks within cultural groups.

Constructivism has become an essential element in postmodernist
thinking by encouraging critical analysis of normally unchallenged
beliefs about how the world functions. Conversation mediates between
personal significance and socially shared meanings based on those
underlying assumptions about important regularities of behavior.
From an educational perspective, constructivism usually refers to
ways of learning though socially shared cognition based on experience,

reflection, and frameworks of understanding. Constructivism underlies most explanations of the stages of cognitive, social and moral development. It informs the rich interpretations of multiculturalism; and it deepens the critique of class, race and gender in society by validating the experi-ences and expressions of historically oppressed groups.

### Multiple Realities

As a philosophical and epistemological system, phenomenology insists that neither objective reality nor intrinsic ideas determine how people make sense of their experiences. Before interpreting an event, consider two prior questions:

"What does this social world mean for the observed actor within this world and what did he mean by his acting within it?" . . . we no longer naively accept the social world and its current idealizations and formalizations as ready-made and meaningful beyond all question, but we undertake to study the process of idealizing and formalizing as such, the genesis of the meaning which social phenomena have for us as well as for the actors, the mechanism of the activity by which human beings understand one another and themselves. (Schutz, 1971, p. 7)

Although the meaning of everyday life originates in the thoughts and actions of individuals, it is shared and modified by interactions with others. In their daily lives, people attribute intentionality to others' behaviors as though everyone acted in response to the same objects and relationships. People speak with others by assuming a "reciprocity of perspectives" and "interchangeability of standpoints" (Schutz & Luckmann, 1973). Over time, key categories and connections (or things and actions) acquire a consistency and "objectivity" that solidifies their existence. In this way, people usually understand what others say. Despite idiosyncratic understandings, individuals usually interact as though everyone perceived a common and reasonably complete account of events.

Words and symbols come to represent personal experiences in ways that can be communicated to others. In ordinary usage, they convey enormous numbers of assumptions. For instance, when we write of households, schools or workplaces, we assume that readers share many beliefs about how they function and their relationships to each other. Common meanings and shared language develop through face-to-face interactions. Gestures and sounds are repeated until meanings become clarified and ideal types identified. While the evolution of terms such as "table" or "truth" lies buried in the past, a similar process is underway for "computer" or "interactive video." As people experience them, they add layers of meanings that then require no further explanation.

Because a "social heritage" that defines relationships and categories is taken as objective reality, it obscures the radical individualism of phenomenology and thereby conceals the social processes of constructing functional meaning systems. It also obscures the influence of powerful groups who dominate interactional dynamics. Traditionally, people in different communities built up their own terminology for plants, soils, weather, and other aspects of daily life through personal interactions. For example, the meaning of gender was constructed by repeated interactions in household production of food, fuel and fiber. Local customs, costumes, and rituals gave meaning to communal life without ordinarily conflicting with different beliefs in nearby areas. Commercial capitalism and then industrialism exposed people to different customs and led to new understandings about locality, social structure, ideology, and culture.

From a perspective of phenomenological sociology, schooling involves a more or less intentional effort to construct shared realities for society. Ways of understanding, acting, communicating, and interacting are practiced and reinforced. As a result, young and old, rich and poor, Black and White, males and females discuss and react to nominally common historical and cultural events. Words and symbols gain significance: the American flag, the Civil War, *Huckleberry Finn*, algebraic conventions, data on gross national product, social tolerance, and fair play. These cultural symbols match the experiences of some students' background, who "learn" their accepted meanings quickly. Others find them alien or demeaning to their social identity.

Communication is easier when others share familiar experiences by attaching similar meanings to common events. In that context, responses are expected, and few issues appear problematic enough to require conscious consideration. Cultural beliefs embody group understandings based on common experiences and values. Some shared attitudes are embedded and unquestioned. Others are loosely linked in webs of significant values. Still others raise persistent dilemmas. Because all humans have much in common, communication across language and cultural differences is possible. Because these meanings are continually reconstructed, cultural patterns are persistent yet ever-changing. Most changes represent adjustments in underlying beliefs, but periodically there is a shift in basic assumptions about what meanings to attach to new interactions.

## Reconstructing Frameworks

All of us are strangers in a postindustrial era. Entering new territory, we lack a "ready-made standardized scheme of the cultural pattern" that can serve as an "unquestioned and unquestionable guide in all the situations" (Schutz, 1971, pp. 95, 99, 105). An immigrant's discovery "that things in his new surroundings look quite different from

what he expected them to be at home is frequently the first shock to the
stranger's confidence in the validity of his habitual 'thinking as usual'."
Faced with different assumptions about the meaning of events, "we first
define the new fact; we try to catch its meaning; we then transform step
by step our general scheme of interpretation of the world in such a way
that the strange fact and its meaning become compatible and consistent
with all the other facts of our experience and their meanings." Outsiders
and members of powerless groups experience similar dissonance between mainstream interpretations and their own perceptions of events.

In depicting knowledge as simultaneously personal, socially constructed, and culturally formatted, Schutz (1971, pp. 283–284) illumi-
nated how we organize thinking around one's individual purposes as
well as shared experiences. Knowledge "is the system of our practical or
theoretical interest at this specific moment which determines not only
what is problematic and what can remain unquestioned but also what
has to be known and with what degree of clarity and precision it has to
be known in order to solve the emergent problem." Those frameworks
establish how sensory inputs are screened and interpreted. As actions
become routine, people plan activities based on those mental constructs,
paying attention only when anomalies appear.

Past experiences and anticipated futures combine to shape what
information seems useful or how to interpret present interactions. As
Schutz (1971, p. 289) noted, "I have to visualize the state of affairs to be
brought about by my future action before I can draft the single steps of
my future acting from which that state of affairs will result." A mental
goal initiates action; each journey brings unanticipated lessons and new
objectives. Both memories and strategic purposes give relevance to
knowledge. Socially constructed in words and symbols, knowledge
enables us to coordinate with others in the present and to plan ahead—
to perform what Dewey called "a dramatic rehearsal in imagination."

---

**Recall a time when you were a stranger or a newcomer in an
unfamiliar setting and had to think about how to act and engage with
others. Did you wonder how others viewed you? Did you then
reconsider your self-identity?**

---

Many voices express perceived problems and tentative directions for
a curriculum designed for life in the 21st century. Yet varied opinions,
values and analytic approaches also feed uncertainty about any action.
Science and pragmatism cannot satisfy a "quest for certainty," as
Dewey (1929, pp. 290–291, 312) affirmed. The world is complex and
plastic—"indefinite interactions taking place within a course of nature
which is not fixed and complete, but which is capable of direction to new

and different results through the mediation of intentional operations."
As he warned, "knowledge by its nature is analytic and discriminating.
It attains large syntheses, sweeping generalizations. But these open up
new problems for consideration, new fields for inquiry; they are transitions to more detailed and varied knowledge."

Constructivism encompasses both stability and change. Categories
and relationships that satisfactorily guide our daily experiences seldom
rise to consciousness. When puzzling anomalies accumulate, they invite
reflection and a conscious reassessment of normal behaviors. Institutional and technological capacities evolve, while transformations in
symbols or underlying frameworks may occur in leaps—followed by
plateaus of understanding. Hopes or fears infect future thinking, and
groups sharply revise interpretation of common events in response to
accumulating tensions or optimistic prospects. When compared with
schools of a century ago, U.S. education looks good; when contrasted to
the many children whose potential remains unrealized, schools are a
failure.

## BETTER FUTURES

For 200 years, Americans focused on increasing production as a
solution to issues of fairness and social stability, but now personal
tensions, group conflicts, and internally contradictory ideological
frameworks obstruct both equity and efficiency. Explicit consideration
of future schools opens possibilities for institutional changes that
markedly transform the options open to students, teachers and other
educators. We wonder what might happen if schools did not reproduce
class, race and gender hierarchies; if international accords led to world
peace; and if social justice substantially assured domestic security.
Perhaps resources now going to arms, police and padlocks might
instead sustain lifelong education, health and comfort. If people trusted
each other, we believe that well-being for everyone on earth could be
raised to a level comparable with industrial nations.

In addition to basic choices between competition and cooperation in
all its many guises in classrooms, playgrounds, workplaces, and communities, the information that people will need—what can be taken for
granted and what must stay in one's consciousness—also depends on
technologies of production and coordination in households, businesses,
and government agencies. Modern families no longer know how to hunt,
skin and clean animals for food. Many have no connection with raising
vegetables, sewing clothes, or maintaining a fire for warmth. At the
same time, many are baffled by programming a VCR, obtaining cash
from an ATM, or downloading files from the Internet. As we explore
these issues, we probe beneath the surface of skills to ask how emerging
information technologies may affect what human knowledge or
competencies are valued.

Finally, to build dialog with teachers about curriculum for a knowledge society, we seek to clarify our theoretical, applied and normative beliefs. Christopher Dede (1990, pp. 85:2, 86:1) depicted the future as shaped by some forces that are highly predictable, some that are "possible, but not plausible," and some "imaginable" but improbable. "Ultimately the single future that occurs is invented (through the interaction of structural certainties, contractual assurances, wild cards, human choices, and indeterminacies in the present)." Sensible futurists direct their efforts toward malleable features that promote desirable changes. Empirical studies and analytic frameworks help locate probabilities in terms of historical development and social situations.

## Functional Learning

In a commonsensical way, most people assume that human knowledge serves practical purposes and varies over time and space. What people need to learn to act efficaciously in their setting depends on their ordinary interactions with things and other people, and what they know affects how they view their experience. Obviously, farmers who loosen soil with a crude hoe know different things about the land and tools than farmers who sit in air-conditioned tractors pulling a six-bottom plow. Daily actions seldom require conscious mental attention because they fit into ordinary categories and relationships. People walk, purchase a daily paper, and exchange friendly greetings without thinking about it or considering alternative actions. What cannot be taken for granted—an accident or storm, committing to a partner, planning a trip, voting in contested elections—requires thought about means and goals.

Without questioning these interconnections between what people know and particular historical, social and cultural settings, it is easy to generalize from personal psychological experience with learning. Each new understanding resolves a perceived anomaly and so appears more useful and true. By extension of that view of personal development, historical societies gradually accumulate better understanding. During a transitional period, some people sense that established values and formal curriculums no longer work well. A threat of impending changes, however, also raises longings for a simpler past—a perceived "golden age." Some react by calling for traditional values embodied in a basic curriculum. Others embrace a technological solution of computer-based access to databases and multimedia images. Instead, educators should ask what knowledge will best serve personal and societal well-being in a better future.

Industrialism was marked by a shift toward formal communication of information—quantities and prices, places and times. In agricultural villages and market towns, everyday relationships with others formed a subtext of taken-for-granted knowledge in face-to-face conversations.

Immediate contexts often supported coordination through signals or words—a factory whistle meant time to start or to stop, depending on the time of day. Most youth learned productive skills through informal apprenticeships within their family and village. As business interactions became sporadic and less personal, instruction came to entail formal identification of things and responsibilities. Specific functions of tools as well as occupational and organizational roles allowed workers to acquire and apply specialized skills while reporting only their needs and outputs to others.

Formal schooling became increasingly useful for industrial workers. It prepared the young to understand abstract meanings embedded in written language or mathematical relationships. Spelling, grammar and vocabulary were standardized. Gradually, speech, writing, arithmetic, and abstract logic incorporated systematic arrangements of knowledge applied to control activities. People became familiar with words and symbols as stand-ins for objects and actions. One did not have to be there to get the point. Specialization of labor allowed individuals to learn within disciplinary or professional boundaries. Finally, the daily routines of the school day prepared workers for time-based schedules and continuous supervision.

Families and schools are challenged to prepare children for adult roles. Sociologist Alex Inkeles (1966, pp. 280–281) compiled the many skills required for "effective participation in a modern industrial and urban society," including

manipulation of language and other symbol systems, such as arithmetic and time; the ability to comprehend and complete forms; information as to when and where to go for what; skills in interpersonal relations which permit negotiation, insure protection of one's interests, and provide maintenance of stable and satisfying relations with intimates, peers, and authorities; motives to achieve, to master, to persevere; defenses to control and channel acceptably the impulses to aggression, to sexual expression, to extreme dependency; a cognitive style which permits thinking in concrete terms while still permitting reasonable handling of abstractions and general concepts; a mind which does not insist on excessively premature closure, is tolerant of diversity, and has some components of flexibility; a conative style which facilitates reasonably regular, steady, and persistent effort, relieved by rest and relaxation but not requiring long periods of total withdrawal or depressive psychic slump; and a style of expressing affect which encourages stable and enduring relationships without excessive narcissistic dependence or explosive aggression in the face of petty frustration.

This comprehensive list suggests that individuals learn skills to keep pace with machines and adapt to existing social arrangements.

By the 1970s, a postindustrial economy was emerging in the United States. Three out of four workers provided services to the one in four who made things on farms or in factories. As markets expanded and products embodied technical improvements, more and more people worked to distribute, sell and maintain those goods. They devoted their time to processing forms, data or money in bureaucracies. Education, health care, recreation, security for persons and property, and welfare were provided by public and private specialists. Unlike personal care providers or custodians, these new service workers developed, processed and transmitted information rather than performing physical tasks. Increasingly, however, even that knowledge work could be handled by electronic microprocessors and data stored in computers.

Schools are caught between a need to prepare students for productive roles and emerging cultural patterns among the young who have grown up in relative prosperity and security. In many surveys, Inglehart (1990, pp. 423, 424) found that affluent youth in industrial countries reject a single-minded pursuit of material gains: "Materialist/Postmaterialist values seem to be part of a broader syndrome of orientations involving motivation to work, political outlook, attitudes toward the environment and nuclear power, the role of religion in people's lives, the likelihood of getting married or having children, and attitudes toward the role of women, homosexuality, divorce, abortion, and numerous other topics." A concern by younger people for ecology, civic participation, and personal self-expression suggests "we may be witnessing a broad cultural shift."

Improving standards of living through industrial modes of production may have reached its limits because of growing contradictions within modes of information in an interdependent, technologically advanced society. Communications designed to coordinate specialized labor break down when command hierarchies foster distrust, when lay persons are less able to assess technological qualities, and when unanticipated consequences of institutional change contradict initial hopes and plans. To date, public schools, economic growth, and equal rights have failed to overcome class, race, ethnic, and gender inequalities that fragment democratic consensus. Meanwhile, affluent societies face a range of choices that require collective agreements on what should be known and done.

## Transforming Knowledge

As an industrial era passes, social critics are becoming aware of previously taken-for-granted stories that had accounted for America's success. These metanarratives were repeated in conversations, literature, history, and social science texts: More Americans attended schools longer, each generation enjoyed a rising standard of living with greater equality; factory production embodied skills in machines and coordination in bureaucratic structures; and the whole was controlled through competitive markets and democratic institutions. Parents, teachers, media, and elites attributed progress to democracy and nationalism, capitalism and competitive markets, science and technology.

As commentators questioned that dominant metanarrative, they discovered coherent themes underlying its social frameworks. Educators had de-emphasized liberal learning in common schools as a basis for democracy and religion to stress efficient preparation of workers and a middle class. Critical theorists in a Marxian tradition depicted how industrialism had shaped household economies, hierarchical organizations, and political processes around specialized roles to produce efficiently. In contrast, postmodern critics stress multiple ways of seeing an event, nonmaterial goals of creativity and community, and a sense of social justice based on outcomes rather than processes. Although it stretches our usual way of thinking, each framework is needed to create a standpoint for viewing the other.

The proliferation of information technologies has redefined under-standings of education, work and well-being because facts, places and relationships compound complexities. Just as earlier mechanical inno-vations molded factories, social patterns, and cognitive styles, today's smart machines manage production and integrate knowledge—thereby redefining organizational strategies and structures. Work has been dramatically transformed by technologies producing "a new medium of electronic text through which organizational events, objects, trans-actions, functions, activities, and know-how could be enacted or observed" (Zuboff, 1988, p. 179). Computers and electronic media facilitate storing, transmitting and manipulating information, but individuals still select what messages they receive, how to interpret data, and what actions to take.

Computers, videodisks and hypermedia are hailed as revolutionary forces for learning and teaching. Most schools currently use live broadcasts and videocassette recorders as well as microcomputers for classroom instruction. In 1981, schools shared each computer among 125 students; by 1995, the ratio was 1 to 12. Computer-aided instruc-tion, intelligent tutoring systems, programming skills, simulations, microcomputer-based laboratories, graphing, database management, multimedia programs, word processing, and electronic networks all claim the capacity to improve learning. As many critics warn, however, drill and practice programs for students simultaneously control and "dumb down" teachers. Do computers facilitate creativity or merely accelerate the transmittal of old ideas? Are children educated or merely entertained by popular video games? Does greater knowledge bring personal satisfaction and social improvement?

An often cited "information explosion" challenges educators. According to mathematician Stanislau Ulam, professional journals publish about 100,000 theorems each year (Louie & Rubeck, 1989, p. 20). "If the number of theorems is larger than one can possibly learn," he asked, "who can be trusted to judge what is 'important'?" Generalists can scarcely scan 1 in 1,000 of the 40,000 scholarly journals; and specialists stay current only by narrowly defining their discipline. Social action, however, needs information from multiple fields. Academics call for transdisciplinary and cross-cultural studies, but the standards for assessing knowledge reside within discipline-based scientific research programs. Who brings expertise into a coherent whole?

Despite stacks of print, film and diskettes, there is no clear evidence that personally held information is exploding. Our great-grandparents did not lack sensory inputs. Imagine all the data in their kitchen—pots and pans, grains and meat, table and chairs, trees and grass glimpsed through a window, and dust settling in late afternoon sunlight. Each artifact present in a room has importance depending on circumstances, and their description varies accordingly. This is Ulam's dilemma in everyday life—how does one screen sensory inputs, remember some, and communicate a few to others? Laments about growing complexities and floods of information may accurately portray a sense of powerlessness over many things that affect our lives; but they also reflect a faith that more learning will somehow resolve all problems.

During industrialization, increasing productivity brought material benefits to most Americans. For them, consumption became a means of self-identity, a measure of one's self-worth. Moreover, economic growth privileged certain kinds of knowledge—technical, scientific, and rational. Now, dramatically lower costs for information transmittal open fresh possibilities. Society as a whole benefits from expanding human expertise, but knowledge can be embodied in individuals who are equal *or* divided hierarchically by class, race and gender. Information may be segmented in disciplines and occupations *or* widely distributed among interactive stakeholders. Information technologies may deskill most workers *or* enable people to take control of their lives. Coordination of complex postindustrial societies will either move toward cooperation and collaboration *or* strengthen competition and hierarchy. Those choices largely determine what children need to learn for the 21st century.

### Normative Beliefs

Normatively, we take a "value-laden stance" that requires openness between authors and readers. Our major beliefs about reasonably certain outcomes as well as personal values shape our thinking, interpretations of others, and practical proposals. Although value judgments are seldom far below the surface of social sciences, academic studies strive to appear objective—based on measurable observations that are evaluated in terms of scientific hypotheses. Causes are identified as factors other than personal choices and surface social dynamics. By contrast, conflicting voices and multiple frameworks ask readers to create meanings through reflection and an implicit dialog. Probably, we emphasize voices and analytic perspectives that point toward a just and affluent society—not to prescribe cures for well-structured problems but to encourage optimism about tentative proposals for reconstructing schools.

Although we see no underlying assurance of progress, we retain an optimism about a human potential to be reasonable, fair, cooperative, kind, and caring in a democracy with equality, constitutional rule, and material abundance. Learning is exciting, self-fulfilling and continuing, and we want public schools to serve everyone fairly. Although we consider most technical panaceas to be incomplete, we are heirs to a tradition of positivist social science reformers. In reviewing literature about schools and society, we have sought to redefine ideals of democracy, equality, multiculturalism, income security, and children raised in loving families for a postmodern era. In that spirit, we submit the following propositions about schools and future societies.

First, educational purposes flow from conceptualizations of better futures that extend from holistic analyses of historical developments and social situations. In general, educators face complex responsibilities with inadequate resources, and those tensions encourage a focus on immediate evidence of student learning. Classroom teachers need personal charisma to motivate their students; yet they also recognize that student aspirations ultimately must fit with their perceived opportunities. Looking for positive outcomes within one's perceived area of authority (e. g., high scores on an algebra test) distracts attention from long-term school improvement. Because meanings are socially constructed out of experiences and aspirations, learning depends on a whole context of interactions with family, peers, schools, and future prospects.

Second, we believe the quality of life depends on perceived choices open to individuals. Those choices critically depend on human capacities to make things and provide services. People working together in families, public and private enterprises, and voluntary associations toward shared goals can efficiently produce goods and services as well as sustain a stock of physical and human capital across generations. Modern science and technology are significant parts of the world's capital stocks—an inheritance from past generations. But industrial patterns of competition, linear thinking, and individualism also block many options that require group consensus. The use or threat of economic power backed by military force can coordinate diverse interests through hierarchies, but people do not willingly surrender their autonomy for long or without reason.

Third, plausible, ad hoc explanations seldom provide a foundation for a consensus-building dialog about a better society. Analytic frameworks can account for phenomena across many situations, but they are incomplete or contradictory. For example, simple group dynamics can account for both stability and change. Competition among individuals and organizations may yield efficient production, but at a cost of unequal power. Democratic processes and a sense of community depend on equality, which is not necessarily an outcome of representative government. Individual choices among a diversity of products, ideas and ideals enhance social welfare—but only when people are educated, organizations flexible, and society just. Our goal is to draw insights from multiple analyses and apply each in relevant areas at an appropriate level of generalization.

Fourth, democracies are stable in one of two positions: Income and rights can be distributed equally or fairly so that diverse people feel reasonably satisfied, or power can be arranged hierarchically and sustained through a variety of controls, including both schools and physical force. For 200 years, industrial hierarchies sustained their privileged position and accumulated vast power. Factories improved the quality of life for most citizens, and historians attributed those gains to increases in education, thriftiness and entrepreneurship. Now, stagnant growth disappoints personal aspirations and undermines a national ideology of progress; but greater equality will entail major changes in economic, political and social institutions. The challenge is for information exchanges to facilitate political agenda-setting among equity, efficiency and choice in pluralistic democracies.

Fifth, anticipating futures is not a well-structured problem with an accepted methodology and information for determining the answer. Citizens can neither predict nor control possibilities. Implicitly, educators make guesses about what ideas will (or should) be useful to their students as adults. Their scenarios about life in the 21st century seldom introduce radically new options such as a society purged of White racism. Empiricists cannot observe and measure what might have happened differently. Most reforms only marginally change institutional patterns. Even tentative projections, however, encourage dialog among stakeholders in future societies—if they are self-aware about how meaning systems shape personal perspectives. Juxtaposing subjective observations with generalizations about modernization or equity can trigger new ideas about one's goals and assumptions.

Finally, we need to question assumptions underlying every statement. For example, in an earlier draft of this chapter, we had asserted a functionalist view: "People act as though they know what will happen tomorrow and a decade from now—within a range of probability. By ignoring major uncertainties as beyond private or public control, they proceed as though rational actions will meet goals." Later, we read a critique of such modernist thinking. From Machiavelli on, functionalism "has constantly been at the same time a 'revolutionary' instrument of destruction of 'Ancient Regimes' and an ideological way of submitting traditional or irrational categories—especially workers, colonized people, women and children—to the rule of an enlightened male bourgeois western elite" (Touraine, 1992, p. 30). That comment reminded us about how much our own thinking has been formed and deformed by Eurocentric and patriarchal social scientists.

These beliefs taken together, we propose, establish a usable base for cultural values built on choice and human potential rather than on economic growth. A metaphor of an information age loosens conventional thinking from institutional and analytical frameworks that presume stable trends for material and social advancement. Technological innovations may shake up habitual behaviors, but they seldom reformat social understandings. When people act collectively to reframe schools and society, they no longer can assume that institutions and opportunities are relatively fixed. An emerging age of information enlarges the context of choices and opens dialog about possible new arrangements.

## RELATED READING

Kathleen Casey, *I Answer With My Life: Life Histories of Women Teachers Working for Social Change* (New York: Routledge, 1993) and Gerald Grant, *The World We Created at Hamilton High* (Cambridge, Harvard University Press, 1988) introduce the importance of educators' voices. For an illustration that the educational reforms proposed in this work have been recognized by prescient educators, see John I. Goodlad, *Facing the Future: Issues in Education and Schooling* (New York: McGraw-Hill, 1976).

Two works extend Alfred Schutz's insights in *The Phenomenology of the Social World* (Evanston, IL: Northwestern University Press, 1967) in accessible, low-cost editions: Peter L. Berger and Thomas Luckmann, *The Social Construction of Reality: A Treatise in the Sociology of Knowledge* (New York: Doubleday, 1966) and John P. Hewitt, *Dilemmas of the American Self* (Philadelphia: Temple University Press, 1989).

# 2

# Schools and Society

Most Americans believe that schools shape future opportunities for individuals and for society—without specifying how curricular decisions relate to either stability or change in economic or political systems. They view their national history as a success story of growing abundance, presumably because public education fostered democratic values and equal opportunities to compete and get ahead. Those who adopt a more critical stance also value fairness and growth, but they emphasize gaps between those ideals and inequalities based on class, race and gender. Because Americans generally associate a growing population and economy with industrialization and urbanization as well as social hierarchies, they have difficulty envisioning more equal, cooperative or empowering alternatives.

Every approach to curriculum, as Ralph Tyler (1949, p. 35) has insisted, asks some variation of the question "should the school develop young people to fit into the present society as it is or does the school have a revolutionary mission to develop young people who will seek to improve the society?" In our interviews, teachers typically started with a hope that all students could learn to function in today's society, and perhaps to make it better. Yet they identified oppressed groups—who see little hope that academics will improve their lives—as problems in their classrooms. A concerned teacher considered how to raise her students' aspiration levels: *"We need to teach our parents that we need to teach the children to have some life goals and life ambitions."* Sometimes educators emphasized individual responsibility for failure and at other times unfair social structures—though neither explanation led to plausible solutions within a coherent analysis of personal and group dynamics.

Our interviews revealed little consensus about what skills will benefit individuals and society or how best to influence future behaviors. When criticized, educators recite various ongoing efforts to achieve equity and efficiency while acknowledging a need to try harder. At the same time, they question whether families prepare their children for school, whether job markets tap the talents and skills of all students, whether governments provide adequate fiscal resources, and whether personal morality matches professed community values. Advocates for public education veer uneasily between citing accomplishments and complaining about a lack of funds or of parental involvement. However, that human tendency to claim credit for successes while blaming others for failures offers little sense about how learning connects to later earnings—or what it might mean if *everyone* did well in school.

Typically, teachers seek to make sense of their dilemmas by addressing immediate issues within familiar cognitive frameworks. Most educators seek to motivate students by relating individual achievement to positive economic outcomes and then account for inequities by noting that it is a "competitive" world. Despite evidence that children can master the curriculum if given time, support and appropriate instruction, educators grade on a bell-shaped curve based on unscientific assumptions about genetically fixed IQ. Alternatively, they attribute below-average grades to dysfunctional families from low-income and minority neighborhoods. Teachers cherish their successes, especially with the higher-level tracks, as evidence that the fault for failure lies with students' apathy or ignorance. Those who want every child to learn cannot offer plausible explanations for unequal outcomes within a dominant American narrative of democratic and capitalist progress.

This chapter explores three puzzles about the relationship of schools to society. First, more schooling correlates with higher productivity and economic development—as well as with persistent class, race and gender hierarchies. Second, although a majority of people could benefit from a more equal education and distribution of income, oppressed groups seldom agree on effective means to improve their general welfare. Third, resistance to school regularities and capitalist ideologies is pervasive, yet it rarely coalesces into politically attractive proposals that focus discontent and mobilize support. Constructivism directs attention to language and popular understandings as a way to explain why unequal conditions due to class, race and gender are largely tolerated in silence, despite an American ideology of equality.

We start with two well-developed accounts of American education. Mainstream histories depict a steady expansion of public schools, economic growth, and equality. Education is described as an investment in human capital: Schooling raises productivity and equal education underlies democracy. By contrast, critical analysts focus on a basic power struggle in which owners of property sustain economic and political dominance, as well as cultural hegemony, through schools, jobs and politics. Next, we sketch how traditional school structures and regularities developed in response to the desire of industrial elites for a docile workforce. Later, organized protests by African Americans and feminists exposed glaring exceptions to equal opportunity. Then, we trace the impact of current stagnation on unequal prospects for children and probe how attitudes toward social equality diffuse discontent. Finally, we explore how low-income youth resist schooling and why many teachers stifle controversial ideas.

## EDUCATION IN A DEMOCRATIC SOCIETY

Mainstream American historians and social commentators picture a people blessed with freedom and abundance. Stable institutions guided a nation through tremendous growth in population, wealth, influence, and power. The eminent historian Lawrence Cremin and others argued that expanded public schooling actualized core values in a democratic and progressive society. The United States never had to overcome a feudal past or a totalitarian government that assigned wealth, rights and power to a ruling elite. Its great conflict of the 19th century was described—at least by the victors—as a moral crusade to end slavery. Liberalism based on equal and responsible individuals was America's traditional political creed, and thus a generally conservative force.

Compared with the rest of the world, most Americans enjoyed democratic rights, abundance, equality, and peace—although European American males dominated indigenous Americans and African Americans as well as exercised patriarchal authority over females. A growing population, a rising standard of living, and national policies to expand democracy all suggested that inequities were being addressed. Universal citizenship among Whites, widespread land ownership, and religious beliefs encouraged an emphasis on literacy, which brought support for public education. In turn, schooling supported democracy and economic expansion. Although native peoples, Blacks and women were omitted from this dominant narrative, they too could point to economic, political and social gains.

Emphasizing the positive, Cremin (1988, pp. 644–645) concluded: "Schooling had become prevalent in the United States by the 1870's, though with considerable variation with respect to race, class, ethnicity, gender, and region; it became virtually universal over the next century." By 1920, 9 of 10 children, age 7 to 13, attended school; 40 years later, over 98% did. Furthermore, 3 of 4 of those who entered fifth grade in 1972 had earned diplomas by 1980. Following a common school ideal, "children of various class, ethnoreligious, and racial backgrounds would attend the same public school building together, however much a variety of modes of formal and informal tracking segregated them from one another."

### Investing in Human Capital

From an economic perspective, schools and society are linked through an investment in human capital—learning pays off in a lifetime of higher earnings. Analytically, an economic good is either consumed in the present or used to enhance future production. Although some learning brings immediate pleasure and is counted as consumption, people support schools in the expectation that their children's employability will improve. Unlike physical investments in plant and equipment, human capital is embodied in a person whose physical and mental health, geographic location, and interactive skills determine whether and how acquired knowledge can be put to use. Like any other investment, formal education is easier if one (or one's family) enjoys a surplus beyond basic necessities.

For two centuries, industrial nations grew richer, more populous, and better educated. Transportation and communication networks sustained urban centers and extended markets. Specialized labor opened career ladders for technical, professional and managerial workers. Public education with expanding opportunities for collegiate training fostered scientific and cultural advances. Mass media from newspapers, phonograph records, radio, magazines, and television surrounded people with information. Formal training supported advances in science and technology as well as managerial and bureaucratic skills. They, in turn, sustained long-term growth in labor productivity, enabling each generation to live better than its parents.

As a result, returns from investment in education have not diminished over time. Expanding academic achievement generated a demand for additional schooling and better jobs. Widespread schooling enabled Americans to advance themselves, communicate in writing, read for amusement and learning, and participate in politics. Business, government and the media all came to count on near-universal literacy. It "rationalized experience, systematizing it on the one hand—thus making possible new technologies of organization—and individualizing it on the other—thereby facilitating not only reflection but also criticism" (Cremin, 1988, pp. 658–659).

Moreover, studies show "a clear and enduring correlation between the level of schooling a person had completed (elementary school, secondary school, college) and the amount of information that person possessed, general as well as specialized, current as well as traditional" (Cremin, 1988, pp. 662–663). Moreover, "there was a less striking but nevertheless clear and enduring correlation between the level of schooling a person had completed and the humaneness of that person's values, the person's commitment to civil liberties, freedom of information, and due process of law, and the person's readiness to grant equal opportunity to members of minority groups."

After World War II, American education flourished as the economy grew. Schools and colleges

provided large numbers of highly trained individuals to fill the needs of agriculture, industry, business, government, and the professions; it drew these individuals from the general population on an increasingly nondiscriminatory basis—at least until the late 1970's; it produced and housed a major share of the nation's most articulate critics—critics of everything from the government's policies to the society's styles of life; it produced a large share of the world's Nobel Prize winners . . . ; and it attracted more candidates for advanced degrees, particularly in the sciences and engineering, from other countries than any other system in the world. (Cremin, 1988, pp. 663–664)

> **True or false:**
> _____ **The United States is the richest country.**
> _____ **Americans are the freest people on earth.**
> _____ **They enjoy the highest standard of living.**
> _____ **America's schools are the best.**
> **What evidence supports your choices?**

Today, investment in human capital—in education, on-the-job experience and health—is more important than investment in physical capital. An individual's earnings typically increase with years of schooling, and advanced credentials usually lead to careers offering lifelong advancement. Anticipated payoffs in future salary and working conditions motivate some students to diagram sentence structures and to solve geometry proofs. Although wage differentials have persisted across occupations, as well as for women and people of color, economic theory attributes higher earnings for well-educated individuals to their greater contributions to national production. Thus, taxpayers earn a return from public schools through equalizing opportunities, diffusing social values, fostering national cohesion, and enhancing productivity.

## Rights to Equal Schooling

If learning determines one's future earnings, then a democratic society should assure that schools offer every child a fair chance to become a productive citizen. Equal protection of the law, as specified by the Fourteenth Amendment, raised constitutional issues about racial separation and pervasive inequalities of resources in public schools. This argument—tracing historical advances to public schools that met minimum curricular standards—informed the *Brown v. Topeka* (1954) decision. For a unanimous court, Chief Justice Earl Warren affirmed the importance of education "in the performance of our most basic public responsibilities, even service in the armed forces. It is the very foundation of good citizenship. Today it is a principal instrument in awakening the child to cultural values, in preparing him for later professional training, and in helping him to adjust normally to his environment." Therefore, schooling "must be made available to all on equal terms."

Although fairness has a broad appeal, schools manifestly discriminate based in part on class, race and gender. Often, educators seek to evade responsibility for inequities by indicting historical patterns or social problems. In 1964, Congress funded a *Report on Equal Educational Opportunity* in the expectation that variations in school resources would account for differences in student achievement—notably between Black and White youngsters. Instead, sociologist and primary author James Coleman (1966) concluded, academic achievement correlated primarily with family income and status. Other inputs such as teachers' experience or credentials, library volumes or science laboratories, and expenditures per pupil showed no consistent relationship to students' test scores.

The Coleman report documented substantial racial isolation and a persistent gap in test scores between Black and White students. Although many interpreted his results as denying that learning could be equalized by a fair allocation of funds for buildings, teachers, or curricular materials, no one seriously doubts that a gap of $1,500 versus $8,500 in per-pupil spending would make a huge difference. Most districts spend roughly similar amounts, so variations often stem from parental inputs or a school's climate. Critics have demonstrated that Coleman's method could not distinguish small but persistent differences in inputs (Mosteller & Moynihan, 1972). Moreover, detailed examinations of classroom curriculums have documented that teachers treat children differently based on their class, race and gender (Rist, 1978; Payne, 1984; Orenstein, 1994).

School finance studies show a pervasive tendency for educational support to correlate with local community wealth. Typically, poor districts tax themselves at rates two or more times higher than wealthy districts and still spend less than half as much per child. For instance, when Fall River, Massachusetts, had $47,000 of taxable property per school-age child, Chatham, a few miles east on Cape Cod, had a tax base in excess of $600,000 per child. In 1988, New Jersey expended an average of $6,564 per student, in contrast to Mississippi's $2,548. Considerable inequities have been tolerated because low-income districts lack political clout, ordinarily pay teachers less, and are partially compensated through state equalization formulas.

The *Brown* decision encouraged an argument that large discrepancies in per-student expenditures violated the equal protection clause of the Fourteenth Amendment. Indeed, the California Supreme Court ruled that funding schools through local property taxes without equalizing state aid "makes the quality of a child's education a function of the wealth of his parents and neighbors." Declaring access to schooling "a fundamental interest," the California court could "discern no compelling state purpose necessitating the present method of financing." Furthermore, public actions such as zoning aggravated inequities by encouraging "economic exclusivity" (*Serrano v. Priest*, 1971). Two years later, however, the United States Supreme Court ruled that substantial maldistribution of fiscal resources in Texas fell short of denying equal protection under the federal Constitution (*Rodriquez v. San Antonio*, 1973).

Subsequently, state courts have decided that interdistrict differences in resources violate assurances of equal education. In 1989, the Texas Supreme Court found that the wealthiest district had $14 million in property per student, while the poorest had about $20,000. The 100 poorest districts levied a rate of 74.5 cents to raise under $3,000 per pupil, while the 100 wealthiest districts assessed property at 47 cents and spent over $7,000 per student. Consequently, Texas school finances violated state constitutional provisions for equal rights, due process, and mandatory "efficiency" in education:

Property-poor districts are trapped in a cycle of poverty from which there is no opportunity to free themselves. Because of their inadequate tax base, they must tax at significantly higher rates in order to meet minimum requirements for accreditation; yet their educational programs are typically inferior. The location of new industry and development is strongly influenced by tax rates and the quality of local schools. Thus, the property-poor districts with their high tax rates and inferior schools are unable to attract new industry or development and so have little opportunity to improve their tax base. (*Edgewood v. Kirby*, 1989)

Mandated rights and state funding formulas alleviate some inequality without upsetting the rank order of money or achievement. Court rulings in California, New Jersey, Connecticut, and Massachusetts failed to induce legislators to vote higher taxes needed to equalize resources. Perhaps Texas, Kentucky or Michigan will prove exceptions to that generalization. Federal and state laws currently mandate equal access for females, extra instruction for those speaking English as a new language, mainstream experiences for students with special needs, and compensatory programs for low-income or low-achieving schools. Nevertheless, no state has equalized resources among districts, much less among and within schools. Hawaii, a partial exception with its single statewide district, inadequately adjusts for concentrations of high-cost students.

## Ambiguous Outcomes

Debates over the purpose of education hinge less on assessments of typical curricula than on judgments about human potential. If people are basically selfish and brutal, then public schools are needed to civilize, socialize and foster a sense of community. Others contend that children will cooperate peacefully if classrooms do not perpetuate competition and hierarchy. National myths emphasize individual initiative and responsibility over collective action for community well-being. Americans cherish an occasional legendary success, such as Abraham Lincoln, as an exception that "proves" rhetoric about meritocratic opportunities, but they resist a rule of equality. Philo-sophical utopias, communal experiments, and comparisons with Sweden or other social welfare states point toward alternative paths without demonstrating the possibility of educational equality on a large scale.

Court orders have been frustrated because elected representatives from wealthier suburban communities resist raising state taxes to provide high-quality schools in every district. With some 15,000 local jurisdictions, many smaller districts lack taxable resources to support a high-quality education, while cities face many competing demands for public funds. Legislative formulas that equalize financing among districts continually fall short because state appropriations fail to keep pace with rising costs. Equalization is complicated by issues of race and longstanding conflicts between urban centers and suburban or rural districts. Legal rights, defined by *Brown v. Topeka*, have not overcome a growing racial isolation in metropolitan regions.

> **Publicly supported schools serve personal and social purposes by preserving traditional knowledge and by creating new arts and sciences. Depending on the context, educators view schools as responding to public *and* to private interests; as conserving established wisdom *and* advancing new knowledge; as rewarding individual merit *and* reproducing class, race and gender attitudes; as reflecting contemporary conditions *and* shaping tomorrow's possibilities.**
>
> **Can students and teachers coherently pursue some or all of these purposes? What priorities do you advocate?**

Liberal historians, economists, and jurists typically express dismay at persistent and pervasive discrimination—after describing major achievements of democratic schooling in the United States. They engage conservative scholars on relatively narrow grounds: Do public welfare programs reduce poverty, or is it better to rely on market incentives to instill personal responsibility? Liberals emphasize a governmental safety net for victims of industrial progress. Conserva-tives stress personal responsibility and competition. Both view school-ing as a production process for equipping the next generation with knowledge, skills and aptitudes related to an expanding economy.

Neither considers it fundamentally contradictory for schools and society to achieve equity and efficiency in a capitalist democracy.

Yet this contradiction generates a persistent tension in American schools and society. Equal economic opportunities and access to civic participation seemingly require that schools offer every child knowledge and values useful for productive citizenship. Commitments to fairness are affirmed in public finance laws, rhetoric about maximizing each student's potential, and a common belief that academic achievement should depend on individual merit. Historically, reforms have expanded opportunities for more students to stay in school longer. Support for public schools remains strong, despite recent efforts by some political leaders to substitute private choice plans that would enable wealthy parents to transfer economic advantages to their children. Nevertheless, relative positions in social status and in academic achievement have proven stubbornly stable across generations.

## SCHOOLS IN CAPITALIST AMERICA

Critical theorists usually start "unpacking" optimistic depictions of American schools along the lines outlined in *Schooling in Capitalist America* by Samuel Bowles and Herbert Gintis (1976, p. 48). The two economists reexamined progressive reforms from a Marxian perspective and found that neither historically nor today have schools systematically promoted equality or interclass mobility. Instead, "the educational system serves—through the correspondence of its social relations with those of economic life—to reproduce economic inequality and to distort personal development." From this perspective, ineffective equalization measures and occasional democratic rhetoric are simply concessions by capitalists to maintain their economic and political dominance.

Reforms extended educational services to a wider spectrum of society and enabled many individuals to exceed their parents' status, but progress toward more equitable outcomes for the powerless were paralleled by gains for the advantaged. Schools for working-class children emphasize obedience and industrial progress with the aim "of forestalling the development of class consciousness among the working people of the state and preserving the legal and economic foundations of the society" (Bowles & Gintis, 1976, p. 173). Preparing able workers and independent citizens through schools entails a fundamental contradiction, because corporations want well-trained employees who also will accede to capitalists' control.

Noting an absence of overt conflict between workers and capitalists, critical theorists subsequently focused attention on the production and reproduction of class attitudes or cultures in schools, media, workplaces, and the nation-state. Public education taught attitudes and values "appropriate" to class, race and gender statuses and thereby perpetuated stable hierarchies within a dynamic economy. Viewing schools as partially independent sites of struggle, critical theorists look for evidence of students' autonomy and resistance. They find it in "tuning out" the formal curriculum as well as assertions by some youth of values that conflict with mainstream norms. Those behaviors partly account for a stable class structure because they divert attention from coherent economic analysis and political action.

### Hierarchies and Control

Because productive activities might be coordinated without hierarchical controls, Bowles and Gintis suggest that technical efficiency fails to account for the characteristic strategies and structures of industrial capitalism. Workers are separated along class, race and gender lines. Men of European background predominate in "primary" labor markets with decent wages and job security in capital-intensive corporations. Youth, minorities and women are relegated to secondary labor markets with lower wages, chronic unemployment, and consequent high labor turnover in firms less sheltered from market fluctuations. A surplus of laborers allows owners to expropriate profits, while divisions among employees block concerted resistance. A growing middle class of managers, technicians and professionals that includes teachers serve capitalists' interests in controlling workers.

Academic degrees justify salary differences and sanction authority. For 150 years, corporate and political leadership has been overwhelmingly White, male, and educationally credentialed. If hierarchy is legitimate, it reconciles "the inherent conflict between capital and labor" (Bowles & Gintis, 1976, p. 83). Machines and workers become interchangeable to capitalists who seek to maintain profits by inducing employees to accept managerial control. "Thus profits are contingent on the ability of employers to elicit proper performance from workers in the face of the latter's lack of concern with the objective of profit, and to reduce the total power of workers by limiting and channeling coalitions among them—divide and conquer." Consequently, labor never organized effective democratic protests.

To support a segmented society, "the school produces, rewards, and labels personal characteristics relevant to the staffing of positions in the hierarchy" (Bowles & Gintis, 1976, pp. 130, 96). Workers should be "dependable (i. e., follow orders) because of the strong emphasis on rules and the complex interrelations among tasks that define the enterprise." They should accept the values of the corporation but "respond to the external incentives of the organization—the crudest being threat of dismissal and the more subtle including the possibility of promotion to a higher status, authority, and pay." Unskilled workers follow orders, while managers coordinate specialized roles and plan ahead to serve capitalists' interests. Over time, those organizational patterns become ingrained, and values are partially internalized.

Factory work and crowded cities diminish an individual's sense of self, creativity, and autonomy as a worker and citizen. Schools reproduce the conditions of alienation through the way they organize activities around adult authority over students, emphasize training for jobs, and establish social relationships. The informal curriculum of bells, rules, teacher supervision, permission slips, and testing trains one to function in modern bureaucracies. "Power and privilege in economic life surface not only in the core social institutions which pattern the formation of consciousness (e. g., school and family), but even in face-to-face personal encounters, leisure activities, cultural life, sexual relationships, and philosophies of the world" (Bowles & Gintis, 1976, p. 148).

Class struggles remain a subtext in educational debates because elites want schools to "sort" or "slot" youths into roles while fostering attitudes that embrace competition and differential rewards. As long as job markets segment workers into hierarchical levels of authority and income that are loosely associated with educational credentials, equity in schools is important. Historically, "parents, students, worker organizations, blacks, ethnic minorities, women, and others have sought to use schools for their own objectives: material security, culture, a more just distribution of economic reward, and a path of personal development conducive not to profits but to a fuller, happier life" (Bowles & Gintis, 1976, p. 101).

## Status Reproduction in Schools?

In an effort to explicate some practical implications from this analysis, critical theorists view schools and industrial firms as parallel institutions with common historical roots:

Schools and workplaces are organized in ways that correspond closely. Both tend to be large, bureaucratic, impersonal, hierarchical, and routinized. Both tend to motivate performance with external rewards such as grades and wages, rather than depending on the value of the enterprise itself. Schools and workplaces alike are dominated by expertise and formal authority; in both there are schedules that determine the timing of work, and regulations that determine its nature. (Carnoy & Levin, 1985, p. 1)

Because schools espouse a rhetoric of openness and equality, however, they expose conflicts between students' aspirations and their unequal prospects. Educators serving low-income and culturally diverse neighborhoods want to believe they can do something to help their students achieve a better life. They wish for economic development in central cities and for less racism and poverty. Public support is never sufficient for teachers to equalize academic achievement—although some exceptional programs demonstrate its possibility. They find themselves troubled by outcomes of both capitalism and democracy.

Likewise, students who see the futility of aspiring to high-status careers resist routine assignments that seemingly lead nowhere.

As long as job markets discriminate and pay is unequal, neither teachers nor parents dare totally ignore class boundaries in preparing the young for real life. Observations of two first-grade classrooms revealed that "parents, school staff, and the state educational apparatus have different expectations for children from upper-middle-class families than for those from lower-middle-class ones" (Carnoy & Levin, 1985, pp. 135, 145). Their combined efforts serve "to produce a labor force with skills, attitudes, and values that fit into the hierarchical division of labor and to reproduce capitalist relations of production" while also promoting "equality of opportunity and occupational mobility through education."

> **Social divisions are continually reconstructed by what happens in schools. For example, working-class children who learn to dislike reading, writing and computing do not aspire to technical, managerial or professional positions. Females may find little support for their interest in math and science.**
>
> **A stagnant economy offers few opportunities for advancement. Do middle-class information workers really want their children to compete fairly for education and jobs with working-class children? Do European American males fear equality with people of color and women?**

Political contests over schools and the curriculum continually redefine the meaning of being Black and White in America. Educators have used intelligence tests as though they measured "native" capacity, thereby implementing racist ideologies long after most social scientists recognized that race is a social construct, not a biological one. They achieve much the same categorization by talking about a culture of poverty, inner city schools, the underclass, welfare mothers, or at-risk children. Complaints about crime, drug abuse, unwed teenage mothers, and gang violence serve to remake the meaning of African Americans and other people of color as seen by comfortable Whites. That language suggests a separation from a desired norm as well as political and cultural controversies.

Patriarchal relations of "traditional" families are replicated in schools, where mostly female teachers guide and assist children under the supervision of mostly male principals and superintendents. Historically, female teachers worked for less money, held fewer after-school positions with pay, and were expected to empathize with children's needs. Moreover, the proportion of female instructors declines from childcare centers through graduate programs. Textbooks, curricular guides, and competency tests effectively determine the curriculum, thereby limiting teachers' discretion. Females lack role models for active leadership among their teachers or in their texts, and many girls are influenced by media images of traditional feminine roles.

Unsurprisingly, teachers feel themselves caught in the middle of conflicting pressures. Bowles and Gintis (1976, p. 49) placed advocates for democratic schools on the side of angels—albeit in an isolated and powerless heaven. "The roots of repression and inequality lie in the structure and functioning of the capitalist economy." Critical theorists urge schools to become "democratic public spheres . . . constructed around forms of critical inquiry that dignify meaningful dialogue and human agency" (Giroux, 1988, p. xxxii). Steps to achieve equitable, inclusive and pleasant schools seemingly conflict with segmented labor markets. Educators remain torn between encouraging children of the working classes to acquire vocational skills as a matter of "practicality" or inspiring them to become professionals, artists or political activists.

## INSTITUTIONALIZATION OF SCHOOL STRUCTURES

From within either a mainstream or a class conflict interpretation, historical developments often appear foreordained—determined by social needs and functional goals. There is little need for further discussion. By contrast, when two or more perspectives are simultaneously entertained, a dialectic or internal dialog is established. Changes then appear as choices that reflect a confluence of many factors, including interests, ideas and ideals. In that context, it is useful to reconsider the development of public schools in light of current dissatisfactions with education and modern society. Reviewing how certain assumptions of democracy and capitalism informed earlier strategies and structures suggests that meaningful school improvements will entail new institutional formats.

For two centuries, modernization—variously seen in commercial capitalism, technological advances, industrialization, mass immigrations, and urbanization—seemed a threat to social stability in the eyes of capitalists and many middle-class citizens in the United States. They looked to public schools to maintain social control in the face of idle youth, immigrants, labor unrest, crime, and poverty—all without blocking desirable growth. Optimists believed that a safe, nurturing classroom could inculcate skills and improve character. Pessimists fell back on hereditarian notions that intelligence was fixed and that racial, ethnic and gender attributes largely determined one's capacities and appropriate roles. More specifically, working-class children, students of color, and females should learn docility within patriarchal and hierarchical structures.

Periods of stability followed by crises and change are understandable in terms of normal processes of institutionalization: "Institutions are the rules of the game in a society or, more formally, are the humanly devised constraints that shape human interaction. In consequence, they structure incentives in human exchange, whether political, social, or economic" (North, 1990, p. 3). They "reduce uncertainty by providing a structure to everyday life." Organizational structures are created in response to historical conditions as perceived by dominant political groups. Over time, those rules and incentives engender unreflective habits with remarkable stability—until new conditions raise fresh questions.

## Public Schools for Social Control

The development of bureaucratic schools has been traced to a confluence of conditions during the transition from commercial to industrial capitalism (Katz, Doucet, & Stern, 1982, pp. 356, 369). New categories of dependency appeared—the unemployed, individuals and families on the move, women, youth, and children, new immigrants, and criminals. "The novelty during the nineteenth century rested in the creation of systems of public education—age-graded, finely articulated, nominally universal institutions presided over by specially trained experts and administrators." Reading, writing and arithmetic contributed to job skills and citizenship, but the focus was on moral values—"sensual restraint, dependability, willingness to work, acquiescence in the legitimacy of the social order, and acceptance of one's place within it—all serviceable traits in early capitalist America."

As revisionist historians Katz, Doucet and Stern (1982, pp. 370, 350, 349–350) concluded, "public education did not represent the institutional culmination of a humane, democratic, egalitarian impulse." Instead, mandatory schooling under professional educators "would promote economic growth and stave off social chaos." Accordingly, common schools sought "the reformation of character rather than the redistribution of wealth or power." In 1851, an educational reformer had argued that "the care and instruction of a kind, affectionate, and skillful female teacher" would overcome "deficient household arrangements and deranged machinery of domestic life, of the extreme poor and ignorant, to say nothing of the intemperate—of the examples of rude manners, impure and profane language, and all the vicious habits of low-bred idleness."

As transportation and communication networks linked the country, the geographic fragmentation of the early republic gave way to social segmentation:

A small, decentralized, localistic, deferential, predominantly rural and relatively egalitarian society was replaced by a new society based on markets in labor, and characterized by transiency, a strident individualism, industrial production, and increasingly urban, unequal, heterogeneous and interconnected. Simultaneously, the social structural conditions of class formation began to take shape: the progressive extension of proletarianization, changes in the opportunity structure (particularly the increasing importance of educational credentials in determining occupational attainment) and ecological patterns of residential areas (particularly the separation of work and residence), and the development of stratified (ethnically, racially, sexually), dual (primary, secondary) and internal labor markets. (Hogan, 1982, p. 46)

Those social and economic developments led to school strategies and structures that legitimized elites and trained workers for docility.

Controlling local schools required political influence, but no party consistently represented working-class interests. Historical factors limited class consciousness: available land and relative scarcity of labor, abundant resources, and hard work leading to affluence, "the size of its middle class and the opportunity for social mobility, widespread home ownership and the power of its individualist ideology, the bloody repression of strikes and radical political activity at key junctures in American history and the racial and ethnic stratification of the working class, the early achievement of liberal democracy and the conservative bent of its trade unions" (Hogan, 1982, p. 38). Trapped between traditional and modern values, recent immigrants fractured along generational and ethnic lines. Because education helped keep pace with technological and sociological developments, working-class families usually supported mandatory schooling, although they also needed their children's labor.

Economic and social developments gradually transformed public education from supporting democracy to a shocking outcome: "Ultimately the moral mission of the schools—as educators would refer to the teaching of attitudes and behavior—was political, for its goal was to legitimize inequality" (Katz et al., 1982, p. 390). Schools enabled capitalists to retain disproportionate power because "children learn to blame themselves for failure." Certified teachers in age-segregated classes insisted that brains and study determined a rank ordering of test scores: "Thus schoolchildren of the last 150 years have received their first lesson in political economy: the unequal distribution of rewards mirrors the unequal distribution of ability."

## Structuring the Status Quo

Early in the 20th century, professional administrators imitated businesslike organizational structures of staff command. Students were "batch processed" through standardized classrooms under the supervision of a principal. School leaders (usually male) imposed their ideas about instruction on students, teachers (mainly female), and working-class voters. Educational reformer Ellwood Cubberley (1947, pp.

527–528, 504) enthusiastically adopted industrial metaphors: "The public schools of the United States are, in a sense, a manufactory, doing a two-billion dollar business each year in trying to prepare future citizens for usefulness and efficiency in life." Literacy no longer sufficed, and workers had to be trained for specialized roles, thereby raising "the danger from class subdivision." Consequently, "more and more has been thrown upon the school the task of instilling into all a social and political consciousness that will lead to unity amid our great diversity, and to united action for the preservation and improvement of our democratic institutions."

The reproduction of social hierarchies in schools is a difficult concept to grasp, but it is clearly visible in a presumption that a bell-curve grading system makes sense. Educators argued that standardized tests enabled the school to chart its progress: "Principals and teachers can tell, from a glance at the results of standard tests, charted on a standard score card, whether or not any room or group of pupils is up to standard; what are the weak points; whether a room or a school is making progress; and in what rooms the load and the teacher are not properly adjusted" (Cubberley, 1947, p. 697). Despite the assumed importance of grades and class rankings, there is startlingly little connection between grades and later success in jobs and careers. Implicitly, preparing for citizenship entailed equality, while training for hierarchical jobs lead toward differential grades, tracks, programs, and outcomes.

By 1900, universal public schooling had redefined educational purposes. "Before 1870," observed historian Marvin Lazerson (1971, pp. 254–255), "educators assumed that children attending the common school needed to learn the same things: the essentials of citizenship, morality, communication, and thought." High schools accommodated "to individual differences. Greater commitments were made to preparing youth for the job market. Pressure for curriculum differentiation intensified, especially on the basis of future occupational destinations. A new ideology emerged that emphasized achievement, measurement, differentiation, and efficiency." Eventually, those features of schools were taken for granted and embedded in behavioral regularities affecting how children experienced education.

As enrollments grew with required attendance, schools focused on training workers less through an academic curriculum than through behaviors imposed on students. According to historian David Tyack (1974, p. 50), urban schools stressed "(1) punctuality, (2) regularity, (3) attention, and (4) silence, as habits necessary through life for successful combination with one's fellow-men in an industrial and commercial civilization." Public education emphasized teacher authority in the formal and informal curriculum, with distinct vocational, technical, commercial, or college preparatory schools. Social studies promoted

"Americanization" for children of immigrants. Health education and physical training were to assure strong bodies (Tyack & Hansot, 1982).

---

Consider the surface arguments and the taken-for-granted beliefs underlying a current proposal for school reform or a metaphor implicit in educational discussions.

What does each assume about student roles and school purposes? How do you think today's discourse will appear 50 or 100 years from now?

---

Although the Great Depression aggravated tensions within industrial economies, schools retained public support. Although New Deal programs and supporters regenerated a laboring class awareness, existing racial, ethnic and regional divisions weakened the political impact. By making concessions to unions on vocational education and by accommodating some ethnic sensibilities, business elites and professionals dominated school boards; and educators gained a license to implement a curriculum serving middle-class interests. With a national work-study program for poor youth to attend college and the GI Bill of Rights after 1945, children of workers and the unemployed chose higher education over political activism based on class identity.

Textbooks and teachers touted the virtue of industrial progress through specialized labor in hierarchical organizations. In classrooms examined by sociologist Eleanor Leacock (1969, pp. 201, 215), "curriculum areas involving social content are approached in a *rationalizing* and *moralizing* spirit, rather than in a *scientific* and *humanistic* one." Schools were "on the whole geared for a rather rigid adaptation to the status quo," and teachers seldom acknowledged that their classroom interactions exacerbated family status differences. Texts sustained "the illusion . . . that the world is not full of questions for children and adults alike, but that it is full of things that are defined and known in terms of either right or wrong." By relating social hierarchies to economic progress, teachers stifled analysis and active resistance.

### Organized Protest in a Postindustrial Era

In the 1960s, a longstanding consensus about the direction of schools and society broke apart. Organized protests developed in response to racial segregation in schools, rights, jobs, and neighborhoods; structural poverty, chiefly in Appalachia and inner cities; and patriarchal domination of females. The Civil Rights Movement, the War on Poverty, and feminist activism initially were led by educated elites who believed that postwar power and affluence could and should be more widely shared. They gained force from publicity because reformers must recruit, educate and politicize their supporters. In a democracy, popular reforms depend on fostering an alternative discourse. Leaders must express dissatisfactions, advance plausible explanations, and propose a political program.

Prior to the 1960s, African Americans lacked economic and political power to protest effectively. Despite a history of slavery and segregation, many Blacks strove to learn in order to gain social acceptance. Students experienced racist derogation in their texts, Jim Crow segregation, and underfunded urban schools. Following the passage of the Voting Rights Act in 1965, Black voters in the South allied with urban counterparts in the North to make their voices heard in party caucuses and elections. Court rulings, federal policies to combat poverty, and growing urbanization gave clout to African Americans, advancing desegregation in the South and Black political power in Northern cities.

Civil rights protests raised several challenges to a traditional curriculum and standardized tests. Ending segregated systems in the South also diminished job opportunities for many Black teachers and administrators. In urban areas, desegregation broke up homogeneous neighborhood schools. Community control threatened the authority of professional administrators who dominated urban districts in an informal alliance with teachers' unions. Despite generalized support for integration among educational leaders, there was visible resentment in many schools where teachers were expected to change their ways and overcome the effects of years of discrimination and miseducation.

Patterns of class and racial isolation in most metropolitan areas meant that integration through busing disproportionately affected some White working-class neighborhoods. Racism as practiced by Realtors, bankers, zoning boards, and municipal service providers continued to exacerbate de facto segregation. Increasingly, schools serving central cities have a majority of "minorities." In the North and Midwest, many White citizens had no children in schools, disliked central cities, distrusted people of color, and shared a self-interest in unequal metropolitan districts. By the 1980s, an idealized common school experience for all had become impractical for most Black students—and, perhaps, unwanted by majorities of White parents.

The African American critique of equality contradicted prevailing ideologies in schools. As Black historian Vincent Harding (1970, pp. 128–229) suggested, once African American experiences became a part of the curriculum, White Americans could no longer view themselves as "a society moving on a straight line upward from perfection to perfection." Oppression of enslaved people, segregation, and urban isolation based on violence contradicted rhetoric about equality. "Failure to face the tragic is failure to mature in national as well as personal spheres, so in the midst of this pabulum view of history a serious implanting of the Afro-American past could be the difference between death and growth—at least spiritually." Nevertheless, White racism is persistent, pervasive and powerful.

Feminists started with middle-class consciousness-raising and gradually developed specific proposals around wages based on comparable worth, childcare, reproductive rights, and the Equal Rights Amendment. Women, unlike people of color, were not a minority; they were, if anything, overrepresented among educators—though typically not in power positions. Starting in the early 1970s, feminists raised awareness of gender discrimination in curriculum, sports, counseling, and other aspects of schools. Women teachers connected feminist critiques with union demands for more-equal pay. The Women's Educational Equity Act of 1974 provided federal support for nonsexist curriculum materials and, together with Title IX of the Higher Education Act of 1972, established national standards for gender fairness.

Educators had long justified women teachers based on presumed nurturing skills and lower salary demands. "The result is continual reinforcement of hierarchy, competition, immediate measurable results, material accumulation, depersonalization, and economic and political expansion" (Bourque & Warren, 1987, p. 176). Feminist critiques cast a new light on prevailing beliefs: "The school and the workplace become cultural and political environments where rules and norms are perpetuated and legitimated by contemporary ideologies of gender-based exclusion, segregation, and avoidance." Women sought leadership roles as principals and superintendents; they challenged gender stereotyping in texts and vocational areas; they pursued athletic activities; and they redefined sex education and family life courses. Public rationalizations revealed patriarchy in families and schools as well as a masculine bias in technology.

Today, there is no vision of schooling as a locus for "a social order of citizens." Critical theorist David Hogan (1982, p. 32) noted that "debates about the public role of schooling in America have been dominated by a preoccupation with issues of inequality: educability, equality of educational opportunity, meritocratic ideology, elite control, desegregation, educational achievement, status attainment, and lately, economic and cultural reproduction." They lead to no institutional restructuring, however, because they ignore "issues of class and class formation." Because class remains largely hidden in American society, its political impact has been concealed in surface debates about funding formulas and curriculum mandates.

Organized to reproduce social control, schools are poorly structured to promote freedom and responsibility. Resistance is diverted and silenced. Teachers rarely explore the ways class, race and gender have interacted historically to sustain economic and political elites. Yet those unequal prospects for their students undercut their best efforts to motivate many students who are ill-fed, ill-housed and without hope.

During much of the past 200 years, Americans could acknowledge social classes and poverty for some while also seeing rising standards of living. People improved their lot by moving from farms to factories, from blue- to white-collar jobs, and from the working class to a growing middle class. Since 1973, that positive prospect has faded.

## UNEQUAL PROSPECTS

America's economic successes from 1946 to 1972 induced a complacent pride among elites in conventional corporate roles within a mixed public-private economy. After 1973, productivity per worker changed little for a decade and then grew slowly. Growth no longer sustained the social expectations raised by the Civil Rights revolution, the War on Poverty, and the women's movement. Small gains in real income per capita probably lagged behind the direct and indirect costs of pollution, crime, and depletion of nonrenewable resources. Most workers, including teachers, experienced a decline in their real as well as their relative standard of living. Inflation eroded their pay; costs for energy and food, in particular, rose. At the same time, record economic growth in Japan and other countries along the Pacific Rim as well as in Europe foretold an end to America's domination of the world economy.

Despite grim prospects, debates in the United States about equity and standards are superficial or so encoded in symbols and images as to defy straightforward interpretation. During the 1990s, the United States stands as the preeminent military power with among the highest standards of living in the world. Yet its people seem perversely discontented, cynical about established institutions, and pessimistic about the nation's future (though often expressing more optimism about their own prospects). Alcohol and drug abuse, violence and theft, rising costs for health and education, deteriorating ecological conditions, stagnant productivity among service workers, and widespread unemployment or underemployment seem beyond public or private solution.

Historically, Americans preferred individual to collective solutions, chose a promise of growth over a policy of redistribution of income or wealth, and sought to pay for social welfare programs out of economic surpluses generated by future expansion. Relative abundance of land and an often buoyant economy eased class conflicts and fed hopes for at least a middle-class lifestyle among most workers. Presently, perceived problems in the schools, health and crime require public solutions, and slow growth leaves no surplus to equalize conditions without taking something from the haves and redistributing to the have-nots. The immediate issue driving social discontent appears in a stagnant economy marked by a widening inequality of income and wealth that started in the 1970s and extended into the 1990s.

## Stagnation and Income Distribution

Normally, competitive labor markets move toward equality over time because potential workers leave low-wage regions and occupations for better opportunities. This century witnessed a tremendous demographic shift from agriculture and the South to industrial cities in the Midwest, New England and West. Recently, families have left decaying Northern cities for opportunities in suburbs or in Southern and Western states. Although educational requirements for skilled positions delay reactions to labor markets, current supplies of teachers, lawyers, and health care providers illustrate that individuals do respond to salary prospects. If equalization by broad sectors continued, then remaining inequalities might stem from individual differences in productive skills within a functioning meritocracy. Because impoverished people have no surplus to invest in new skills, however, private spending for health and education tends to widen the gap in income.

As economist Frank Levy (1987, pp. 5–6) has clarified, "the link between slow wage growth and inequality . . . involves the way the economy and political process have divided a slow-growing pie." Overall, the distribution of income by quintiles (segments of 20% each) has changed little since 1945: "But *within* this constant shape, substantial rearrangements have taken place. Incomes of the elderly have moved up while incomes of younger families have moved down. Fewer families have at least one worker while more rely on government benefits. Regional income gaps have closed but city-suburban income gaps have grown larger, a reflection of the growing number of city families headed by single women." Although current income data show only a slight flattening of distribution with more poor and more rich, "there is a rapidly increasing *inequality of prospects*, an inequality in the chance that a family will enjoy the 'middle class dream.'"

In 1947, median family income was $14,100; by 1973, it had doubled to over $28,000 (both in 1984 dollars). From 1973 to 1984, median income in real terms for middle-aged men fell significantly, although family incomes dropped slightly from $32,800 to $31,400 as more spouses worked for wages. Labor force participation for those 20 and older rose from 59% shortly after World War II to 66% in 1984. Between 1979 and 1989, income for the bottom fifth fell by 2.1% while the top fifth rose 20.4% (after adjustments for taxes and transfers). Well-educated, technologically skilled workers earned more than ever. The top 5%, about 3.1 million households, earned over $73,000 (16% of the total). The top 10% earned over one-fourth of all wages, salaries, and reported dividends, interest and profits. Yet half of all families with children are worse off now than in 1973.

Between 1979 and 1987, the share of earnings for working and middle classes (the second through seventh tenths of the income distribution) fell—first during a recession intended to curb inflation and then during the subsequent recovery. In part, that outcome reflect-ed a pattern of second wage earner households, but more importantly, salary differentials widened. Progressiveness in federal taxes declined, and public burdens were shifted to states and localities that typically relied on regressive levies. Experienced workers continued to do fairly well after 1973—if they were protected by unions and seniority, owned their home, or were retired on inflation-indexed pensions such as Social Security.

Recent figures confirm these trends. Fewer families are having children, and more children are raised by single parents. In 1973, average family size was 2.87 persons per household, with 1.39 wage earners. In 1991, family size had fallen to 2.40 persons with a drop in earners to 1.28. That is, in 1973 each worker supported 2.06 persons; in 1991, a worker supported less than 1.9 persons (Table 2.1).

TABLE 2.1
Distributions of Families and Persons by Family Type

|  | Number of Families (thousands) | | | |
| --- | --- | --- | --- | --- |
|  | 1973 | 1979 | 1989 | 1991 |
| Total | 73,166 | 84,229 | 101,663 | 104,522 |
| Families with children | 31,098 | 32,166 | 34,768 | 35,482 |
| Married couples with children | 24,798 | 24,166 | 24,378 | 24,227 |
| Single mothers with children | 4,126 | 5,650 | 7,123 | 7,768 |
| Nonelderly without children | 28,183 | 35,730 | 46,467 | 47,873 |
| Elderly without children | 13,884 | 16,331 | 20,428 | 21,166 |

Source: Compiled from U.S. Congress, Committee of Ways and Means, 103rd Cong., 1st Sess. (1993). 1993 Green Book. Washington, DC: Government Printing Office, p. 1398.

Changes in family income by various methods of calculation indicate a slow growth in real income from 1973 to 1991 mainly due to more wage earners per family unit. The income figures for 1991, of course, reflect depressed business conditions during that year (see Table 2.2).

Another way to look at this change is to consider the mean adjusted family income by quintiles, weighted by number of persons per household in comparison with poverty level adjustments for family size. Table 2.3 illustrates that someone in the top fifth was 7.6 times better off in 1973 than someone in the bottom fifth (with adjustments made for economies of family size). In 1991, the person in the top fifth was 10.6 times better off than someone at the bottom.

Today, young people entering the workforce and beginning families face rising costs for health and education. At the same time, federal

**TABLE 2.2**
**Income Trends for All Families, 1989 Dollars**

|  | 1973 | 1979 | 1989 | 1991 |
|---|---|---|---|---|
| Total family cash income (billions) | 2,220 | 2,591 | 3,353 | 3,265 |
| Mean family cash income | 30,341 | 30,764 | 32,978 | 31,236 |
| Mean family income per capita | 10,718 | 11,922 | 13,743 | 13,007 |

*Source*: Compiled from U.S. Congress, Committee of Ways and Means, 103rd Cong., 1st Sess. (1993). *1993 Green Book*. Washington, DC: Government Printing Office, p. 1399.

**TABLE 2.3**
**Mean Adjusted Family Income by Quintile (Person Weighted)**
**as a Proportion of the Poverty Level**

|  | 1967 | 1973 | 1979 | 1989 | 1991 |
|---|---|---|---|---|---|
| Lowest | .69 | .90 | .90 | .86 | .79 |
| Second | 1.54 | 1.94 | 2.06 | 2.09 | 1.97 |
| Middle | 2.26 | 2.82 | 3.07 | 3.27 | 3.12 |
| Fourth | 3.16 | 3.94 | 4.32 | 4.77 | 4.56 |
| Highest | 5.67 | 6.87 | 7.39 | 8.84 | 8.38 |

*Source*: Compiled from U.S. Congress, Committee of Ways and Means, 103rd Cong., 1st Sess. (1993). *1993 Green Book*. Washington, DC: Government Printing Office, p. 1402.

programs for community and regional development are blocked by commitments to military spending, interest on a burgeoning national debt, Social Security and Medicare transfers to retirees, and needs-based programs. For instance, Head Start enrolls only a portion of those eligible. During the 1980s, lower federal tax rates protected the personal consumption of wealthy citizens; a rising national debt was not matched by personal saving or public spending on capital improvements. Those decisions to invest in neither physical infrastructures nor children foretell further declines in well-being and national power.

## Our Children's Prospects

Today's youth have seen their families' economic prospects diminish over their lifetime. Parents, teachers and administrators lack credibility when asserting that studying diligently, working hard, and obeying the rules will assure a decent life. Teachers and parents whose own aspirations have turned sour scarcely can instill hope and determination in the next generation. Voters repeatedly fail to equalize school resources. An expanding economic pie no longer motivates students, many of whom face ongoing discrimination in labor markets. A

metanarrative of academic achievement leading to economic success
rings hollow after more than two decades of stagnation and growing
income inequality.

Edelman (1987, p. 31) focused a reverse angle lens to reveal a chill-
ing future for children who are educationally cheated in schools:

One in four of today's preschool children is poor; one in nine is living in a
household with income less than half of the poverty level. Only 16 percent of
these eligible poor children are enrolled in Head Start, and only half can
expect to be given compensatory education when they go to elementary school
in the next couple of years. One child in six lives in a female-headed household, one in eight has no health insurance, and one in ten has not seen a doctor
in the past year. One in two has a working mother, but only one in five has
adequate day care. One in six lives in a family where no parent has a job, one
in five is likely to become a teen parent, and one in seven is likely to drop out
of school.

The consequences are dire: "We invest in children because the cost to
the public of sickness, ignorance, neglect, dependence, and unemployment over the long term exceeds the cost of preventive investment in
health, education, employed youth, and stable families."

Children have replaced elders as the largest group living in
poverty—with markedly different social consequences. In 1990, the
United States ranked in the bottom third among industrial nations in
statistical indicators of well-being for children. In a recent study, it
placed 14th out of 16 industrial nations in spending per elementary and
secondary student (Rasell & Mishel, 1990). African American sociologist
William J. Wilson (1980, 1987) argued that a Black underclass in urban
ghettoes is raising children in an environment deformed by crime and
poverty. Many employed women have major responsibilities for family
childcare. Working-class parents send children to neighborhood public
schools that are isolated by class and race. Today, one in three children
are Native Americans, Latinos, Asians or African Americans, half of
whom live in poverty.

Historically, a large middle class with growing incomes has amelior-
ated conditions for the poor and limited the power of wealth. Following
the *Brown* decision in 1954, a generation witnessed giant steps toward
civil rights and income equality. By the 1980s, however, conservatives
blamed those protesters for the stagnant industrial economy. Stagnation feeds a conservative reaction, and public debate over schools
focuses on standards, accountability, and "excellence." Children of poverty are blamed for not striving—however realistically they appraise
their prospects. Today, "the stark inequalities in American education
that are now so deeply embedded in social geography and in the political
economy raise new and fundamental questions about access and citizenship" (Katznelson & Weir, 1985, p. 221).

Faced with a crisis of confidence in their prospects, Americans can either retreat into nostalgic solutions or explore radical reforms. Basically, the choice is to equalize incomes directly or to provide health and educational services for children that entitle them to anticipate a fairer and brighter future. Fearing that innovations and reallocations of resources might worsen their position, powerful interests have resisted change. Low rates of saving pushed up real interest rates, thereby discouraging investment in education, research and development, or plant and equipment. Dominant groups used their political clout to reduce public spending to equalize schooling and other social services. Political processes seemed gridlocked, and children face a prospect of growing inequalities.

## INJUSTICE AND POLITICAL INACTION

In the face of persistent hierarchies along class, race and gender lines, educators reiterate an achievement ideology that academic credentials assure later success. Earlier studies showed that "intergenerational mobility across all socioeconomic levels is consistently upward, but also consistently modest" (Hochschild, 1981, p. 13). During the 1970s and 1980s, those opportunities largely disappeared. Although young, well-educated females (including Black women) who work full time have nearly achieved income parity with males, earnings for women and African Americans remain about 60% of those for White men. Unemployment, underemployment and family responsibilities of caring for those who are young, old or ill disproportionately affect women.

Although people attribute economic advancement to education, many blame poverty on the victims. Low grades and low incomes are taken as evidence of personal shortcomings. Typically, Americans discuss intelligence as though it were biologically determined. Presumably, children of affluent parents do well in school because of inherited intelligence, not because educators reward their cultural baggage. A gap in academic achievement between Blacks and Whites is attributed to variations in gene pools, despite repeated refutations of that view (Kamin, 1974; Lewontin, Rose, & Kamin, 1984). Norm-referenced tests and apparently fixed IQ scores excuse unequal academic outcomes—without indicting teachers or schools. Given the range of human potential and evidence that every child can successfully learn, it is foolishly dangerous to argue backward from unequal outcomes to innate differences.

Genetics scarcely accounts for persistent gender differences, unless a Y chromosome also determines brain power or motivation. But discrimination and socialization patterns clearly can. Schools replicate gender differences in status, income and influence in the workforce. Texts either omit women or present them in domestic roles. Guidance counselors still encourage female students into secretarial, health care, and childcare roles that generally offer lower salaries. Apparently, educators assume that women are naturally less autonomous and more passive and nurturing than men. Although most teachers are female, schools have neither eliminated gender biases nor addressed class inequalities.

### Attitudes toward Distributive Justice

Given critical activists such as Bowles and Gintis and liberal political leaders, why have oppressed groups not used their vote to level the playing field? Political scientist Jennifer Hochschild (1981, pp. 1–2) tellingly defined the conundrum: "more people would benefit than would lose from downward redistribution. And yet never has the poorer majority of the population, not to speak of the poorest minority, voted itself out of its economic disadvantage." Since 1970, income disparities have grown despite equalizing trends such as rising rates of labor force participation, greater educational attainments, a declining gap in years of schooling between Blacks and Whites, more government transfer payments, and relative gains in labor's income share. Meanwhile, other industrial democracies, such as Sweden or Germany, more nearly equalize take-home pay and provide a higher floor of income security.

Based on extensive interviews with many citizens, Hochschild (1981, pp. 82, 184) found that ideas about distributive justice depended on the issue under consideration: "Respondents usually start from a principle of equality, and use mainly egalitarian norms, when they address the socializing and political domains; they usually start from a principle of differentiation, and use mainly differentiating norms, when they address the economic domain." Class or ideological position made little difference. Almost no one articulated a sense of how taxes and social programs actually function. "With the exception of tax loopholes," Hochschild noted, "respondents are much less aware of social policies that redistribute within one class or upward than of policies that redistribute downward."

Within that framework, Hochschild (1981, pp. 114, 143) found considerable ambivalence and variation of issues based on the educational and class background of her respondents. Most poor persons vented not against inequality per se but against a perceived unfairness of specific inequities. A domestic worker was trapped by her conflicting views:

Maria is in a bind. She *knows* that she works as hard as she can, that she hasn't enough money, that her employers underpay her, that many people deserve neither their wealth nor their poverty, and that her descendants seem destined to relive her frustrations. But she *believes* that the rich should keep their wealth, that a hardworking cleaner deserves less than a lazy executive, that work and education are supposed to bring upward mobility, and that wages should not reflect need or promote equality. She tries to subsume her knowledge of economic injustice under her differentiating economic beliefs. The result is discouragement, helplessness, and confusion.

Neither rich nor poor believe "that America really is the land of equal opportunity." They agree that the poor should not be blamed for their plight but lack a consistent sense of class formation. Most Americans "define themselves as members of the middle class, no matter how poor or rich they are."

In considering government programs and taxes, Maria and others seek equality of political and civil rights and denounce privileges bought with money. "They want tax and social welfare policies mainly to take from the rich and give to the poor and middle classes" (Hochschild, 1981, pp. 181, 183). Specific public welfare programs based on revenues raised from the wealthy often generate ambivalent feelings because they conflict with views about economic incentives. Most assign a privileged position to private property over community needs. They favor progressive taxes on income but reject inheritance levies. "With regard to welfare and social policies, respondents no longer begin by thinking about private property; hence they start out and remain egalitarian." Health insurance, public higher education, housing subsidies, expanded Social Security, and job programs attract popular support.

---

**How should teachers fairly distribute grades in a class? How should schools impartially support women's and men's sports, and programs for special needs and the gifted? How should an equitable society allocate resources such as income and wealth?**

---

Hochschild (1981, pp. 264, 266, 275) identified several responses to possible redistribution. First, some people endorse existing inequalities and view the disjuncture between economic and political spheres as "the very essence of Western liberalism": "Belief in the necessity and justice of economic differentiation permits political equality to exist; belief in the existence of political equality permits economic differentiation to persist." Others acquiesce because they envision no alternative, and they "feel helpless, bitter, resigned, or withdrawn when they consider their beliefs." Many feel this way because "political and social institutions express the dominant world view." A small number of citizens in Hochschild's sample opposed current distributions of income but could not "generate and sustain a complete oppositional orientation on one's own." A few others appeared indifferent, mainly because they focused on family, religion or other interest.

Although public demands for income redistribution remain weak, social scientists have analyzed how democracy and private markets generate injustices:

Theoretically, capitalism, in which private vices generate public virtues, is the most productive and efficient economic system possible. And yet we all know about free riders, money wasted through advertising and superficial style changes in products, planned obsolescence, simultaneous inflation and depression, total ineptitude in managing energy needs. In theory, our democratic republic is the most free and responsive political system possible. And yet we all know about entrenched special interests, gerrymandered electoral districts that avoid minority representation, laws that give symbolic rewards to the needy and material rewards to the wealthy, violent repression of dissent, bureaucracies immune to budget-cutters. (Hochschild, 1981, p. 283)

The logic of seeking more-equal distributions of income through democratic processes remains powerful. It follows from self-interested behavior by large numbers, perhaps four out of five voters, who hold no net wealth. Citizens seldom analyze complex social phenomena, view social institutions in a critical fashion, consider themselves competent to devise fairer systems, or build a consensus on reforms. Many poor adults lack educational skills to promote viable redistribution policies, and elites have a vested interest in the status quo. Manifest contradictions between America's liberal creed and longstanding inequalities generate pressures by have-nots for a share of a growing economy—not for radically equal incomes.

Students neither experience justice in schools nor analyze social conflicts generated by inequalities. Equality may be definable and achievable only in separate spheres. For instance, schools may define justice in terms of access, but uniform treatment of diverse students penalizes some learners while rewarding others. An assigned essay helps expository writers; multiple choice benefits those who recall fragmentary information. Standardized tests suit "good" students whose family's cultural background fits the mainstream. Perhaps a portfolio of various performances allows students to present their strongest evidence of their competencies. Equal academic achievements might not reduce income differentials, nor would equal incomes and status of families assure equitable schools, but both represent steps toward greater justice.

## STABILITY AND CHANGE IN SCHOOLS

After observing behavioral regularities in many classrooms, Sarason (1982, p. 217) depicted an implicit "constitution" that subordinates students. Teachers set the rules because they share a number of beliefs, including:

5. Children should be governed by what a teacher thinks is right or wrong, but a teacher should not be governed by what children think is right or wrong.
6. The ethics of adults are obviously different from and superior to the ethics of children.
7. Children should not be given responsibility for something they cannot handle or for which they are not accountable.

An embedded assumption of teachers' authority and control paradoxically ends up frustrating their hopes to inspire learning.

When school and society deny autonomy to students, they may resist or accommodate or both. Most students sabotage classroom learning because they sensibly resent industrial-age patterns. Adolescents separate into peer groups such as athletes, brains or socializers, which reinforce particularistic identities. Three in five work outside of school, and almost everyone devotes more time to television than to schoolwork. They refrain from asking questions that personally matter, opting for boredom over engagement. Their resistance seldom appears overt or becomes channeled into action for social change. Instead, teachers and students act out ritualized performances that regularize the presentation of blandly unexceptional selves.

Public schools make organizational and curricular adjustments to social problems as identified by powerful groups but consistently act to sustain adult control. In an affluent, capitalist democracy, those responses neither praise a narrow elitism nor meet the needs of oppressed groups. Instead, they reiterate a promise of respectability to all—although that message favors middle-class children. Historically, a growing economy with some intergenerational mobility satisfied most citizens, at least enough so dissenters seldom organized political alternatives. Somehow, "within this context, children act as active theory builders and relatively autonomous, certainly active, participants in their own development—and for many, entrapment" (Hogan, 1982, p. 62).

Resistance is real but lacks effective outlets. This conundrum has been explained by examining student responses to social hierarchies and classroom interactions with teachers. First, schools contain and deflect resistance from relatively powerless students whose needs are met by neither schools nor society. Second, teachers contradict their personal and pedagogical values in order to accommodate to a perceived demand for order by administrators. There are important implications about how schools must transform strategies and structures in order to empower individuals and groups.

## Defusing Discontent

Because schooling involves two generations in crucial dialog—students and parents or teachers—modernization built discord into their interactions. Children of immigrants learn English and a different heritage, creating a cultural dislocation within families and ambivalent attitudes toward schools. That started with European immigrants a century ago and has continued for Latino and Asian newcomers in the present. During the 1960s and 1970s, working-class parents wanted schools to emphasize discipline and basic skills because they feared their children would get into trouble and be frustrated by a lifetime of drudgery (Rubin, 1976, pp. 86-88). This pattern explains some of the popularity of "back to basics" in schools as well as weak support for an openly political agenda of resistance to oppression in low-income communities. For instance, some Black parents oppose an Afrocentric curriculum that might de-emphasize basic skills.

Ambitious individuals among low-income students hope to become exceptions to class stability. By echoing attitudes that make sense only among educated elites, they seek acceptance. According to a 1990 survey, they anticipated working "for a *big* company" because of promotion opportunities: "I'd like to keep going up and up and up until I croak, I guess." Overall, high school students expected to earn $58,000 a year in real terms within a decade—more than twice then-current average incomes (*Fortune*, 1990, p. 221). Faced with such unrealistic ambitions, adults may squelch the dreams of youth or allow job markets to do so later. Although an achievement ideology holds true for some, few escape from their parents' class and status. Taken individually, each case obscures coherent analysis of subordination in social institutions.

In an ethnographic study of low-income male youth, Jay MacLeod (1987, pp. 156, 112) demonstrated that "American society is not as open as we like to think; the ladder of social mobility is not accessible to all, nor are its rungs easy to grasp." Those at the bottom of the social structure "feel so trapped in their subordinate position that they do not even aspire to move upward." After extensive discussions with two youth groups in a public housing project in the Boston area, MacLeod concluded that "the regulation of aspirations is perhaps the most significant of all the mechanisms contributing to social reproduction; however, aspirations themselves are largely a function of structural mechanisms." Although White youth resisted middle-class ambitions more actively than Black youth, neither group achieved upward mobility.

Schools, including those serving low-income neighborhoods, value the views, experiences, preferences, and aspirations of middle-class children. Their daily routines and teachers' messages encourage "individuals in a stratified social order . . . to accept their own position and the inequalities of the social order as legitimate" (MacLeod, 1987, pp. 112–113). On a day-to-day basis, visible oppression is less crucial than an achievement ideology that "maintains that individual merit and achievement are the fair and equitable sources of inequality of

American society. If merit is the basis for the distribution of rewards, then members of the lower classes attribute their subordinate position in the social order to personal deficiencies. In this way, inequality is legitimated." In conversations, low-income youth expressed mixed views—asserting their determination to get ahead, denouncing the rich for having opportunities denied the poor, blaming themselves for not learning more in school, and criticizing teachers for ignoring their needs and values.

Youth who were antagonistic to the achievement ideology of the school assessed their life chances realistically. Although occasionally they speculated about earning a good living, they faulted low grades for their menial job prospects. "By internalizing the blame for failure, students lose their self-esteem and then accept their eventual place-ment in low-status jobs as a natural outcome of their own shortcomings. If individuals are convinced that they are responsible for their low position in society, then criticism of the social order by subordinate classes is deflected" (MacLeod, 1987, pp. 113, 148). Though reinforced by experiences of parents and older siblings, diminished expectations owe much to educators: "The school's valuation of the cultural capital of the upper classes and its depreciation of the cultural capital of the lower classes are the most important mechanisms of social reproduction within the educational system, but the discriminatory effects of tracking and of teachers' expectations also inhibit the academic performance of lower-class students."

---

Recall instances of resistance in a familiar classroom or work-place—for example, students putting down their teacher or workers slacking off when unsupervised.

How often do you see individuals or groups consistently engaged in productive activities? What examples of cooperation or sharing of personal feelings and choices have you witnessed?

---

Socialization for girls follows a different pattern than for low-income boys but has a similar consequence of diffusing protest. At a private school in upstate New York, Carol Gilligan and her colleagues found that confident and self-assertive 10- and 11-year-old girls grew into compliant, unsure and confused teenagers. Adolescence brought complex developmental issues of connection, relationships and resistance. "Insecurity and self-doubt" followed from sensitivity to how others are responding: "The loss may be of a sense of self as a moral, caring self and of trust in a logic of interdependence and responsiveness derived from personal experience" (Brown, 1990, p. 108).

Noting different degrees of overt resistance to dismal prospects, MacLeod (1987, p. 148) recognized that neither actual opportunities in labor markets nor institutional pressures in schools fully determined the responses of individuals or groups. "Aspirations," he argued, "provide a conceptual link between structure and agency because although they are rooted firmly in individual proclivity (agency), they also are acutely sensitive to perceived societal constraints (structure)." Students of color, those living in poverty, and many females seek to maintain a healthy self-image without many positive role models or visible opportunities in the adult world around them. As a result, they often turn to activities and dreams outside affluent, male definitions of success.

## Silencing Controversies

When schools adopt bland, middle-class, Eurocentric, and patriarchal values in their curriculum and treat them as noncontroversial, they stifle dialog with many working-class families, people of color, and females. In large public schools, most students feel themselves subject to teachers' rules and mindless bureaucratic regulations, so they agree to orderly behaviors in return for reduced academic efforts and more space for peer interactions. During informal discussions in corridors or before and after school, students feel most comfortably themselves. By muting or segmenting resistance to the status quo, teachers undercut their students' sense of control over personal or group prospects. Alienating environments devalue students' pride in learning.

Certainly, discussions about class, race and gender discrimination might invigorate American history and civics. Observing social studies classes in four high schools serving predominantly middle-class neighborhoods, Linda McNeil (1986, pp. 192, 193) found mainly "defensive teaching." Lectures presented fragmentary knowledge, mystified complex topics, or omitted controversy (including most current events). Neither a teacher's philosophy nor preparation significantly affected classroom behaviors. "What is interesting in these social studies classes is that the political and economic content processed through defensive teaching confirmed the message conveyed by the nature of instruction; the economy, like the classroom, works best when students/clients/ consumers are passive recipients of its benefits rather than active participants." Teachers traded reduced efforts for nominal acquiescence to their authority: "The parallel implication for social studies instruction is that we should trust the system, trust the experts and learn only a little to get by; we are receivers of public policy, not shapers of it."

In reality, teachers knew far more about social inequities than they included in the curriculum. "Their stated goal of making sure students understood 'how things work' was tempered by their expressed fear that students might find out about the injustices and inadequacies of their economic and political institutions" (McNeil, 1986, p. 159). Students might act on their knowledge of gender or class biases, as when they had protested American involvement in Vietnam. Although most teachers favored inquiry approaches, praised critical thinking, and thought their subject should connect to the real world, they taught differently: *"Their patterns of knowledge control were, according to their own statements in taped interviews, rooted in their desire for classroom control."*

Defensive teaching that served the school administration's desire for orderly appearances also deskilled teachers and students as active learners. It separated personal, experiential knowledge from scholarship valued only to obtain credits that accumulated to earn a diploma. Although social studies addressed democratic citizenship, an underlying message urged acceptance of the status quo, because questions interfered with most teachers' expressed goal of covering the syllabus. Consequently, the system effectively controls them—just as assembly lines set a pace for factory workers. By deskilling jobs through curriculum packages and moving "unfinished" students through sequential classrooms on a regular schedule for 180 days, the system pressures teachers to view students as passive receptors for bits of information.

Although control reflects social class, educators also avoided issues of race and gender oppression. White teachers in Midwestern schools with high enrollments of students of color reacted angrily to suggestions that American society is not open to all, although majority students got disproportionately more As while Blacks received Ds and Fs. Asked to participate in a racism workshop, these teachers resorted to familiar strategies. "Many simply refused to 'see' color. Others searched for 'positive' associations with race by drawing on the European ethnic experience, which points toward petrified vestiges of immigrant culture" (Sleeter, 1993, p. 168). A European bias in the curriculum manifested itself mainly by omissions of people of color, while multicultural education concentrated on contributions of interesting foods and customs from various groups. "Discussing race or multiculturalism meant discussing 'them,' not the social structure." Social justice requires teachers to "expose, challenge, and deconstruct racism rather than tacitly accepting it."

Issues of patriarchy or female submission are so deeply embedded in school patterns that only extensive analysis and reflection reveal their multiple facets. Women are presumed suited for jobs in the helping professions because their caring and concern for others reinforce a nurturing role. At the same time, teachers, nurses and social workers carry low status, in part because of the predominance of females in their ranks. Discrimination in labor markets as well as pay, reinforced by ongoing disrespect and harassment, has socialized many female teachers to ignore institutions and political struggles that so powerfully shape prospects for children and society.

### Education and Society

Schools connect to future societies in at least four ways:

- teaching skills for productive citizenship;
- socializing for class, race and gender roles;
- screening or slotting workers into existing jobs, mainly by legitimizing professional and managerial power; and
- setting aspiration levels according to the fit between a student's cultural norms and those of schools.

Each function accounts for some observed phenomena, but none explains the many exceptions in specific settings. Schools are simultaneously viewed "as an arena of tension between processes of cultural production and reproduction, as a locus of human activity, and occasionally as a locus of a form of class conflict between the official, bourgeois culture of the school and the informal cultural creations of its working-class constituency" (Hogan, 1982, p. 58).

Schools avoid potentially controversial subjects related to a less hierarchical, racist and patriarchal society, as McNeil (1986) reported. Adults hold ambivalent views that frustrate group analysis and action, as Hochschild (1981) described. Neither controversy in social studies classrooms nor clear thinking by adults will by themselves improve society. Certain dilemmas are inherent in a democracy—neither rights nor pragmatic considerations always prevail. Although decentralized groups may arrive at decisions and agree on a sense of justice, local units lack the size needed for efficient production in technologically advanced societies. In the 20th century, schools waver on these dilemmas—wanting to be effective functional units while valuing democratic equality of rights.

Historical linkages between schools and society need not mean that patterns will persist. For two centuries, democracy and industrialization liberated and equalized individuals. Yet their association enabled capitalist-corporate interests to sustain an advantaged position—without social responsibility attached to their privileges. Democratic and capitalist rhetoric honored rational persons acting in their selfish interests, but powerful technologies and huge organizations raise profound questions about how to control autonomous individuals. Schools—especially public and parochial schools serving the masses—emphasized domination by adult authorities and bureaucratic procedures. As school structures divided and paced teachers, they no longer saw children in contexts of their capacities and aspirations or their families and communities.

Control in school is linked to power in society. Economic interests—whether in enhancing public welfare or in perpetuating status—are translated into school strategies and structures through political processes involving class, ethnic, racial, and gender differences. In the past, abundance and economic growth muted struggles over income inequality, but unequal schooling threatens a bleak prospect for a majority of students. Political consensus on equality is complicated by class and occupational isolation, together with resurgent demands for cultural respect and autonomy. Neither teachers nor students can justify their interactions in terms of democratic rights or pragmatic benefits, but change is difficult because of institutionalized strategies and structures that shape schools.

Many students and teachers sense a deep contradiction between their roles and their ostensible purposes—without actively seeking alternatives. What would happen if teachers and students discussed declining prospects for children as well as intergenerational disagreements about lifestyles and values? What would it take for teachers and students to design a curriculum that explains organizational stagnation, economic inequalities, social injustices, and political gridlock? Suppose the public applauded and supported those educators who succeed through hard work and charisma in relating daily instruction and informal practices to an emerging knowledge society. We believe renewed purpose and support for schools will come when people work together to make sense of the multiple realities of a fragmented, postmodern society.

## RELATED READING

For a powerful account of school inequities today, see Jonathan Kozol, *Savage Inequalities: Children in America's Schools* (New York: Crown Publishers, 1991). In addition, see Frank S. Levy and Richard C. Michel, *The Economic Future of American Families: Income and Wealth Trends* (Washington, DC: Urban Institute Press, 1991).

Current analyses of schooling from critical perspectives include Michael W. Apple, *Teachers and Texts: A Political Economy of Class and Gender Relations in Education* (New York: Routledge and Kegan Paul, 1986) or *Ideology and Curriculum*, 2nd ed. (New York: Routledge, 1990); Henry A. Giroux and Peter L. McLaren, *Critical Pedagogy, the State, and Cultural Struggle* (Albany: State University of New York Press, 1989); and Ira Schor, *Empowering Education: Critical Teaching for Social Change* (Chicago: University of Chicago Press, 1992).

# 3

# Learning and Teaching in Schools

Every fall over 3 million five-year-olds arrive in kindergarten anxious, active and hopeful. By contrast, many older students barely tolerate classes they find dull, purposeless and demeaning. Few experience excitement and self-fulfillment from applying knowledge to understand themselves and the world around them. Despite civic rhetoric about the importance of education, one in four youths leaves before graduating. American adults seldom read serious books, and over 50 million are functionally illiterate. Although most parents express positive views about their children's school, public education as a whole receives low marks in opinion polls. What is it about formal education that erodes high expectations among the young?

Teachers begin in September determined to inspire their classes and improve society. By June they appear exhausted from intense interpersonal and organizational demands. In casual conversations, they seem to depict students as "the enemy." Seeking to make sense of their work, some teachers emphasize a functionalist approach: basic skills, individual achievement, and structured competition aimed at employment or higher education. Others favor making schools pleasant places through a humanistic, child-centered, and socially relevant curriculum. As problems and frustrations accumulate, educators assign blame elsewhere— willful kids, lazy colleagues, bureaucracy, television, immigrants, a moral decline. What fosters group dynamics of misunderstanding and mistrust among students and teachers?

Typical organizational patterns of schools and endemic tensions between students and teachers contradict natural processes of human learning through exploratory activities. Between ages 5 and 18, most Americans spend 6 hours a day, 180 days a year, in regularly scheduled, teacher-dominated classrooms with 20 to 30 others. Characteristically, schools segment students by age and by rank-ordered tests into hierarchical tracks or programs. Students are categorized, and that message squelches or distorts a young person's desire to express personal beliefs or risk failure. It takes extraordinary effort for teachers to build trust so students raise questions and purposefully move toward personal and social goals.

In this chapter, we explore some simple yet amorphous puzzles. Why do so many children who are engaged learners outside of school settings perform so poorly in age-segregated, adult-controlled classrooms? Why do teachers who start with eagerness and idealism so often end up blaming kids or their families, complaining about bureaucratic details, and avoiding issues that excite the curiosity of learners? How do teachers make sense of education systems where between 25% and 75% of the students are marked for failure by their family's status or an IQ score? Throughout, we seek to present these dilemmas less as an explanation for the status quo than as potential building blocks for reconsidering the meanings of teaching and learning.

We introduce constructivist-developmental stages of cognitive development and a perspective on learning as a pragmatic, lifelong activity of making sense out of personal experiences and perceived events. We juxtapose traditional school structures and behavioral regularities that emphasize order, training for docility, and rank-ordered tests against Paulo Freire's vision of teaching as liberation from cultural oppressions. Popular reform proposals that advocate more instruction and higher standards conflict with natural developmental processes and an expansive view of human potential. Currently, economic stagnation, rising enrollments, and new racial and linguistic populations both compel and impede a reconsideration of educational practices. Finally, we briefly examine how educators view their preparation and development as active creators of classroom interactions.

## EXPERIENCING LEARNING

Learning requires taking risks to try out new activities and ideas. In nonstructured environments at home or with peers, young children act, make mistakes, try again, imitate others, and explore the complexities of larger settings with adult guidance. Constructivists depict normal stages of developing cognitive understandings. Between birth and age three, children discover their immediate environment and learn to speak, develop ideas about past and future actions, and imagine possibilities by combining ideas in new ways. From three to eight, children share their ideas with others and learn essential skills for reading, writing and arithmetic as formal mental operations. By age nine, children view other people, things, and ideas as independent of their own interactions with them.

In modern terms, human development proceeds through incremental gains in the capacity to act purposively. It is "the process through which the growing person acquires a more extended, differentiated, and valid conception of the ecological environment, and becomes motivated and able to engage in activities that reveal the properties of, sustain, or restructure that environment at levels of similar or greater complexity in form and content" (Bronfenbrenner, 1979, pp. 288–289). Ideally, throughout their lifetime people learn to function in increasingly power-filled settings by addressing relevant problems. They should experience success in specific performances and trust that failure will lead to another chance.

Despite the way classrooms are tracked and tests scored, educators have ample evidence that practically all children can acquire the basic competencies taught in schools. After 40 years of research, Benjamin Bloom (1985, pp. 4, 3) concluded that "what any person in the world can learn, *almost* all persons can learn *if* provided with appropriate prior and current conditions of learning." He asserted that "the middle 95% of school students become very similar in terms of their measured achievement, learning ability, rate of learning, and motivation for further learning when provided with *favorable learning conditions*." Great achievements are not the result of native genius but "a long and intensive process of encouragement, nurturance, education, and training."

Readiness to learn depends on past experiences, one's developmental frame, and a sense of how learning connects to personal aspirations. Self-directed learners require a base in information and cognitive processes. That framework has to start someplace: "Before knowledge becomes truly generative—knowledge that can be used to interpret new situations, to solve problems, to think and reason, and to learn—students must elaborate and question what they are told, examine the new information in relation to other information, and build new knowledge structures" (Resnick & Klopfer, 1989, pp. 5, 9). Learners need practice in linking skills to content around activities that have personal meaning. Moreover, a good classroom conveys to students "that all the elements of critical thought—interpretation, questioning, trying possibilities, demanding rational justifications—are socially valued."

## Stages of Cognitive Development

To explain how individuals make sense of events at different ages, constructivists propose multiple stages of intellectual and social development. Developmental changes occur rapidly for infants and more slowly for adults. Each person maintains a meaning system whose integrity imposes order on values and actions. These stages, with labels such as "impulsive," "imperial," and "interpersonal," are artificial constructs or researchers' categories that cannot explain how young people may see events in their own terms. Nevertheless, stages covering approximate age levels help educators address the needs of students as they mature. For example, a multicultural lesson in the first grade should not assume that a six-year old can visualize himself or herself in another's role.

Contained within the notion of stages is an insight that, at various points in their lives, individuals reconstruct interpretations of familiar events. During a child's second year, a crucial development occurs—a capacity to hold diverse mental images marking a new sense of self as an actor. According to social psychologist Jerome Kagan (1989, pp. 236, 242), "the half year that begins with the first smile following completion of a puzzle and ends with the embarrassed statement, 'I can't do that,' contains one of the most significant sets of competences to appear in our species." Between 18 and 24 months of age, most children develop "(1) an appreciation of standards of proper behavior and (2) an awareness of one's actions, intentions, states, and competences." Self-awareness depends on "at least five competences: recognition of the past, retrieval of prior schemata, inference, awareness of one's potentiality for action, and, finally, awareness of self as an entity with symbolic attributes."

For 50 years, Jean Piaget watched children solve various puzzles in order to learn about their physical and cognitive developments. That research suggested a sequence of four eras, with various stages in each. From two to five years of age, children offer intuitive or nonlogical explanations for phenomena based on what they see. For instance, in one of Piaget's often-cited experiments, a fixed amount of water poured from a tall, thin beaker into a short, fat one appears as a smaller quantity to young children, and vice versa. There is no contradiction of a principle of conservation of matter in a five-year old's mind. They offer such explanations as the red liquid (from the tall jar) must have spilled or the green liquid (in the short vessel) got bigger.

In another experiment, Piaget (1980, p. 6) asked children five to seven years old about a series of seven disks with slightly increasing diameters. Comparing adjacent disks by eye or physical congruence revealed no discernible difference; yet, the last (G) appeared larger than the first (A). One youngster reported them as the same, including A and G. When invited to look again, he corrected to "all except G and A. So G is the same as what?—As B C D E F.—And A?—That's the same as B C D E F. And A and G?—They're the not the same.—Is that a good explanation?—Don't know." Although adults find these responses illogical, young children show no concern about their reasoning.

Some seven- and eight-year olds recognized the transitivity (a < b < c) but could not resolve the contradiction (Piaget, 1980, pp. 11, 16–17): "So what's happening?—That one [C] is changing its size! I don't know, I can't see it properly.—So sometimes it's big and sometimes it's little?— . . . I must see if I made a mistake." Again he checks D against E, and laughs: "I did make a mistake. G and F are big and the rest are little." A 10-year old reasoned that many small differences would not add up to a significant one. The idea of same size disks prevailed. By age 11, a student "overcomes the contradiction by accepting the existence of imperceptible differences of magnitude capable of being progressively added to produce a visible inequality." As one commented, *"they're all equal but there's such a small difference that several small differences makes one big difference."*

As children enter school, they develop a capacity to separate their own point of view from the "objects" around them: "With the capacity to take command of one's impulses (to have them, rather than be them) can come a new sense of freedom, power, independence—agency, above all. Things no longer just happen in the world; with the capacity to see behind the shadows, to come in with the data of experience, I now have something to do with what happens" (Kegan, 1982, pp. 89–90). No wonder elementary teachers find their students so exciting, vulnerable, frustrating, and unpredictable. They are forever poised between earlier impulses and a newly found control over self and environment.

During elementary school, most children think concretely, learning to put named objects or relationships into categories. At this stage, children "manage" external objects by assigning them to categories according to defining features. For example, students memorize lists of typical products, common foods, and religions for geographic areas. Gradually, they learn logical operations such as "included within" (A $\subset$ B), transitivity, arithmetic functions, and conservation of matter. Reasoning and skills from one area are applied or recombined to cover new situations. Students may ponder "what if" questions in history or literature and focus on key elements or relationships in algebra or scientific laws. Moral reasoning becomes increasingly based on generalized principles or empathy.

Purposive competence in arenas beyond an immediate situation requires formalized concepts. Without that critical step, events appear as personal, fragmentary phenomena. Developing the implications of Piaget's epistemology, Eleanor Duckworth (1987, p. 14) linked concrete events to abstract analyses. Learners need a foundation of information and relationships from which to extend their understandings. Mastery of auto mechanics or geometry builds awareness of standard cognitive processes. "Knowing enough about things is one prerequisite for wonderful ideas." Connections become established between existing knowledge and new experiences to create complex interpretations.

Despite their accomplishments, neither elementary nor secondary students are developmentally ready to understand some cognitive frameworks used by adults. Young children do not reason abstractly apart from specific concrete illustrations, imagine counterfactual situations, or make generalizations that account for large, multifaceted systems. They cannot hold in balance both their own preferences and those of another within "mutual interpersonal relationships"; nor can they effectively prioritize their personal needs and strategies. By high school graduation, most youth have learned to reason abstractly about hypothetical situations; to recognize "shared feelings, agreements, and expectations"; and to balance personal perspectives with empathic understandings of others' points of view (Kegan, 1994, pp. 30–31).

Constructivism highlights several crucial points about how children learn that contradict a metaphor of the mind as a "blank slate" gradually being filled with knowledge. By age two, children have frameworks for making sense of phenomena. Their cognitive formats usually generalize to explain many events more or les consistently. As they mature, new frameworks transform existing understandings. Stages are "products of interactional experiences between the child and the world, experience which leads to a restructuring of the child's own organization rather than to the direct imposition of the culture's pattern upon the child" (Kohlberg & Gilligan, 1972, p. 152). There are substantial overlaps among stages of cognitive development across cultures and groups, as well as differences based on class, race and gender. In this respect, development is neither linear nor logical; instead, it depends on the association between cognitive frameworks and perceived experiences.

## Learning In and Out of School

Commonly, productive competencies are learned through apprenticeship roles in which gathering information and practicing skills are an incidental part of observation and participation with an experienced practitioner. Socially valued goals are usually implicit in the contributions that apprentices make to ongoing production. Experiential learning or internships "teach" skilled practices that cannot be described fully in abstract, rational language. For example, a cooperating teacher may resolve a specific problem without generalizing to all situations. Experience takes time, however, and there are advantages in structuring knowledge and transmitting it through group instruction in sequential courses. Sometimes novices are coached on specific skills as well as collaborative problem solving in ways that resemble classroom instruction.

Effective instruction entails organizing information into underlying structures so that a few concepts "explain" large numbers of actions or events. According to social psychologist Jerome Bruner (1977, p. ix), "emphasis should shift to teaching basic principles, underlying axioms, pervasive themes, that one should 'talk physics' with students rather than 'talk about' it to them." Bruner envisioned a spiral curriculum: "One approached knowledge in the spirit of making it accessible to the problem-solving learner by modes of thinking that he already possessed or that he could, so to speak, assemble by combining natural ways of thinking that he had not previously combined. One starts somewhere— where the learner *is*. And one starts *whenever* the student arrives to begin his career as a learner."

Moreover, Bruner (1977, pp. ix, xiv–xv, 12–13) insisted, "any subject could be taught to any child at any age in some form that is honest." New information becomes usable when learners engage in personally meaningful interactions in settings that reinforce a sense of self as a purposive actor: "So much of learning depends upon the need to achieve joint attention, to conduct enterprises jointly, to honor the social relationship that exists between learner and tutor, to generate possible worlds in which given propositions may be true or appropriate or even felicitous: to overlook this functional setting of learning—whatever its content—is to dry it to a mummy." Deemphasizing "facts and techniques" in favor of underlying principles reinforces a view "that the basic ideas that lie at the heart of all science and mathematics and the basic themes that give form to life and literature are as simple as they are powerful."

Because usable information builds on existing competencies, concepts and values within contexts of personal expectations, schooling means most to those who anticipate having power in a knowledge society. By revisiting ideas in light of new purposes and proficiencies, students reconstruct frameworks of categories and relationships. "To be in command of these basic ideas, to use them effectively, requires a continual deepening of one's understanding of them that comes from learning to use them in progressively more complex forms" (Bruner, 1977, pp. 13, 14, 17). Learning depends on intrinsic motivation, intuition to make a "courageous leap to a tentative conclusion, " and anticipated utility: "Learning should not only take us somewhere; it should allow us later to go further more easily."

---

Recalling our experiences in school, most of us associate learning with a difficult class—spelling, a new language, algebra, or Shakespeare. Those memories may undervalue learning through informal interactions, listening to music, enjoying games and hobbies, or sharing thoughts about the meaning of life.

Are there differences between what you learned in formal classes and what you "picked up" through daily experiences, associations, or mentoring?

---

Intelligence, as psychologist Robert Sternberg (1988, pp. x, 75, 65, 70) describes it, "can be understood as *mental self-management*—the manner in which we order and make sense of events that take place around and within us." IQ tests and schools "measure only a narrow spectrum of our mental self-management skills." As a result, "all existing tests tend to favor certain groups over others, and the favored groups are virtually always the societal 'in-groups.'" He depicted a "triarchic theory" of mind wherein "intelligence in everyday life is defined as the *purposive adaptation to, selection of, and shaping of real-world environments relevant to one's life and abilities*." Achievement tests omit "(a) adaptation to, selection of, and shaping of real-world environments; (b) dealing with novel kinds of tasks and situations; and (c) metacomponential planning and decision making."

Whether embedded in taken-for-granted frameworks for interpreting events or used to process sensory inputs related to a possible course of action, knowledge is valued because it helps us function in our daily lives. Conditions of factory production in market economies led Americans to elevate a narrow range of mental skills that served powerful socioeconomic forces. In turn, schools privileged knowledge appropriate for that system. Today's information technologies raise other possibilities for human cognition that will elevate new forms of practical knowledge and creativity.

## Constructing Postmodernism

Most learning occurs in incremental steps that build on prior knowledge and involve frequent failures until certain patterns are mastered. At times, however, underlying frameworks shift dramatically, causing revisions in many previously assumed relationships and opening fresh areas for exploration. Developmental constructivists see a basic movement toward increasing differentiation or complexity of viewpoints. Preschoolers see only themselves in relation to their feelings and movements; school-age children fill in descriptions around durable categories of things and other people; late adolescents begin to apply cognitive operations to categories (including other people) and to conceptualize abstractions that include themselves in relationship to others; and adults who have adopted a modern framework operate effectively within institutional settings and conceive of their world as interrelated complex systems.

Each new way to make sense of experience, however, is not readily understandable to those who are embedded within an earlier developmental framework. When experts offer advice to parents, workers, leaders, and educators from a postmodern framework, they often add to the demands of modern life. In social psychologist Robert Kegan's (1994, p. 303) summary, people today are urged to

Exercise critical thinking

Examine ourselves, our culture, and our milieu in order to understand how to separate what we feel from what we should feel, what we value from what we should value, and what we want from what we should want

Be a self-directed learner (take initiative; set our own goals and standards; use experts, institutions, and our resources to pursue these goals; take responsibility for our direction and productivity in learning)

See ourselves as the co-creators of the culture (rather than only shaped by culture)

These prescriptions make sense only to those adults whose cognitive framework includes both self and system. They are beyond the reach of youth who are struggling to learn facts, relationships and self-identity in terms of their preferences and prospective social roles.

Many adults have difficulty moving to a fourth level of consciousness, which Kegan called "modern." Modern thinkers move from abstract entities to abstract systems, from ideals to ideology. The focus shifts from interpersonal relations based on mutuality to institutional contexts that shape roles and relationships. The result is multiple contexts and roles. The self is seen as something to be authored and regulated—sometimes to maintain connections and sometimes to advance in an organization. From this perspective, advice to others can be balanced and contingent, based on general principles and empathy. Youth and young adults who are still trying to fill in their understanding of the characteristics of durable categories—and who are encouraged in that pursuit by an emphasis on right answers in school—find it hard to grasp how one can simultaneously see oneself in relation to organizations, cultural norms and ideals.

As new meanings of knowledge and self-identity are renegotiated in social interactions among diverse individuals, they undermine prevailing notions of universal truths or essential concepts and principles. In words that reflect the complexity of cognition, Jean Lave (1991, p. 67) asserted "that learning, thinking, and knowing are relations among people engaged in activity *in, with, and arising from the socially and culturally structured world.*" Nature and classrooms alike are generated "in dialectical relations between the social world and persons engaged in activity; together these produce and re-produce both world and person in activity." Meanings arise out of those relations, and neither can be described separately—or fully explain the other.

Because learning is contextual, its meanings are transformed by historical developments. Traditionally, people acquired knowledge and identity through apprenticeships in which "learning is recognized as a social phenomenon constituted in the experienced, lived-in world, through legitimate peripheral participation in ongoing social practice" (Lave, 1991, pp. 64, 67). Industrialism segments skills and workers in hierarchical structures that disengage identity from instrumental knowledge. Neither schools nor workplaces induct novices into a craft and a way of life by encouraging greater participation with communities of practitioners. At the same time, both settings seek explicitly to teach and control—perhaps enforcing "the trivializing decomposition of forms of activity" into unrelated "facts" or "principles" for transmission to others. That insight may start to explain why today's schools and workplaces seem so alienating.

All this poses an extraordinary challenge for educators and this text: As teachers, we try to present ideas in cognitive frameworks that are meaningful to students, within their perspective and vocabulary. At the same time, we raise dilemmas and offer words and ideas that build bridges to postmodern frameworks. Socially constructed knowledge becomes problematic as young adults move into complex settings, try to resolve endemic tensions in organizations, experience changing conditions, or seek to actualize values. We want to construct more inclusive, less marginalizing, more contingent categories and roles. This may lead to greater readiness for an encompassing framework or to confusion. Our accounts shift among traditional, modern and postmodern perspectives in order to encourage deconstruction and reconstruction.

## TEACHING IN TODAY'S SCHOOLS

Teachers necessarily disturb established meanings. New ideas continually bump against taken-for-granted views. An exciting class introduces different perspectives, allows students to explore, and generates alternative courses of action. Students "create" new understandings when they relate personal ideas to their assignments. They "write" history through inquiry into varied sources and rearranging a narrative. They "discover" science by manipulating wires, batteries and light bulbs. When novel ideas raise doubts about long-held beliefs, traditional ways of classroom management discourage the sharing of ideas. When teachers present academic subjects in imitation of a college course based on a scholar's disciplinary paradigm, it is three-times abstracted from their students' lives.

From a constructivist orientation, teachers make ideas, behaviors and frameworks real to others. To make information accessible, they engage in personable interactions, drawing from their experiences to fill in gaps between a student's existing framework and new ideas. Selecting from a vast array of facts, principles and values, teachers choose what lessons to present and when. They seek to address the varied interests and learning styles among their students. Ideally, an ongoing dialog around issues that matter to both parties creates common understanding, but reconsidering personal knowledge to connect with the frameworks and goals of others is an exhausting, hit-and-miss task. Educators treasure moments when students connect ideas to fresh contexts.

In complex educational organizations, teachers' viewpoints emerge from endemic tensions between learning and school regularities based on adult control. Repeated studies validate a conclusion that teachers "picture themselves as constrained, under supplied, and under appreciated; their aims and their context do not jibe" (Lortie, 1975, p. 185). Only when instructing their classes do they feel in charge. Typically, teachers lecture to an imagined "middle" group because hands-on activities, personal reflections, and individualized approaches appear confusing and student-centered. They seek those elusive "good" moments when the class responds positively but "believe that high points require a lucky conjunction of moods." Over time, teachers develop an occupational "ethos" characterized by conservatism, a tendency to live day to day, and an absence of dialog about what they hope to achieve.

All teachers report frustration at times with crucial aspects of their work (Boyer, 1983, pp. 154–185):

- the low status accorded educators by the public;
- their hectic daily routines, myriad duties, isolation from other adults, and in some schools, fears of physical violence;
- school settings characterized by inadequate materials, equipment, and facilities;
- unorganized intellectual supports and uninspired leadership;
- the difficulty they have in deriving psychological rewards from their job; and
- the belief that teaching is more like a "trade" than a "profession."

Teachers ask for administrators and parents to acknowledge the importance of their role in educating the young.

## Isolated and Overburdened

Teachers struggle to integrate multiple and conflicting responsibilities—individual productivity and democratic citizenship, equity and efficiency, traditions and innovations. They work as a lonely professional in a crowded room. Every day, educators make thousands of decisions to solve immediate problems and perform multiple roles: caring for and supporting students; collaborating with parents; planning, organizing, scheduling, communicating and assessing curriculum; researching new ideas and approaches; developing programs that provoke thought and reflection; and modeling adult behaviors (Heck & Williams, 1984; Dollase, 1992).

Feelings of personal powerlessness and frustration recurred in our interviews with educators. *"It is tough in the classroom,"* said one teacher. As a solution to burnout, he urged going *"back to school, learn some new stuff to give you new tools. You may find out that you are not burned out at all, just frustrated because you don't have the tools or knowledge to deal with the situation."* Unsupported by colleagues and administrators, he observed that, whatever his principal proposed, *"I am the one who ultimately decides exactly what will be taught in that classroom. Therein lies the real power in the teachers."* That authority is negated, however, by the *"organization and isolation of teachers. Some teachers never see each other. They can't share their ideas—not really a networking system set up."*

Much of a teacher's felt experience revolves around "surviving" or "coping" with some 25 restive learners. Classroom management requires planned activities. Unlike professionals who charge for their time or operate within bureaucratic procedures, teachers face unlimited demands for their attention. Students need personal attention for instruction, assessment and guidance as well as time to support their mental, psychological and social development. Forced to make organizational-bureaucratic decisions about whom to serve and how, teachers fall short of their idealistic wish to help all students. Not their intentions but "the routines they establish, and the devices they invent to cope with uncertainties and work pressures, effectively *become* the public policies they carry out" (Lipsky, 1980, p. xii).

Facing limitless demands on their attention from eager learners, teachers typically act in isolation "to salvage service and decision-making values" under adverse conditions "in a corrupted world of service" (Lipsky, 1980, p. xiii). Wanting to help others, teachers lack time for personable interactions with every student. Instead, they rely on coping strategies that contradict their knowledge about how best to facilitate learning. They establish classroom routines that ignore differences among their students. They modify goals to emphasize those easiest to achieve. They discourage curiosity that strays from a set curriculum, thereby rationing services and controlling students.

---

**After establishing orderly classrooms, teachers focus on aspects of the curriculum within their control. They assign readings and homework, lecture and conduct class discussions, and periodically give tests in an effort to cover a proscribed subject matter.**

**Yet student learning is facilitated by choices from a rich array of materials, activities and assessments that foster en gagement and self-directed learning. Those classes may appear unplanned or out of control.**

**What desirable outcomes, or problems, do you foresee with a student-centered curriculum in schools?**

---

When asked, teachers in a middle school readily acknowledged their familiarity with common tactics to implement varied coping strategies

(Bratiotis, 1982). They utilized seatwork, copied or modified from workbooks, in order to individualize assistance to one or two. They emphasized basic skills over critical thinking. They performed triage to sort out a "teachable" group while ignoring others as beyond hope as well as those able to learn on their own. Although all teachers stifled student motivation occasionally, they credited their own good intentions somewhat more than those of their colleagues. Several suggested that others adopted similar coping tactics for reasons of laziness or ignorance rather than to reassert personal autonomy in the face of endless demands for attention.

Teachers find it difficult to escape from routines and normal expectations in schools. Innovations raise questions about fitting in with a school's culture—its established behaviors and values. Asked what it would take to do away with tracking, an administrator in an urban district noted the ineffectiveness of outside experts: *"Teachers have to be convinced that it [an innovation] can work; and those who have not tried it for the most part don't believe it can work, so it means finding a small group of people in the school that are willing to try it."* Wanting to implement cooperative approaches, teachers also recognized that student grades and evaluations would have to be justified to skeptical colleagues.

Schools present mixed messages about their expectations for students and teachers. If students are seen as irresponsible, then teachers must monitor homework and supervise corridors and bathrooms. Schools may hold high expectations for students' behaviors or for their interest in learning, but rarely both. Typically, only extracurricular activities such as music or athletics call on students to exercise initiative and to represent their school with maturity. Likewise, state-mandated competency tests suggest that no one trusts teachers to perform without bureaucratic oversight. Personal autonomy, creative risk taking, and a sense of playfulness have been squelched or channeled in ways that create and sustain an alienating workplace for most teachers as well as for students.

## Elementary and Middle School Structures

Elementary and secondary teaching often seem quite distinct occupations reflecting stages of student development and characteristic organizational patterns. Elementary teacher roles have been sensitively described as responses to six "major dilemmas":

- More subjects to teach than time to teach them
- Coverage vs. mastery
- Large-group vs. small-group instruction
- When to stay with a subject or a routine and when to shift

- How to discipline students without destroying the class
- How to deal with isolation from other adults. (Lieberman & Miller, 1992, p. 82)

Typically, elementary schools place 24 to 30 children, segregated by age, in self-contained classrooms. In most schools, instruction covers reading, writing, social studies, mathematics, science, art, music, and health. Academic subjects are taught during scheduled times. Self-directed individual and group activities are reserved for the youngest students, for those with special needs, and for "honors" groups. Most buildings serve 300 to 600 students with 12 to 24 classroom teachers in order to gain organizational economies of scale. They are supported by building administrators, counselors, reading specialists, special educators, bilingual teachers, physical education, art, music and other auxiliary subject instructors, health care providers, aides, food service workers, custodial staff, community liaisons, bus drivers, and parent volunteers.

In his classic study of *Life in Classrooms*, Philip W. Jackson (1968, pp. 7, 8, 9, 10) found a remarkable sameness to the 7,000 hours that children spend in elementary schools. Classroom routines proceed without overt notice or protest. "Each student has an assigned seat and, under normal circumstances, that is where he is to be found." Instruction follows well-established rules—"no loud talking during seatwork, do not interrupt someone else during discussion, keep your eyes on your own paper during tests, raise your hand if you have a question." Schedules recur, and "everyone can tell at a glance what will happen next." Students soon adapt to *"crowds, praise, and power."* Children are dominated by teachers and "pawns of institutional authorities."

Somewhere between the ages of 10 and 12 (grades four to seven), children move from a system that is predominately one teacher covering all subjects to schools where different staff members teach different subjects in different rooms. Typically, these schools serve 500 to 800 students who are establishing social identities and maturing sexually. Control can no longer be assured by a teacher's physical strength or restrictions on students' movement. Their rapidly shifting moods, interests and aspirations conflict with demands for orderly, scheduled classes:

Every 50 minutes, perhaps 6 or 7 times each day, assemble with 30 or so of your peers, each time in a different group, sit silently in a chair in neat, frozen rows, and try to catch hold of knowledge as it whizzes by you in the words of an adult you met only at the beginning of this school year. The subject of one class has nothing to do with the subject of the next class. If a concept is confusing, don't ask for help, there isn't time to explain. If something interests you deeply, don't stop to think about it, there's too much to cover. (Carnegie Council on Adolescent Development, 1989, p. 37)

Traditional structures and programs ill-serve one in four of the 28 million teenagers: "Young adolescents have a great need for intimacy, yet we put them in large, impersonal schools" (Carnegie Council on Adolescent Development, 1989, p. 36). They "need to make their own decisions, yet we put them in environments of review and rote learning." They ask, "Who are my friends?" "What should I learn?" "What can I do?" Socially, they cope with physical and emotional changes that place them uneasily between family and society. Warned against drugs, they question why their parents and other adults smoke and drink. Sex education emphasizes biological functions and abstinence, while sexual allurement pervades popular media. Likewise, the Golden Rule seems contradicted by class, race and gender biases. When students attempt to reconcile disparate messages, they find few connections between their search for identity and academic subjects.

Bells and rules offer few choices to students who also are expected to think critically and determine whom they want to become. Schools do not have to be that way. Many elementary and middle school teachers arrange classrooms around multiple activity centers, engage students in small-group projects, encourage student decisionmaking, and collaborate with parents. Elite academies usually offer independent study and many extracurricular activities in which students exercise leadership. Structures that facilitate learning based on student choice and cooperation are far better preparation for a modern and post-modern world than traditional schools.

## Secondary School Structures

Most older adolescents attend large, impersonal, comprehensive high schools that enroll 1,000 to 5,000 youths—often divided into "houses" or programs with 200 to 500 students each. Secondary teachers specialize in math, English, science, social studies, foreign languages, and fine arts as well as a range of technical, vocational, and commercial areas. To graduate, students must take at least three years of English or communications, two years of social studies including U.S. history, and a year each of mathematics, science, and fine arts. Four years of physical education and a year of home economics or shop round out a student's requirements. Many districts mandate typing or computer literacy. Students elect almost half their courses from predesignated college preparatory, technical, vocational, commercial or general programs.

Those who teach in middle and high schools feel closer to adult issues and to their academic discipline, but lack autonomy:

For secondary teachers dilemmas are rooted in the complexity of the formal and informal system, such as:
- Personal vs. organizational constraints
- Dealing with the classroom and with the whole school
- Packaging and pacing instruction to fit into allocated time periods
- Proportioning subject matter expertise and affective needs in some way
- Figuring out how to deal with mixed loyalties to the faculty and to the student culture. (Lieberman & Miller, 1992, p. 82)

Secondary schools acknowledge the near-adult status of their students with cooperative or vocational programs. Four out of five teenagers hold part-time jobs. Most schools give credit for paid work during the school day as well as offer training in a school-based auto shop or snack bar. Some provide childcare for teenage parents, clinics that dispense condoms, and meeting space for political or religious clubs. One auxiliary professional for every two teachers handle student discipline; security in the hallways and bathrooms; academic scheduling; guidance, career, and drug and alcohol counseling; and coaching or advising for extracurricular activities.

Commenting on the organization of curriculum and learning in secondary education, Powell, Farrar, and Cohen (1985, pp. 12-13, 38, 11, 309) described a comprehensive high school as a shopping mall. It offers many introductory courses with limited advanced sequences; an "extracurriculum" of clubs and sports, each serving a small number; and a "services curriculum" devoted to students' physical and psychological well-being. Like mall operators, educators assume "variety makes prosperity possible for all." Students "do their own thing. In general the customer is always right. Finally, the institution is largely neutral about the choices students make." Educators cite egalitarian principles in defending consumer mathematics and remedial English; such choices raise questions about a curriculum "exclusively governed by consumer choice."

Despite their apparent options, many students perceive high school classes as something to endure or to ease through. Most teachers adjust their expectations to fit community norms. In some suburban high schools, 90% graduate, and of those as many as 85% advance to postsecondary education. In low-income urban schools, as few as half graduate; of those one in four intends to pursue education the following year. Issues of drugs, pregnancy and violence appear more pressing than Scholastic Aptitude Test scores or college application forms. In schools that have a class and racial mix of students, the academic and vocational programs effectively segregate students within the building—except in physical education or music.

School size makes a difference. Complex organizations with multiple subunits (departments, houses, or alternative programs) and specialized staffs discourage participation. Smaller units encourage personable interactions, cohesive programs, and flexibility. For example, in many small elementary schools all the staff meet in the principal's space for coffee in the morning. As a result, schedule adjustments, comments about parents or students, and curricular suggestions are handled informally. Nevertheless, small administrative units do not guarantee a positive social climate. Some organizational features such as meetings, schedules, classes and degrees become rituals to legitimize existing arrangements rather than serving to coordinate learning activities.

---

**Imagine a school based on the proposals of a former chancellor of the New York City schools ( Scribner & Stevens, 1975) :**
- **children enter on their fifth birthday;**
- **buildings are open all year, and families choose vacation days;**
- **every younger child has a tutor and, later, tutors others;**
- **students apprentice with craft workers, artists, or professionals;**
- **high schoolers periodically engage in restructuring their setting as a part of their academic program;**
- **districts allow parents to govern each school; and**
- **external evaluations of performance determine grades and degrees.**

---

Despite autonomy within their classrooms, teachers feel constrained by their colleagues' work norms as well as their students' expectations: *"Well if there's going to be change, it's going to have to start with the teachers, certainly, and what they bring to that classroom. I mean, you can have a billion administrators but they're never going to be there and help you to do your job, really. They can provide you with some materials but it's your own creativity and training that you can bring into that class. . . . That's what drives me crazy. I want to do all of these things, but I'm limited by their system."* Impersonal regulations, strict disciplinary rules, and distinctions between staff and students perversely prevail in schools serving poor and minority neighborhoods where positive role models and flexibility are most needed.

With extrinsic rewards from high school diplomas declining, teachers find it increasingly difficult to control the curriculum and students. Public school teachers complain about bureaucratic restrictions and demands, but they gratefully use them to reduce their own discretionary role. There are inherent conflicts "when rationalizing structures are applied to work that is not wholly rational; when schools are organized as if pedagogy could be prescribed, instruction delivered in uniform doses to clients in large groups, and the products of learning measured and summarized for public scrutiny" (Johnson, 1990, p. 107).

## EMBEDDED LESSONS

Organizational patterns in schools establish a powerful culture whose taken-for-granted assumptions constrain the range of plausible alternatives. Asked to recall behavioral regularities from their school days, students in our teacher education classes recited answers to familiar questions—names of presidents, rules of English grammar, multiplication tables. Gradually, they raised questions about the cultural values implicit in school rules governing student behaviors— such as raising hands to obtain a teacher's attention, punctuality, dress codes, hall passes, and alphabetical seating arrangements. They recalled adult justifications for those rules—maintaining order or respecting the teacher's authority. They identified other value-laden activities, including homework, textbook assignments, a daily pledge of allegiance, emphasis on correct spelling and proper grammar, sex-segregated sports, and assemblies to foster school pride.

One group saw these features as realistic preparation for life. Another stressed how regularities regimented people, silenced some, limited choices, induced disengagement, privileged book knowledge over personal beliefs, and labeled certain racial groups as inferior. Others fell in between, with some values viewed positively and others negatively. No one addressed the prevalence of testing and grades to rank-order students or of age segregation within a typical classroom. Apparently, it seemed natural that youngsters should all be within a year or two of the same age and study discrete subjects where all questions have a correct answer.

These prospective teachers viewed uniform rules imposed on students, despite their individual needs and desires, as problematic. They envisioned a more flexible and student-centered school that, nevertheless, maintained most existing regularities. As young men and women who had performed well in school, they supported book learning for others. They valued grading systems from which they had benefited. Questioning underlying assumptions about education created discomfort. One objected to the exercise as another criticism of the United States; several worried about losing control of a class with individualized programs. When those issues arose, many retreated to a belief that teachers should determine classroom rules and curriculum.

### School Realities

Scholars have puzzled over the failures of popular reforms from the 1970s such as alternative schools, community-based programs, and humanistic education to promote smaller, less-bureaucratic units. They looked at schools as experienced by teachers and students. Their ethnographic studies focused attention on organizational structures and prevalent attitudes that disempowered professionals (Boyer, 1983; Hampel, 1986; Johnson, 1990). They confirmed Charles Silberman's (1970) earlier observation that schools are dull, boring and purposeless. When engaged outside of classrooms, teachers appear inquisitive and aware of current social issues; yet, as Goodlad (1984, p. 192) found, "large numbers of secondary teachers resort to practices designed to keep students passive and under control just at the time when adolescents should be taking more charge of their own education."

American educators officially proclaim widely shared goals for schools—starting with academic skills and proceeding through vocational preparation; social, civic, and cultural learning; and personal development. Under each category, Goodlad (1984, pp. 51–56) identified specific competencies. For example, under intellectual development, he listed "the ability to think rationally, including problem-solving skills, application of principles of logic, and skill in using different modes of inquiry." A part of interpersonal understandings emphasized "the ability to identify with and advance the goals and concerns of others." In order to be socialized, students should "develop an awareness and understanding of one's cultural heritage and become familiar with the achievements of the past that have inspired and influenced humanity."

In classrooms, Goodlad (1984, p. 236) found a pervasive emphasis on the traditional three Rs (reading, writing and arithmetic). What he did not find were teachers developing those qualities commonly listed under "intellectual development." "Only *rarely* did we find evidence to suggest instruction likely to go much beyond mere possession of information to a level of understanding its implications and either applying it or exploring its possible applications. Nor did we see activities likely to arouse students' curiosity or to involve them in seeking solutions to some problem not already laid bare by teacher or textbook." Moreover, "this preoccupation with the lower intellectual processes pervades social studies and science as well."

Goodlad (1984, pp. 237, 239) also identified "a general failure to view subjects and subject matter as turf on which to experience the struggles and satisfactions of personal development." Typically, educators have sought to inculcate "understanding differing value systems; developing productive and satisfying relations with others based on respect, trust, cooperation, and caring; developing a concern for humanity; developing the ability to apply the basic principles and concepts of the fine arts and humanities to the appreciation of aesthetic contributions of other cultures; and developing an understanding of the necessity for moral conduct." Further, schools aim to develop competencies "to use leisure time effectively, to criticize oneself constructively, to deal with problems in original ways, and to experience and enjoy different forms of creative expression." In practice, however, grading fosters individual competition, and school rules induce a docile conformity.

Behavioral regularities imposed on schools by an overarching demand for order stifled motivation and discouraged active learning, except in advanced or "unimportant" courses: "From the beginning, students experience school and classroom environments that condition them in precisely opposite behaviors—seeking 'right' answers, conforming, and reproducing the known. These behaviors are reinforced daily by the physical restraints of the group and classroom, by the kinds of questions teachers ask, by the nature of the seatwork exercises assigned, and by the format of tests and quizzes" (Goodlad, 1984, pp. 241, 267). Outside innovations provoke defensive "mechanisms that protect conventional practices." As a result, "replacing all the principals and teachers tomorrow would change only the actors. The play would go on as before."

Faced with unending demands for their attention, teachers lack time to consider each student's needs. Driven in part by mandatory competency tests, teachers largely determine the acceptable discourse—citing the importance of book knowledge, praising American democracy and capitalism, defining two-parent heterosexual families as the norm, and vaguely supporting tolerance for cultural differences. Usually, they emphasize opportunities for their students to get ahead by studying and working hard. Those whose background, prospects or values do not fit in soon learn that they are deficient and cannot expect to succeed either in school or later in a job. By sorting students into ability groups and academic or vocational schools, teachers largely determine future social hierarchies.

### Testing and Tracking

When teachers make sense out of their role by assuming that they have important information to be conveyed to youngsters' empty minds, then much of what happens in schools fits with their assumptions and reconfirms their belief. Educators emphasize formal subject areas with facts and figures that then are tested at regular intervals. Assuming that intelligence is largely fixed, measurable by IQ scores, and distributed across a "normal" bell-shaped curve, teachers design tests or scale their grades to give roughly two-thirds Cs or Bs, with the remainder divided between As and Ds or Fs. Faced with student resistance to their authority, teachers engage in daily struggles to increase "time on task" in order to raise scores on standardized achievement tests.

National tests rank students, schools and even states. Students who earn the Bs and As, or about half of a class, have little reason to question that way of making sense of schools. In most cases, their scores and their school's reputation suffice for acceptance at a college that offers a reasonable chance to graduate with credentials leading to a better-than-average job and salary—especially for White males. They may resent boring homework and difficult tests, but they presume that the process benefits them in the long run. Students in the bottom half usually blame themselves, although their "below average" scores follow from the school's grading pattern and a prevailing denigration of knowledge held by low-income families as well as by linguistically and culturally diverse children.

Teachers observe, and national studies show, that educational outcomes are unequal and unjust. Nevertheless, educators continue to justify multiple-choice tests in the name of fair procedures and administrative convenience. Students have varied readiness and experiences: A few have traveled abroad, some use computers at home, many cope with poverty in latchkey households, others speak Spanish or Khmer, most have work or family responsibilities. For 20 years, researchers have known "that 'standardized' tests and experiments are, in reality, intricately negotiated and manifestly *non*standard forms of social interaction whose dynamics and structure must be understood in terms of the social contexts of which they are a constituent part" (Cole, 1991, p. 407). Students bring cultural knowledge from home as well as prior experiences with teachers and tests to their way of interpreting the intent of each question.

Homogeneous ability groups divide and label students hierarchically. Tracking practices are deeply ingrained—educators "*assume* that it is best for students*" (Oakes, 1985, pp. 6, 7). Three out of four schools separate students "on the basis of perceived ability, as determined by standardized test scores, student academic performance, less formal teacher assessments, and/or parental and student input." Reviewing research on ability grouping, Jeannie Oakes flatly concluded: *"no group of students has been found to benefit consistently from being in a homogeneous group."* Contrary to prevailing belief, high-track students do just as well on standardized tests when placed in heterogeneous groups. Because tracking effectively isolates students by class and race, all groups are denied opportunities to interact and learn from their diversity.

When tracked, student contacts are limited socially and academically. Students recognize that a B in a vocational or general course is not the same as a B in advanced placement. Self-esteem in a school setting follows from the way they perceive others view them:

A student in a high-achieving group is seen as a high-achieving *person*, bright, smart, quick, and in the eyes of many, *good*. And those in the low-achieving groups come to be called slow, below average, and—often when people are being less careful—dummies, sweathogs, or yahoos. . . . On the basis of these sorting decisions, the groupings of students that result, and the way educators see the students in these groups, teenagers are treated by and experience schools very differently. (Oakes, 1985, p. 3)

Within their classrooms, teachers structure an appearance of fairness by using a textbook, group assignments, lectures, and objective assess-ments—seldom acknowledging that their decisions favor Eurocentric, middle-class cultural experiences. Consequently, norm-referenced tests and tracking convey embedded lessons of class and race. Those tests also measure only a small part of the seven intelligences identified by Howard Gardner (1983): linguistic, musical, logical-mathematical, spatial, bodily-kinesthetic, intrapersonal, and interpersonal. Scholars honor certain categories—notably, observable and measurable quanti-ties arranged in hierarchical subunits that can be presented in writing or manipulated mathematically. They privilege logical and material aspects of life over affective, procedural and relational considerations. Skills in managing time, talents in the fine arts, or abilities to establish rapport with others are seldom rewarded and then usually in extra-curricular activities.

---

**Think about different competencies that you have learned at home, in school, or on the job (such as skating or riding a bicycle, playing a game or musical instrument, exploring a nearby woods or urban neighborhood, using a map or a computer).**

**What roles did other learners have in the process? Were groups divided according to proficiency level? Did you contribute ideas to others and feel good about sharing your skills or knowledge?**

---

National assessments reveal that little of a formal curriculum lasts beyond final exams. Few questions covering commonly taught facts could be answered by 60% of 17-year-olds in a national sample (Ravitch & Finn, 1987, p. 59). For example, only 41% selected Jane Addams from a list of four women as someone associated with settlement houses. Although some researchers interpret such failures as arguments for rigorous homework, longer classes, and regular tests, one might equally well question why academic ignorance matters so little to otherwise competent adults. Perhaps the formal curriculum has little utility for most people, except those who become educators. What lasts is a social-ization implicit in a hierarchy of power based on grades or advanced degrees.

For instance, White, middle-class, healthy college students learn many things that will serve them well in later life—little of which relates to their courses. They learn to function in bureaucratic organiza-tions; to work long and effectively to meet deadlines imposed by others for work that has little personal meaning; to present a competent and conventionally ambitious persona in social situations; to draw from a variety of sources and to apply those lessons selectively; and to adopt elitist attitudes about gender roles and families, media and recreation, politics and religion, class and race. Many also learn to socialize around alcohol, to establish personal relations with others outside their family, to conceal anger, to cope with loneliness, to handle sexual feelings and identity, to mix fresh challenges with successes. Few think critically about their special advantages.

From a critical theorist's perspective, widespread dissatisfaction attests to the fact that "reproductive processes are not carried out in a smooth, uncontested manner in the schools, and they are accomplished only at a substantial price" (Carlson, 1987, pp. 305, 306). Mandating higher standards or bureaucratic procedures subordinates teachers and "generates more discontent and further alienates teachers and students from managerial goals." If students and teachers engage in a democratic dialog to determine their curriculum, then they may opt not to "use their newfound power, or define excellence, in ways that are consistent with corporate and state interests." Currently, alienating conditions in schools raise questions about entrusting students and teachers with power to reform education from the bottom up. Meanwhile, new economic and social prospects erode the logic of existing strategies and structures.

## APPROACHES TO REFORM

At some point in their careers, most educators say they love teaching but hate the school. In our interviews, people expressed personal enthusiasm for an innovative program or approach and also vented frustrations at rules and stick-in-the-mud attitudes. As teacher educators for over two decades, we have seen many novices entering classrooms determined to inspire learning and foster a positive climate for all students. They complain about bureaucratic procedures and opposition from an experienced but tired staff. By now, however, we recognize that those veteran teachers are the ones who started out with high hopes in previous years.

If schools generate so much frustration and criticism, why are they so hard to change? Popular reforms reveal how educators and citizens socially construct the meaning of schooling. Fundamentally, most schools meet the needs of dominant groups, while those who are educationally cheated lack resources or influence to change them. Embedded school structures effectively block exploratory dialogs around personally meaningful or socially controversial topics. As a consequence, educators hear mixed signals about what students, businesses, public agencies, or community members expect from them *and* will support financially. Simple solutions are popular; effective programs take time, commitment and an awareness of the context. Simple, good solutions are a figment of rhetoric.

Previously, school structures, embedded lessons, and the skills and attitudes demanded by capitalists in an industrial era were consistent. Rank ordering through tests, tracking and limited access to higher education served to separate out enough technicians, professionals and managers while preparing others to follow orders. In the future, productive citizens will need skills of cooperation, engagement in group decisionmaking, and management based on readily accessible information. In that context, the inertia of schools threatens growing dysfunction, rising resistance in classrooms, and dissatisfaction among taxpayers.

## Top-down Proposals

Although key institutions for social change, schools are peculiarly resistant to reform. In the United States, 2.8 million teachers instruct approximately 47 million young people in over 84,000 elementary and secondary schools at a public cost exceeding $280 billion a year. Another 2 million principals, librarians, counselors, clerks and paraprofessionals along with uncounted childcare providers support those teachers. The costs of over 3,500 institutions of higher education with over 800,000 instructors serving nearly 15 million students exceed $180 billion annually. Public agencies, nonprofit organizations, and businesses spend over $100 billion on formal training programs. Total spending on investment in human capital approximates 10% of the total domestic product.

Seeking to overhaul schools as a national priority, educators and governors met with President George Bush in 1990 to set goals for "America 2000" (now included in President Bill Clinton's "Goals 2000"):

1. All children in America will start school ready to learn.
2. The high-school graduation rate will increase to at least 90 percent.
3. American students will leave grades four, eight, and twelve having demonstrated competency in challenging subject matter, including English, mathematics, science, history, and geography; and every school in America will ensure that all students learn to use their minds well, so they may be prepared for responsible citizenship, further learning, and productive employment in our modern economy.
4. U. S. students will be the first in the world in science and mathematics achievement.
5. Every adult American will be literate and will possess the knowledge and skills necessary to compete in a global economy and exercise the rights and responsibilities of citizenship.

6. Every school in America will be free of drugs and violence and will offer a disciplined environment conducive to learning. (U.S. Department of Education, 1991, p. 3)

Several items repeated goals previously set by President Ronald Reagan to be achieved by 1990. These lofty standards implicitly condemned schools as inadequate, without addressing classroom interactions or students' aspirations.

Efforts to reform schools with a panacea from the top have small chance for success. There is little evidence that competency tests, rigorous evaluation procedures, differential pay systems, mandatory coursework, or other suggestions compel teachers or schools to improve. The Rand Change Agent Study of federally funded innovations in the 1960s and 1970s concluded that professional development of teachers must be integrated "with other aspects of school change such as curriculum development and administrative reform." According to the study, 1) teachers possess the best available "clinical expertise"—although class-room realities often fall short of those instructional possibilities; 2) innovations are implemented in a local setting through "adaptive and heuristic" approaches; 3) "professional learning is a long-term, nonlinear process"; 4) ongoing inservice training for staff must be viewed as a "program-building" process in schools; and 5) teacher development depends on "organizational factors in the school site and in the district" (McLaughlin & Marsh, 1978, pp. 89, 91).

No one controls enough of the warp and woof of the educational system to design and implement widespread changes in learning or teaching. Educators lurch from one crisis to the next, from one panacea to the next, muddling their goals, hedging their bets, and avoiding political controversy. "The problem of power thus is critical to the effective behavior of people in organizations," Rosabeth Moss Kanter (1977, p. 205) concluded. "Power issues occupy center stage not because individuals are greedy for more, but because some people are incapacitated without it." Persistent powerlessness among teachers as well as working classes and the poor, minorities and women undercuts the capacity to work toward fairer schools and society. Teachers and students need a "hope factor" to invest in learning directed toward positive goals.

## Teaching for Liberation

In a powerful metaphor, Paulo Freire (1968, pp. 57, 58, 59) depicted traditional methods of schooling as resembling a central bank filled with information that teachers redeposit into their students' minds. Facts are "detached from reality, disconnected from the totality that engendered them and could give them significance." Accordingly, "knowledge is a gift bestowed by those who consider themselves knowledgeable upon those whom they consider to know nothing." Classroom practices confirm teachers' dominance: They choose and "students comply"; "the teacher acts and the students have the illusion of acting"; educators select the curriculum "and the students (who were not consulted) adapt to it"; teachers believe expert knowledge bolsters their control over scheduling and discipline "in opposition to the freedom of the students."

Tests are occasions for verifying to official auditors that appropriate facts are still "on deposit." Perhaps no one expects that the causes of the Civil War, factoring a quadratic equation, or diagramming a sentence will relate to real life. Instead, each year of schooling prepares one for the next level. Eventually, one's highest degree signals her or his socialization to prospective employers. Along the way, most students acquire some general knowledge that they put to use in their own lives—to manage money, to communicate with friends, to keep records of baseball teams or popular music. Few students find opportunities to build dialog around identity and representation, to raise questions about embedded values and beliefs, or to imagine themselves as shapers of their own future.

Proposing that teachers reject manipulation and dominance, Freire (1968, pp. 176, 177, 182) advocated "cultural action . . . to clarify to the oppressed the objective situation which binds them to the oppressors, visible or not." A teacher necessarily becomes a "witness" with "increasingly critical knowledge of the current historical context, the view of the world held by the people, the principal contradiction of society, and the principal aspect of that contradiction." To transform society, witnesses must display "*consistency* between words and actions," "*boldness*" or risk taking, "*radicalization*" stimulating "increasing action," "*courage to love*" without "accommodation to an unjust world," and "*faith* in the people." Teachers engage in "a mode of action for confronting culture itself, as the preserver of the very structures by which it was formed."

Critical teaching from a democratic perspective appears "political" and controversial, although it draws on key documents that define American beliefs in liberty and equality. Oddly, a common curriculum justifying the status quo of business-dominated public agendas is viewed as neither controversial nor political. Mainstream histories address issues of oppression in conjunction with their presumed redress: Yellow-dog contracts and company union practices are cited in conjunction with laws that established labor's right to organize and bargain collectively in the 1930s; Jim Crow segregation enters U.S. history texts when civil rights advanced from *Brown v. Topeka* to the Public Accommodations Act of 1964; and patriarchy is discussed primarily to explain women's liberation struggles during the 1970s. Nevertheless, class, race and gender inequities continue to shape the lives of most Americans

Liberation requires critical approaches that reenvision new personal and social possibilities. In a recent study, students, parents and educators in four schools representative of ethnically diverse communities told researchers that they would welcome open dialog about personal and social issues (Institute for Education in Transformation, 1992, p. 14). They consistently cited seven key elements for discussion—relationships; race, culture and class; values; teaching and learning; safety; physical environment; despair, hope and the process of change. Everyone wanted more communication. "Parents, teachers, students, staff and administrators of all ethnicities and classes, value and desire education, honesty, integrity, beauty, care, justice, truth, courage and meaningful hard work," although these concerns seldom were discussed in school.

Teachers who present these issues will have to be open to controversies, personal values, and student concerns influencing classroom agendas. For instance, when one teacher asked her class about possible topics for community service, they proposed stopping violence. She regarded the topic as divisive and possible activities as unsafe. Contemporary issues of White racism that are raised by news accounts seldom fit into the required curriculum. Although class differences are implicated in school finance inequities, teachers are reluctant to challenge the existing distributions of power and authority. Teachers who are frustrated and feeling powerless scarcely can bear witness to a common hope for caring, justice and truth.

If education facilitates a sense of control over one's life, then the curriculum should focus on issues that learners perceive as major stumbling blocks in meeting their goals. Typically, schools have focused on an adult's view of what children should know. When that is not learned, individuals are labeled as deficient. Almost all students perceive learning to read, write and compute as basic skills needed by everyone. As their ideas expand to include the worldviews of others, they sense constraints based on class, race and gender as well as religion, national origin, disabling conditions, sexual orientation, appearance, dialect, or accent. If such social barriers affect a student's prospects for productive citizenship, then they legitimately belong within the formal curriculum.

## CHANGING CONDITIONS

Three major factors have changed the meaning of school practices that seemed entrenched as late as the 1960s. First, young Americans face diminished prospects for a secure career in light of stagnant productivity and increasing inequality of income and wealth. Except for the few who can afford elite colleges and graduate programs, the potential rewards from education seem uncertain. Second, for the first time in U.S. history, public school enrollments declined in the 1970s, marking a smaller constituency of supporters. Third, students of color now comprise about 30% of public school enrollments based on recent immigration and differences in birth rates. An achievement ideology, faith in growth, and the Eurocentric content of academic disciplines subvert meanings of established practices even while industrial-era school structures and ideologies persist.

## Declining Expectations

Although it is difficult to measure the impacts of diminishing economic prospects for most Americans (wages have grown only for those in the top one-fifth), youth realistically appraise their employment prospects as bleak—despite occasional expressions of their dreams for a high-paying job. Upward mobility seems a distant hope in America's inner cities, on Indian reservations, throughout rural areas, and in working-class neighborhoods. Ebbing opportunities for meaningful careers for a majority of young adults, reinforced by diminished real standards of living for most Americans since 1973, contradict those teachers who seek to motivate students through an implicit promise that academic achievement will lead to success in later life.

Without a promising future, students and teachers reasonably will not invest time and expense in order to acquire knowledge and academic credentials. During the 1980s, only those fortunate enough to have investment funds, an executive position, or innovative ideas enjoyed higher earnings. Persistent deficits (driven by a cut in progressive tax rates and soaring military budgets) led to reduced federal spending for community development, elementary and secondary education, and preventive health care programs. High interest rates, intended to attract funds to cover unprecedented federal borrowing, discouraged investment in capital equipment or education. In the meantime, commitments to Social Security programs, especially medical costs, sharply pushed up federal and state spending for the elderly, often pitting their interests against the young.

From the mid-1970s through the mid-1980s, public school teachers experienced a decline in well-being and prestige. Nationally, salaries lost ground to inflation until the mid-1980s. Only a few exceptional suburban communities or urban districts with a strong union raised teachers' salaries to a level where they might afford a college education for their children. Subsequently, teacher pay scales have risen slightly, and more new teachers are being hired. Beginning salaries in 1990 averaged about $21,500. A slight gain in real income reflects additional years of experience by an aging staff, as reflected in Table 3.1.

During the 1980s, most states enjoyed rising revenues from sales taxes and higher property values, so they could compensate for federal cutbacks. Spending for schools increased mainly for special education and bilingual programs mandated by law or in states that had historically lagged behind in per-pupil costs. The outcome was predictable. Once most voters experienced a net decline in their

**TABLE 3.1**
**Profile of Teachers in U.S. Public Schools**

|                          | 1976                       | 1991      |
|--------------------------|----------------------------|-----------|
| Number                   | 2,189,141                  | 2,323,204 |
| Percent female           | 67.1                       | 72.1      |
| Median age               | 32                         | 42        |
| Median years of teaching | 8                          | 15        |
| Average annual salary    | $12,600                    | $32,880   |
|                          | ($32,382 in 1992 dollars)  |           |

*Source*: *Digest of Education Statistics*. 1991. U.S. Department of Education. Washington, DC: Government Printing Office, pp. 75, 80.

well-being, taxpayer revolts followed, often bankrolled by business groups. For example, the High-Technology Council in Massachusetts supported Proposition 2-1/2, which limited local property taxes and forced school districts to compete with libraries, recreation, police and fire protection, water and sewage, and public works. When states faced economic recession in the early 1990s, many cut local aid to schools as well as social welfare programs.

Teachers lobbied for support and campaigned for or against political candidates, but those districts most in need typically had the least taxable property per student. Some districts faced added costs for children with special needs because of poverty, poor health care, limited English proficiency, or family dysfunctions. Superintendents responded to political pressures for greater economies by reducing athletics, extra-curricular clubs, and health and family services (which had kept some students in school despite their boredom with academics). They hired long-term substitutes and postponed purchases of textbooks, computers and software. Given smaller families, as few as one in five voters had children in public schools. Meanwhile, wealthy families often opted for private education. Under such conditions, teachers found it hard to sustain positive attitudes toward the future or to motivate their students.

## Enrollment Prospects

A baby boom from 1946 to 1964, followed by a sharp drop in birth rates through 1973, first intensified the historical expansion of student enrollments and then brought significant declines to most districts. During World War II, birth rates reached 3 million per year, about the level of the 1920s, following low fertility during the Great Depression. For seven years starting in 1956, more than 4.2 million babies were born each year. In 1965, when birth rates fell below 4 million, 4 in 10 Americans were under the age of 20. School enrollments crested in 1971, about 11 years after the peak in births (when those children were in the sixth grade). Moreover, school enrollments increased because of higher graduation rates.

When school-age populations declined in the 1970s and 1980s, no reservoir of underserved youths could be attracted to stay longer, especially in light of declining prospects for employment. In 1965, more seniors graduated than five-year olds started kindergarten. Thereafter, births fell to 3.1 million in 1973. Those children reached school 5 years later and affected enrollments for another 12 years. By 1980, enrollments had started to grow in kindergarten. The bottom of the trough for total enrollment occurred around 1986, although high school enrollments continued to decline through 1991. These declines were greater in New England and the Midwest, in central cities, and among middle-class families of European descent. Table 3.2 depicts historical shifts in school-age population.

Changes in enrollments have exaggerated impacts on demands for new teachers. With a normal turnover from retirements, relocation or career shifts of 5% annually, a 3% growth in enrollment means hiring 8% of a staff each year. On the downward side, a decline of 3 to 4% annually cuts vacancies to 1 to 2%. Nationwide, the proportion of first-year teachers fell from 9.1% in 1971 to 2.4% in 1981, rising slightly to 3% currently. During the 1980s, urban districts in New England hired almost no regular classroom teachers. Only those newly certified teachers who were strongly motivated found employment in their chosen field. More than three out of four were women. Many sought

**TABLE 3.2**
**Population and School Enrollments**

| Year | Total Population (thousands) | Population Ages 5–17 (thousands) | Percent of Population Ages 5–17 | Enrollment K–12 (thousands) |
|---|---|---|---|---|
| 1879–80 | 50,156 | 15,066 | 30.0 | 9,867 |
| 1889–90 | 62,948 | 18,543 | 29.5 | 12,723 |
| 1899–00 | 75,995 | 21,573 | 28.4 | 15,503 |
| 1909–10 | 90,492 | 24,009 | 26.5 | 17,814 |
| 1919–20 | 104,512 | 27,556 | 26.4 | 21,578 |
| 1929–30 | 121,770 | 31,417 | 25.8 | 25,678 |
| 1939–40 | 130,880 | 30,150 | 23.0 | 25,434 |
| 1949–50 | 148,665 | 30,168 | 20.3 | 25,112 |
| 1959–60 | 179,323 | 43,881 | 24.5 | 36,087 |
| 1969–70 | 201,385 | 52,386 | 25.8 | 45,619 |
| 1979–80 | 224,567 | 48,041 | 21.4 | 41,645 |
| 1985–86 | 238,741 | 44,975 | 18.8 | 39,509 |
| 1989–90 | 248,239 | 45,330 | 18.3 | 40,526 |

*Source: Digest of Education Statistics.* 1991. U.S. Department of Education. Washington, DC: Government Printing Office, p. 47.

certification in special education, bilingual, or English as a second language areas where there were openings. With a surplus of candidates, states raised their certification standards—especially in the area of information technologies. Enrollments in teacher education programs plummeted.

In the 1990s, there is renewed interest in teaching careers. The large influx of new teachers in the 1950s meant an aging instructional staff in the 1980s. Consequently, educators project a need for replacing about half of all teachers in the decade after 1994. Furthermore, between 1990 and 2005, the 1.5 million elementary teachers will grow by about 21%, with most of that growth occurring after 1995. The 1.3 million secondary teacher population also is expected to increase, with most new job openings before 1999, as the children of baby boomers reach adolescence. Such swings in job openings in schools force difficult readjustments among teacher preparation programs.

When 1 in 12 teachers were newly hired each year and many beginning teachers enrolled in master's level professional development programs, there was a straightforward transfer of innovative methods and ideas from higher education to public schools. In recent years, universities have promoted whole language approaches to writing and reading, multicultural social studies, and a range of constructivist approaches in mathematics and science, but channeling these ideas into practice has seemed painfully slow. Staff development among experienced teachers seldom proved a satisfactory substitute, particularly around computers and other instructional technologies. As teaching careers now open up, both teacher preparation programs and schools will be challenged to take advantage of possibilities for rethinking education.

## Students of Color

During the 1990s, 5 million children of immigrants—over 40% from Southeast Asia and 40% from Latin America—will attend schools. Their arrival follows from changes in U.S. immigration policies. In 1924, Congress had restricted annual immigration to 150,000 (outside this hemisphere) based on the national origins of residents as of 1920 (later, as of 1980). In 1965, a new law opened the doors to immigrants from the relatively poor and populous southern hemisphere. Millions of Filipino, Vietnamese and Central American immigrants are an unanticipated outcome of American imperialism. Newcomers from many non-European nations are enriching the racial and linguistic composition of the United States, but they face significant learning barriers in classrooms where English is the language of instruction.

Of the 42 million public school students in 1991–92, 6.9 million were Black (16.4%), 5 million were Hispanic (11.8%), 1.4 million were Asian (3.4%), and 420,000 were Native American (1%). One in 4 New Yorkers is Black, 1 in 5 Hispanic, and 1 in 20 Asian. "By 1986, approximately

2.3 million of that city's 7 million residents have been born outside the country. In 1986 alone, 90,000 new immigrants came to New York from 153 countries" (Fuchs, 1990, p. 304). Diversity increasingly means Dominicans, Mexicans, Chinese, Jamaicans, Indians, Koreans, Haitians, and others typically grouped as Black, Hispanic and Asian. In 26 California cities, no racial or ethnic group makes up half or more of the population.

Nearly 40 years after the Supreme Court declared segregated schools unconstitutional, the overwhelming majority of students of color go to schools in which minorities predominate (Orfield, 1993). More than half of Black students in urbanized states attend schools that are 90 to 100% segregated: Illinois (59.3%), Michigan (58.5%), New York (57.5%), and New Jersey (54.6%). In the largest cities, 15 out of 16 African American and Latino students attend schools that are pre-dominantly minority. By contrast, formerly segregated Southern states such as Alabama and Mississippi enroll only 36% of Black students in schools that are more than 90% racially isolated. In New Mexico, California and Texas, more than one in four students are Hispanic. For Latinos, 55% were in segregated schools (more than half students of color) in 1968. By 1991, that proportion had risen to 73%.

Although beginning teachers can expect to work in a school with significant minority populations, state legislatures, school committees, and teachers remain overwhelmingly European American. Although classrooms should enroll three limited-English-proficient students on average, in fact, they are overwhelmingly concentrated in urban districts and, thus, isolated from suburban students. Changing demo-graphics in many central cities has left an aging White staff in charge of education for a majority of Black, Latino and Asian students. By 2010, 11 states plus the District of Columbia will enroll half of the nation's 64.4 million youths, and over 40% of them will be students of color. In Texas, Louisiana, California, Florida, and New York as well as Hawaii and the District of Columbia, White students will be in the minority.

Within a generation, terms like "minority" and "students of color" will lose their power to include and exclude. According to Census Bureau projections, the population in 2050 will be around 383 million, a 50% growth in 60 years. This will include "82 million people who arrived in this country after 1991 or who were born in the United States of parents who did" (Pear, 1992, p. D18). Around 2013, Latinos will out-number African Americans, with both groups over 42 million. Asians will "double by 2009, triple by 2024 and quadruple by 2038," reaching 41 million by 2050. Americans of European descent will stabilize at about 208 million around 2029. An increasing part of international trade will be with Asia, Latin America, and Africa.

Declining expectations, shifting enrollments, and increasing diversity undercut embedded understandings about U.S. schools as a source of progress that builds on and extends Western democracy, productivity and culture. One outcome has been signs of resistance among majority groups—demands for English only, attacks on multiculturalism, reading texts based on old morality tales, and choice plans that would use public funds to support private and religious schools. Despite the successes of many individuals, some Americans are promoting nativist fears and raising discriminatory barriers. Perhaps more crucially, questions about education have become part of a broader critique of modernism from critical theorists, feminists and ecologists. What knowledge will be important in the 21st century?

## DEVELOPING EDUCATORS

Students enrolled in one of our introductory teacher certification courses described themselves as wanting to make a difference in the lives of the young. Their experiences with former teachers surfaced as key motivators. About half the class recalled that parents and other adults had praised their success as "good" students. They reported always wanting to teach. A science major described education as *"always a silent force in our family. In high school I would look at the teachers, particularly three whom I greatly respected, and would try to picture myself up there teaching."* Others described negative experiences as students. Reflecting on *"numerous teachers who just don't seem to care,"* a language major sought *"to break away from the rules and have a more humane relationship with my students."*

Whether reacting to positive or negative role models, prospective teachers hope to improve schools and society. A graduate student who had taught overseas *"wanted to work with social issues"* and therefore pursued certification in social studies. *"I feel the kids are able to think in a more complex way and I want to make them more socially aware."* A woman recalled that *"over the years, I have not really enjoyed any of my past computer programming jobs. I am tired of doing a job only for money and prestige. . . . Physics turns me on, and I would like to turn kids onto it."* A science major saw secondary teaching *"as a chance to help those kids to keep an honest outlook on life and shape it so they can use it to their advantage when they are older. . . . Children are our most precious asset and we all should be doing something to improve the quality of young people's lives."*

Many young adults seek personal satisfaction from actualizing their desire to help others in the classroom, not too different from those who chose teaching as a career in earlier generations. In the 1970s, Lortie (1975, p. 33) found that prospective teachers wanted to work with children, to contribute to social betterment, to pursue personal intellectual interests, and to have job security with long vacations. Although women now have alternative career opportunities and educators have less job security and status, not much has changed in the motivations of prospective teachers. As Lortie documented, however, school cultures generated "a reiterated emphasis on conserving the past rather than changing educational institutions"; "conventionality rather than a special, deviant point of view"; and "a bias toward continuity."

## Rethinking Teacher Preparation

Nearly 500,000 preservice teachers are enrolled in over 1,200 institutions of higher education nationwide. According to conventional critiques, less talented undergraduates opt for careers in education, teacher education programs in colleges and universities lack academic substance and rigor, and new teachers enter the classroom with insufficient knowledge about their subject fields and the methodologies of teaching. The Holmes Group (1986) recommended a sequential model, with arts and sciences courses preceding professional preparation. The Carnegie Forum on Education and the Economy (1986) called for a national board of teaching standards to issue certificates to those candidates who demonstrate expertise. These reports assumed better instruction follows from tougher standards and a longer preparation.

---

**Recall the qualities shared by teachers who inspired and demanded learning from you. How might teacher preparation programs assure that effectiveness among their certification candidates?**

---

Seeking a sense of efficacy, some reformers reduce teacher development to a well-structured problem: What are the knowledge, skills, and aptitudes needed by teachers? Asked that question by a national commission, Lee S. Shulman (1987, pp. 4, 7, 8) defined a teacher's knowledge base as "a codified or codifiable aggregation of knowledge, skill, understanding, and technology, of ethics and disposition, of collective responsibility—as well as a means for representing and communicating it." Educators must know about learners, instructional approaches, and a subject area. Able teachers "can transform understanding, performance skills, or desired attitudes or values into pedagogical representations and actions." Prospective teachers, "at a minimum," should learn:

— content knowledge;
— general pedagogical knowledge, with special reference to those broad principles and strategies of classroom management and organization that appear to transcend subject matter;

— curriculum knowledge, with particular grasp of the materials and programs that serve as "tools of the trade" for teachers;

— pedagogical content knowledge, that special amalgam of content and pedagogy that is uniquely the province of teachers, their own special form of professional understanding;

— knowledge of learners and their characteristics;

— knowledge of educational contexts, ranging from the workings of the group or classroom, the governance and financing of school districts, to the character of communities and cultures; and

— knowledge of educational ends, purposes, and values, and their philosophical and historical grounds.

Shulman's comprehensive list raises no questions about established cultural norms and common understandings, especially those of scholarly research. When scrutinized critically, however, an exhaustive list of competencies raises contradictions. Who defines how much or whose history of schooling will be taught? Should teachers follow Cremin or Bowles and Gintis? Suppose everyone mastered each instructional strategy: Would schools become pleasant places or student outcomes dramatically improve? As conditions change, static depictions lose validity. Besides, teachers view the world through "pet frameworks" and assess organizational development "autobiographically" (Lightfoot, 1983, p. 9). Considerable evidence suggests that students learn most when teachers care about them and talk with them about their future.

From a constructivist perspective, specific competencies for teachers cannot be readily identified, codified and then taught in universities. Teaching is not a set of skills that novices can copy from expert practitioners. To a large extent, "in formulating recommendations about what beginning teachers need to know, we have failed to consider what novices think they already know" (Barnes, 1989, pp. 13:2, 15, 17:1). Subject knowledge and exemplary repertoires do not assure effective instructors who process information to make rapid decisions in a context of ever-changing classroom interactions. Teachers need "the ability to see what is happening, to interpret events, and to generate and consider alternatives." While working with children, they should "question, criticize, and reformulate assumptions about the nature of their work."

Engaged in making their knowledge accessible to students, teachers continuously interact—seldom pausing to consider what to do or why. Effective teachers, as Johnson (1990, pp. 4, 5, 4, 5–6) found, define their role as "necessarily interactive and people centered"; educational goals are "multiple and sometimes conflicting"; learners at all levels "are varied and unpredictable." Teachers must reach students "as they find them and move them what distance they can along the course of their education and development." Moreover, "the technology of teaching is neither well defined nor widely accepted. . . . There are no proven, standardized procedures that all teachers agree constitute good practice." Consequently, teaching is "a predominantly unspecialized yet interdependent enterprise which requires autonomy for teachers and defies close oversight and assessment by superiors."

Teacher development starts long before college and continues throughout a lifetime. Ethnographic studies depict curriculum and instruction "as classroom events" only slightly related to lesson plans or intentions (Carter, 1990, pp. 306, 307). Methods courses provide after-the-fact rationales rather than usable blueprints for instruction. Teachers construct mental frameworks based on their personal educational experiences, their disciplinary studies, and their philosophical beliefs that influence "their planning and instruction, the goals they set for themselves and their students, the organization they developed for different units of study, and the means of communicating their own ideas and values about the content to students." Equally competent teachers typically follow quite distinct strategies to present similar information to a class. Their knowledge is "experiential, procedural, situational, and particularistic."

Complex organizational demands largely account for a recurring pattern in teachers' work lives. Beginning teachers start out as problem solvers, eager to expand their instructional repertoire. As they gain a measure of success, student interests and local policies shift, and they must begin anew. Gradually, teachers distance themselves from their work, resist innovations, and sustain a status quo marked by adult control. Older teachers have seen reforms come and go—"new math," flexible scheduling, educational television, open education, management-by-objectives, competency-based courses, computer literacy, and teacher empowerment. In the meantime, students bring different aspirations based on their parents' status and an evolving community ethos.

It makes a difference how educators understand their personal and social roles. Teachers, who view students as passive recipients of knowledge and as sources of disorder, resist structural innovations and narrow their professional concerns. Yet in the 21st century, cooperation in flexible organizations may displace competitive hierarchies. Even effective instructional techniques that actively involve students seldom raise critical and controversial issues about preparing productive citizens whose well-being depends as much on household arrangements and learning outside of school as on job-related skills. If education becomes liberating for oppressed groups, democratic practices will reinvigorate debates about public policies that express values of equity, efficiency and choice. The next three chapters reconsider productive efforts, organizational structures, and political processes in light of their impact on stability or change.

## RELATED READING

Jacqueline Grennon Brooks and Martin G. Brooks's *In Search of Understanding: The Case for Constructivist Classrooms* (Alexandria, VA: Association for Supervision and Curriculum Development, 1993) introduces Piaget for teachers. Seth Kreisberg's *Transforming Power: Domination, Empowerment, and Education* (Albany: State University of New York Press, 1992) and Kathleen Weiler's *Women Teaching for Change: Gender, Class & Power* (New York: Bergin & Garvey, 1988) address issues of power and autonomy in teacher development.

Anne Wheelock in *Crossing the Tracks: How "Untracking" Can Save America's Schools* (New York: New Press, 1992) documents resistance to heterogeneous grouping and offers practical strategies for reform. For African American education, see Kofi Lomotey, *Going to School: The African-American Experience* (Albany: State University of New York Press, 1990) and Martin Carnoy, *Faded Dreams: The Politics and Economics of Race in America* (New York: Cambridge University Press, 1994).

# 4

# Work, Well-being, and Information

Educators like to think they are preparing the young for work and citizenship. Indeed, this belief is so embedded that it is seldom stated—unless someone asks about the mission of schools. It underlies assertions that history or geometry will prove useful in one's adult life. It supports a belief that competitive testing and rank-ordered grades in schools prepare students for real life. It becomes explicit in guidance offices, where labor market forecasts and evidence of higher earnings by graduates are recited as encouragement for students to stay in school. In our interviews, it surfaced directly in statements that students needed to become familiar with computers in order to hold a high technology job. Indeed, our thesis about a social transformation also rests on presumed interconnections between today's schools and tomorrow's conditions.

For the most part, the formal curriculum in elementary and secondary schools aims to provide students with a range of facts and characteristics about things and other people that they will apply later. By placing specific objects into general categories, students assume a fixity of roles and relationships. "Reality," then, is composed of durable categories beyond one's power to change. To satisfy one's wants, preferences and sense of self, a learner has to adjust to those realities. In developmental-constructivist terms, most school-age children as well as many young adults view themselves as coping with an "objective" world (or one that is determined by the beliefs of others). They lack an outside standpoint from which to understand organizations or societies as modifiable entities with their own internal dynamics.

Without a framework for seeing oneself as a self-authoring person within productive households and workplaces that are also socially constructed, students and young workers lack both vocabulary and perspective to describe adult roles as partly their own responsibility. For most people, experiencing oneself as subject with roles and mutual reciprocity comes only from on-the-job activities or, perhaps, college-level study. Even as people transformatively achieve a modern framework, they internalize their experiences with organizations as relationship-regulating structures. At the same time, productive citizens are urged to take ownership of their work, to "be self-initiating, self-correcting, self-evaluating (rather than dependent on others to frame the problems, initiate adjustments, or determine whether things are going well)" (Kegan, 1994, p. 302).

Teachers who support positive identities that empower learners as workers and citizens cannot ignore the context of incentives set by current wages while recognizing how little is known about what skills and competencies will be used in future roles. Market wages often have slight relationship to a job's unpleasantness or its contribution to society—note the salary differences between professional athletes and elementary school teachers. More critically, a widespread assumption that individuals must adjust to "the real world" leaves students relatively powerless to do anything other than to accommodate to the roles offered by economic, political and social systems. Even affluent youth who develop concerns about lifestyle choices, ecology and fairness see few ways to break down class, race and gender barriers.

To raise questions about what "productive citizenship" entails, this chapter explores emerging meanings of living and learning from an economic perspective. Time becomes the crucial scarcity, but its "value" is determined by employment opportunities. Current household production and careers no longer fit an industrial-age myth of male providers supported by women who raise families and care for others. To gain fresh insights into work, well-being and information, we describe time allocations among households, jobs and learning. As technologies open new economic roles for women and children, longstanding patriarchal patterns become contested terrain. Next, a review of labor market projections indicates their limitations for educational or career planning. Finally, we consider how new informational modes separate speakers from listeners and elevate abstract, decentered ideas over concrete, personal and commonsense views.

## ACHIEVING WELL-BEING

For thousands of years, the crucial economic problem was production—making and maintaining things to feed, clothe and shelter a growing population. Continued economic growth became necessary to sustain standards of living. More production supported large families, and, in turn, they supplied labor for further rises in output. Regional advantages and urban economies attracted mass migrations from rural areas to cities and from Europe and Africa to the New World. Today, over 5 billion people crowd the planet, depleting nonrenewable resources and polluting the biosphere. Families weigh the costs of raising and educating children; many consciously limit births. In addition to ecological considerations, economic growth is constrained by difficulties in assuring cooperation or consensus. Negative effects spill over to others in the neighborhood, and social conflicts erode personal security and satisfaction.

In postindustrial economies, the critical problem involves determining what to make for whom in ways that sustain the environment and promote peaceful social adjustments. In much of the world, people struggle to feed growing populations and to raise living standards. With relative material abundance, individuals and groups can choose what kind of life they wish for themselves and their children. Affluent people, however, wonder why material plenty has not brought contentment and peace. During the 1970s, a post–World War II consensus on full employment and growth gave way to disputes over environmental regulations and lifestyle values. In the United States today, poverty results from unequal distributions of education, jobs and wealth, not from a lack of productive techniques.

An impending information age has two hallmark features—workers offer services to others, and their productive efforts require trustworthy communications. In low-income economies today, seven in ten laborers raise crops or reshape materials into usable objects. In affluent countries, three out of four workers provide supportive services to those engaged in farming, manufacturing, mining, or construction as well as to each other. For 40 years, most new jobs have opened in the human services—education, health care, public security, or legal assistance. More people design, plan or coordinate production as well as distribute and sell goods than grow, fabricate or assemble physical objects. For these workers, the crucial skill is to apply knowledge to interactions with people.

### Allocating Time

Rational individuals consciously or unconsciously allocate their time among various activities to maximize their well-being. Their choices reveal how they perceive their opportunities and preferences. Most adults spend their waking hours "getting and spending" to satisfy their needs for food, shelter, clothing, affiliation and self-expression. Modern adults specialize, unlike Robinson Crusoe who picked berries, built a shelter and looked for Friday's footprints. They apply acquired skills and information to tools in locations suited to particular tasks. They then share their output with others in a household, or they exchange it through markets to obtain other goods and services. Over their lifetime, individuals divide their hours among paid employment, nonmarket activities in households, learning, or leisure.

To make sensible choices for a lifetime, youth need an awareness of wage and price structures, technological and market trends, together with ways to learn about these factors. Crusoe acted on local and personal information; today individuals need public and general knowledge to decide what to do with their lives. Crusoe's independence has its appeal, but he remained an amateur at most tasks. No one has the knowledge, skills and experiences to be proficient at everything— nor access to the right tool in the best place. The quality of modern life follows from complex, lengthy modes of production with specialized labor coordinated within workplaces and households. Formal education and ongoing exchanges of information gain importance and occupy increasing amounts of time.

Most adults do something for others, receive a paycheck or a share of profits, and then purchase what they need. Money facilitates indirect exchanges, thereby concealing an underlying trade of labor for goods or services. Indeed, competitive markets use information about prices with remarkable efficiency. Economists focus attention on how adults allocate approximately 14 hours each day, or 100 hours a week, among producing for pay or in household activities, seeking information, and enjoying leisure (Jorgenson & Fraumeni, 1989, pp. 321–322). To decide whether to plant radishes or buy them, for instance, one needs to know their price and availability together with an estimate about how much time, equipment and land it would take to raise them.

Potential hourly wages (or opportunity costs) heavily influence how people value their time and, thus, how they allocate it during the rest of the day, including their hours of sleep. Few persons devote the majority of waking hours to paid labor (an average of 27 hours per week for full-time workers). Individuals devote most of their time to sleep, personal care, or intimate relationships (almost 80 hours per week). For most Americans, nonmarket activity in the household contributes somewhat more to personal well-being than wages or salaries. The second largest block of time goes to household and nonmarket production— including commuting, cooking, cleaning, caring for the young and infirm, volunteering community service, reading, gardening, exercising, entertaining, and recreating (a bit over 40 hours per week).

Over a lifetime, uses of time for education, production and leisure vary dramatically. Formal schooling is concentrated from ages 5 to 24, thereby allowing a longer period to earn a return on one's investment. In the United States, teenage students devote 30 hours per week to schooling, 8.7 to working at home or on a job, 7.0 to games and sports, 14.2 to watching television, 6.7 to personal care, and 68.1 to eating and sleeping (Juster & Stafford, 1991, p. 480). Many healthy, ambitious adults work extraordinarily long days. Others lack education, stamina, mental balance, or opportunities to advance in a career. Childcare takes little time for those over 44. Sleep and passive leisure increase to fill the hours as demands for schooling, sports, work, and childcare diminish.

In all industrial nations, time allocations among work, personal care and leisure show comparable patterns for men and women who are employed full-time (Table 4.1). In the United States, women work 54.4

**TABLE 4.1**
**Cross-national Time Use for Employed Workers**

| Activity | Men | | | | Women | | | |
|---|---|---|---|---|---|---|---|---|
| | United States 1981 | Japan 1985 | Former Soviet Union 1985 | Sweden 1984 | United States 1981 | Japan 1985 | Former Soviet Union 1985 | Sweden 1984 |
| Total work | 57.8 | 55.5 | 65.7 | 57.9 | 54.4 | 55.6 | 66.3 | 55.5 |
| Market work | 44.0 | 52.0 | 53.8 | 39.8 | 23.9 | 24.6 | 39.3 | 23.7 |
| Commuting | 3.5 | 4.5 | 5.2 | 3.8 | 2.0 | 1.2 | 3.4 | 2.1 |
| Housework | 13.8 | 3.5 | 11.9 | 18.1 | 30.5 | 31.0 | 27.0 | 31.8 |
| Personal Care | 68.2 | 72.4 | 67.8 | 70.9 | 71.6 | 72.1 | 69.8 | 73.8 |
| Sleep | 57.9 | 60.0 | 56.9 | 55.3 | 59.9 | 57.0 | 58.2 | 56.9 |
| Leisure | 41.8 | 40.3 | 34.6 | 39.0 | 41.9 | 40.3 | 32.0 | 38.5 |
| Adult education | 0.6 | 1.2 | 1.0 | 1.0 | 0.4 | 2.2 | 2.6 | 1.0 |
| Social interaction | 14.9 | 8.0 | 7.8 | 9.6 | 17.6 | 7.0 | 9.6 | 11.2 |
| Active leisure | 5.6 | 5.3 | 4.- | 7.2 | 4.2 | 3.6 | 3.0 | 8.4 |
| Passive leisure | 20.8 | 25.5 | 21.7 | 21.2 | 19.8 | 27.5 | 16.8 | 17.9 |
| Television | 12.7 | 17.3 | 14.5 | 13.4 | 11.5 | 21.4 | 11.2 | 10.8 |
| Total | 168.0 | 168.0 | 168.0 | 168.0 | 168.0 | 168.0 | 168.0 | 168.0 |

Source: Juster, F. T., & Stafford, F. P. (1991). The Allocation of Time: Empirical Findings, Behavior Models, and Problems of Measurement. Journal of Economic Literature 29(2), 475.

hours to men's 57.8, but women devote 30.5 hours to housework, compared with 13.8 for men. Personal care and leisure activities, including adult education, vary slightly across countries and between sexes. Surprisingly little time is devoted to adult learning and active recreation compared with television viewing and other passive leisure.

A family's well-being depends on combined pay and contributed labor. Potential earnings largely determine how individuals mix time with purchased goods or services in nonmarket activities. In the 19th century, men increasingly worked outside the home or farm for pay, while women performed household tasks. In the 20th century, both paid and unpaid work by adults has declined in a typical week. Women have worked more for pay and significantly reduced their household labors. From 1965 to 1975, household work for women aged 25 to 44 in urban households dropped by 9 hours to 35, while paid employment increased from 3 to 16 hours per week. Married men, aged 18 to 44, increased their household work from 13 to 15 hours. Recently, men's wages and work hours have fallen, while women's employment stayed about the same.

## Household Choices

Knowledge, skills and aptitudes contribute to what one can do on the job and at home. Most productive competencies are learned by doing— cooking, raising children, repairing trucks, or supervising personnel. Some tasks involve mainly repetitive routines—picking strawberries, folding laundry, assembling radios, or filing correspondence. In these cases, veteran workers earn little more than novices and seldom advance in pay or responsibility. By contrast, technicians, managers and professionals anticipate promotions as they gain experience. In households, information enhances the availability of goods and services over wider geographic areas. Literate persons read about sales, public services, preventive health measures, enjoyable books, and potential shifts in work requirements. People listen to the news in order to anticipate risks from storms, wars, taxes, or civil disorders as well as to contribute to social interactions.

---

**Think about your activities and how long they take during a typical day. Assign them to categories of school, paid job, commuting, housework, personal care, sleep, leisure, television.**

**What activities do you consider an investment in your future? How much time do you devote to maintaining physical and mental health?**

---

Because well-being depends on productivity on the job and at home over one's life span, time patterns offer important insights into family differences. Each person decides how to spend her or his time based in part on personal preferences and in part on how much she or he can make while gainfully employed. Consider three prototypical households with markedly different opportunity costs: a surgeon whose specialized skills are in high demand, two school teachers who raise a family on a modest income, and an unskilled, underemployed street person who occasionally relies on charity or welfare. The value of their time is a crucial factor in their lifestyle choices.

Highly educated and visibly pressed for time, the surgeon sees patients, performs operations, and keeps up with the latest techniques. Annual earnings of $160,000 place her in the top 2% of U.S. incomes. She buys goods and services that bring a high level of personal satisfaction—a housekeeper prepares evening meals, newspapers and magazines are glanced at and discarded, and a travel agent arranges vacations. She selects a lawyer, an accountant, and a dry cleaner for their reliability and convenience rather than their fees. Her schedule does not include shopping at sales or long walks on the beach. A decision about having a child looms as a major financial sacrifice in time away from her practice as well as direct costs for childcare.

By contrast, the school teachers have a combined salary of $58,000 as determined by their district's contract, placing them at about the 70th percentile for married couples. Time is relatively more plentiful than money, and they use time to enhance their overall well-being. Their work schedule is convenient for raising two children and enjoying family vacations. They mow the lawn, paint the house, and play tennis at a public park. Through informal communication with colleagues as well as browsing in a library, they discover bargains and scenic bicycle trips, substituting information for money. Their awareness of current events and participation in community affairs complement instructional responsibilities. Before the municipal budget crises in the 1980s, their jobs seemed protected by tenure rights and union contracts. Their income precludes foreign travel, private colleges for their children, or savings to cover a disabling illness, although their lifestyle appeals to many who are uneasy about materialism.

An underemployed street person apparently has time on his hands, but everyday tasks such as fixing meals, staying warm, getting to places, finding a job, or coping with bureaucratic procedures take extraordinarily long by middle-class norms. To learn about odd jobs, he hangs around on street corners. To maintain personal security, he talks with others who are jobless and homeless about how the police respond to panhandling or sleeping in the park. Few adults willingly choose a life of unemployment and poverty. Most low-skilled and part-time laborers come from families that lacked the means to provide stable home environments supportive of health and education. Periodic misfortunes, the difficulties of living without means, and a lack of social services help perpetuate a cycle of destitution and despair, marked by few productive options.

Over the past two decades, choices for young couples have become particularly difficult. Many entry-level positions and new occupations offer low pay, forcing both adults to work in order to maintain a middle-class lifestyle. Temporary and unskilled jobs are interrupted by layoffs, accidents or family crises. Regional recessions and substantial down-sizing by major corporations foster job insecurity that discourages long-term commitments to buying a house or raising a child. Costs for health care and education (especially college) have risen faster than wages or other prices. Single parents seldom earn enough to provide adequate housing or medical treatment, and they, like many two-wage-earner professional families, find little time to spare for their children's needs.

## Thresholds for Proficient Learning

A flow of information about tasks and costs allows individuals to allocate their effort efficiently and purposefully. People study new pro-ductive techniques and market opportunities, scan ads for consumer items and prices, follow local and national news, and try out leisure activities. They seek to maintain expertise, to learn about possible trade-offs, and to anticipate general risks. Few decisions can be treated in narrow cost-accounting terms because multiple goals conflict and the future is uncertain. Often, they learn from the perceived successes and failures of family members and friends or other role models. The point is that actions (or inaction) require decisions, and no one deliberately acts against their best interest—as interpreted within their framework of knowledge.

Information seeking enables people to get more out of life and to contribute more to group efforts. People may hold 50,000 to 100,000 facts in their mind, enabling them to connect with sensory inputs from their immediate surroundings. Modern people understand their world less from direct experiences with land, tools and products than through their capacity to utilize expert service providers and information technologies. Today, knowledge "is irretrievably split into two parts: one related to the actual performance of the task, another related to finding and using the reified or personal carriers of the former" (Bauman, 1992, p. 90). Words (including numbers, symbols and images) and the exper-tise of others are crucial for making and distributing things. General information links personal experiences with role models, scientific principles, and cultural values.

Learning is an investment in future productivity that occurs in homes, schools, the military, workplaces, voluntary associations, and social and civic events. There are a number of barriers to proficient

information seeking implicit in that statement. First, schooling establishes a critical threshold of competencies for modern adults. Reading
offers rapid access to knowledge, especially for complex technical or
social issues that require an abstract framework. Computation and
writing are essential for processing information and communicating it
to others. Unfortunately, many educators believe low-income or minority students lack intellectual capacity for anything beyond memorization or physical labor, and too many reinforce math and computer
anxiety among females. Particularly because wages are lower for
unskilled jobs and female-dominated occupations than for engineering
or accounting, those attitudes have social consequences.

A second threshold affects those who live in substandard housing
or in communities with inadequate public amenities. With the introduction of electrical appliances and inventories of consumable supplies,
married women who are employed full-time have reduced housework
from over 50 hours a week to about 18. Without income for decent
housing, the poor devote more hours to shopping, cleaning, cooking,
and childcare. They lack time and comfortable spaces for varied activities that encourage family harmony, the accumulation of books, or
home computers. Without access to transportation, there are few
choices for working, shopping and recreation. Although many single
adults earn enough for a satisfactory lifestyle, they have little interest
in supporting public schools, parks and housing for other people's
children.

A third threshold involves the characteristics of one's primary
occupation. Many poor people are discriminated against based on their
skin color, language, or residence in high crime areas. Barriers based on
educational credentials, race, gender, and previous work history shunt
many workers into dead-end jobs. Bosses set their schedules and
prescribe their tasks; workers experience boredom and powerlessness.
Repetitive performances, whether physical or mental, are soon understood and offer few opportunities for complementary learning. Without
decisions to be made, curiosity or innovation seems irrelevant. By
contrast, chief executive officers, nuclear engineers, and surgeons talk
with colleagues or clients to ascertain the situation at hand and to act
wisely.

Achieving these basic thresholds in a postindustrial economy rests
on the productivity made possible by earlier investment in physical and
human capital when population growth, technological improvements,
and optimism about progress encouraged public and private investments in the young. Output grew as competitive markets expanded
based on new transportation and communication technologies, lower
costs from economies of scale in production, higher personal incomes,
and fewer restrictions on trade. Since 1900, sustained investment in
education and on-the-job training as well as in plant and equipment
enabled Americans to enjoy a 600% increase in real per capita income.

Material abundance flowed from scientific, technical and managerial advances; organizational structures for coordination over space and time; and coherent social values related to work, material consumption and community. But they may no longer generate higher incomes!

If everyone had education and skills to earn a decent living and was assured of income security, personal or family well-being should be more equal than taxable income. Once every individual has achieved these thresholds, differences of preference, taste, creativity, and values should be welcomed. Some people may work for pay and purchase many things. Others may opt for less demanding work roles to obtain satisfaction through household activities. Some will communicate with friends, while others maintain privacy. Some adults will prefer work in a helping profession or in manipulating things, while others pursue creativity or aesthetic appreciation. Because individuals like to do different things and each decision affects future choice sets, people develop varied competencies and interests over their lifetime. When unconstrained by arbitrary or historical inequities, those differences need not conflict with fairness.

## FAMILIES AND CHILDREN

In our interviews, educators struggled to make sense of their students' families. Some expressed concern or frustration over "dysfunctional" behaviors. Others wanted adults to do more in preparing children for school. Single parents, separation and divorce, teenaged parenting, latchkey children, or nontraditional households concerned teachers; yet these arrangements may be solutions to other problems. As welfare payments have declined in real terms, single parents have to work, and many families rely on two wage earners to maintain a standard of living. Despite widespread publicity about a crisis in American families, there is no coherent and widely shared analysis of the forces reshaping how men and women interact and raise children.

Traditionally, families were primary centers of nonmarket economic activity characterized by divisions of labor across sex and generational lines. When crops had to be harvested, everyone worked in the fields. When illness struck, family members provided care. Although early deaths, impoverishment, slavery, and family brutality often contradicted this image of working together on largely self-sufficient farms, that myth accurately described many household economies. Raising children was a "joint product" with other activities. From a young age, children performed light chores. Everyday skills passed from one generation to the next through natural apprenticeships. Moreover, the elderly often relied on grown children for support.

The onset of industrialization changed the economic role of married women from partners in household production to unequal power relationships where women either worked as homemakers or earned less money than males in factories, schools, hospitals, and many other businesses. Those restricted opportunities subsidized household production to the advantage of married men. By the 20th century, more women sought full-time salaried employment, gave birth to fewer children, and had less tolerance for unhappy marriages. Yet patriarchy persisted—despite its contradiction of democratic and capitalist ideologies. Justifications for gender roles based on the physical force required to handle a plow or lift sacks of cement (tasks designed for male upper body strength) have given way to a truism that only women can give birth.

With urbanization, working-class children held jobs in mills or mines or they were on the street. Prisons, asylums and poorhouses signaled the inability of families to provide for everyone. Factory owners sought to enforce discipline and orderly behaviors on mobile, young workers whose cash wages allowed for dissolute behaviors. Later, school boards asked teachers to compensate for perceived failures of some parents, especially among recent immigrants. Today, many middle-class youth have no meaningful role in household production and assume no responsibility for others. At the same time, children in poverty have adult tasks thrust on them. They supervise themselves, care for younger siblings, and sometimes cope with neglectful parents.

By 1900, industrial cities still propelled America's economy, but suburbs seemed the ideal settings for families—thereby reinforcing class segmentation with geographic isolation. Men worked in an office or factory some distance from a home where their wives cooked, cleaned, and cared for children or the ill. As real per capita income rose during the 1950s and 1960s and fertility rates remained high, middle-class, White male observers believed that this arrangement satisfied nearly everyone. Poverty among African and Hispanic Americans, especially women and children, remained hidden. Indeed, if productivity doubled every 25 years, all Americans would soon enjoy a middle-class standard of living. Technology would protect the country militarily and sustain abundance.

Over time, small differences in family prospects can grow large. In part because so much household production is shared, individuals tend to marry others who share similar tastes and values. Commonalities simplify choices about meals, recreation, where to live, what to watch on television—thereby tending to match people by income and educational levels. Poorer families have less household equipment and services, lower opportunity costs related to outside employment, and greater reliance on the public for parks, schools and health care. Accordingly, their out-of-pocket expenses and foregone earnings for raising children are markedly less; their children, however, typically miss the social capital offered by interactions with educated parents as well as quality schooling and other amenities provided in suburbs.

## Gender Discrimination

Industrialization had the effect of isolating married women, as economist Claudia Goldin (1990, p. 12) observed: "From 1850 to 1950, the working time of married women within the household was separated first from their spouses and other workers, next and most ironically from their own children, and finally from other married women who had entered the work force." As long as married women contributed to household economies, overt discrimination based on sex did not clearly manifest itself in wage differentials. Traditional gender roles and engendered occupations obscured inequities of power that sustained patriarchy. Today, full-time employed women earn about 70% of what comparably educated men receive. After factoring out differences attributable to lower wage scales in female-dominated occupations and greater time off, significant discriminatory practices in labor markets remain.

From the outset of industrialization in the United States, young White women worked in factories, but throughout the 19th century, employment generally ceased with marriage. In 1900, three out of four female workers were single and 20 years old on the average: "They were docile, educated, and had few home responsibilities" (Goldin, 1990, p. 175). Some women worked for pay throughout their lifetime, often as a household domestic or boardinghouse operator. A few unmarried women taught school or held other professional roles. More commonly, they earned some money through part-time tutoring, picking crops, or selling household products. Fewer than 1 in 20 White women worked for pay after marriage, although nearly half of Black women held jobs—mainly in agriculture or in someone else's house. Recent immigrants often worked in sweatshops or at piecework in their living quarters.

After 1900, household tasks took less time or were displaced by store-bought goods, thereby reducing women's role in the home while opening opportunities for paid employment. Large American corporations harnessed chemistry and electricity to generate new products for information processing, communication and home maintenance. Dramatically lower costs for assembly line manufacturing opened jobs in accounting, distribution and sales that required detailed accuracy—education rather than physical strength. Efficient factories and retail outlets successfully competed with household production of items such as clothes, canned foods and baked goods. As the standard work week dropped from 55 hours in 1900 to 44 hours in the 1920s, more women combined homemaking with outside employment. Married women who opted for fewer children could work for wages without violating patriarchal norms.

Early in the 20th century, Progressive-era laws aimed to protect the health of women and children by prohibiting women from excessive hours or unsafe occupations—characteristics of highly paid industrial work. During the 1920s, corporate personnel departments established policies against hiring married women in advanced positions. A majority of school districts excluded them from teaching. Because most married women soon quit their jobs, companies may have gained from discrimination. As Goldin (1990, p. 116) noted, "by segregating workers by sex into two jobs ladders (and some dead-end positions), firms may have been better able to use the effort-inducing and ability-revealing mechanisms of the wage structure."

Discrimination in labor markets has puzzled economists. If a person produces more (or the same) output for a lower wage, profit-seeking firms should hire those workers until competition brings wages in line. Historical evidence of powerful anti-Black prejudices as Africans arrived in Virginia in 1619 offers a partial explanation for developments that transformed indentured servitude for Africans into chattel slavery. Once institutionalized in slavery, racial bias perpetuated itself through legal and de facto segregation. Also, capitalists may promote racial and ethnic divisions in order to hinder unionization (Reich, 1981). Overt patterns of discrimination against women are harder to explain, although patriarchy has a long history. After all, wage differentials and outright bans applied mainly to married women.

Nevertheless, discrimination against employing married women had real consequences. It discouraged younger women from seeking careers: "They might become typists and possibly machine operators, but they had less incentive to become accountants. The bars also prevented firms from recognizing the hidden labor supply of older married women" (Goldin, 1990, p. 178). Significant exceptions suggest that discrimination aimed at keeping women from advancing to power positions: "Smaller firms without personnel departments hired married women and did not fire single women when they married. Sectors such as banking, insurance, and public utilities, however, were off-limits to married women, as were a large percentage of local school districts around the country." During the Great Depression, firms justified patriarchal policies on the basis of men's role as the primary breadwinner. Despite the contribution of women in many jobs during World War II, they lost ground in the immediate postwar years.

In 1950, just over one in five married White women held paid jobs. Thereafter, participation rates rose by 10% each decade, reaching nearly three in five by 1990. Starting in the 1950s, many college-educated women continued to work after marriage and were passed over for promotion. As a result, wage discrimination became painfully obvious. Career-minded women demanded equal opportunities, rights and pay. That generation raised consciousness about subordinate roles for women, overt discrimination in laws and the marketplace, and traditional patriarchy. In 1957, a survey of female college graduates indicated that within three months, 84% had jobs (54% in teaching and 5% in nursing) and 38% had married (with 77% employed). Only 8%

indicated no plan to work, 71% anticipated stopping work with marriage (although more than half intended to return), and 14% planned to pursue a career. Seven years later, 4 out of 5 had married, and almost 2 in 3 had children. "While the 1957 comments convey complacency, those in 1964 communicate growing frustration" (Goldin, 1990, p. 207).

Ample evidence remains of discrimination against women in a patriarchal society. Through 1980, women earned just about 60% of wages for males—in part because many were inexperienced on the job. In the 1960s and 1970s, men added to their leisure time while women put in more hours at work than they gained in household efficiencies. If divorced, women generally are stuck with lower salaries and responsibility for any children. Although the feminization of poverty is not new, women are 50% more likely to experience poverty than men. Historically, women's labor force participation followed from "sectoral shifts in demand toward the service sector, increased education, reduced hours, increased real wages, technological change, and decreased fertility" (Goldin, 1990, p. 213); today, those forces are weak.

Currently, women are entering traditionally male-dominated fields. A smaller percentage of young women prepare to be teachers, nurses or secretaries and more aim to become doctors, lawyers and engineers. Women have forcefully demonstrated for abortion rights, equal pay for comparable work, provision of childcare, and punishment of abuse and rape. They have broken barriers in higher education, notably in law, medicine, engineering, and management. They seek leadership roles. Women exercise growing political clout, despite the failure to pass the Equal Rights Amendment. Social beliefs about work and family will adjust—and so will schools.

### Costs of Children

Traditionally, American society has counted on families to invest enough in children to raise living standards and sustain national power. In 1980, out-of-pocket expenses to rear a child to age 18 ranged from $75,000 to $135,000 ($112,000 to $200,000 in 1990 prices). Costs varied "depending on the parents' socioeconomic status (SES), number of children, and wife's employment status" (Epenshade, 1984, p. 2). Wealthier families spent somewhat more, as did families where both parents worked (about $1,000 more per year in 1980). Budgetary allocations were similar across SES levels: About 30% of a family's budget went to a first child, while a second required another 10 to 15%. Middle-income families allocated those expenditures as follows: 25% to transportation, 25% to food (both in the home and outside), a bit less for housing, almost 10% for recreation, 7% for clothing, and 6% for health care.

Estimated expenses of $200,000 omit costs for higher education and foregone earnings from parents' time as well as any subsequent inflation. College costs at four-year institutions range from $50,000 to

$120,000 per student. Estimating opportunity costs for parents raises subjective issues about how to value time with children. Should family trips to the zoo count as childcare or as recreation? Some tasks—feeding, cleaning and watching after a baby, caring for a sick child, establishing disciplinary rules, or driving to scouts—clearly resemble work. Foregone earnings vary dramatically with one's wage rate (although high SES families also spend more for diaper services, daycare, and separate rooms for children). Even conservative estimates add up. Parental time of 10 hours per week for 14 years and 5 hours per week for 4 more years at $8 per hour (median wages in 1990) totals over $64,000 per child.

If one parent leaves the paid workforce to care for children in the home, unpaid household time exceeds 50 hours per week. Young adults might assess foregone earnings as at least $14,000 per year (median wages plus fringe benefits less marginal taxes), or $252,000 over 18 years. When company policies and social norms barred married women from working in many occupations, opportunity costs for women were artificially lowered. Also, marginal costs for additional children dropped dramatically if one spouse was already committed to staying home. Today, women who want children make a major time commitment (women still do most of the cooking, cleaning and childcare). Maternity leaves of two or more years usually shunt one off an ideal career track with prospective higher salaries.

Family planning has major economic consequences. There are few useful roles for children in households, and higher education is costly. When females earned college degrees in education or nursing, they simultaneously prepared for work and for raising children, but those choices represented a subsidy to society's future paid for largely by women. Gender-limited career choices impede growth and help account for poverty among children raised in single-parent households. Raising a productive adult in a technologically advanced society now costs $200,000 to $500,000. Unsurprisingly, many middle-income families opt for fewer children—though some argue that, in economic terms, they are "high quality," because more is invested in them. In contrast to middle- and upper-class households, most children do not have family support for postsecondary education, and they now comprise the largest group living in poverty.

## Household Trends

What does this mean for the future? Married women who can and do work outside the household will have greater independence—even if their compensation lags behind men for many years. "Traditional" families as crystallized in the 1950s will decline—as will time devoted to household production, poverty among women, a demeaning double standard of sexual license, and male dominance, including abuse or rape. As patriarchy erodes, shared household roles will be a source of conflicts. There will be fewer children, more unmarried adult partners, and more burdens on schools to support children during periods of family instability. More women with advanced degrees will crack a glass ceiling blocking promotion to positions of power.

Although more of the adult population will work for wages, it does not assure a corresponding gain in well-being. Persistent wage discrimination raises emotional issues over traditional gender roles. Harried workers reduce their time in household chores by eating out, hiring landscape gardeners, subscribing to relevant media, and scheduling packaged vacations. Paid employment will decline somewhat, with more holidays and time off for medical care. Because the United States offers less support for children than most industrial nations, caring parents often make great sacrifices, although long-term benefits accrue to society as a whole. Mothers with low opportunity costs have fewer barriers to having additional children than those households more able to afford the $200,000 required to prepare youth for technological work. Too often, children will be the big losers in terms of quality of life.

Affluent households face different issues in raising children. The values of getting ahead and earning a decent living that motivate parents are not easily transmitted to their children, who are less concerned about material things and more interested in ecological balance and personal values. In earlier decades, Civil Rights and protests against the war in Vietnam raised these generational conflicts. Students in elite colleges questioned authority and explored alternative lifestyles. Today's parents are at a loss when children try drugs, listen to heavy metal or rap music, join New Age cults or fundamentalist sects, manifest eating disorders or steroid use, become active sexually with risks of AIDS, appear apathetic or attempt suicide.

For 200 years, families have adjusted to the destructive effects of industrial capitalism. During much of that time, they have been viewed as "havens—preserves of cooperativeness, sharing, and love arrayed against an impersonal public realm in which competition, self-interest, and rational calculation prevail" (Dizard & Gadlin, 1990, pp. 223–224). That goal became a primary responsibility of women, requiring "selflessness, in a society otherwise committed to the celebration of self-interest." Moreover, "the business cycle, the advance of technology, and the steady expansion of the commodity form have cumulatively robbed the family of its sources of stability: parental authoritativeness, self-sufficiency of the family unit, and reciprocal bonds of dependency."

Students need to see consistency between their aspirations and prevailing social values. Why learn when one's prospects include boring classes, alienating work, subordination to others, violence, and alcohol and drug abuse? Because more children live in poverty and experience racial or language bias than the rest of the population, they see starkly unequal prospects. Middle-class professional or managerial roles seem beyond their reach. But if students fail to become productive, civic-minded adults, national income and well-being will decline. Perhaps the only solution is to incorporate values of caring, concern and connection into our public institutions so that families can sustain personal emotional bonds. Thus, public policies should encourage investing in children to assure at least minimal thresholds of education, housing, and jobs. In turn, an equitable and growing economy will motivate students to invest in their future.

## NEW MEANINGS OF WORK

In an emerging information age, human interactions occur within artificial environments. Instead of seeing, touching, hearing, smelling, and tasting objects that serve personal purposes, words or images on a videoscreen convey "reality." Whereas hunting and gathering societies relied on custom and priestly auguries for advice, modern farmers tune their radios to agricultural extension agents. In the 16th century, Erasmus admonished sausage makers not to wipe their noses on hands or clothing; today, computer chips are "cooked" in dust-free rooms. In the 17th century, farmers and artisans owned a few multipurpose tools; contemporary workers oversee power-driven, specialized machinery costing millions. In 1850, human power accounted for 15% of the energy used in farm and factory production and animals contributed 79%—a century later, they were less than 3% and 1%, respectively.

Prior to the 19th century, when most work was organized by communicating with others who shared a location, activities and a visible goal, there was less need for explicit words of instruction. As individuals, workers anticipated and coordinated purposeful activities intracranially. They interpreted relevant inputs and adjusted their actions to fit a perceived environment. Typically, information was processed in response to immediate sensory inputs. A homemaker or a craftperson responded to sight, sound, smell, taste, and tactile impressions within a context of previous experiences. Adding a pinch of salt or repainting a cabinet did not require specifying a quantity or color code. Supplies were acquired, tasks organized, adjustments made, and accomplishments enjoyed, all without necessarily speaking or recording those thoughts.

In 1820, 7 in 10 workers engaged in farming, with household production of food, fuel and fiber more important than production for sale. By 1900, fewer than 4 in 10 farmed, and commercial agriculture dominated. Now, only 3 in 100 work the land using machines, fertilizers and pesticides to raise genetically selected plants and animals. The proportion of industrial jobs peaked at 39% in 1920, with 10.7 million laborers out of 27.4 million employed. Today, about 18% of the workforce (or fewer than 20 million workers) are employed in manufacturing. Retail and wholesale sales employ more than any other occupations.

Technicians, professionals and managers outnumber those directly engaged in production.

Occupations provide clues about educational background, income, lifestyle, and many social values. Industrial jobs segment people as dramatically as region and locality did in the 18th century when most Americans lived on largely self-sufficient farms. At that time, plowing, spinning, cooking and heating with wood fires established common references in everyday lives of Americans. Soil conditions, access to transportation, and closeness to the frontier shaped local variations on those national experiences. An important exception was slavery for African Americans and slaveholding among some Whites. Today, movies and television establish common references, and most adults find social identity through—but not in—a primary economic role.

## Alienation and Satisfaction at Work

Higher living standards do not always bring personal satisfaction and social harmony. Modern work is less physically tiring, though many jobs require limited repetitive motions or entail high levels of stress. It is cleaner, though unseen chemicals and radiation can be as threatening to health as filth. Local weather conditions, personalities, external events, and religious beliefs affect work less; secular knowledge about technology, organizational strategies and structures, mass tastes or preferences, and global interactions also seem beyond one's control. Purposeful actions draw their physical and psychological context from a socially constructed environment of machines and specialized roles in organizations. Stress is mental rather than physical.

Just as American productivity entered two decades of relative stagnation, a national report documented widespread worker dissatisfaction:

Because work is central to the lives of so many Americans, either the absence of work or employment in meaningless work is creating an increasingly intolerable situation. The human costs of this state of affairs are manifested in worker alienation, alcoholism, drug addiction, and other symptoms of poor mental health. Moreover, much of our tax money is expended in an effort to compensate for problems with at least a part of their genesis in the world of work. A great part of the staggering national bill in the areas of crime and delinquency, mental and physical health, manpower and welfare are generated in our national policies and attitudes toward work. (U.S. Department of Health, Education, and Welfare, 1973, p. 186)

An updated study would have to add only sections on violence, job insecurity because of corporate takeovers or spin-offs, and a tendency to blame schools or foreigners for declining real wages.

Since Karl Marx, social scientists have attributed alienation to factory labor that manifests itself in apathy, anger or displacement of interests to consumption or leisure. Sociologist Kai Erikson (1990, p. 23) identified two key sources of alienation: "first, those structures in the modern workplace that subdivide labor into narrower and narrower specialties, and second, those structures in the modern workplace that limit the amount of control workers exercise over the conditions in which they work." Yet, today, more jobs expect intelligent judgments as well as reliable oversight of machinery. Specialization segments workers but also affords time and reasons for communications. Many innovations deskill existing producers and then reskill them or others.

The loss of autonomy in industrial jobs had negative effects on workers' sense of self. Studies designed to show the effect of work on personality identified conditions related to "a worker's place in the organizational structure, opportunities for occupational self-direction, the principal pressures to which the worker is subject, the principal extrinsic risks and rewards built into the job" (Kohn, 1990, p. 41). Workers do not like being controlled by bosses and bureaucratic systems. They resent dull routines, close oversight, time pressures, dirty conditions, and long hours. In particular, they object to "being held responsible for things outside one's control, the risk of losing one's job or business, job protections, and job income."

> How many of your typical activities combine physical skills with active decisionmaking? How many serve multiple and complementary goals, for example, attending a concert, doing homework with a friend, or counseling at a summer camp?

Following a period of rapid economic growth in the 1960s, work did not become more onerous or exploitive. Instead, widespread affluence suggested that life could mean more than a high-paying but boring job to support a consumption-oriented household: "the discontent of women, minorities, blue-collar workers, youth, and older adults would be considerably less were these Americans to have an active voice in the decisions in the workplace that most directly affect their lives" (U.S. Department of Health, Education, and Welfare, 1973, p. 186). Many studies confirm that "exercising self-direction in work—doing work that is substantively complex, not being closely supervised, not working at routinized tasks—is conducive to favorable evaluations of self, an open and flexible orientation to others, and effective intellectual functioning" (Kohn, 1990, p. 42).

### Workers' Knowledge

Throughout most of history, work was not a separate sphere of activity with specialized roles. It was part of an ongoing struggle to survive in a physically brutal, sometimes desperate, search for food, warmth and personal safety. Thought and action occurred together, or in close time and spatial proximity, and in harmony with tribal or village customs. With industrialization, factories structured roles so that most workers adapted to the pace and demands of power-driven machinery. Workers on assembly lines often coped with speed and monotony by letting their minds drift while staying alert for signs of trouble. They combined physical and mental awareness to respond to anomalous events.

For a familiar illustration, consider a driver's thought processes while moving in city traffic. She might monitor speed by the engine's sound as well as the speedometer, learn about congested streets by radio as well as visually, and follow traffic signs that contradict the compass—all the while focusing on the truck ahead.

Fringe awareness and selective attention are integrated when the operator can integrate the three modes of knowing: dense perception of physical processes, heuristic knowledge of production relationships, and theoretical understanding of the production process. Heuristic knowledge helps the operator make normal production decisions while paying conscious and selective attention to long-term goals, such as quality and timeliness. Density of perception supplies fringe awareness with anomalous data—data that might otherwise go unnoticed because it is unexpected. Finally, theoretical knowledge helps the operator understand the anomalous data so that he can overcome previously established rules of action and create new ones appropriate to the novel situation. (Hirschhorn, 1984, p. 93)

Schools face perplexing challenges in preparing knowledge workers who handle symbols only vaguely connected to the natural world or their implementation in organizations. In order to think about how to perform everyday tasks in computer-based settings, knowledge workers must translate back and forth from images on the screen to concrete meanings in technical or organizational contexts. Neither microelectronics nor global operations are subject to visual oversight. Sometimes it is hard to put a human face to the statistical depictions of trends or organizational charts that sum up policymakers' decisions. At the same time, anecdotal evidence may mislead by emphasizing exceptional cases.

Information technologies force workers to rearrange how they approach many everyday tasks. Shoshana Zuboff (1988, pp. 71, 72) described the new skills and attitudes in a computerized paper mill: "Immediate physical responses must be replaced by an abstract thought process in which options are considered, and choices are made and then translated into the terms of the information system." Rather than rushing to close a valve when a vat overflows, operators scan a video-screen and punch commands into a keyboard. "As one operator put it, 'Your past physical mobility must be translated into a mental thought process.'" Managers must "convince the operator to leave behind a world in which things were immediately known, comprehensively sensed, and able to be acted upon directly, in order to embrace a world that is dominated by objective data, is removed from the action context, and requires a qualitatively different kind of response."

Knowledge workers deal with information that extends the range of possibilities beyond what is immediately sensed in one's work and living situation. In time, those new contexts become familiar and within one's competence. Zuboff (1988, pp. 72, 75-76, 95) distinguished between "action-centered" work done in close physical association with the production process and information work that required "intellective skills" marked by "a shift away from physical cues, toward sense-making based more exclusively upon abstract cues; explicit inferential reasoning used both inductively and deductively; and procedural, systemic thinking." Human cognition is adjusting to these new participants, called "computers."

---

**What information technologies do you use, for example, pocket calculator, VCR, ATM, PC, Internet, or mobile phone? Has a computer made your daily tasks easier? Do representations on video monitors affect the way you think about and interact with the world? Describe continuities or differences.**

---

How do professional and technical workers know what to do? Imagine a self-employed person who defines goals in three slightly different ways: satisfied customers, cost efficiencies, and best technical practices. Nothing makes these goals coincide automatically. Satisfaction is an ambiguous criterion: An easy A on a quiz or an engineer's assurance about a cheaper bolt may yield immediate satisfaction but long-run disaster. One might reduce costs by doing things quickly and covering up shoddy or unsafe work. Characteristically, studies of alternative approaches in any discipline leave considerable discretion about specific applications. Narrow training increases the likelihood that a customer's problems lie outside one's area of expertise.

Typically, engineers, teachers and managers see little connection between their academic courses and their first job. Mathematics educator Lauren Resnick (1987, p. 16) contrasted school activities with work experiences:

Briefly, schooling focuses on the individual's performance, whereas out-of-school mental work is often socially shared. Schooling aims to foster unaided thought, whereas mental work outside of school usually involves cognitive tools. School cultivates symbolic thinking, whereas mental activity outside school engages directly with objects and situations. Finally, schooling aims to teach general skills and knowledge, whereas situation-specific competencies dominate outside.

Classroom assignments entail manipulating symbols without organizational or physical contexts.

As adult competencies are reconstructed, the process reverses familiar ways of learning in school that proceed from concrete examples to abstract rules. Adults first approach new situations as a novice self-consciously searching for relevant facts; as they acquire competence, those facts appear in clusters of relevance. At a stage of expertise, conscious thought and planning are minimized because such activities as playing chess, air traffic control, nursing, or teaching feel natural and intuitively understandable. "What should stand out is the progression *from* the analytic behavior of a detached subject, constantly decomposing his environment into recognizable elements, and following abstract rules," as Dreyfus and Dreyfus (1986, p. 35) concluded, "*to* involved skilled behavior based on holistic pairing of new situations with associated responses produced by successful experiences in similar situations."

There are several ways to view this split between cognitive approaches taught in schools and the interconnections among information acquired through experience that constitutes expertise in complex roles. It might reinforce a view of schools as a sorting machine (partially based on merit) that legitimizes class hierarchies. Or it might suggest that academic disciplines with their awkward descriptions of phenomenological experiences are a useful step toward gaining familiarity with abstract symbols. In this interpretation, text and test routines expand cognitive approaches without conveying immediately usable job skills. Indeed, routine behaviors are more efficiently transmitted by machines, computer programs or expert systems. That second interpretation suggests that the formal curriculum serves only indirectly to prepare one for work.

## JOBS TODAY AND TOMORROW

In our interviews, educators sensed a tension between basic skills and the latest in scientific and technological developments. Noting that many future jobs are unknown today, a school principal sought "*to prepare kids in the basic skills and in the technology and in the world of the future as well as we can—giving them coping skills, learning skills, and study skills—and working-with-each-other skills. Just encourage them to be open to everything. We have a responsibility at the same time to keep our eyes out on what is out there on the edge career-wise.*" An instructional director aimed for students "*to think and get information (whatever that information is, wherever it may be) and be able to analyze it with some sense of confidence—not to have the competency in all areas.*" Another educator urged that students "*learn how to work through different processes.*"

Presumably, schools help prepare youth for appropriate roles, although few educators have analyzed how that occurs. Over 120 million Americans work in 12,000 occupational categories. Four in five work for someone else, often in large corporations. Some 30 million make things; another 20 million transport, distribute, and sell those things; another 30 million plus provide managerial, technical or professional services. As jobs are segmented along sequential production and distribution channels, the nature of work is poorly conveyed by job titles or principal responsibilities. Furthermore, the skills of a particular worker gradually redefine the job.

Usually, occupations are described by titles and competencies. A primary school education suffices for tasks requiring physical stamina or sociability, such as manual work, delivery, or a waitperson. Such laborers make up 20% of the workforce. Data processing and clerical duties (15%), skilled crafts (7%), and retail sales (19%) require a high-school diploma, often with modest vocational training. Technicians (10%), professionals (13%), and managers (13%) typically require post-secondary training although only about one-third now hold a bachelor's degree. These 35 million workers handle sales, accounting, teaching, engineering, medicine, and management. Although three out of four new entrants into fast growing high tech areas are college graduates, post-secondary enrollments will meet projected demands.

## Forecasting Jobs for the 21st Century

In discussing possible careers, school counselors and employment officers typically fall back on a technocratic approach: Project labor demands and encourage youth to acquire relevant skills. The Bureau of Labor Statistics (BLS) urged that their forecasts be used for "planning curriculum and program offerings in educational institutions, formulating policy by government agencies, and conducting market research and personnel planning by business organizations," as well as in selecting a career (Abramson, 1987, p. 2). If projections were accurate, then students might decide on their preferences and schools slot them into relevant job training. A closed system uses resources efficiently, however, only if goals and techniques remain largely fixed for long periods. Note, America's educational system has perversely demonstrated that sort of efficiency in areas of persistent biases—i. e., schools have rationed their services along class, race and gender lines.

In fall 1991, the Bureau of Labor Statistics's (BLS's) "Outlook 1990–2005" predicted that labor participation would grow by 20%— from 122.6 million in 1990 to 147.2 million in 2005. By that date, baby boomers will be 40 to 60 years old, and the labor force will include substantially more women (47%), Asians (4.3%), Hispanics (11.1%), and Blacks (11.6%). The South and West are forecast to grow faster than other regions. Basic industries and defense might see declining employment, while "services and retail trade industry divisions will account for three-fourths of the growth in employment" (U.S. Department of Labor, Bureau of Labor Statistics, 1991, pp. 2–3). Expanding areas include health care (from 8.9 to 12.8 million), business services (5.2 to 7.6 million), education (9.4 to 11.7 million), and social services (1.1 to 2.9 million). Meanwhile, retail trades would rise 26% from 19.7 to 24.8 million.

From 1975 to 1990, the labor force as a whole showed a sharp gain in educational credentials as older and less educated workers retired. In 1990, over 1 in 4 workers aged 25 to 64 had 4 or more years of college. BLS projected a continuation of those trends: "Three out of the 4 fastest growing occupational groups will be executive, administrative, and managerial; professional specialty; and technicians and related support occupations" (U.S. Department of Labor, Bureau of Labor Statistics, 1992, p. 9). High school graduates will compete for semiskilled jobs with workers outside the United States. Those without literacy will have trouble finding any position. Computers and internationalization of production reduce demand for routine skills while augmenting a need for interpersonal and analytical competencies.

The abundance of information, however, about possible occupations makes it easy to get lost in the data. If students plan their majors with an eye to possible careers, then two key facts affect those choices. First, larger occupations hire more people in a given year within any geographic area. New openings depend on a fairly predictable number of retirements or relocations plus or minus changes in overall employment. Specialized fields are inherently volatile in their labor demands within a particular year or location. Second, new occupations based on a technological innovation often peak quickly. For instance, computer programming and keypunch operators experienced major shifts. Moreover, labor markets are dynamic. People will seek out substitutes for high-cost services or goods—for example, going to nurse practitioners when doctors' fees rise.

Educational planning to prepare workers for future jobs is complex. New openings have been primarily in services that pay less than most manufacturing jobs. Despite labor protests, companies move abroad or buy parts from Japan, Korea or Taiwan. A sharp inflation at the end of the 1970s and recessions in 1980, 1983 and 1990 upset previous expectations. A rolling recession affected regions differently. The Midwest became the Rust Belt, and then the Sun Belt states with petroleum-based industries went through a long downturn. In 1989, strong economic growth in the Northeast faded as demand fell for defense contracts and computer technologies. Without a national sense of crisis, political majorities did little to stabilize employment. A graduate's immediate prospects depend on the place and timing of one's entry into labor markets.

Preparing teachers should be more predictable than other major occupations. First, birth rates provide 5 to 13 years' lead time on enrollments. Second, states determine certification requirements, and they fund institutions of higher education where most teacher preparation occurs. Given population data and predicted retirements (based on the age distribution of current instructional forces), a state or region might project demand for new teachers, and collegiate programs then could expand or contract. Indeed, Massachusetts supported such a study largely because the sharp decline in school-age population after 1972 resulted in an aging instructional force. At first glance, there should have been a sharp rise in demand for newly certified teachers in the 1990s, but some combination of previously certified teachers not employed in schools, budget stringencies, and delayed retirement diffused demand.

Even accurate projections provide little guidance for planning by students. In part, this situation follows from multiple locally controlled institutions. Colleges, including major state universities, seldom take on responsibility for adjusting supply to probable demand. Traditionally, higher education does not limit students' choices of majors—except when institutions recruit too few faculty in areas of high student interest. On the demand side, hundreds of local districts—although heavily dependent on state funds—act as though their personnel decisions (qualifications, salaries, working conditions, and opportunities for promotion) have no implications for the region as a whole. For instance, districts in New England recruit bilingual teachers from outside the area, although shortages are nationwide. College offerings and student interests respond to market demand with a time lag. Accordingly, careers requiring academic credentials experience cycles of mismatched supply and demand.

Working conditions and qualifications that form the basis for projecting educational needs are only loosely tied to academic courses. According to the BLS, "kindergarten and elementary teachers spend most of their time moving about the classroom" (U.S. Department of Labor, Bureau of Labor Statistics, 1992, pp. 135, 139). They enjoy "introducing children to the joy of learning and seeing them gain new skills" but "may have to deal with disruptive children." Secondary teachers "work the traditional 10-month school year with a 2-month vacation during the summer." They "lecture and demonstrate to students, and may use films, slides, overhead projectors, and the latest technology in teaching, such as computers and video discs." What is appropriate training for these roles?

Despite a rising income gap between high school and college graduates between the 1980s and 1990s, there appears no shortage of trained technicians and scientists. Although educational critics urge more math and science, personnel offices seek prospective employees who demonstrate "no substance abuse; honesty; integrity; follow directions; respect others; and punctuality, attendance" (Berliner, 1992, p. 33A). Among the least important criteria were "mathematics, social sciences, natural sciences, computer programming, and foreign language." Although business leaders would like schools to prepare more potential workers from whom they might select those who seem most suited to their organizational demands, they will have to restructure workplaces before many more workers can utilize advanced training on the job.

In sum, labor market projections are a poor guide to curriculum development or career planning. Existing occupational structures may not attract individuals who have vague preferences and face local constraints of school curriculum and economic opportunities. Job requirements are not fixed by technological relationships, and workers continue to learn on the job. Within limits, productive activities accommodate to adult skill levels—machines and organizations will adjust to many low-skilled, low-wage workers. Moreover, education is not limited to job skills; it includes household and citizenship competencies. If computer-driven machines readily produce the necessities for a comfortable lifestyle, then interpersonal relations, aesthetic creativity, and healthy leisure activities may gain priority in an information age.

### Knowledge Workers

Although most Americans recognize the increasing importance of information in economic activity (or the decline of physical contributions to output), it is difficult to separate out knowledge workers from others. Fritz Machlup (1962) estimated that in 1958 about 29% of the gross national product (GNP) flowed from a "knowledge industry" that employed about 32% of workers. In 1977, the Department of Commerce issued a nine-volume study of *The Information Economy* that distinguished a primary information sector from a secondary one that contributed to the output of other goods. It attributed 25% of GNP to the primary sector in 1967 and 21% to the secondary sector. An OECD study estimated a range of primary sectors from 14.8% in Australia to 24.8% in France and the United States in 1978–79 (Organization for Economic Cooperation and Development, 1981). Information workers ranged from 27.5% in Finland to 41.1% in the United States.

These estimates spurred predictions of continued growth, but for the past 20 years knowledge production has involved about one-third of

**TABLE 4.2**
**Cost of Knowledge Production (Includes Foregone Earnings)**

|  | 1958 | 1963 | 1967 | 1972 | 1977 | 1980 |
|---|---|---|---|---|---|---|
| Education | 57,238 | 86,334 | 128,578 | 188,644 | 280,187 | 351,362 |
| Research and development | 10,711 | 17,059 | 23,146 | 28,477 | 42,982 | 62,222 |
| Media of communication | 37,234 | 48,645 | 66,991 | 100,849 | 166,719 | 227,135 |
| Information machines | 9,878 | 15,239 | 22,696 | 29,149 | 54,418 | 90,210 |
| Information services | 23,764 | 33,803 | 49,398 | 85,142 | 156,665 | 236,980 |
| Total | 138,825 | 201,080 | 290,809 | 432,261 | 700,971 | 967,909 |
| Adjusted GNP | 485,439 | 648,416 | 872,106 | 1,275,556 | 2,051,671 | 2,823,251 |

*Percent of Adjusted GNP*

|  | 1958 | 1963 | 1967 | 1972 | 1977 | 1980 |
|---|---|---|---|---|---|---|
| Education | 11.8 | 13.3 | 14.7 | 14.8 | 13.7 | 12.5 |
| Research and development | 2.2 | 2.6 | 2.6 | 2.2 | 2.1 | 2.2 |
| Media of communication | 7.7 | 7.5 | 7.7 | 7.9 | 8.1 | 8.0 |
| Information machines | 2.0 | 2.4 | 2.6 | 2.3 | 2.7 | 3.2 |
| Information services | 4.9 | 5.2 | 5.7 | 6.7 | 7.6 | 8.4 |
| Total | 28.6 | 31.0 | 33.3 | 33.9 | 34.2 | 34.3 |

*Source*: Rubin, M. R., & Huber, M. T. (1986). *The Knowledge Industry in the United States: 1960–1980*, p. 19. Princeton, NJ: Princeton University Press.

GNP. The percentage spent on education fell, while information services grew (Table 4.2).

Mainstream commentators see opportunities for steadily rising real incomes as more workers find positions in well-paid knowledge industries. Optimists predict that as many as seven in ten new workers will need a college degree. Pessimists point to a growing inequality in income and education with a decline in high school graduates holding secure, well-paying industrial or service jobs. For instance, Mishel and Teixeira (1990, pp. 1–2) foresaw little rise in real incomes from projected skill requirements or new members of the labor force:

Growth in skills levels from occupational upgrading will actually *slow down* in the 1990s. . . .

The projected employment shift towards low-paying industries will lower hourly compensation by 1 to 1.5 percent over a ten-year period. As a result, projected future changes in the job structure should *depress* wage and compensation levels, at the same time as skill requirements increase.

Sluggish wage and income growth is projected to continue into the 1990s, along with a continuing increase in the hours worked per adult. It seems unlikely that the earnings of large segments of the workforce will ever recover to their levels of the late 1970s by the year 2000.

All sides, however, continue to advocate more schooling and retraining.

> In a sense, the school's mission to prepare productive citizens resembles training for an unknown contest. Will the future be a 100 meter dash or a marathon? When jobs are uncertain, students seek a general education with a focus on probable opportunities. When jobs are plentiful, they can choose the work and recreation they prefer and anticipate a lifetime of learning new roles.
>
> How would you describe your own educational planning and preparation for the future? Does an uncertain future leave you reluctant to articulate your hopes and aspirations?

If information workers remain a separate class, their position may permanently segment American society rather than communicating a common knowledge that binds people together. Urban planner Manuel Castells (1989, pp. 228, 353) warns about a dual city where 3 in 10 people

hold the strategic position of information producers in the new economy, enjoy a high cultural and educational level, are correspondingly rewarded in income and status within the stratification system, and control the key to political decision-making in terms of their social influence and organizational capacity. This new professional-managerial class, that by and large is white-dominated and male-dominated, is spatially organized, in terms of residence, work, and consumption activities, and tends to appropriate an increasingly exclusive space on the basis of a real estate market that makes location in that space a most valuable asset.

Meanwhile, unskilled workers are increasingly fragmented geographically and occupationally. To loosen class stratifications, households and workplaces must reintegrate "knowledge and meaning into a new Informational City."

In light of new work roles emerging among professionals such as teachers as well as workers in computer-controlled manufacturing, it makes sense for schools to focus on general skills, cooperative approaches, and development of personal autonomy. Today's youth typically will hold five to eight different jobs over their lifetime—half in occupations that do not currently exist. Educators should encourage active learning around developing identities defined by more than traditional or occupational norms. Adults should have a commitment to personal and social values that enhance everyone's security and well-being through cooperation. To that end, schools, households and workplaces will need to expand access to knowledge and meaningful decisionmaking.

## INFORMATION AND COMMUNICATION

As knowledge sustains modern productivity, its transmission and replacement become increasingly critical social functions. It costs little to disseminate, nothing to dispose of, and can be made available to everyone without diminishing anyone's holdings. Economic returns from human capital acquired at home, in school, and from adult activities account for about half the total gains in national output. As hours working for pay or in households decline, formal and informal education will increase as part of both paid and unpaid work. As jobs are less dangerous, stressful, boring and alienating, they should enhance self-esteem and personal satisfaction.

Although individuals seek information in anticipation of its future uses, much as they do with other investments, knowledge has some peculiar characteristics. Despite towering piles of scholarly journals, proliferating subdisciplines, and stupendous leaps in computers' speed and capacity, an age of information is not distinguished by unmanageable quantities of data. Available sensory inputs always exceed the mind's capacity to make sense of it all. The brain functions as a screen to prevent repetitious and irrelevant information from intruding on conscious thought. From a constructivist perspective, communication depends on some "preprocessing" in order to select concepts or ideas that are understandable to others. In modern times, that preprocessing involves "symbolic" inputs of words, numbers and pictures that are interpreted through "artificial" frameworks based on social and natural sciences.

Industrial structures used information with enormous efficiency by standardizing specialized roles that a worker needed to learn. Manufacturers set sizes and tolerances so that multiple parts fit together and served their purpose. Accountants calculated how many labor hours went into a refrigerator or average costs per student in a primary school so that efficiencies could be compared. Factories coordinated repetitive routines so that workers quickly learned their functions. Time clocks and interchangeable parts replaced individualized adjustments. Knowledge was expressed in measurable scales, technically defined categories, or policies and procedures. Functional relationships for coordinating work sequences or accessing bureaucratic services generated formal protocols specifying periodic provision of data.

In a postmodern era, the symbol displaces the object or act. Today, a person is granted credit, pays for vacations, or receives a license to drive a car according to symbols on paper. Informally, local communities may worry about someone's driving skills or dedication to work, but those judgments seldom supersede publicly available records. A personal identification number establishes access to checking accounts and other databases. E-mail allows anonymous communication about fantasies. Virtual reality on a videoscreen displaces physical sensory inputs. The consequences for teaching and learning of these multiple realities are still unknown.

## Characteristics of Available Information

Knowledge-based services consist of professional judgments about what information to transfer and how to allocate effort equitably. Technical consultants, planners, counselors, troubleshooters, and coordinators share previously acquired expertise in brief interactions with others. Interpersonal skills and trust among coworkers enhance that communication. Teachers, police, social workers, public defenders, and many health care providers whose time is not directly charged to clients, however, must cope with unlimited demands for their services. Their initial preparation and organizational cultures shape how they determine their responses to daily dilemmas in classrooms or in meeting demands of other clients. Providers have unusual power over what facts are conveyed to whom and in what detail.

On the demand side, potential purchasers can ascertain their potential payoff in new knowledge only after paying for media and investing the opportunity cost of time to learn it. Repeated purchases of products yield clear expectations of benefits, but exploration, research and development, or discoveries are inherently unpredictable. A competitive economy will spend suboptimal amounts for research because of well-understood market flaws: The costs of invention occur prior to discovery, dissemination of ideas scarcely can be prevented, and endemic uncertainties discourage risk-taking by individuals and firms (Arrow, 1962). Public agencies and foundations inadequately fund basic research requiring multiyear support, while most university faculty conduct surveys or experiments within existing research programs with an eye to publishing before perishing.

Information (and misinformation) are practically infinite, but their availability depends on effective demand and on organizations that supply knowledge. Creativity and research respond to those with purchasing power—whether wealthy buyers or mass markets for those with common tastes, as in television programming. Individuals with idiosyncratic tastes, rare diseases, or cultures that diverge from the mainstream offer only niche market opportunities. Competitive firms focus on immediate profits, which discourages their interest in basic scientific research. Moreover, they may opt for air pollution or unsafe workplaces over lower profits. On the other hand, large communities correctly view such external effects as costs.

People understand complex systems by decomposing them into hierarchical subparts with varied levels of specificity. Scientific disciplines basically define themselves as sets of answerable questions. By structuring problems around methods for testing those hypotheses, scientists explain many phenomena as manifestations of a handful of underlying laws or principles. Averages, medians, standard deviations, and survey outcomes with a stated margin for error all serve to reduce multiple data to a single figure. That statistic can then be compared with either implicit expectations or comparable numbers over time or among nations. Computers crunch data to compare rates of job growth with investment tax credits to illustrate production functions.

Publicly communicable information is highly dependent on formal schooling for generalized contexts. A small number of identifiers, measurable quantities (often based on arbitrary scales), and protocols or bureaucratic procedures for collecting data yield results not dependent on specific contexts. Measured quantities invite statistical treatments and describe analytic concepts that have little intuitive meaning to outsiders. As a result, communication is segmented among insiders, and each discipline constructs a view of the world that is clearly "artificial" from a perspective of a person trying to act purposefully based on sensory inputs and local knowledge. Finally, there are no a priori reasons for assuming that modern organizing categories are "better" than earlier myths and local patterns of knowledge.

Despite marvelous achievements in natural and social sciences, many problems fall between explanatory systems (disciplinary paradigms) or extend beyond their range. Our awareness of interdependencies in a postindustrial society exceeds any discipline's coverage. Sequential functions aided by machines sharply increased efficient assembly of standardized parts, as Henry Ford demonstrated, but unanticipated outcomes such as smog and congested highways now stifle cities. Policy studies illuminate interrelated technical, economic and social problems, but decisions are made locally and selfishly. Individuals, private firms, academic disciplines, and national governments seek information that enhances their autonomous control. The United Nations collects useful statistics and issues reports on global concerns, but no powerful actor has a comprehensive view of the world.

Low-cost information should do more than assist familiar patterns in schools, households and workplaces. Because private suppliers have an interest in devising easier ways to perform common tasks, those markets will be supplied and consumer products seem continuously improved or revolutionized. It is far harder to imagine ways to do new things or to serve smaller markets where those aware of productive possibilities may not recognize a potential demand. For instance, cohousing arrangements may save on cooking and laundry functions, outdoor recreation, and entertainment spaces while allowing considerable privacy. Mixtures of common and personal spaces and furnishings might foster communal arrangements among like-minded groups that substitute for extended families. The key is to envision a better society and then focus efforts in every sphere toward moving in those directions.

## Information Technologies

A second major cluster of characteristics of information today flows from the potential of information technologies that have developed over 150 years. In a preindustrial era, printed words reached only literate members of society. Newspapers served local areas, and books or pamphlets depended on limited distribution channels. Theater and lectures reached a more mixed audience, but human vocal cords limited the size of audiences. With telegraph, telephone, modem and fax machines, ideas are transmitted around the globe in seconds. Photography, rotogravure printing, motion pictures, television, and contemporary computers add images to words, numbers and sounds to strengthen messages.

In this world of mass communication, some people develop expertise in influencing others. Newspapers, popular magazines, radio, and television combine editorial messages with entertainment to attract an audience for the advertisers, who basically pay for production. That shift reverses an author's concern from "what do I want to say" to "what does the largest possible audience wish to hear." In a democracy with a broad middle class and abundant goods, information technologies encouraged mass marketing, national advertising, and a conformity to popular opinion first observed by Alexis de Tocqueville in the 1830s. In a world of symbols and artificial realities, communication techniques tolerate discrepancies between rhetoric and reality. For example, advertisers may encourage speech about democracy and equal opportunity to mask hierarchical structures and capitalist dominance over consumer choices.

With advanced personal computers, communication is individualized yet open to large groups. Desktop publishing brings low-cost printing of words, tables and images all within the budget of many individuals. Images are manipulated to heighten a message or to mislead. Hypermedia and large databases offer redundant information and invite users to devise their own searches. Although low-cost data may suggest a reduced need for human memory, an information overload shifts the key choices from producers to users. Previously, the cost of calculating a new total, rearranging a list, or generating another chart forced producers to ration publication and seek a broad market. Now, learners weigh their needs against the time required to obtain new knowledge.

Computer-based networks change how people access information and how people view human competencies. Those possibilities, however, stimulate reconsideration of how earlier technologies shaped common ways of thinking about ideas. Printing facilitated multiple copies of the same text that could be shared by many individuals across time and places. Nevertheless, text "confronts the knowledge worker with the fundamental problem of an information retrieval system based on physical instantiations of text—namely, that preserving information in a fixed, unchangeable linear format makes information retrieval difficult" (Landow, 1992, p. 18). Electronic text can easily be altered, adapted, presented in multiple formats, and customized by author and reader.

When words, images, and sounds are combined in various ways without regard for time or location, meanings are disembodied. Contemporary information technologies separate speakers and listeners in a way that "allows a reconfiguration of the relation between emitter and receiver, between the message and its context, between the receiver/ subject and representations of him or herself. These reconfigurations, which I call wrappings of language, in turn impose a new relation between science and power, between the state and the individual, between the individual and the community, between *authority* and law, between family members, between the consumer and the retailer" (Poster, 1990, pp. 14, 15). It is "increasingly difficult, or even pointless, for the subject to distinguish a 'real' existing 'behind' the flow of signifiers, and as a consequence social life in part becomes a practice of positioning subjects to receive and interpret messages."

Considering postmodern possibilities for work and well being suggests how many facets of our lives are affected by current technological capacities. We can mass-produce almost anything as long as willing buyers exist and products do not overrun space or ecological limits. Moreover, households and workplaces can facilitate informational exchanges within pleasant and safe settings. Addressing a problem (such as the sameness of television programming) with a technical solution (such as fiber optic cables with 500 channels) avoids asking about what people want and why. Low-cost information technologies, in particular, raise questions about traditional purposes and structures of schools, hierarchical coordination, and democratic agreements.

## Overlapping Multiple Realities

A third characteristic of information today follows from a recognition that individuals in groups construct meanings based on the ways they interact with the physical environment and with each other. These multiple realities involve considerable overlap, or else communication would be implausible. That overlap suggests possibilities for learning several things at once and for links among disciplines and cultural perspectives. Philatelists pick up geographical facts in passing; managers acquire skills in social psychology, and organic farmers study natural insect predators. Experienced learners fit new observations into established frameworks, and new disciplines seldom upset one's views.

When information and communication depended on local meanings and vague terms, then preprocessing related more to specific settings and visible references. Discovering a global perspective was difficult until trade and broad markets introduced exotic products and manufactured goods. Language and communication often emphasized differences rather than similarities. Travel and international relocation of persons and enterprise forced an acknowledgment of cultural mixtures within all countries. Current interdisciplinary approaches suggest how academics have segmented discourse. Transdisciplinary and multicultural perspectives open understandings of global interests in peace, trade, health, migration, and so on.

In Schutz's terms, strangers in a new territory reframe their understandings by building on existing vocabularies. Historians, sociologists, economists, psychologists, and novelists depict similar situations from their own perspectives, and each has something to learn from the other's analytic concepts. Patriotic histories often foster divisions, but enough common ground exists for cultures to communicate their essential humanness. Although Marshall McLuhan projected a media-based "global village," organizational structures continually reconstruct personal meaning systems. Military power, trade policies, and entertainment currently dominate international relations, but an interdependent world requires people to share some values while respecting diversity in others.

Often information directly contributes to self-awareness and community spirit rather than just enhancing earning and spending. Those purposes shape what parts of one's capacity to perform usefully can remain part of subconscious routines and what parts require conscious thought. As tools and goods embody many skills, people engage in fewer routine activities (or routines are repeated less often and include fewer physical cues). For instance, a point-and-shoot camera may include so many buttons and options that one needs to keep its instructions handy, whereas one soon learned to set aperture, focus and film advance on earlier single-lens reflex cameras without conscious thought. Other adjustments can be recalled because of analogous actions.

As a result, language shifts its role in conveying images of a subject and purposeful action: "Instead of envisioning language as a tool of a rational, autonomous subject intent upon controlling a world of objects for the purpose of enhanced freedom, the new language structures refer back upon themselves, subverting referentiality and thereby acting upon the subject and constituting it in new and disorienting ways" (Poster, 1990, pp. 17, 18–19). Postmodernists suggest "that the political metanarratives of emancipation from the eighteenth and nineteenth centuries that have served as frames and reference points for the disciplines of history, literature, philosophy, sociology, anthropology and so forth now appear to be losing their powers of coherence, their ability to provide a groundwork of assumptions that make it appear natural to ask certain questions and to think that the answers to those questions define the limit and extent of the problem of truth."

An information society has far-reaching implications for schools. "Producing" well-being entails different competencies and a new framework of social understandings. Our conscious categories and relationships are less visible and tangible—purposeful actions involve ideas that motivate other people—yet, well-being is still largely a matter of physical and social arrangements. The question is how to prepare adults for that world. For 20 years, progressive educators have urged an emphasis on processes rather than facts, on how to look up information rather than memorization, on problem solving and creativity rather than simply learning theories, histories and heritages. The puzzle has been that it seemed an add-on in which ever more information would be required to equip students to perform new jobs and roles.

A new framework that includes cooperation, democratic processes, and a just society can transform the nature of public discourse. When low-cost information enables each worker in households and workplaces to share in the effort and contributions of others, then cooperation and democratic governance are easier. When engaged in creative and useful roles that include learning as a complementary benefit, people gain satisfaction from their daily activities wherever they occur. If school and "work" become less onerous and alienating, then people have less need for mindless or destructive distractions. Engagement in constructing positive visions of the future encourages ongoing learning throughout all experiences and a sharing of new purposes and possibilities with others. That vision suggests a way to reconstruct work and well-being.

## RELATED READING

Understanding how information relates to work and households is difficult because so many of our experiences are taken for granted. Victor R. Fuchs, *How We Live: An Economic Perspective on Americans from Birth to Death* (Cambridge: Harvard University Press, 1983) shows how foregone earnings affect time allocations to shape our daily routines, and Lillian B. Rubin, *Worlds of Pain: Life in the Working Class Family* (New York: Basic Books, 1994) shows stress within households. Juliet B. Schor, *The Overworked American: The Unexpected Decline of Leisure* (New York: Basic Books, 1991) offers intriguing details about the uses of scarce leisure among employed workers. David W. Hornbeck and Lester M. Salamon, eds., *Human Capital and America's Future: An Economic Strategy for the '90s* (Baltimore, MD: Johns Hopkins University Press, 1991) suggests a range of public programs for investing in people.

# 5

# Purposeful Organizations

People everywhere work together to do things that are beyond the scope of individual effort. They naturally interact with others for companionship as well as the efficiencies of specialized or shared endeavors. Yet no one can perform all the specific skills in a modern society, nor does anyone know enough to optimize their purchases of goods and services from others. Although the word "organization" elicits images of military command, government bureaucracy, or corporate management, cooperative activities range from voluntary groups such as a children's kickball game through multipart corporate structures. Largely self-perpetuating institutional arrangements allow for predictable behaviors, thereby reducing a need for new information.

Despite their importance and familiarity in everyday life, organizations are poorly understood. Educators in our interviews lacked a useful vocabulary for conceptualizing how schools or workplaces might be restructured to serve new strategic goals. Organizations differ widely in their interactional patterns, their adaptability, and their attention to clients, customers or students. Located midway between the individual and the nation, organizations cannot be explained simply as a rational means to a specific end. As sites of human interactions, they are both socially constructed and sources of evolving meaning systems. As such, they exhibit "cultural" characteristics—that is, members share a vocabulary, norms and values that give stability to their behaviors.

Despite the mission of educators to prepare youth as productive citizens, there is almost nothing in the formal curriculum about how adults will spend much of their working life within organizations that have powerful internal dynamics. Industrial-era enterprises designed for mass production and sales persist with little challenge, muting dialog about alternative ways to work and live together. People interact in diverse organizational structures that range in size from partners in households to the United Nations. They specialize efforts within a decisionmaking group in order to do things efficiently. People make sense of their experiences through social interactions, but in modern societies, face-to-face interchanges are supplemented by organizational and ideological "actors." Over time, persons, purposes, structures and external environments shape group norms.

We start by contrasting a view of organizations as rationalized, efficient command structures with nonrational, socially constructed ways of working together. Next, we briefly discuss industrial firms, their impact on modes of thinking, and their current crises. Stagnant economic growth exposed inherent dilemmas of hierarchical supervision of knowledge workers. Neither professionalism nor principal-agent controls provide satisfactory solutions to unequal distributions of information. Then, we describe three innovative postindustrial firms that achieve coordination without top-down commands in a manufacturing, service, and knowledge enterprise. Finally, we depict effective schools as a prototype for adaptive and flexible learning communities.

## PERSPECTIVES ON ORGANIZATIONS

There are at least three different meanings attached to organizing and organizations. First, people in proximity groups specialize and coordinate their contributions through informal exchanges. Adult family members divide tasks to provide a comfortable home for themselves and their children—often renegotiating roles and responsibilities within a lifetime commitment. Other voluntary associations are short term or focused on a single goal. For instance, barn raisings, quilting bees, and crime watches suggest how neighbors get together so that many hands make light work. Individuals pursue worship, a hobby, or civic activities and gain satisfaction from membership in a like-minded group. In these cases, cooperation is fostered because people know each other, share cultural beliefs, and expect reciprocal returns.

Second, some units have a formal structure with a defined hierarchy of command, often with procedural rules for decisionmaking. Historically, nation states, commercial ventures, and industrial enterprises undertook to coordinate large-scale and long-term projects. Governments fostered command structures based on loyalty to rulers and built bureaucracies to collect taxes and to supply military forces. In the 17th century, European exploitation of colonial areas stimulated the development of private corporations with royal charters. With industrialization, organizations became a central part of most people's lives. Wages and managers replaced informal exchanges. Profit-seeking firms, not-for-profit agencies, and government bureaus coordinated multiple workers over space and time by paying salaries to subordinates in hierarchical structures.

Third, longstanding groups and organizational structures become institutionalized, dividing social roles without visible supervision. Normal interactive patterns among these structured groups allow people to count on others without explicit agreement. For instance, a contract for painting a house assumes a legal system as well as a weathered building, a paint store, a ladder company, and insurance agents, but these elements never hold a meeting in order to plan the job. Organizational theorist Karl Weick (1979, p. 100) described such interactions between disparate individuals as "mutual equivalence structures." Ordinarily, they "can be built and sustained *without* people knowing the motives of another person, without people having to share goals, and it is not even necessary that people see the entire structure or know who their partners are."

American society may be viewed as a stew of associations or organizations—each defined by purposes and external boundaries and surrounded by space unmarked by control systems. People take for granted that children will be raised by families, educated by schools, and informed by media; in time, they will replace their parents as producers and consumers. Entities called "businesses" offer goods and services for consumption in "households." Governments protect persons and property, establish ground rules of personal responsibilities and entitlements, and punish misbehaviors. Distinct purposes reduce conflicts among organizations and ease mutually beneficial exchanges through markets, yet they also hinder agreements to modify existing customs.

## Complexity and Information

What enables a group to function internally or externally in relation to others? Mission statements, tables of organization, and strategic planning capture only a small part of the story. As people interact, they repeat words and actions in recognizable roles. Weick (1979, pp. 3-4) proposed an inclusive definition:

Organizing is like a grammar in the sense that it is a systematic account of some rules and conventions by which sets of interlocked behaviors are assembled to form social processes that are intelligible to actors. It is also a grammar in the sense that it consists of rules for forming variables and causal linkages into meaningful structures . . . that summarize the recent experience of the people who are organized. The grammar consists of recipes for getting things done when one person alone can't do them and recipes for interpreting what has been done.

After the fact, organizational leaders offer accounts that stress rationalized structures and downplay personal, accidental or ambiguous factors.

Most formal organizations emerge from informal working relationships. On self-sufficient farms or in family businesses, relatives share tasks, perhaps hiring someone during a busy season. Amateurs may perform a drama or play a game without a director or coach. In small groups, each contribution matters, and peer pressure encourages cooperation. Players fill roles based on their physical capacity, experience and skill—gaining from their diversity. Because teamwork enables the group to accomplish more than its members could singly, early accomplishments motivate mutual support. Over time, members may chafe at their roles and question the value of cooperation. They continuously renegotiate roles and responsibilities to mesh self-interests with organizational goals.

If subunits follow regular rules while taking other parts as given, the whole can "make sense" without a comprehensive blueprint drawn up in advance. For example, plant maintenance and payroll functions have their own expertise and dynamics whether applied to canning tomatoes or generating electricity. Functional subunits relate to each other in partial ways, each with a particularistic impression of the complex whole. That is, custodians may sweep the shop floor and the manager's office, noting the differences in lighting and quantity of dirt. Their knowledge of replacement bulbs or type of vacuum cleaner need not affect anyone's assumption that their space will be clean and well-lit. Moreover, as long as a paycheck appears, janitors can ignore the skills that accountants bring to their joint enterprise.

Organizations use information efficiently to coordinate complex activities over space and time. Systematic subunits are necessary because no person, bureaucracy or computer can handle all the data needed to arrange the logistics and contingencies of everyday life. Once organizational patterns are established, only those "events" that require a decision enter into an individual's conscious thought. By assuming that others know their job, people act as consumers, clients or colleagues based on familiar roles and relationships. For instance, shoppers seldom think about how bananas are picked and shipped to local grocers or wonder what a store manager does beyond approving personal checks. Moreover, a hierarchy of command arranges information in functional subunits. Following bureaucratic procedures, each level reports selected measures of its activities to supervisors. Then, executives make decisions and seek to hold staff accountable.

Individuals who decide to work together need to coordinate activities so that specialization is possible. Within families and other voluntary groups, altruistic cooperation prevails—based on traditional roles and mutual accommodation. Small numbers can organize teams around immediate benefits, such as a bucket brigade for fighting fires. Proximity and limited aims facilitate communication about personal needs and desires as well as what each is willing to contribute to a collective endeavor. Markets for goods and services entail mutually beneficial exchanges and seem free from coercion. In contrast, corporations as well as government and nonprofit agencies rely on paid employment and command structures that often generate miscommunication and resentment among workers.

## Managing Groups

All organizations serve multiple and nonobvious purposes. For instance, customers interact with a local bookstore in different ways that might puzzle an outside observer. Those who come to browse find a pleasant and friendly place to interact around ideas. They examine new titles, pursue personal interests, talk with staff or other like-minded individuals, and sometimes buy a book. Those who know what they want proceed briskly to get help in locating titles and expeditious handling of their credit card. Some customers appear overwhelmed by shelves overflowing with books, fail to formulate questions to narrow their search, and wait in a line at the cash register. What appears a simple transaction—$19.95 for a novel—often conceals complicated and somewhat unpredictable outcomes.

A purposive organization needs management, as economist Peter Drucker (1973, p. 567) insists: "It does not possess clarity unless the team leader creates it. It has poor stability. Its economy is low; a team demands continuing attention to its management, to the relationships of people within the task force, to assigning people to their jobs, to explanation, deliberation, communication, and so on. A large part of the energy of all the members goes into keeping things running." As a result, small groups recognize some as leaders, seek a coach or outside expert, and continually adjust to evolving skills and player turnover. Yet, as Harlan Cleveland (1985) quipped, the more power a manager accrues, the less he or she knows what frontline staff actually do.

Bookstore managers seek a profit through a series of choices: What titles to stock, how to conduct sales, where to advertise, whom to hire? They have expenses for staff, rent and inventory but charge only for those items selected by walk-in customers. Lengthy inquiries, extensive collections of children's literature, and bibliographical guides add significantly to costs without earning a direct return. Employees want a sense of autonomy, responsibility and a fair wage; nevertheless, owners may not trust them to order wisely and ring up every sale. Typically, managers seek to enhance their control over staff and resources while minimizing costs. From a social perspective, however, bookstores disperse knowledge in their locality as part of a large informational system—though no one in the store has that as a conscious goal or assigned role.

Managing a classroom raises these issues of control and efficiency in a knowledge society. Somewhat naively, some start with an idea that teachers set schedules, make assignments, and grade the quality of performances, all with an eye to efficiently transmitting a standard curriculum to a class. Although an orderly climate is essential, it is not sufficient. Other educators, perhaps equally naively, see students as naturally motivated to learn if provided with resources and support for their interests. Although students do want to learn, their motivation as well as readiness is neither uniform nor necessarily congruent with statewide curricular goals. A third group of teachers have essentially given up on positive educational goals to focus on order. They may use grades as punitive measures or negotiate light assignments in exchange for quiet in class.

> Traditional teachers try to motivate students through competition for rank-ordered grades. Extracurricular activities such as clubs or sports foster cooperation and enthusiasm that inspire students to volunteer time and effort. Either pattern structures activities toward some predictable outcomes.
>
> Reflect on your feelings about each approach. How do they differ in communication patterns?

Teachers assume control by virtue of their age and knowledge of the school setting and a need for someone to initiate activities and facilitate agreement, but their authority is seldom unquestioned. Despite these complexities, effective teachers do set a few rules and norms of behavior and build on students' interests that relate to curricular goals. They do this mainly through personable interactions with students, parents and colleagues that uneasily balance multiple goals. Their achievement resembles new managerial techniques in innovative organizations, but those lessons need to be seen as part of larger reenvisioning of working and learning together.

In large manufacturing companies, varied, amorphous roles are formalized in distinct subunits. Typically, several product lines are supported by a research and development laboratory, central accounting, sales and service, and a top management charged with allocating internal resources. Firms may provide custodial or childcare services or subcontract with others. Subunits have operational goals that may or may not coincide with overall objectives: A production unit strives to meet monthly quotas; accounting aims to minimize costs; research dreams of inventing faster machines; sales wants satisfied customers; and management directs efforts toward investors' profits. To link those parts, businesses develop bureaucratic information systems characterized by regular reports.

Government agencies, though usually providing services rather than products, have their purposes defined by laws and regulations. Typically, those goals are general, hedged by political constraints, and initiated by a perceived social problem. Managers struggle to gain political support for appropriations and to motivate civil service workers or political appointees. Although government bureaus serve the common good as defined in legislation, each focuses on one aspect of an individual's life and may work at cross-purposes with others. For instance, schools seek to integrate races and educate for citizenship while zoning board restrictions isolate communities by class or income levels. Segmented by expertise or clientele, each agency strives to enhance its reputation. Only rarely can strong political leaders harmonize public services.

In performing necessary functions, organizations generate endemic tensions between personal autonomy and prescribed roles. Any rule or custom that regularizes behaviors simplifies what people need to know, but that segmentation means that few ever grasp a sense of the whole. Perhaps industrial-era schools—with their isolated classrooms, bureaucratic procedures, and accountability through periodic testing—prepare adults for a hierarchical society. Powerful managers constrain individual freedom, and most people sense a conflict between personal autonomy and the opportunities opened by being a member of a large organization. The challenging question today is whether new information technologies can meld personal autonomy and cooperation within and among groups.

### Dilemmas of Cooperation

At first glance, organizations appear made up of people who share goals and activities. Yet workers taken individually have no self-interest in cooperating with supervisors' directives. Moreover, managers' interests may differ from those of owners. Economist Mancur Olson (1968, pp. 1, 2) puzzled over why organizations exist at all in light of the "logic of collective behavior." Most people presume that "if the members of some group have a common interest or objective, and if they would all be better off if that objective were achieved, . . . [then] the individuals in that group would, if they were rational and self-interested, act to achieve that objective." Instead, Olson concluded, cooperation ensues only in small groups or coercive situations: *"rational, self-interested individuals will not act to achieve their common or group interests."*

Many interactions within and among organizations take on a puzzling dynamic associated with the "prisoner's dilemma" because individuals view situations selfishly. Although all members (potentially) benefit from working together toward common goals, each individual faces incentives to defect or to deny their share of responsibility for the group's output. For example, the matrix in Figure 5.1 illustrates the additional effort required by two teachers to raise student achievement scores. If Ann and Bev cooperate in supporting high expectations for students, then each contributes an extra hour a week (upper left quadrant). If Ann accepts responsibility while Bev loafs, Ann must devote

**FIGURE 5.1**
**A Teacher's Dilemma**

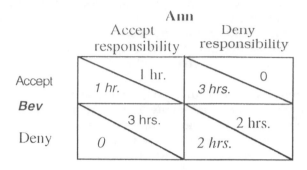

three extra hours to motivate students (lower left). If neither contributes and the principal demands extra commitment to overcome low scores, then each must work two hours extra (lower right).

This payoff schedule is often depicted as a dilemma facing two prisoners who must decide whether to cop a plea by implicating their partner in crime. Responses depend on a broad context of organizational rewards and expectations. In large groups, workers hope that their freeloading will not matter. For instance, some teachers evade their share of advising extracurricular clubs or arranging an open house for parents, counting on others to make an extra effort. In competitive settings, however, slackers induce similar behavior among coworkers. When colleagues assume they must win in order not to lose, they distrust the other's word, look out for "number one," and seek to mislead others about their intent or performance. Distrust and defection predictably occur when relatively anonymous players pursue nonrecurring games with high payoffs.

In long-term relationships, trusting others builds trust, so that cooperating often leads to cooperation. Members recognize a tit-for-tat strategy through repeated interactions and so opt to build trust through teamwork. In small elementary schools, teachers easily see themselves working together to achieve an orderly and pleasant environment, and principals can establish positive norms through friendly persuasion and a positive example. Modest payoffs and small risks allow altruistic teachers to elicit mutual support. In larger, less personal settings, supervisors continually seek to control and evaluate to limit defection, without eliminating a temptation to slack off or to freeload on the group's efforts.

Related issues are sometimes discussed under the heading of "free riders" or "exploiting the commons." Free riders are prevalent in democracies where citizens see little reason to participate in selecting candidates or voting. They underreport their interest in public goods, complain about taxes, and still demand public services for themselves. In the case of a common resource, such as fish in the ocean, individuals pursue their immediate interests, although overfishing results in smaller catches for every boat. In another example, a school's failure to educate a youth is like polluting a river. A district may lower its expenses by discouraging high-cost students from continuing in school, but the rest of the community then loses the contributions of a productive citizen, while usually paying more for police and welfare.

Some large voluntary organizations thrive because economies of scale make the individual's benefits commensurate with a relatively small contribution. For instance, dues to the Audubon Society buy reduced fees for bird sanctuaries, a monthly magazine, as well as enhanced lobbying for conservation. Union members gain from collective bargaining, grievance procedures, and political support for unemployment benefits. Churchgoers and computer groups are rewarded by companionship and shared activities. Citizens vote and write their representatives because taxes and regulations are coerced and their expressed preferences may influence policy choices.

To coordinate their efforts, families rely on bonds of affection as well as face-to-face communication and traditional social roles. Governments protect fundamental rights and duties of individuals and organizations through legal authority backed by force. Competitive markets entail free exchanges by both parties. Firms rely on managerial control, but a degree of trust between workers and managers and between the firm and its customers is necessary. As public policy analyst John D. Donahue (1989, p. 39) concluded, "a culture's capacity to get things done depends greatly on the quality of the institutions it develops to allow people to delegate tasks to others, or to undertake tasks for others, without fear of exploitation."

## INDUSTRIAL STRATEGIES AND STRUCTURES

The evolution of competitive firms and worker roles in industrial America offers insights into how organizations impact on modern times. Corporations developed in response to extended markets made possible by commercial capitalism and mechanical inventions. They evolved in contradictory directions, imposing a visible hand of management on previously self-reliant farmers. Owners of capital promulgated an ideology of free markets to justify their control over others' labor. Internally, they insisted on hierarchical supervision and control; externally, they competed against rival individuals and firms. As suppliers and buyers extended beyond trusted associates or personal oversight, they relied on a cash nexus through impersonal markets to purchase resources and labor from others.

In the 19th century, American entrepreneurs learned to put together productive units by harnessing energy and labor to machines in

sequential order. They built different organizations to handle distribution and sales of factory-produced goods. Sears Roebuck filled warehouses with goods and distributed them to customers' mailboxes in
response to order codes. Early in the 20th century, Henry Ford
successfully assembled standardized parts along moving lines to mass-
produce cars under control of a prototypic multiunit, hierarchical
structure. As steel and rubber turned into Model Ts along an assembly
line, a reverse flow of paper with designs, costs, and tolerances recorded
their movement through the factory. Management struggled to devise
systematic structures to facilitate parallel flows of products and
information.

Management applied bureaucratic systems and new information
technologies to coordinate flows of workers, goods and consumers over
space and time. When railroads moved things faster than human
speeds, managers sought speedier means to communicate and process
information (Beniger, 1986). The telegraph enabled trains to be
rescheduled when an accident or weather interfered. Double-entry
accounting practices helped businesses process cash flows in heavily
capitalized firms engaged in long-term or distant activities. Managers
focused their efforts on control through a sequence of subunits that
resolved problems at the appropriate level while preserving oversight at
the top. After the fact, they argued that a rational predictability was an
intended outcome of hierarchical forms.

According to economic historian Alfred Chandler (1977, pp. 8, 11),
"once a managerial hierarchy had been formed and successfully carried
out its function of administrative coordination, the hierarchy itself became a source of permanence, power, and continued growth." Increasingly, top managers had technical skills earned in professional degree
programs. By the 1920s, managers of large corporations had displaced
markets in "the coordination and integration of the flow of goods and
services from the production of the raw materials through the several
processes of production to the sale to the ultimate consumer." By the
1950s, corporate saving had sustained new investment, and America's
leading firms dominated world markets for steel, electrical equipment
and appliances, chemicals, food processing, tobacco, jet engines, and
automobiles.

Multilevel firms with interlocking subunits proved enormously
effective structures for coordinating mass production, mass retailing,
and mass transportation. Thousands worked for the same firm. During
the 1950s, the 500 largest U.S. corporations "produced about half of the
nation's industrial output (about a quarter of the industrial output of
the free world), owned roughly three-quarters of the nation's industrial
assets, accounted for about 40 percent of the nation's corporate profits,
and employed more than one out of eight of the nation's nonfarm
workers" (Reich, 1990, pp. 46, 51). To coordinate these vast corporate
organizations, managers adopted bureaucratic structures "featuring

chains of command, spans of control, job classifications, divisions and division heads, and standard operating procedures to guide every decision."

As specialized roles become knowledge-based, information systems no longer adequately convey what is done or translate into orders to frontline workers. Moreover, large operations encompass multiple and unexpected functions. For instance, many firms and universities operate medical clinics, restaurants, childcare and recreation centers, building and grounds departments, drug and alcohol counseling, print shops and television studios, and public safety units. Although wages or salaries motivate cooperative efforts, workers may ignore orders, mislead their supervisors, and sabotage engineering potential to protect their position. Nevertheless, top-down control over multiple, sequential roles was more efficient than free market arrangements for much of the economy.

## Machines, Production, and Consciousness

For two centuries, language and meaning systems have been shaped by work with machines in bureaucratic organizations, thereby reducing resistance to managerial control. Following a burst of inventions during the early 19th century, industrialism became a dominant economic force. Anthropologist A.F.C. Wallace (1978, pp. 478, 479, 481) noted that a key innovation "solves a limited problem but does so in a way which opens up a whole new line of development." He depicted a chronological progression from a technological (or structural) discovery through new behaviors to "the ethical, philosophical, religious, and political justifications" offered by insiders to each other. A social transformation occurs in stages: "innovation, paradigmatic core development, exploitation, functional consequences, and rationalization."

A revolution in work, community patterns, and socially constructed meaning systems occurred as people adapted to factory discipline. The logic of faster machines and higher output per laborer increased specialization, thereby dividing manual workers from managers. Moreover, it separated mechanicians who improved the jennies and looms from merchants, professionals and political leaders—whose thoughts involved words and concepts, not designs and models. Workers struggled to keep pace with machines, and owners worried about credits, advancing technologies, and new markets. Initially, a mobile workforce adjusted machinery to suit local conditions, and managers relied on their personal reputation for honesty. Later, metals, speed and finance required formal training as well as an induction period of learning on the job.

Industrialization brought hierarchies of income, information and power based on the organizational size needed for economies of scale under private ownership of capital. For example, mining anthracite coal required drilling shafts thousands of feet deep, ventilation systems, lifts, crushers, sorters, railroad connections, and crews of 100 to 200 workers. Seeking immediate profits, owners skimped on safety and conservation. Accidents closed mines as well as maiming or killing miners. Capital costs and specialized labor encouraged "centralization and social control" (Wallace, 1987, p. 408). They were justified in part by public rhetoric about lazy or careless workers, heroic inventors and industrialists, and social progress through competition (in which some were losers). Mine owners promoted schools for children of workers where "the moral message conveyed in the primers emphasized, above all, obedience."

By the 1920s, efficient and resilient firms had adopted functional multidivisional structures that separated semiskilled workers, mechanics, engineers, accountants, and managers by roles, salaries, training, and status. "The visible hand of management replaced the invisible hand of market mechanisms," as Chandler (1977, p. 372) summarized the change. Personal relations with owners or buyers gave way to separate roles under bureaucratic procedures and managerial decisions. Major organizations set the terms of trade for independent professionals and small entrepreneurs. Segmentation marked the U.S. economy: "In order to succeed, individuals had to concentrate on a single specialty; in order to survive, they had to rely upon an array of specialists in those many critical areas beyond their knowledge" (Wiebe, 1975, p. 24).

Mid-20th century Americans demonstrated an identifiable cognitive style around machines, assembly line production, measurable output, and large organizations (Berger, Berger, & Kellner, 1973, pp. 27, 28):

- First, "everything is analyzable into constituent components, and everything can be taken apart and put together again in terms of these components."

- Second, outcomes depend on sequential actions "because the components are continuously interdependent in a rational, controllable and predictable way."

- Third, components serve various ends—for instance, bolts and gears fit either clocks or missiles.

- Finally, factory work occasions *"implicit abstraction,"* especially identifying others by a functional role. Rather than a tailor measuring and stitching to order, nameless garment workers cut shirts to standard sizes and sew cuffs or collars for unknown customers.

Industrial workers construct a social reality that views their roles as *"both* concrete individuals *and* anonymous functionaries" (Berger et al., 1973, pp. 32, 50). Physically separated from family and community and psychologically divided between feeling unique yet serving standardized roles, members of modern organizations experience a pervasive sense of alienation—"the homeless mind." As citizens, they interact with a public bureaucracy which "presupposes *general and autonomous organizability*," follows orderly procedures, and tries to treat everyone alike (and thus impersonally) in the name of fairness. Competitive specialists in their work lives, many Americans express their personality through where they live, what they buy, and how they spend their leisure time.

Schools reinforced images of standardized, but rank-ordered, individuals trained for functionality in a modern society. Educators imitated organizational patterns "found in the factory, the army, the newly created police departments, and even the railroad" (Tyack, 1974, pp. 30, 40, 54). Superintendents acted to "replace village forms in which laymen participated in decentralized decision-making with the new bureaucratic model of a closed 'nonpolitical' system in which directives flowed from the top down, reports emanated from the bottom, and each step of the educational process was carefully prescribed by professional educators." Teachers strove to control low-income students "by keeping each child busy at a specific task every minute, by competition for that scarce commodity, praise, and by the 'terror of degradation.'"

> In a traditional classroom or factory, students and workers are watched and evaluated. Yet no teacher or supervisor knows what goes on in someone's mind—how resentment induces slowdowns or silences useful ideas.
>
> Reflect on your experience resisting control by others, concealing or fabricating information, and pursuing personal goals. Do you respond better to group support or to a competitive challenge? Does your ability to succeed affect your motivation to cooperate or compete?

Many Americans came to assume that industrial efficiency required workers to follow orders in specialized, though alienating, roles. In keeping with a machine age, people identified themselves by their functional role in an efficient sequence of production. Schools did not prepare most adults to think critically, creatively or holistically. Instead, they honored empirical and rational approaches that privileged materialism and individual autonomy—but only for those with authority or means. Those embedded approaches blocked perceptions of ill-structured problems and loose organizational patterns that affected cooperation. With relative abundance and fading memories of the Great Depression and World War II, young Americans in the 1950s viewed themselves as components of rationalized organizations and as avid consumers.

## Stagnant Growth

Since 1973, stagnant growth has challenged America's ideological framework. For the first time since the industrial revolution, young workers in the 1980s anticipated a lower standard of living than their parents enjoyed. Examining the economy from 1929 to 1982, Edward F. Denison (1985, p. 30) highlighted education and technological know-how as sources for rising productivity among those employed in non-residential businesses. Potential output grew by 1.7% annually because of the following sources (weights indicated by percentage): advances in knowledge (64%), education per worker (30%), economies of scale (20%), improved resource allocation (19%), and additions to capital (10%). That total of 143% was reduced by fewer hours per week (−23%) as well as other factors such as less land per worker and changes in the legal and human environment (−21%). After 1973, a growing labor supply from immigrants, women and baby boomers sustained modest growth in national output, while the usual sources for higher productivity made no discernible contribution.

After considering possible explanations for lagging productivity, Denison (1985) discarded all the usual suspects: laziness did not become pandemic in 1973; regulations and lawsuits did not suddenly misallocate resources or slow the rate of innovation; taxes did not rise nor public services erode at times that might account for falling labor efficiency. Other commonly cited explanations such as inflation, unemployment, dysfunctional families, and undue burdens from government regulations and revenues had no noticeable affect on employment, labor force participation, capital spending, or utilization rates. Perhaps, he speculated, the underlying beliefs, activities and structures of the industrial system—aspirations, education, scientific advances, and corporate organizations—no longer meshed.

The available evidence suggests that widespread inflation triggered by limitations on petroleum output in 1973 induced a collapse of social practices that had moderated the inefficiencies attributable to hierarchical segmentation. Relative prices became unstable, and wages adjusted erratically to inflation. A social compact had been broken. Workers no longer could count on salary increases to sustain a rising standard of living. Neither giant corporations nor labor unions could sustain their accustomed roles.

Once the blaming started, economic shocks fed a conservative reaction. Manufacturers automated, relocated factories or purchases to low-wage areas, and bought or sold assets, leaving consumers unsure about brand names and employees insecure in their positions. Unions failed to protect workers from inflation or layoffs. Neither corporate nor governmental responsibility assured workers' jobs and health or consumers' safety. Everyone paid more because earlier generations had depleted natural resources and degraded soil, water and air. An initial distrust fed by uneven inflationary spurts perpetuated itself as selfishness at work and in consumption.

Historically, higher productivity per worker depended on skills acquired through specialization of labor (production for markets); accumulated knowledge (science and technology); physical plant, equipment, and an infrastructure for transportation and communication (capital accumulation); the organization of production, distribution and consumption (economies of scope and scale); and generally stable and peaceful conditions (rules of law under constitutional procedures). Small wonder that, when given a choice, most people opted for industrialization, democratic governments, and modern values. Industrial America harnessed workers in efficient, profit-making structures that yielded unequal outcomes of income and power. Workers surrendered autonomy and creativity in return for high and secure wages. Although many groups resented corporate or governmental power, they assumed that the system worked to their advantage.

With stagnation, industrial corporations no longer sustained economic progress nor governments their promise of civil rights and an end to poverty. Faced with industrial competition from Europe and Japan, a postwar political consensus collapsed: business no longer supported New Deal programs (notably Social Security and labor's right to organize) in return for peaceful relations with workers and U.S. government support in foreign markets. Some charged that families, firms and public institutions failed to discipline themselves or missed new possibilities. While liberals advocated less reliance on military force abroad and more equitable entitlements at home, conservatives argued for greater emphasis on personal responsibility for one's income and lifestyle, a powerful national presence abroad, and reduced social programs.

Under President Reagan, reductions in federal income taxes benefited the rich while most others paid more in Social Security taxes than they gained from income tax cuts. Revenues fell far short of military and domestic spending. The result was a sharp rise in borrowing from abroad, higher domestic interest rates that discouraged business investments, and a failure to address long-term issues of poverty, racism and environmental degradation. As economist Benjamin Friedman (1989, p. 198) concluded, "Reagan's new fiscal policy delivered not more capital formation but less, not faster growth in productivity but slower, and an economy that is not a stronger but a weaker competitor." Net business investment fell from a postwar average of 3.3% to 2.3%.

Although business investment in new equipment directly enhances labor productivity (and thus the goods and services available for social well-being), public investment in transportation, communication, education and health sets the context for market decisions. Public investments in the infrastructure fell from a postwar peak of 6.9% in 1952 (with a second peak of 4.4% in 1965) to an average of 1.5% in the 1970s and 1.2% during the 1980s. Schools, hospitals, roads, sewers and other public works took about 30% of state and local budgets through the 1960s, dropped to 17% in the 1970s, and fell to 13% in the 1980s. After growing 3.5% annually for 30 years, net public investment "has slowed to just .9 percent since 1980" (Friedman, 1989, p. 205).

As a consequence of declining births, probusiness and military-oriented priorities, and tax cuts, Friedman (1989, pp. 206, 208) concluded, "we have been cheating our future in all these respects—not just in business capital formation but in government infrastructure and education too." During the 1980s, productivity grew in key manufacturing industries, primarily because employment fell by over 1.5 million between 1979 and 1987. Several factors enhanced productive potential: Baby boomers acquired work experience, inflation subsided, business spent more on research, and environmental regulations weakened. "But . . . with a *lower* net business investment rate than in any period since World War II—none of these reversals, nor even all in combination, proved sufficient to turn our productivity growth around."

Symbolically, that break in a long-term pattern of a rising standard of living marked the end of industrialism. Over the past two decades, traditional organizations in the United States have appeared less effective, and a bond of trust in their stability and fairness has eroded. In asking for greater effort and accountability from workers, management too often destroyed old loyalties instead. Electronic technologies eliminated many jobs and sharply revised skill requirements for others. Users could not easily assess the value of varied, technologically complex, and risky goods and services. Although violence, alcohol and drug abuse, and widespread loss of standards earlier had been attributed to working conditions, it was easy to condemn schools—especially elite colleges where opposition to the war in Vietnam struck an older generation as unpatriotic and "unmanly."

## INFORMATION AND CONTROL

Productivity is sapped by inappropriate organizational structures that are ill-prepared to induce cooperation among knowledge workers. Efficiency requires technicians, professionals and managers to communicate relevant information, to agree on goals, to share group benefits, and to encourage multiple initiatives. Output by human service or technical workers is not easily observed or measured. Now that computers can control routine processes and provide everyone with access to relevant information, people can make nonroutine decisions, innovate, connect products with consumers' needs, and protect workers and consumers from environmental dangers.

Paradoxically, efforts to tighten accountability and get quick results push postindustrial organizations into counterproductive behaviors. Their time horizons and perspectives narrow and shorten. Human service personnel, overburdened with responsibilities, emphasize their personal strengths while ignoring group synergy. Bureaucracies collect and synthesize misleading data that support managerial decisions in favor of existing products and practices. Meanwhile, long-term economic growth depends more on workers' educational backgrounds, the scale of organized production, public goods, and negative by-products of technology. Moreover, important investments in human capital through education, health, and personal security require either public programs to assure their equitable allocation or a general equality of income.

In an increasingly interdependent and global economy where productivity depends on coordinating multiple resources and workers, people have to trust others whom they can neither see nor effectively hold accountable after the fact. A common industrial-era solution has been to seek ever more facts about products and people—more tests, reports, standards, managers, and laws to punish those who provide misleading data. Teachers may find that computerized scheduling and attendance reports provide them with more information sooner but also with more demands to file reports, leaving less time to talk with students about what is important to them. In that sense, larger databases may communicate less about what matters to effective instruction.

## Asymmetrical Knowledge

All communication is asymmetrical: Not only do people know different things, but their understandings about what others mean differ even when attempting open and honest discussion. When most knowledge needed for everyday production and consumption is tangible and grounded in common experiences, people establish trust through ongoing observations and ordinary conversations. Multiple interactions reward those who keep their word, but information is power and tempts its holders to use it for selfish gains. Hierarchies of status and power systematically bias access to information and provide reasons for parties to mislead each other. Long-term investment in physical and human capital multiplies the importance of abstract analyses about distant consequences and thus the accuracy of data and the adequacy of analysis.

Labor markets shaped by asymmetrical information exaggerate the importance of academic credentials. Applicants or candidates for advancement put their best foot forward in light of what they view as desired qualifications. Employers rely on proxies such as degrees and references to determine who can do the job. College degrees are easier to verify than job-related competencies. A similar pattern prevails on the job. An educated agent is hired to do something that the employer does not know how to do—for example, program a computer. Other proxies, such as rapport with staff, measure job performance. To protect their position, employees may conceal their problems or strategies for efficient output from their supervisors.

If information and bargaining were costless, corporate functions of coordination, planning, and risk reduction could be carried out through market transactions, including an active market in future contracts. In fact, negotiations are time consuming and uncertain—especially when land, building, equipment, supplies, and labor serve specialized functions. When Fisher made car bodies for General Motors, for instance, both sides would lose in any disruption of their relationship. Hence, price and quality were negotiated within a range set by the short-run cost of developing alternative suppliers. Two-party agreements such as union contracts depend on the bargainers' skills and how each interprets the other side's signals. An indeterminacy of salary applies particularly to knowledge workers but also to all others who are not paid for piecework rates.

A dream of open facts about others for purposes of social control has extended from Jeremy Bentham's panopticon prison to modern databases. According to Poster (1990, p. 91), "in capitalist society, regulation takes the form of discourses/practices that produce and reproduce the norm. The school, the asylum, the factory, the barracks to greater or lesser degrees and with considerable variation all imitate the Panopticon." Software programs that handle many routine tasks also enable electronic monitoring. Students who perform homework on video display terminals may discover that a record of their time on task and responses is available to administrators. Today, surveillance scarcely requires presence of an overseer because people voluntarily provide information about age, sex, health, purchases, debts, income, and political affiliation. Meanwhile, computers record their work, purchases, messages, and possible correlations.

Moreover, Poster (1990, pp. 95, 97) contended "that the database imposes a new language on top of those already existing and that it is an impoverished, limited language, one that uses the norm to constitute individuals and define deviants." The categories are fixed, often numerical and impersonal. Interconnected electronic files become "a means of controlling masses in the postmodern, postindustrial mode of information." As a result, current efforts to apply informational technologies to acquire and process more data about more activities may degrade the value of knowledge. Rather than communicating directly and openly, people present themselves in ways designed to mislead or to manipulate others. Sometimes extensive data or multiple messages overwhelm an observer's capacity to determine their significance.

Labor markets are mediated by socially constructed views about a fair wage and a fair day's work because no one knows what a worker will be able to contribute over a day or a career (Solow, 1990). Moreover, continual recontracting is peculiarly onerous, taking into account every headache and downturn or uptick in demand. Everyday knowledge about cooperation comes from working with colleagues, sharing ideas and responses, constructing group meanings and gaining confidence in them. We consider two responses for establishing control when specialized skills and knowledge are divided hierarchically: new uses of information or markets to resolve accountability issues between principals and agents and explicit standards for professionals.

## Principals and Agents

Commonly, organizations contract for an employee's time and attempt to specify appropriate responsibilities and tasks to maintain a sequential flow of goods. Parallel to that flow of goods and activities is a bureaucratic system that handles information. In capital-intensive firms with many workers, no clearly measurable product can be attributed to a specific machine or employee. Moreover, specialized products that suit a single buyer result in bilateral negotiations for price and quality: Consequently, buyers with contracts detailing performance expectations and salaried workers participate in periodic performance reviews. New ideas and techniques generate calls for ever more information.

Specialization creates issues of asymmetrical knowledge and control because the parties have different information and goals. Those issues grow as work depends more on knowledge and less on visible physical effort and outputs. Donahue (1989, p. 38) summarized the core issue involved in hiring a worker in public or private organizations: "A *principal* commissions an *agent* to act on the principal's behalf. In general, the agent's interests do not entirely coincide with those of the principal; and the principal does not have complete control over the agent; the agent has only partial information about the principal's interests; and the principal has only partial information about the agent's behavior." Moreover, industrial-era hierarchies with overt conflicts between workers and management left a residue of distrust and uncooperative habits that was revived by widespread layoffs in the 1980s and 1990s.

Complex choices in a modern economy make organizational stability attractive—especially an assurance of long-term employment. As Donahue (1989, pp. 43, 44) noted, "in all but the simplest undertakings, participants will not know at the outset just what will be needed at each stage along the way. New information—about the task at hand or the goals to be pursued—may make the original contracts obsolete." Renegotiation, as is common for new weapons systems, is costly to everyone. Long-term employment offers a remedy, enabling managers to "amend the agent's mandate in line with shifting priorities and opportunities." Open-ended contracts diminish interest in misleading about quantity or quality of output: "A more structured relationship may permit better monitoring, and ease communication between the principal and the agent."

On the other hand, agent-principal relations generate many problems. Friendships may diminish efficiency and profits. Rigid protocols prevent employees from using their knowledge or responding to anomalies. People in organizations, whatever their relationship, have reason to mislead each other. Agents may exaggerate their capacities and achievements. Principals seek to elicit desired behaviors with minimal payment and supervision. By emphasizing partial truths, each seeks to influence the other's response. For example, students try to minimize homework assignments and to maximize grades by tales of midnight "booking," while teachers tell students that learning to spell, completing a paper, and scoring well on tests will lead to future happiness.

Managers continually struggle to hold workers accountable for designated responsibilities and tasks: "The relative appeal of *employing* people, as opposed to *contracting with* them, increases (1) the more the task at hand is uncertain at the outset and prone to revision, (2) the harder it is to measure the value of the production, (3) the more disruptive it is to switch agents in midstream, and (4) the more the principal knows about the best means to accomplish his task" (Donahue, 1989, p. 45). A shift to customized goods and services that depends on highly knowledgeable workers who can elicit needs from would-be buyers and capacities from technicians and production people marks a move from physical to mental capital, an increasing dependence on symbolic communication (with opportunities to mislead), and a reliance on more trust and less oversight. Information is often intangible, and judgment follows no set procedures.

By understanding the basis for seniority and tenure rights as sharing a stake in the school, teachers may gain insight into organizational practices in most firms. With an implicit lifetime contract, teachers and other workers have a shared interest in the long-run success of their school or firm. Freed from worrying about losing their job, experienced staff have a reason to show novices how to perform more effectively. Professional development and mentoring make sense in that context. Furthermore, employees reasonably devote time and thought to governance and planning in order to adjust to new or altered circumstances. Although tenure has particular applicability to protecting academic freedom for teachers, it makes sense in any organization that pays salaries to an ongoing staff because it builds trustworthy communication.

## Professionalism

Professionalization is a traditional way to impose responsibilities on information workers who are neither easily supervised nor employed solely by one organization. In the 19th century, knowledge workers sought to promote autonomous careers by asserting special authority and status. Arguing that laypersons could scarcely assess their qualifications or the quality of their work, they claimed a morally superior position based on their credentials—usually academic training—and a collegial enforcement of high standards. They sought state laws covering licenses to practice law, to teach, to cut hair, or to design highways. Potential clients had to trust experts about what risks and knowledge applied to their particular situation. As sociologist Andrew Abbott (1988, p. 318) concluded, professionals created careers for "somewhat exclusive groups of individuals applying somewhat abstract knowledge to particular cases."

Academic knowledge grew in importance in part because learning on the job was long and risky. Drivers counted on competent highway engineers; people with a toothache sought well-trained dentists. Expertise was embodied in individuals and signaled by academic degrees or special licenses, although the boundaries around disciplines were threatened continually. For years, medical doctors enjoyed community respect; as health costs rose, their area of expertise was eroded by nurse practitioners, physical therapists, radiologists, chiropractors, and others. Neither engineers nor teachers ever successfully limited access through rigorous training or special examinations for their professions.

Although teachers advocate for professional status, they are blocked on a number of fronts. Professional standards become less useful when many adults share responsibility and knowledge to perform a particular service or role, such as child development. Millions of certified teachers are not employed in schools. When shortages develop, states usually lower requirements rather than letting salaries rise. Abstract pedagogical techniques have to be adapted to suit time, place, and personalities of learners. Teachers want to earn a decent salary and community respect for their crucial role in preparing youth for work and citizenship; but pay scales scarcely sustain pretensions to upper-middle-class lifestyles. Nor is there much prestige from associating with children. Most importantly, teachers are subordinated to bureaucracies that direct their activities.

Today, professional status generally is threatened by embodying expertise in commodities or organizational structures. Low-paid workers with smart software keep financial records, design blueprints, write wills, or check medical symptoms in an expert diagnostic system: "Multiprofessional firms in accounting, information, and architecture, the team concept in medicine and social services, elaborate professional bureaucracies in engineering and law, all encode professional knowledge in the structures of organization themselves. Much current expertise resides in the rules of these and other organizations of professionals, most of which are either overtly heteronomous or governed by professionals more or less openly identified as professional administrators" (Abbott, 1988, p. 325). Constrained by bureaucratic procedures and group cultures, many knowledge workers become replaceable parts in organizational systems.

Hierarchies block the flow of information from frontline workers and consumers to managers. Specialization alienates workers from a sense of achievement, creativity and responsibility; it erodes "commitment to others, trust, identification with the organization, cooperation, and a sense of common organizational objectives" (Liebenstein, 1987, p. 150). Capitalism fosters inequalities of wealth that exceed human grasp—the wealthiest persons make more per hour than the average per capita income in the United States. Huge corporations diminish a sense of human scale or control. Mass media bolster conformity and apathy. Bureaucratic procedures are impersonal and dehumanizing, although preferable to personal favoritism, bribery or arbitrary acts.

Distinctions between managers and workers, technicians and mechanics, or men and women as well as across skills and disciplines interfere with the open dialog and trust needed to build larger understandings that encompass specialized knowledge within group contexts. These issues of asymmetrical information never can be fully resolved, as a constructivist would guess. Yet coordination among specialists is possible through a kind of holographic image of the organization. Each worker holds a general sense of organizational functions and goals with a detailed knowledge about one's specific responsibilities. The function is seen at the group level, and one's participation is cooperatively and collectively developed in terms of the team's output.

## POSTINDUSTRIAL STRUCTURES

The sharply reduced costs of information in today's world make it possible to work together in organizations that are less hierarchical—more flexible and responsive to workers, consumers and clients. Knowledge workers contribute their best thinking in open structures. Layers of bureaucratic reports and permissions impede reactions to emerging markets or technologies. A focus on one or two well-established rules of thumb for setting policies, such as market share or a projected profit of 25%, may distract attention from new problems or opportunities. Ignoring connections to public policies for health, environmental protection and community development causes firms to cling to outmoded products and practices, for example, tobacco in the 1990s.

Longstanding assumptions about roles and job security were shaken in the 1970s despite a continuity of firms and brand names. Chandler

(1990, pp. 621, 623–627) noted that, "intensified inter-nation and inter-industry competition began to reshape the strategies of growth, the internal organization of managerial enterprises, and the relationships between individual firms and between owners and managers." Diversification "often led to a separation, that is, a breakdown of communications," between top executives and those managers responsible for operations. Executives focused on quarterly returns, reducing diversification, or seeking to decentralize "the planning, control, and resource-allocation functions of the corporate office." These changes interfered with a crucial function of industrial organizations—"constant reinvestment in order to maintain and improve product-specific facilities and to maintain and develop product-specific technical and managerial skills."

Different organizational strategies and structures will evolve to serve a knowledge society. Firms, public agencies, nonprofit associations, and schools face an evolving context of choices based on information about technological feasibility, professional knowledge, and mutual equivalence structures (see Table 5.1 for key differences for coordinating activities).

Innovative firms have adopted new organizational structures to foster a strategy of rapid changes based on customer needs and knowledge held by frontline workers. We present three illustrations—teamwork in a manufacturing plant, a family-owned business that stresses values and fair treatment of employees, and a research firm that encourages internal entrepreneurship. Although older tensions remain, each organization flattened structures and encouraged agreements that better aligned personal interests with the company's growth. Each experienced a period of marked success associated with these changes.

## Manufacturing in Teams

In the mid-1980s, American Saw & Mfg. Company in East Longmeadow, Massachusetts, a leading manufacturer of saw blades and hand tools for an international market, reorganized its production and sales procedures to create a team-oriented workplace. One middle manager explained, "in years past, we hired people for their hands, their backs, their muscles" (Goldberg, 1991, p. 4). Shared decisionmaking creates "a 700-headed brain, because truly none of us is as smart as all of us." Internal cooperation is seen as a way to meet external competition. Teams also deal with pressing concerns—telephone time, carbide processing, scrap reduction, paper recycling, childcare, coil stock, and employee recognition.

Self-managed teams oversee manufacturing and assembly, as computers greatly reduce production time. Workers solve problems on the assembly line; foremen act as coaches or collectors of ideas rather than as managers of people and processes. Utilizing group

**TABLE 5.1**
**Industrial and Information Organizations**

|  | Industrial Age | Information Age |
|---|---|---|
| Modes of production | Mass production for non-local markets. Specialization of labor and capital in rationalized structures with increasing returns to scale—based on low-cost energy, shipping and communication. | Diversified and specialized output for nonlocal markets utilizing automated techniques and flexible organizations. Information needed for technical, electronic and design refinements. |
| Typical products | Output included machines for farm and factory, semidurable brand-name consumer goods, or personal services. | Diverse products and services incorporate scientific and technological designs. Automation for continuous processes. |
| Managers' roles | Oversight to supervise production, set sequential processes, and coordinate with marketing, research and development, and accounting. | Foster culture of professional autonomy with shared values and goals. Group processes to coordinate and plan. |
| Structures | Multitiered hierarchy of functional units with information controlled through bureaucratic channels. | Shallow, flexible subunits. Accessible information shared "holographically." |
| Accountability | Standardization of parts and processes, visual oversight by supervisors, control through accounting systems, and top-down orders. | Common values link diverse goals and uses. Quality and technical values depend on pride in work and close connections with users. |
| Images of organization | Table of organization shows subordinate and coordinate relationships of functional parts. Unwieldy bureaucracies. | Flexible, shifting roles and relationships tied together by a shared culture. Loosely coupled internal structures. |

problem-solving techniques, employees aim to ship hand tools within 24 hours and saw blades within 48 hours. Orders arrive by telephone or fax, products are boxed by machine, and some are out the door in less than an hour. Viewing one another as internal customers and suppliers displaced a traditional pattern where workers took for granted the roles and responsibilities of coworkers.

American Saw's reorganization rested on a set of corporate princi-ples. The purpose of the business is to "manufacture and distribute consumable products and related services for materials separation that provide exceptional value" (American Saw & Mfg. Company, 1990). The company defined its mission to:

- Achieve a global market base of satisfied repeat customers by selling quality products and services that provide exceptional value.
- Maximize profits for the long-term benefit of end users, distrib-utors, employees, suppliers and shareholders. Improve competi-tiveness, minimize costs and increase sales through a continuous improvement process.
- Provide a trusting and participative environment.
- Create the opportunity for each individual to develop his or her full potential.

American Saw's "Corporate Principles" reflected its effort to build trust within and outside the firm by emphasizing such values as "satisfy the customer," "communicate effectively," "make it simple," "do what is right," and "people make the company."

Today, many manufacturers allocate more time to information—research and development, advertising and sales, accounting and man-agement—than to producing and distributing tangible things. An educated labor force works together to redesign materials for manu-facturability and quality. Employees "are asked to use judgment and make decisions, management layers disappear as front-line workers assume responsibility for many of the tasks—from quality control to production scheduling—that others used to do" (Commission on the Skills of the American Workforce, 1990, p. 2). Future workers will understand customers' needs, retool and retrain quickly, and resolve complex problems rather than acting to control machinery in sequential output.

An MIT Commission on Industrial Productivity found that success-ful firms transform workers' roles from "passive performance of narrow, repetitive tasks to one of active collaboration in the organization and fine-tuning of production" (Dertouzos, Lester, & Solow, 1989, pp. 137, 131). Competencies are continually refined on the job: "Restructuring job categories, flattening hierarchies, broadening responsibilities, and taking on new tasks in regular job rotations—all of these produce a work force capable of responding rapidly and creatively to new problems." Eventually, "the convergence of market forces, consumer preferences, and technological opportunities suggests the possibility of 'totally flexible' production systems, in which the craft-era tradition of custom-tailoring of products to the needs and tastes of individual customers will be combined with the power, precision, and economy of modern production technology."

## Humane Organizations

Channing L. Bete Company (CLB), located in South Deerfield, Massachusetts, is an educational publisher selling concise, easy-to-read information materials to other businesses, public agencies, and volunteer groups. Since its founding in 1954, the company has sold over half a billion booklets, more than 66 million in 1990 alone. CLB booklets in "scriptography" combined text and graphics to convey key ideas about health, business, government, religion, education and community services in a few pages. "Magnetic Resonance Imaging," "Money Management," "Protecting the Earth," and "Stop the Pain of Child Abuse" were some of the 1,500 titles available. CLB defined its mission as one of "people helping people communicate" in order to "make this a better world" (personal visit).

To foster information sharing and reduce resistance to ongoing reassignments of tasks and responsibilities, CLB created a flexible and humane environment for over 200 researchers, writers, artists, marketing and sales personnel, and production workers. At the center of the company's operations is its main facility—two interconnected, open-space buildings that were designed with input from employees. There are many windows, carpets, movable partitions, and large and small meeting rooms. A restaurant serving low-cost meals features a fountain, trees and other plantings behind a three-story glass wall overlooking open fields. Employees set flexible schedules, redesign modular workstations, provide regular input into products and procedures, and take pride in CLB's rapid growth.

Channing Bete starts making the world a better place in its own plant. Printing and paper handling take advantage of rapidly improving technologies. The company encourages everyone to continue their education. It buys recycled paper despite its higher cost. The building is smoke-free and features both indoor and outdoor exercise facilities. For many years, CLB covered the costs of medical care, including eye, dentistry, and annual physical checkups. Currently, a shared-cost plan includes incentives for employees to reach healthy levels of weight and cholesterol. No year goes by without significant reorganization in some aspect of the firm, and the sense of a clean, pleasant and open environment helps workers cope with the predictable anxieties of innovation.

Many companies now stress the importance of a humane environment; amenities for workers foster stability, trust and organizational loyalties. An employee-centered company culture promotes a sense of engagement with their jobs without intrusive supervision and control. In 1992, General Electric's boss, John Welch, Jr., known in the 1980s as Neutron Jack for his ruthless elimination of divisions and staff, changed his tune (Holusha, 1992). After asking "what we are and what we want to be," he sought to encourage a manager who performs as expected and "shares the values of our company." He called for "trust and respect" rather than "management styles that repress and intimidate." As Welch insisted, "we know that without leaders who 'walk the talk,' all of our plans, promises and dreams for the future are just that—talk."

## Organizing Information

Research firms such as Science Applications International Corporation (SAIC) adopted new structures to organize knowledge production (adapted from Jones & Maloy, 1993). Founded in 1969 by experts in nuclear weapons' effects, SAIC has expanded and diversified its consulting services to include software and communication systems. In 1988 its revenues reached $693 million, and the firm projects growth to $5 billion by 2009. In essence, SAIC sells a promise to develop information for government agencies or firms based on the best estimate of cost by highly specialized experts. Within SAIC, experts in submarine surveillance through fiberoptic sensors may know little about coworkers assessing hazardous wastes in the oceans; and upper level executives can seldom direct or supervise engineers and computer programmers investigating ill-structured problems.

Managerial hierarchies for planning, coordinating and accountability functions make little sense in this context. After a decade of growth, Science Applications International Corporation (1984) defined itself: "SAIC is a company for professional people who want to perform superior scientific and technical work, who are willing to work hard to do it, who want to have a say in the policies and management of the company . . . , who want to be exposed to a minimal number of distracting outside influences and pressures, and who want to be fairly rewarded for doing good work." The firm operationalized that mission in 12 guiding "Principles and Practices of SAIC." First, autonomy for workers "Responsible individuals in the company use this freedom to conduct their business with a straightforward, generally decentralized, approach to matters." Second, at SAIC the "quality of our technical efforts must always come first." Third, corporate growth "provides opportunities for individuals to expand their technical areas of interest and to advance in management responsibility." Fourth, profits make the firm "an attractive investment to its employees."

Fifth, SAIC's belief system rests on employee ownership in proportion to their "contribution and performance." The next three principles promise sound investments and rising productivity to safeguard stock values by supporting technological innovations and "minimizing layers of management and decision making in order to focus on responding to its customers." Ninth, SAIC offers "three parallel career paths," technical, management/administrative, and marketing, in recognition that "internal competition has always been a complex matter in SAIC, as it is in most companies in which aggressive, entrepreneurial people abound." Cooperation and teamwork are reiterated messages in company communications. SAIC combines employees into groups organized around themes such as defense technology or energy each with "autonomy at the operating level," including major responsibility for marketing. Group-level planning makes sense only when overall objectives are "known, understood and accepted throughout the company."

Employees determine SAIC's business less through ownership than their ability to market their track record of usable research. By cooperating informally, they avoid bureaucratic structures and rigid procedures. By operating as a series of "nested" profit centers ranging from an individual project manager to the group, SAIC helps with start-up costs or arranges for new outlets while rewarding achievement. Workers know about the company's goals and culture. They carry out its technical, marketing and management functions in a structure that encourages cooperation, flexibility and innovation. SAIC regards its challenge as sustaining profits through growth while staying true to the "kind of company we want to be."

Many knowledge-based organizations are trying out new structures to encourage cooperation along the lines envisioned by Zuboff (1988, p. 394):

The traditional system of imperative control, which was designed to maximize the relationship between commands and obedience, depended upon restricted hierarchical access to knowledge and nurtured the belief that those who were excluded from the organization's explicit knowledge base were intrinsically less capable of learning what it had to offer. In contrast, an informated organization is structured to promote the possibility of useful learning among all members and thus presupposes relations of equality.

In future workplaces, group projects bring together workers' interests, and the organization functions as a "learning community."

The critical organizational challenge lies exactly in taking structures designed to reproduce activities in long-term, yet difficult-to-specify relationships for mass production and transforming them into flexible, innovative, and people-centered organizations. American Saw, CLB, and SAIC suggest different ways to coordinate and plan in an age of information and international markets. Not all workers adjust well to teamwork, a humane environment, or an entrepreneurial climate; but over time personalities and cultures accommodate. Then, open communication and consensus help coordinate rapidly changing flows of technical products and services.

What does all this have to do with schools? At the beginning of the 20th century, educators consciously borrowed management techniques from business, which became institutionalized. Now, innovative firms are replacing hierarchical control structures with teams, humane environments, and worker ownership. Immediately, that shift indicates that the still-widespread practice of schools training students for docility is inappropriate preparation for participation in many firms. Schools cannot simply imitate innovative firms, though various features may be incorporated to unblock communications and innovations. There are also good models among the many effective schools and universities that have built a cultural context incorporating the multiple goals of learning for an uncertain future.

## MEETING MULTIPLE GOALS

In conceptualizing purposeful organizations for an information age, educators should start by recognizing that they have multiple goals. Instead of rationalized structures, they must deal with images and vocabularies that describe group interactions within a culture of participation and dialog. Organizational images of rationally arranged sequential steps to maximize a desirable purpose probably never characterized industrial firms, and they certainly seem inappropriate for all but the narrowest tasks within a school. Typically, coordination starts from personal negotiations about how to work together, and informal agreements and friendships continue to ease organizational interactions. Those informal relationships, however, are seldom seen as a part of the formal structure.

As public organizations, schools have multiple, often-conflicting goals. Taxpayers want to lower costs, while teachers always need more and better resources to individualize instruction and motivate students. Parents want the best for their children but often define that as a high rank in grades, so only a few can be satisfied. Democratic citizenship implies a commitment to equality, participation, fairness, and time-consuming dialog; employers apparently want schools to train in specific skills of spelling, writing, numeracy, and attention to time frames and deadlines. Students may learn as much from peers as from texts, and teachers are undecided about whether to insist on orderly classrooms or to engage students in active learning. These and many more adjustments occur daily and are mainly affected by the overall culture or climate of the school.

### Rational versus Nonrational Organizations

A commonsense view that organizations are powerful assumes they have some leeway to act willfully or, perhaps more commonly, to fail to respond quickly to new conditions. Not every managerial blunder or inefficiency causes a firm's demise. Moreover, giant corporations with dispersed ownership and internal savings have considerable power over suppliers, workers and customers. In the 1990s, firms big enough to compete internationally can escape from national regulations of monopoly, occupational safety, or environmental impacts. Yet economists normally describe firms as rationalized structures for efficient output. Although managers appear to have discretionary power, in economic theory they act like a well-programmed computer continuously calculating cost curves and technological frontiers. Their decisions are thus presented as reasoned assessments of what is best for the group.

If that were the whole story, organizations would be of little concern. Their behaviors would be effectively determined by their goals and the best strategies given technological possibilities, relative prices, and consumer or client preferences. Routine skills could be easily assessed; other differences in wages would reflect economic rent attributable to scarce talents or innovations. Indeed, if information were truly costless, organizational command structures would be redundant because workers could combine through market bargaining to perform the specialized roles involved in complex productive processes. In the real world, however, wages may as much determine a laborer's marginal contribution as be determined by that additional output.

In complex environments, information is costly and ambiguous. Few decisions are determined by clear goals, known production functions, or painless transitions. According to James March (1988, pp. 255, 414), organizational theory usually presumes "that thinking should precede action; that action should serve a purpose; that purpose should be defined in terms of a consistent set of pre-existent goals; and that choice should be based on a consistent theory of the relation between action and its consequences." Detailed examinations of decisionmaking reveal that "most organizations and individuals often collect more information than they use or can reasonably expect to use in the making of decisions." Yet they seek ever more data in order to legitimize decisions and plans.

After noting how ambiguities interfere with a manager's ability to maximize any goal, theorists such as Simon and March "characterize organizations as garbage cans into which are dumped problems, people, choice situations, and solutions" (Weick, 1979, p. 21). Seeking to sustain their role and the firm or agency, leaders engage workers in elaborate decisionmaking rituals to justify action or inaction. Viewed as a garbage can, an organization entails "a continual stream of people, solutions, choices, and problems." Issues and answers collide and realign themselves rather randomly. Quick action often fails to resolve a problem, while delay allows a different solution to coalesce. Computer models simulate organizations that tackle certain problems, ignore others, and often seek survival rather than maximization of output or profit.

Most educators acknowledge that multiple realities, changing goals, and persistent ambiguity characterize teaching and learning. Although sometimes adopting bureaucratic controls and rationalizing procedures, most teachers see their role as personable, interactive, and based on professional judgments. Effective schools depend on a culture or attitudinal climate, rather than resources or techniques. They result in nonrational (not irrational) organizations (Table 5.2).

**TABLE 5.2**
**Rational and Nonrational Goals**

| Rational Goals | Nonrational Goals |
|---|---|
| There is a single set of uniform goals that provides consistent direction for us. | There are multiple, sometimes competing sets of goals that attempt to provide direction for us. |
| The district goals are clearly stated and specific. | The district goals are somewhat ambiguous and general in nature. |
| The goals remain stable over a sustained period of time. | The goals change as conditions change. |
| Organizational goals are set via a logical, problem-solving process. | Organizational goals are arrived at through bargaining and compromise. |
| The goals for the district are determined by the leaders of the organization. | The goals for the district are set by many different forces, both in and out of the organization. |

Source: Patterson, J. L., Purkey, S. C., & Parker, J. V. (1986). *Productive School Systems for a Nonrational World*, pp. 40–41. Alexandria, VA: Association for Supervision and Curriculum Development.

There are good reasons for working with others by following routines in established roles—and good reasons for resisting those limitations on personal autonomy. Groups can undertake enterprises beyond any one person's capacity or understanding. At the same time, they generate resentment by constraining individual autonomy and judgment. An emphasis on rational structures, however, leads most leaders to perceive their role as imposing discipline on somewhat recalcitrant subordinates. Recognizing nonrational aspects is a first step toward building a vision of how people construct meanings for their interactions. It points toward ways that cooperation reduces uncertainties by pooling risks to insure against random ill fortune.

## Lessons from Effective Schools

"Why not run a business like a good university?" asked Robert L. Woodbury, former chancellor of the University of Maine system. Educational organizations have long incorporated practices now urged on the private sector:

Decisionmaking is highly decentralized. The fundamental work of teaching and learning is controlled by the faculty member, the "front-line" worker. Management's job is to provide the tools, encouragement, and security for faculty to use their creativity and imagination. The enterprise is daily in touch with the consumer. Opportunities for professional renewal, growth, and continuing education are well developed. Universities are structured in a mode of "shared governance," a relatively flat bureaucracy, and open information across the entire enterprise. Finally, universities and colleges seek long-term results. (Adapted from Woodbury, 1993)

Effective schools foster organizational climates that limit the destructive impact of "free riders" and "prisoner's dilemmas." Staff and students work together toward goals that are arrived at through dialog and a public discourse that includes parents. Educators discuss their professional and bureaucratic dilemmas: their isolation, fears of failure, and personal coping strategies. They work together toward a vision of what education in a democracy should achieve. Members of the school collectively implement responsibilities, make decisions, welcome innovations, and adapt them to their purposes. Broad participation sustains "a style of work that is open, task oriented, and nonaccusatory" (Payne, 1984, p. 171). Effective schools stand for something—equality, academic excellence, community development, or whatever—and staff loyalties sustain positive efforts. They demonstrate that principal-agent controls and professional associations are only a part of the story of coordinating learning and teaching.

All effective schools are marked by five characteristics that demonstrate the importance of multiple goals to achieve cooperation (Edmonds, 1982):

- positive leadership,
- consensus on goals and objectives,
- high expectations for all students,
- an orderly environment, and
- continual monitoring of students' learning.

Effective schools are important precisely because they adjust their curriculum and maintain high expectations without regard to family status. In overcoming the effects of class, race and gender biases, teachers are motivated by a belief that all children can learn. Most schools that are regarded as successful, however, serve upper-middle-income communities whose graduates advance to higher education. Though seeking to credential merit, educators more often succeed in replicating family status, an outcome now taken for granted by many parents and teachers.

Puzzled by that association of academic failure with low-income families and students of color, educational researcher Ronald Edmonds examined those schools where student achievement contradicted Coleman's (1966) conclusion that academic rank correlated with family income and status more than with variations among school resources. After identifying many cases in all kinds of communities, Edmonds (1982) and his colleagues looked at what made them different. Neither money and programs nor advanced degrees for teachers necessarily built a positive school climate and staff ethos, but working together to build a positive climate of achievement and high expectations did.

---

**Often efforts to assure accountability for learning and standardized procedures for treating students generate resentment, alienation and misinformation that contradict the fundamental goal of schooling.**

**Identify ways that a college or other familiar knowledge organization seeks to coordinate people and activities over space and time. Which behaviors illustrate a reliance on trust and cooperation? Which rely on surveillance and control?**

---

Prototypical knowledge organizations, such as effective schools, overcome the limitations of bureaucratic rules and procedures to serve multiple constituencies and goals. Public and private managers share "common preoccupations—with goals, people, organization resources, and constituencies" (Lynn, 1981, pp. 124, 136). Leaders in government and business "spend much of their time meeting with people with whom they must compromise to achieve their goals; they must choose a leadership style that motivates rather than inhibits subordinates; they must deal with substantive and organizational complexities." Nevertheless, many public managers succeed in serving both equity and efficiency. They create a shared climate of information and positive expectations that enables all participants—both paid staff and those being served—to work together toward some larger community ends.

If pedagogical techniques assured success in transferring knowledge into the minds of others, then a top-down command structure might enable schools to adapt quickly to new demands. As Weick (1985, p. 121) observed, however, education is a loosely coupled system:

For actors and observers alike, the prediction and activation of cause-effect relations is made more difficult because relations are intermittent, lagged, dampened, slow, abrupt, and mediated.

Actors in a loosely coupled system rely on trust and presumptions, are often isolated, find social comparison difficult, have no one to borrow from, seldom imitate, suffer pluralistic ignorance, maintain discretion, improvise, and have less hubris because they know the universe is not sufficiently connected to make widespread change possible.

The upshot of the story is that schools, like other organizations, cannot be rationalized to achieve a single goal with efficiency. For instance, many schools find that when they focus on reading, math suffers; mapping skills improve, but spatial relationships test poorly. Yet their management is not irrational. Through their interactions, participants in schools construct a culture that shapes their understanding of learning, teaching and achievement. By encouraging positive dialog and experiences, many schools help the young develop into productive citizens. In turn, that record of engagement, participation and accomplishments builds a sense of empowerment for individuals and for organizations.

In our interviews, educators were attracted to teacher empowerment and site-based management, but few teachers described a "self-authoring" role in their school. Most adults consider organizations as similar to other actors—with a history and a point of view—in order to establish functional relationships. In Chapter 3, we described schools in terms of their size, staff and function marked by certain characteristics—age-segregated and rank-ordered students controlled by underresourced and bureaucratically structured adults. We ignored how schools "regulate" behaviors so that people who differ in philosophy, political views, interests, and thoughtfulness end up seeming so remarkably similar in that setting. That analysis entails a capacity to hold in mind both an organizational and an educator's perspective and to see how their cultural patterns interact with each other. From a postmodern perspective, however, organizations are "relationship-regulating forms" (Kegan, 1994, p. 315).

## Limits on Organizational Power

Today, loosely linked, somewhat independent institutions maintain stability and continuity for most people because no one controls all aspects of their own life. At the same time, purposive organizations are counted on to adjust to new conditions. Productive groups are large enough to gain from specialization and yet coherent enough for internal communication and decisionmaking. They capture economies of scale by coordinating labor and machinery, yet remain manageable in pursuit of limited goals. Varied roles in functional organizations both extend and limit workers' autonomy. Often, their scope and scale overwhelm individual choices, yet even powerful governments and corporations may lack power to assert their will in a global economy.

Effective schools and innovative firms such as American Saw, CLB, and SAIC are still rare. The challenge becomes how to include multiple organizations in a democratic discourse. Most public schools, hierarchical workplaces, and bureaucratic agencies discourage individual judgments and have no place for stakeholders to participate in decisionmaking. Students and teachers engage in barely covert hostilities so that even friendly gestures seem just another control device; a similar pattern prevails between workers and managers in many firms. Their climate is impersonal and alienating. In essence, they treat everyone as though they were unruly children who lack knowledge about what needs to be done and a willingness to contribute their fair share.

Imbued with a characteristic distrust of government, many Americans regard schools as hopelessly inefficient because they are public agencies. Yet profit-seeking firms operate with bureaucracies and live under multiple public mandates such as collecting taxes, protecting the environment, and selling only safe products. Public managers in many agencies as well as effective schools demonstrate great skills in motivating and coordinating their staff to serve public goals. Although managers of government agencies focus more on public perceptions of their success or failures and private executives more on profits, both face complex uncertainties with only a limited capacity to change the organization.

A growing mismatch between schools and what youth and employers want feeds a distrust of educational organizations. That distrust generates conflicting demands that are impossible for anyone to meet. Students and most organizations prepare for cutthroat competition, even while recognizing that cooperation would be a better solution. The logic of the fallacy of composition and the prisoner's dilemma for individuals applies to organizations and institutions in the whole society. For example, a principal working with teachers and parents might generate positive publicity for one school, but high test scores, articles in the newspaper, and awards for innovation and excellence mean that other schools suffer by comparison.

A noted educational researcher, David Berliner (1992) responded to a steady drumbeat of charges against American schools that demanded longer school days, more tests, and tougher standards. He analyzed common indictments of low achievement, falling scores, and unfavorable international comparisons. Point by point, Berliner showed that, on the whole, U.S. students perform better than in the past by most measures of achievement. Reported scores are lower because norms have been raised or because more students from lower ranks of classes take tests for college admission. Other data show that the United States spends less on elementary and secondary students than most industrial nations and that American students who had taken algebra performed as well as their Japanese counterparts.

That positive news in no way contradicts ample evidence for sharp inequities in American education. Oddly, evidence exists that Department of Education officials as well as many political leaders have exaggerated negative views raising a suspicion that they do not want to acknowledge or deal with those inequalities:

Perhaps Americans have been lied to, because when nations have economic difficulties or go through social change, their leaders look for scapegoats, and the American school system is a handy one. Perhaps we are changing into a plutocracy, where a wealthy elite chooses not to use the public schools, and participates in undermining confidence in that system so as to promote the conception of schooling as a commodity, to be bought like medicine, to be regarded as a privilege rather than a right of every American. (Berliner, 1992, p. 6)

Herein lies a contemporary political dilemma. Organizations are created and sustained as elements of social governance—they structure choices and regularities within which individuals can plan their lives. Current arrangements evolved in response to industrial-era production possibilities, and generally they complemented each other. Less autonomy at paid work was compensated for by more leisure and consumption choices. Democratic governments supported schools and a social welfare system that protected workers from the vagaries of competitive markets. As information technologies make it plausible to coordinate a complex, interdependent economy through voluntary cooperation based on democratic decisionmaking, organizations find that hierarchical controls generate resentment and miscommunication. Those with positions of authority may then blame other associations and institutions for the failure to work together.

That reaction reinforces some internal cohesion, but it undermines trust among groups that need to collaborate to adjust to a changing world. Once legitimacy is questioned, then it takes a broad public endorsement sanctioned by governing bodies to reestablish implicit relationships among organizations and with individuals. In today's global economy, multinational corporations as well as environmental issues ignore boundaries separating governing units, but there is no worldwide political body capable of enforcing peace, establishing guidelines for competitive markets, or conserving the environment. Free emigration, for example, is a necessary condition for assuring democracy, yet existing inequalities of income among regions creates an almost unstoppable pressure of immigration into affluent areas. That situation triggers conflict between insiders and outsiders that feeds racist and xenophobic reactions.

Low-cost information opens possibilities for multiple understandings to facilitate cooperative interactions among fragmented groups in a postmodern world—as well as misunderstandings that serve the interests of currently privileged groups. In open organizations, everything does not have to be conceptualized in advance if their structures foster autonomy and cooperation among adults who continue to learn and who continually reenvision how to work together and toward what ends. Openness of information and communication patterns—all eased by new technologies—allow verification, break down divisions, and build confidence in the accuracy of communication. To take advantage of ready access to low-cost information exchanges that facilitate adaptation to changing conditions, democratic governments must sustain a sense of fairness for basic spheres of human activity.

## RELATED READING

There is a rich and growing literature on organization effectiveness. For current views, see Gareth Morgan, *Images of Organization* (Beverly Hills, CA: Sage Publications, 1986); Terrence E. Deal and Kent D. Peterson, *The Leadership Paradox: Balancing Logic and Artistry in Schools* (San Francisco: Jossey-Bass, 1994); Michael G. Fullan and Suzanne M. Stiegelbauer, *The New Meaning of Educational Change*, 2nd ed. (New York: Teachers College Press, 1991); and Peter M. Senge, *The Fifth Discipline: The Art and Practice of the Learning Organization* (New York: Doubleday/Currency, 1994). For school leadership through organizational cultures, see Linda T. Sheive and Marian B. Schoenheit, eds., *Leadership: Examining the Elusive* (Alexandria, VA: Association for Supervision and Curriculum Development, 1987).

# 6

# Social Choices and Public Policies

Most Americans regard public schools as a key institution for equalizing opportunities to learn and get ahead as a basis for democratic fairness. They sense a tension between education as socialization (preparing youth for work and citizenship in communities marked by class, race and gender biases) and as liberation (escaping from fixed occupational and social roles). Although most teachers profess democratic values, schools shortchange many students who are marked by their parents' low income, a language or dialect other than academic English, their perceived racial/ethnic origin, being female, or a district's low property values. Educational inequities are aggravated when higher education legitimates careers that confer a lifetime of economic advantages.

The curriculum is political because it influences "who gets what, when and how," in Harold Lasswell's (1958) memorable phrase. School boards, state legislatures, and Congress mandate what should be taught and to whom. In turn, academic attainment partly determines earnings and social status. In our interviews, many educators commented on a political dimension of sustaining community support. An administrator asserted that public demands kept growing for higher achievement levels: *"Yet I believe a great deal is rhetoric; in other words, they are not willing to put the resources behind what they are asking."* Nonmainstream topics such as Afrocentric philosophies, feminist perspectives, or teenage sexuality generate even less support from dominant groups in society.

Just as frontline educators seldom analyze organizational dilemmas, they lack frameworks for thinking about policy issues in a federalist democracy. Teachers are torn between covering state-mandated topics for standardized tests and an ideal of reaching "the whole child." They express ambivalence: *"When I entered education I felt that my obligation was to help students basically in the core areas, teach them to read, write, compute, be capable of listening accurately, etc. I also recognize today that we have to deal with values. We have to deal with the issues that society thrusts upon us—sexuality, nutrition, homelessness, the cultural diversity that we are facing."* Small wonder that teachers feel overburdened and leery about engaging in open dialog about controversial issues facing youth.

Schooling is simplistically depicted as a straightforward transmittal of facts and values to the young. Presumably, voters know what information and experiences children will need and how to transfer it at the lowest cost. That common narrative of collective decisionmaking as a rational-technological process shapes how students view democracy. As long as democratic procedures are viewed as a nonproblematic expression of the will of the majority, a split between a mission of preparing productive citizens and a perceived reality of reproducing class, race and gender categories will continue to mystify. It will frustrate a democratic discourse among students and teachers.

This chapter is guided by four propositions about how governments establish institutional contexts, or choice sets, for persons and organizations.

- First, liberal democratic theory usually depicts the state as a constitutional contract among citizens to provide collective services in return for limited restrictions on one's freedom.
- Second, effective laws gain broad public support because they sustain individual security, common justice, and community development.
- Third, as voters and taxpayers, citizens sensibly lump together local, state and national taxes, and they view public benefits as a whole involving private and governmental acts.
- Fourth, democratic governments sustain their legitimacy as well as basic rights and opportunities for citizens by maintaining an open dialog.

We first examine endemic flaws in democratic process and competitive markets that preclude easy solutions to social well-being. These dilemmas impose innumerable possible choices between equal rights and individual freedoms—with many people lacking the means to act on their rights. Next, we briefly consider why civic discourse pays little attention to issues of social justice. In particular, corporate power truncates social policy debates about income distribution through the government's management of the economy. Then, we use education to illustrate tradeoffs among equity, efficiency and choice. Finally, we argue that individual security to explore personal and social choices entails maintaining equality in critical spheres of activity.

## DILEMMAS OF INDUSTRIAL DEMOCRACY

Historically, democracies have flourished in relatively affluent nations with industrialized economies. Representative governments established a framework for capitalism (property rights and legal contracts), restrained behaviors with negative consequences to others (criminal law), and subsidized investments in human capital (notably education). They also provided public goods where it would be costly to exclude people from benefits—such as schools, highways, parks, a safe environment, and national defense. Over the past century, governments regulated businesses, professions, many products, and some markets in response to perceived abuses of power. Social Security and welfare programs insured individuals against common risks due to industrial fluctuations. During the past 150 years, economic growth allowed most regional and class conflicts to be compromised without upsetting the dominance of capitalists.

The Constitution charged the United States government to "form a more perfect Union, establish Justice, insure domestic Tranquillity, provide for the common defence, promote the general Welfare, and secure the Blessings of Liberty to ourselves and Posterity." Shared values among people who defined themselves by ideas derived from John Locke facilitated agreements. Government was a contract among individuals who held an inalienable right "to life, liberty, and the pursuit of happiness." Over two centuries, those ideals have expanded to ban slavery and to include voting rights for former slaves and finally women. Current debates about justice and liberty hinge on assuring adequate education and income for everyone to enjoy their rights and freedoms.

One of the major lessons of 20th-century social science has been an awareness that no recipe—neither voting procedures nor competitive markets— automatically leads to desirable personal or social outcomes. Constitutional democracies and market-driven capitalism substantially advanced equity and efficiency, but each has endemic flaws. Ideally, they work together in an uneasy tandem, contributing their strengths while not interfering in a central way with the other. People who operate from a modern cognitive framework may elevate government or markets to a privileged status, seeking a panacea that will then yield desired outcomes. In a postmodern world, problems and solutions are complex, giving rise to multiple interpretations.

### Pluralist Democracy

In liberal theory, democratic governments are viewed as functional organizations serving public rather than private purposes, guided by votes rather than dollars. In effect, democracy is treated as a "black box" into which individual voters place their preferences and from which appropriate public policies emerge. Legal rights and prohibitions set parameters around individual behaviors. Taxes and spending affect income distribution as well as what public goods are produced. At their best, democratic governments articulate and legitimate widely shared social norms while opening other issues to debate. For example, all states cover the basic costs for kindergarten to grade 12 schools, but they vary widely in spending for computers, the arts or athletics.

Representative governments, however, cannot assure rational or consistent voter preferences through democratic principles, unless only two options exist. In practice, the outcome of voting depends on what choices are presented to a group. As economist Kenneth Arrow (1963, p. 60) demonstrated, given "a wide range of individual orderings, the doctrine of voters' sovereignty is incompatible with that of collective rationality." Table 6.1 illustrates a pertinent case of differently ordered preferences among three citizens whose votes determine whether to improve schools, lower taxes, or desegregate students. If the choice is between better schools or lower taxes, then voters A and B prefer to spend more for public education. If the choice is between lower taxes or desegregation, voters A and C vote for lower taxes. If the choice is better schools or desegregation, voters B and C form a two-thirds majority for desegregation.

**TABLE 6.1**
**Voter Preferences for Schools**

| Voter | Order of Preferences | | |
|---|---|---|---|
| A — has children in public school | Better schools | Lower taxes | Desegregation |
| B — has never married | Desegregation | Better schools | Lower taxes |
| C — has children in private school | Lower taxes | Desegregation | Better schools |

No voting procedure can resolve this dilemma of pluralist democracy. Voters with clear preferences make group decisions that fail an elementary criterion of rationality—illogically, society prefers A to B, B to C, but C to A. The outcome depends on who determines the choices. As James Madison and others argued in the *Federalist Papers*, a large republic containing many regional interests would find democratic majorities for little save national defense and international relations. It went without saying that a weak government served to protect the status quo or the position of those with private power embodied in land or capital.

In practice, information costs (election campaigns, drafting complex legislation, voting) restrict options. Political parties select candidates to run for office. Legislative committees report out bills. Interest groups lobby, support candidates, and shape public agendas—thereby powerfully influencing laws, regulations and nominees. With modest stakes in public policies, ordinary citizens reasonably ignore such details, thereby ceding great power to groups that are organized, funded and self-interested. According to an epigram cited by political scientist Robert A. Dahl (1982, pp. 100, 54), "votes count but organizational resources decide." America's "civic consciousness that stresses egoism rather than altruism or benevolence" further weakens a sense of a common good. Modern welfare states are continually frustrated by an inability to identify majorities for a specific plan to implement even popular policy goals, such as health care reform.

Public ownership under a central bureaucracy also escapes democratic control. First, legislative compromises result in ambiguous goals so that many policies are effectively determined by street-level bureaucrats. Second, costs of accurate information and continual renegotiations rise with high technology, making both public and private oversight more difficult. Third, government directives offer few incentives for efficiency. General rules cannot treat people or situations equitably; examples of injustices generate negative publicity, leading bureaucrats to conceal their failures.

Dilemmas of democratic decisionmaking are increasingly important in interdependent economies because individual options are framed by public policies and institutional practices. Many social outcomes are determined by capitalist opportunities. For example, corporations are seldom challenged in their control over when, where, and how much most people can earn. Important decisions about income allocation or a right to medical care seldom rise to the level of public debate. Despite their presumed efficiency, profit-seeking firms do not necessarily make better social choices about resource allocations, the mix of outputs, or curricular outcomes. Although some issues are publicly debated, modern societies are governed largely through customs and nongovernmental institutions. In general, a truncated public debate allows those who have power to win by default.

## Flaws in Competitive Markets

Over the past century, government oversight and direction of economic practices has grown dramatically in response to endemic flaws in competitive markets. In theory, competition leads to desirable social outcomes—if the distribution of wealth is fair at the outset, all prices and qualities are known (including future ones), no single buyer or seller influences market prices, and a good's costs and benefits affect only its users. No market meets those conditions, and few come close. As a result, every industrial democracy has enlarged its public sector in response to excessive market power or economies of scale, externalities or public goods, and uncertainties or information costs. Moreover, popular support for education, health care, and income security—now over one-fourth of the U. S. economy—mean a large government role in the overall economy.

Government programs grew in order to protect individuals against the power and vagaries of industrial capitalism. After 1850, businesses achieved important economies of scale in transportation, communication, heavy industry, and mass marketing. Capital-intensive corporations chartered by states and municipalities coordinated long-term and large-scale projects that brought specialization to mass assembly and distribution. Earning huge profits for their owners, they overwhelmed potential competitors. Their wealth and monopolistic power dominated free markets as well as democratic procedures. Workers organized unions as a counterbalancing force. Citizens pursued protection against monopolies in transportation and communication through antitrust suits and rate regulations.

During the three decades around the beginning of the 20th century, Progressive reformers regulated big business and also opened political processes to voters through referendum and recall petitions, direct election of U.S. senators, and women's suffrage. Public agencies tamed blatant monopolistic practices, inspected food and cosmetics, proscribed unfair competitive practices, and provided a flexible currency under the Federal Reserve System. Cities built parks, inspected milk, and required tenements to include windows and bathrooms. In addition, laws regulated working hours and conditions for women and children. The federal government supported vocational training, and urban schools sought to "Americanize" recent immigrants.

In response to the Great Depression, the New Deal enacted a social welfare system. With one in four workers unemployed, federal relief programs offered a dole and jobs. The National Labor Relations Act (1935) established rights of labor to organize and bargain collectively. The Social Security Act (1935) mandated contributions to a pension for old age and survivors' benefits. It also covered those adults unable to work because of blindness or other handicaps. Unemployment insurance offered short-term benefits to those who lost their jobs. States and localities provided temporary relief for anyone not otherwise covered. In 1946, the Employment Act established a federal responsibility to use fiscal and monetary policies to stabilize employment and prices.

Under Presidents John F. Kennedy and Lyndon B. Johnson, welfare rights were extended to poor and minority residents. Civil rights and a war on poverty tackled two structural limitations on productivity, while Social Security covered medical care for the elderly and poor. The Elementary and Secondary School Act of 1965 extended federal support to local districts serving low-income and minority students. The Higher Education Act of 1965 expanded access to loans for postsecondary students. Housing and health measures were key parts of a broad strategy to induce investment in human capital, especially among discriminated-against groups. During Nixon's administration, occupational and environmental protection was extended.

With public spending and regulations governing one-third to one-half of the total market economy, all industrial nations including the United States have intertwined private and public controls. Increasingly, property rights are both assured and limited by laws. Governments protect consumers and workers because technological developments create unanticipated hazards. Currently, 25 cents of every consumer dollar is spent on products regulated by the Federal Trade Commission. New issues of bonds or stocks disclose information required by the Securities and Exchange Commission; the Occupational Safety and Health Administration sets standards for pesticides and machinery. States license lawyers, barbers and teachers, among others. In most areas, land use is regulated by zoning restrictions and building codes.

During reform eras, strong political leaders only partially tamed corporate interests. Over time, regulatory agencies collaborated with those they monitored. The public benefits of full employment were diverted by military spending and weakened by fears of inflation. The Civil Rights Movement overcame legal segregation, but many forms of private discrimination persist. For example, bankers and Realtors collude to maintain racially isolated neighborhoods. Affirmative action opened some positions for women and "protected minorities," but it did little to equalize income levels for women, Blacks or Latinos. Although business remained dominant, much of 20th-century politics has revolved around finding a balance between government efforts to assure justice and business insistence on liberty to do whatever earns high profits.

As this brief summary of public policies reveals, teaching for citizenship in a modern economy requires knowledge about programs, their intentions and effects, and alternative possibilities. Even a simple program such as federal assistance to the blind generates pages of regulations designed to clarify the exact degree of vision loss that constitutes a disability. Neither ideology nor self-interest explain citizens' varied responses to government management of the economy; paradoxically, it aims to enhance competition by limiting unfair business practices, reducing industrial fluctuations, stabilizing money and credit, and sustaining a healthy, well-educated workforce. Understandably, few teachers are prepared to explore topics such as the Federal Reserve System that are central to the allocation of economic resources.

## Equity, Efficiency and Choice

One way to start making sense of the mix of government agencies and private functions is to assess them in terms of equity, efficiency and choice. Rather than letting the details of each law and program dominate the discussion, educators should ask some key questions. Who benefits, and what are the distributional implications? Does the program advance a more equal society? Who is responsible for deciding what is feasible and efficient? Do they have to live with consequences? What choices are left to those most affected by the program or regulation? Are there options for people with different preferences or beliefs? Finally, are there open channels for feedback from users to policymakers?

Equity—defined by equal rights *and* by raising revenue for public purposes based on ability to pay—is best assured within large units. Individual rights and fairness cannot be limited to small areas of a nation without arbitrarily declaring some people more worthy than others. Assuming diverse histories, social situations, and personal preferences, efficiency is best assured by leaving crucial decisions in the hands of those most affected by the outcomes. Efficiency is a preeminent feature of markets because voluntary transactions allow individuals to maximize satisfactions within their budget constraints. Flexibility, or adaptation to evolving understandings, depends on maximizing voice for stakeholders while assuring a safety net so that individuals can explore options without fear of disaster. When people sense that their decisions make a difference, their actions serve as indicators for social equity and efficiency.

Equity is a prerequisite for meaningful efficiency. Otherwise, microefficiencies increase social unfairness. John Rawls (1971, esp. pp. 60–117) linked individual self-interest and a primary preference for equality of basic rights. Asked to accept a social contract without knowing one's place or status, a risk-averse citizen would reasonably choose equality for each member. Equivalent welfare ordinarily requires compensation for those with physical or mental handicaps. A just society would tolerate unequal authority in order to coordinate organizations and governments—as long as most of the gains from management accrued to those who accept subordinate roles.

Because risk-averse individuals who cannot count on a favorable class, race or gender position have a strong motive for defining justice as equal conditions, a powerful case exists for viewing governments as aiming for both primary rights for all and the opportunity to exercise those freedoms. We interpret that goal as substantive equality for educational outcomes; a secure income sufficient to sustain health, learning and work; and insurance against disaster. Once those basic thresholds are in place, then individuals may choose a mix of activities and discourse that meets their preferences and aspirations.

In order to devise a mix of policies that complement rather than conflict with each other, voters need a coherent vision of a good society. Relatively advantaged individuals lean toward personal freedom, liberty and rights that limit government's capacity to interfere. They dominate public rhetoric and foster a compelling vision—often in stark contrast to totalitarian control. The less advantaged rely on the government for mundane things like good schools, health care, safe neighborhoods, job opportunities, decent housing, and a chance for their children to develop their potential. Granting political rights without the means to exercise them effectively denies the poor their freedoms.

Democratic dialog takes time. Deciding on individual versus community responsibility for schooling, crime, or housing requires information of all sorts—evaluations, projections, cross-national comparisons, and so on. All stakeholders need access to relevant facts so they can learn from experience and continually adjust to evolving conditions. To hold a long-term, public perspective, everyone needs to see reasonable opportunities for learning, working and enjoying life. Each person has preferences and knowledge about how to do things at the lowest costs to themselves and society, but large bureaucracies, whether public or private, promulgate procedures aimed at treating everyone alike— thereby stifling flexibility and innovation. At the same time, some rights or processes must be assured and structured so that individual or corporate actions do not distort the choices available to others.

When individuals feel free to choose among several opportunities— at least some of which are desirable—then society has functional equity with efficiency. Psychologically, individuals sense enough control over their own futures to act purposefully. As plans turn into acts, they learn new things and shape new self-identities. Likewise, their sense of fairness evolves in relation to their spheres of activity. Modern societies that defined social justice in terms of individual choices among voluntary communities (based on occupation, residence, friends, religion, political affiliation, and hobbies) have difficulty arriving at a sense of a larger community. Competition pervades schools, workplaces and social groups and erodes a sense of caring as well as standards of fairness.

Allocating responsibilities for various activities to firms, government agencies, voluntary associations, or individuals is enormously challenging because they set underlying frameworks of power in an interdependent society. Whatever the arrangements, specific boundaries and principles must be adjusted continually in order to maintain a balance among interests. That requires a broad awareness of how the parts fit together and evolve in accord with relevant analyses and socially constructed understandings. It also requires a sense of social justice. The crucial political discourse involves which rights are considered necessary in a just society, such as education or full employment, and what issues are regarded as debatable, such as tax rates or levels of spending.

## COMPLEXITIES OF CIVIC DIALOG

Governments incorporate social choices into public policies that set contexts for how individuals interact, plan their futures, and agree on cultural values. That process requires democratic processes to foster dialog around personal, organizational and public purposes. Labor markets, corporate charters, taxes, social security, and needs-based welfare programs all affect the distribution of income. In turn, one's income, experiences, values, and interests affect how laws are perceived. Many rights and institutions are regarded as fundamental, despite periodic objections about how they are used. People support free speech without approving every message. Access to education is considered a right, but the curriculum continually stretches to include new topics.

Governments delegate tasks to organizations that then hold quasi-public authority. For example, corporations, labor unions, schools and universities, voluntary groups, and lobbyists serve social ends as well as self-interests. If such units become overly powerful, they restrict the choices of individuals or organizations. Outlawing associations, however, would deny fundamental freedoms of individuals to communicate and cooperate. Moreover, they meet local needs while stabilizing interactions in an interdependent economy. As Dahl (1982, pp. 51, 52) noted, "the sheer complexity of organized pluralism" requires ever more facts: "Yet in modern democratic countries the complexity of the patterns, processes, and activities of a large number of relatively autonomous organizations has outstripped theory, existing information, and the ability of representatives—or others, for that matter—to comprehend it."

A familiar maxim holds that knowledge is power. Certainly the spread of literacy and low-cost newspapers in the 18th century was crucial for the American Revolution and establishing a representative democracy. The reverse also is true: Without a sense of power or efficacy, there is not much incentive to learn how political and economic systems function or how to increase one's effectiveness within those systems. Feelings of powerlessness encapsulated in the adage that you cannot fight city hall are confirmed by low voter turnout and public opinion polls.

We attribute apathy toward civic participation to three factors: First, America's ideology favors individualism over government. Second, public and private motives within civic and individual acts are intertwined and unclear; and ambiguous concepts are harder to convey than clearcut normative judgments. Third, a division of responsibilities among multiple levels of local, regional, state and national agencies complicates program implementation and evaluation, although federalism is essential to preserve both equity and efficiency. Consequently, most curriculum treats history as a march of progress marked by notable achievements to be memorized and literature as lessons on individual values from the past.

## An Ideology of Individualism

Historically, a majority of Americans shared a number of interlocked beliefs that discouraged public programs designed to alleviate inequalities of power and wealth brought by industrial capitalism. The American creed defined a normative ideal of equality, liberty, individualism, constitutionalism, and democracy that

unite in imposing limits on power and on the institutions of government. The essence of constitutionalism is the restraint of governmental power through fundamental law. The essence of liberalism is freedom from governmental control. . . . The essence of individualism is the right of each person to act in accordance with his own conscience and to control his own destiny free of external restraint, except insofar as such restraint is necessary to ensure comparable rights to others. The essence of egalitarianism is rejection of the idea that one person has the right to exercise power over another. The essence of democracy is popular control over government, directly or through representatives, and the responsiveness of governmental officials to public opinion. In sum, the distinctive aspect of the American Creed is its antigovernment character. (Huntington, 1981, p. 33)

Antistate attitudes are amplified by alienation among workers and widespread resentment of bureaucrats and intellectuals. Surveys show few citizens participate in politics beyond voting, less than half can name their legislators, and only a handful can describe the contexts or consequences of major bills. Lawmakers, lobbyists and bureaucrats speak of "markups," "out-years" and arcane exemptions. Politicians have overpromised so many things—for instance, a balanced budget or a drug-free society—that few pay attention to their platforms. Academic experts lean in an opposite direction—documenting failures, unanticipated outcomes, and weaknesses of bureaucratic management. Yet political decisions and government programs affect everyone's life, and a tendency to compromise combined with bureaucratic inertia has institutionalized many policies. A shift in parties usually brings only marginal changes.

Despite the importance of laws and regulations, Americans have no formal mechanisms for assessing the health of their society. Newspapers present assorted social trends as well as stories revealing local conditions but seldom connect the dots to show a coherent picture. Late in President Johnson's term, he initiated a social accounting analogous to the *Economic Report of the President*. The first summary commented on social mobility, environment, income distribution, personal safety, contributions of "learning, science, and art," as well as "community and alienation" in a segmented society: "People need a sense of belonging, a feeling of community, in some small social group. If such associations are lacking, they will feel alienated; they will have a tendency either to 'cop out' of the central life of the society, or else try to reverse the direction of society by extreme or even violent methods" (U.S. Department of Health, Education, and Welfare, 1969, p. 88). Subsequent reports presented statistics with little text and lacked systematic recommendations for bringing people together.

American thinking about social control is locked into three ideological options: pure democracy "untroubled by a multiplicity of relatively autonomous organizations," perfect competition with "voluntary transactions among free individuals," and "bureaucratic socialism" (Dahl, 1982, p. 204). Those narratives structure discussions in ways that benefit capitalists. Social scientists who define trade-offs between equity and efficiency—between politics and markets—ignore other choices. Ideally, however, democratic voices would infuse corporations, and competition would invigorate public enterprises. In particular, Dahl urged democratizing workplaces—"for their decisions which most affect their lives all the employees of an economic enterprise must be included in the demos." Work and citizenship are not separate spheres with different normative rules.

A dialog limited to narrow choices frustrates educators because students' prospects are increasingly affected by laws, regulations and standard operating procedures. Governments act to implement ideals of social justice but are blamed for any resulting interference with personal freedoms. For example, most people approve of integration, though many dislike the idea of crosstown busing. Ambivalently, drivers approve of traffic safety but practice a "rolling stop" at intersections. Such divided judgments make teaching about postindustrial societies very difficult. Students come to expect correct answers; yet either a positive or a negative judgment about current programs omits the diversity of opinion. Truth may lie in the details, but there is little time to weigh scholarly studies or the multiple realities of our postmodern world.

### Government as a Policy Instrument

Although Americans proclaim a belief in freedom, no one can do whatever they want with their own life or their children's lives while also drawing on the resources of a complex economy. Certain acts are defined as criminal and punished accordingly. Others are declared public nuisances, such as making loud noises or blocking entrances and exits to property. Individual liberty is shaped to meet community standards of morality and assure public safety. For instance, people cannot own artillery or certain drugs; taxes discourage consumption of whiskey and cigarettes; cars and drivers are licensed and subject to inspections and traffic rules; children cannot work full-time, buy alcohol or cigarettes, or attend schools without vaccinations. Some activities with positive impacts on others are publicly subsidized—notably home ownership and education.

For two decades, public spending in the United States has totaled about one-third of the net domestic product. Roughly a third of that sum transfers funds across life spans through old-age and survivors benefits or welfare payments for dependent children. Another third pays for salaries of government workers from city hall custodians to national park rangers. Educators comprise the largest group with 3.2 million—compared with a peacetime peak of 2 million in military service. The remaining third goes for purchases of goods and services by governments, military contracts, environmental cleanups, consultants on energy policy, and so on. The federal government spends about 14% for salaries and 21.6% for goods and services, with huge transfers through Social Security, interest on a burgeoning national debt, and aid to states. State and local governments spend 36.3% on outside purchases and over half their budgets on salaries (3 million state employees and 9.7 million local government employees).

> **A major debate in schools today concerns whether to adopt a single textbook or to use multiple readings in a history course.**
> **Identify what features in each proposal have implications for equity, efficiency and choice.**

Administering public programs is difficult because "we want better management and greater competence in the federal government, but we do not want to rely on strong, competent executives to help achieve it" (Lynn, 1981, pp. 4, 10). New responsibilities and tasks are assigned to public managers—just as they have been added to schools—but decisionmaking capacity has been hedged by procedural rights and requirements. Social welfare programs "are characterized by vague or uncertain technologies, strong ideological and value commitments on the part of staffs and organized interest groups, the dominance of trained professionals, and the near impossibility of defining measures of effectiveness and standards of efficiency." Programs to redistribute income "provoke strong resentment," while flexible policies generate jurisdictional conflicts.

Because politics ordinarily reconciles divergent interests, government bureaucracies practice a "muddling through" approach. Usually the status quo benefits by their failure to act. A majority may prefer cleaner air and better schools yet disagree on how to achieve those ends. Meanwhile, people's trust in institutions—including schools, universities, and notably Congress—has declined. Over the past two decades, calls for making public services more businesslike or efficient have overwhelmed voices for democratizing private enterprises. Such public services as garbage collection, institutional care for the disabled, and schools have been contracted to profit-seeking firms. At best, the results are mixed.

Successful privatization of public functions depends on three steps: clarity about desired outcomes, competition for contracts, and managerial autonomy. Definable goals, however, remain a pipe dream for 75% of government spending because votes convey "information about interests [that] is aggregated, imprecise, and only indirectly conveyed to the people—whether civil servants or profit-seekers—who do the work" (Donahue, 1989, p. 85). Without a set bottom line or competitive threat and without shifting political winds in mind, bureaucrats seek multiple goals; they monitor and evaluate for political support as well as performance of central mission. Indeed, such apparent laxness sometimes characterizes many established, successful corporations.

In practice, public and private agencies mix social and selfish goals. For example, the Department of the Interior has to protect the environment, conserve resources, spend as little as possible, balance the interests of nature lovers and timber companies, and win congressional approval for appropriations. Similarly, private organizations do not single-mindedly pursue profits without concern for worker and consumer safety. Many of these responsibilities are "delegated" to firms, with only occasional inspection or enforcement from government. In general, the public sets norms and contexts while relying on local decisionmakers to implement them.

## Coordination under Federalism

Most Americans live in overlapping governmental units that evolved to meet new needs. Local governments—symbolized by New England town meetings open to all residents—once covered most public services: schools, roads, a constable, and a tree warden. Now, many towns cannot support a comprehensive educational system—much less provide for waste disposal, water supplies, mass transportation, crime prevention, and so on through the range of services provided by public agencies. Furthermore, local governments no longer rely primarily on property taxes, long favored because they were not easily evaded or shifted. Now public agencies mingle revenues derived from federal, state and local sources in a mix of services that address human needs, foster community development, and advance national goals.

Multiple levels of democratic government incorporate different majorities around specific interests. Public programs (whose location and structure depend largely on which goals are central) seek to balance equity, efficiency and individual choice. Responsibilities are assigned to the federal level; state or local governments; quasi-judicial agencies such as the Federal Trade Commission, Securities and Exchange Commission, or National Labor Relations Board; quasi-independent administrations such as the Tennessee Valley Authority or National Aeronautics and Space Administration; the courts; local administrative agencies; or citizens. Firms pay for many required inspections, collect

Social Security taxes, and, often, cover health and pension benefits. Individuals fill out income tax forms, insure their motor vehicles, send children to school, and pay for mandatory treatment of the dead.

In general, federalism enables each level and agency to serve appropriate functions in response to relevant constituencies or legal mandates: "The central government is responsible for regularizing relations with foreign countries, for maintaining the nation's prosperity, and for sustaining social welfare and other redistributive services. Local governments concentrate on operating efficiently those services necessary for maintaining a healthy local economy and society" (Peterson, 1982, p. 247). Many public functions benefit from adjustments to local needs and oversight by those who are most affected. Transportation, public safety, education, health and recreation, income security, and community development activities may be implemented best by local governments or quasi-independent agencies. Funding, however, often includes state and federal sources because taxable resources vary widely among localities.

The national government, as historian Arthur M. Schlesinger, Jr. (1977, pp. 26–27) pointed out, "protected the Bill of Rights against local vigilantism"; "protected national resources against local greed"; "civilized our industry"; "secured the rights of labor organization"; and "defended the livelihood of the farmer." Moreover, "only the national government can relieve such problems as racial justice, unemployment, inflation, urban decay, environmental protection, and the nation's need for health care, education, housing, and welfare." Those who criticize government power seek to preserve "the freedom to deny a tenth of the population their elementary rights as citizens, the freedom to loot and waste our resources, the freedom to work small children in mills and immigrants in sweatshops, the freedom to offer squalid working conditions and pay starvation wages, the freedom to lie in the sale of goods and securities."

Educational policy entails a complex mixture of governments, businesses, and family influences. The national government sets standards, for example, no discrimination based on race, sex, or handicapping condition. It also offers financial support for certain inequities—low-income or low-achieving districts, districts under desegregation plans or those with military bases—and for gathering statistics, pioneering innovations, or research. States set minimum standards for teachers, the curriculum, and the condition of the school. Local districts hire teachers, schedule buses, buy texts, enforce attendance, and set a general level for satisfactory performance of students. Families get children ready for schools; businesses offer jobs. Federalism gains when schools and other organizations share understandings of everyone's common interests as well as particular goals and roles for each governmental unit.

Getting people to work together is difficult, whether through hierarchical management or democratic dialog. Yet our overall efficiency depends on complex linkages among public and private agencies, with many beliefs and behaviors taken for granted. Federalism is not a rational system in the sense of serving to maximize a single goal or criterion by applying appropriate techniques. But it is a system that makes a great deal of sense. It takes advantage of special strengths in a variety of organizations and governmental units. It seeks to command through loyalty and incentives rather than coercion and punishment. It relies on cultural legacies and institutional practices to simplify the ways a restless and powerful people interact with each other.

## ECONOMIC POWER IN DEMOCRATIC AMERICA

The national discussion that might ensue from a consideration of equity, efficiency and choice in economic and political institutions is difficult at best but is vastly complicated by the power that capitalists or businesses have exercised in both sectors. As long as capitalists generally delivered on a promise of personal freedom, growing well-being, and national power, there was little incentive to consider alternatives. Earlier compromises no longer hold during a time of stagnant wages for most workers, rising threats to the environment, and a growing sense of insecurity about health, education, a job, and old age pensions. A two-decade rise in income inequality and heightened resistance to equal rights for people of color and women adds to feelings of alienation from the polity.

Government programs aimed at alleviating social inequalities under capitalism have sharpened political struggles: "The distribution of income, for example, is increasingly decided by government decisions on taxes, public education, public housing, health care, pensions, disability and unemployment compensation, and other transfer payments. As these decisions move from market to government, there is more to fight about in politics and a greater burden, consequently, on whatever political devices there are to keep the peace" (Lindblom, 1977, p. 353). With economic stagnation and rising costs of public services, redistributing income cannot be financed out of growth.

The divisions by occupations, class, race, and gender revealed in recent elections and opinion polls raise questions about how to reestablish a consensus on social justice during a period of slow economic growth and widening inequalities of income and, perhaps, of education. Negative campaigning and seemingly rapid shifts in public opinion suggest a high degree of public anxiety about future employment and public policies. In terms of the visible public debate, those concerns have fed a national "blaming game," with finger pointing all around. That mistrust erodes productive actions on everyone's part because self-protective acts contribute little to organizational goals or social justice.

## Resistance to Equality

Although business in general benefits from fair competition, full employment, and unbiased labor markets, some firms see short-run gains in monopoly pricing, misleading advertising, unsafe products, and unhealthy working conditions. Established firms complain about competitors who exploit labor in sweatshops, ignore health and safety regulations, or advertise falsely. Capitalists' support for racial and gender discrimination is more puzzling but probably relates to fostering divisions among workers in unions and political movements. Corporations and individuals seek both to exploit their advantages and to insist on equity where they are disadvantaged. The outcome is a distorted public discourse in which ideology and demands for rights seem instruments to conceal self-interests and dominant power.

During the 1970s, popular opinion shifted from supporting active government roles to fears that bureaucratic regulations and spending were a drag on innovation and productivity. Owners resented safety and environmental regulations, and they chafed at affirmative action requirements. A sharp rise in energy costs did not overcome political resistance to conservation measures, nor did investment in capital equipment keep pace with baby boomers entering the workforce. Real wages dropped, and high-wage earners opposed taxes to pay for social welfare services. Conservative interests argued that "to rectify unemployment, inflation, declining investment, and slowed productivity growth, the failed policies of the past, and with them the government's expansion in all its forms, had to be turned around" (Schwarz, 1983, p. 119).

Although this indictment ignored alternative explanations for economic stagnation, it had business support and effective political leadership. Liberals had grown demoralized when attacks on poverty and racism failed to yield quick victories. They could not muster majorities to tax oil imports (for cleaner air and a lower trade deficit) or to spend more on education and rebuilding a transportation and communication infrastructure. Protests against the war in Vietnam together with a youth counterculture and feminist objections to patriarchy divided a liberal coalition that formed during the New Deal. Conservatives blamed big government, encouraged private consumption (especially by the wealthier half of the population), spent for a massive military buildup during a period of relative peace, and borrowed from abroad to cover the federal deficit.

Business clout in government became especially visible during President Reagan's first administration. Taxes for high income brackets declined. For example, a family earning $10,000 to $20,000 paid $573 more for Social Security and $387 less for income taxes, or a net increase of $186. For those who made ten times as much, Social Security taxes rose by $5,979 while income taxes fell $8,248, yielding a gain of $2,269. Meanwhile, major cuts in domestic spending affected every income level but hit those making less than $10,000 per year with a dollar loss three times greater than for those making over $40,000 per year. Conservatives successfully argued that the rich needed more money to induce them to work, save and invest, while the poor would work only when welfare and social service programs offered less. Federal support for public schools declined in real terms and shifted toward loan guarantees for students in higher education.

Political choices are crucial to government management of the economy: "The distribution of income and wealth in a democratic country goes to the heart of its political ethic, defining the basic contours of a nation's sense of justice and equity as it pursues economic growth, and determining how the benefits of growth, or the burdens of decline, will be shared by its citizens" (Edsall, 1984, pp. 18, 19). Public policies affect who gets what in all spheres: "At the federal level, the size and mix of domestic spending, the structure and distributional consequences of the tax system, and the permitted rate of growth in the money supply are central factors in determining the rate of inflation, the rate of unemployment, the rate of interest on borrowed money, and the proportion of families living below the poverty level, as well as of those living in great wealth." In advanced economies, private markets as well as social spending affect "the well-being and economic status of individual citizens, classes of citizens, categories of workers, geographic areas, sets of corporations, and racial and ethnic groups."

White racism disrupted political coalitions aimed at addressing inequities in income and power, as it has done for a century. Following Reconstruction in the South, White Democrats used race baiting against Republicans and Populists. In the 1960s, Governor George Wallace of Alabama campaigned nationally against Washington bureaucrats who enforced civil rights and welfare rights. In the 1970s and 1980s, presidential candidates Nixon, Reagan, and Bush appealed to racial fears among White voters: "Race has crystallized and provided a focus for values conflicts, for cultural conflicts, and for interest conflicts—conflicts over subjects as diverse as social welfare spending, neighborhood schooling, the distribution of the tax burden, criminal violence, sexual conduct, family structure, political competition, and union membership" (Edsall & Edsall, 1991, pp. 5, 3). As the Edsalls concluded, "race and taxes have permitted the Republican party to adapt the principles of conservatism to break the underlying class basis of the Roosevelt-Democratic coalition and to build a reconfigured voting majority in presidential elections."

In the United States, crosscutting differences based on ethnic origins, religion, regional loyalties, and diverse business interests complicate a central cleavage along class lines that might sustain social welfare programs. Although existing distributions of power, income and knowledge have commanded legislative majorities, a less segmented people might support more equal standards, similar to those in European democracies. At some point, a society divided along racist lines will no longer find political means to establish equality, despite the social costs of dysfunctional cities and families resulting from past and present discrimination. In the long run, however, business and society benefits from well-educated and well-paid workers who use information technologies, cooperate with others, and purchase the goods and services of a postindustrial economy.

## Income Distribution and Public Welfare

A division of authority along federalist lines with democratic procedures incorporated into functioning organizations might offer access and voice to all groups—if market-oriented societies were not dominated by capitalists. As long as Americans focused on material production and business delivered the goods, entrepreneurs had a controlling influence. If government taxes or regulations seemed too threatening, their spokespersons announced that businesses would have to close their doors and lay off workers. Moreover, an ideological commitment to individualism combined with a legal decision that corporations had rights as an "artificial person" gave firms and the wealthy great leeway to do as they pleased.

Indeed, as political economist Charles Lindblom (1977, pp. 188, 224) concluded, "the entire industrial structure is largely the result of business decisions on the whole sanctioned and sometimes implemented by responsive government officials." Capitalists "determine the size of plants and firms, the location of industry, the organization of markets and transport—hence the configuration of cities, on the one hand, and the bureaucratization of the workplace, on the other." A person's employment controls many other options. One's community, church, dialect, politics, and education reveal class differences. Moreover, "one class contains most wealthy persons," political leaders, corporate executives, "some professionals and academics (depending on their income, their institutional affiliations, or their clientele), some journalists and other public figures" who share "a common package of traits."

Modern welfare states ostensibly regulate business and offer income security in response to industrial fluctuations, but in the United States, that has not gone far to redistribute income. Most equalization has occurred as a direct result of rapid growth as better jobs opened up for women, minorities and the unskilled. Despite a litany of complaints about high taxes and high living by some welfare recipients, Americans pay less in taxes and provide less income security than other industrial democracies. As of 1992, tax breaks that benefited those making over $20,000 (150% of the poverty level) exceeded $150 billion. By comparison, direct aid based on need through food stamps, Medicaid,

Supplemental Security Income, and Aid to Families with Dependent Children totaled about $140 billion. Over half of Social Security pensions and Medicare benefits go to families earning over $20,000 per year.

Sharply progressive income tax rates always included many exclusions, exemptions and deductions, while the lower and flatter taxes passed during the 1980s more obviously benefit the rich, whose expenses for basic needs do not rise proportionately with income. Moreover, a rising share of public revenues is derived from regressive sales and Social Security taxes that disproportionately affect the working poor. Although majorities are willing to provide welfare to alleviate visible signs of hunger and homelessness, there is little support for education and community development programs that would enable the poor to obtain a job, live in a safe neighborhood, send their children to high quality schools, and acquire adequate medical care. Contemporary public policies resemble capitalism in the 19th century in offering something for most people without changing the rank orders of class, race or gender.

> **Consider three uses of public funds that concern you as a citizen—national standards for high-school graduation, magnet schools to attract a racially and culturally diverse student body, or computer technologies that reduce instructional costs.**
>
> **Who is likely to influence decisionmaking in each case? What symbols and arguments might sway public opinion? What potential coalitions and values generate support for more equitable schools.**

On balance, American capitalists use the power of the state to enhance their own position and to limit income redistribution. Major spending programs for defense, highways and education scarcely advantage the poor. "In its central role of backing up U. S. foreign policy, military spending probably most greatly helps the most wealthy, owners of property, and especially owners of capital invested abroad" (Page, 1983, pp. 212–213). Interstate highways and environmental protection benefit Americans roughly in proportion to their income. By and large, schools reward wealthy taxpayers by reproducing class structures. "Finally, the Constitution and the legal system clearly provide foundations for a capitalist economic system. Thus, the income distributional effects of that system are themselves products of government action."

A functioning democracy has economic implications, as Arrow (1974, p. 23) noted: "A commitment to democratic values strongly implies an ideal of redistribution of income and wealth." Capitalist competition stratifies classes: "A hierarchical society marked by great inequalities in power and esteem will surely not tolerate the liberties of those most disadvantaged." A perception of fairness is needed for people to work together: "The strong element of truth in all social contract theories is that the Hobbesian nightmare can be avoided only if the bulk of society feels in fact incorporated and accepted in it." In every industrial nation, public programs redistribute income. The United States, however, relies primarily on creating equal opportunities through public schooling— raising the consequences of unequal educational outcomes.

Only an inclusive discourse will heed now-silenced voices and help reconstruct meanings for common schooling. Yet aggressive conservative voices, mainly White males, regularly challenge efforts to equalize educational achievement and incomes. Their rhetoric equates excellence with high test scores on traditional Eurocentric knowledge and associates lack of discipline in school with noncompetitiveness in international markets. A subtext of racism appears in terms such as "urban schools," "inner-city violence," "drug abuse," "busing," and "low test scores." When teachers avoid controversy, they present these issues as unimportant, undebatable and beyond anyone's ability to influence through democratic dialog.

## PUBLIC AND PRIVATE MOTIVES FOR LEARNING

Education exemplifies the intermingling of public and private interests and motivations. People acquire knowledge in order to enhance their earnings, effectiveness as consumers, capacity to learn, knowledge about the world, and enjoyment of leisure. If that were the whole story, schooling could be left to individual decisions just as consumers in a grocery choose which items, within their budget, best meet their needs. Unequal family resources might be addressed by assuring students of access to loans. Because learning predictably pays off later on, reasonable students would borrow to cover their out-of-pocket costs while contributing through their foregone earnings. The consequences of schooling, however, will be known only far into the future, and then they will be affected by what others learned and want to do.

All industrial societies subsidize schools and usually require attendance. They are supported in part because everyone benefits from well-educated, well-behaved neighbors who take care of themselves, contribute to the community, share similar tastes, perform services for others, and in general cope well without continuous oversight or public services. Moreover, citizen participation is easier if adults can cope with industrial, urban, bureaucratic, and secular conditions. Mandatory schooling indicates a strong public interest in a literate citizenry as well as a fear that some parents do not know what is best for their children. For example, educators cite child abuse, dysfunctional families, and special educational needs as evidence of parental inadequacies.

Focusing on public expenditures and state requirements, however, misses the extent of family and student control already present in schools. Teachers deliver only part of the learning associated with normal human development. Parents or other adults in a child's life shape how one interacts with others and responds to problems or opportunities. By monitoring television viewing, enriching vacation activities, providing educational materials in the household, and discussing controversial issues, many families compensate for what schools leave out. Normally, parents increase their attention to school outcomes when they discover that a child is not learning or dislikes the teacher. If one child dislikes academic study, parents try to reinforce book learning or to support alternative aspirations.

### Privatization of Schools

Although private schools long have competed with public ones, the idea of applying market principles to education gained prominence from conservative economist Milton Friedman's (1973, pp. 22, 65) radical proposal: "Eliminate compulsory schooling, government operation of schools and financing of schools except for financial assistance to the indigent." Each child would receive a voucher (based on existing average costs) that could be redeemed at any public or private school. He saw the common school ideal as a false issue for metropolitan areas where "the public school has fostered residential stratification, by tying the kind and the cost of schooling to residential location." Vouchers did not raise new issues about common benefits from "promoting a stable and democratic society"; the plan "forces us to face this issue rather than evade it." Indeed, Friedman argued, "nothing could do more to moderate racial conflict and to promote a society in which black and white cooperate in joint objectives, while respecting each other's separate rights and interests."

Although Friedman (1973, pp. 67, 69) expressed "great sympathy" for compensatory spending because "governmental expenditures benefit disproportionately middle- and upper-income groups," he dismissed it: "In the first place, the political facts that account for the present bias in government spending will also pervert compensatory vouchers. In the second place, equal per-child vouchers, while falling short of the ideal, would be a great improvement over what now exists." He would privilege a freedom to spend: "Can the egalitarian say, it is all right for the well-to-do to spend any income that the tax collector leaves them on riotous living, but they must be penalized (by being denied a voucher) if they try to spend more than the publicly specified sum on schooling their children?" He accused liberals of patronizing the poor as unable to choose a school wisely and forecast "a larger total sum spent on schooling, with that sum, if anything, more evenly divided."

Although critics feared that the exit of middle-class students would weaken public schools, Friedman (1973, p. 71) saw it as competition working to eliminate the unfit:

Such a sorting-out process goes on now, but, it can be argued, the voucher plan will greatly accelerate it, so that many public schools will be left with "the dregs," society's rejects, and will become, by virtue of the well-documented effect of the students on a school, even poorer in quality than now.

As the private market took over, the quality of all schooling would rise so much that even the worst, while it might be *relatively* lower in the scale, would be better in *absolute* quality.

Starting with a liberal concern for inequities, sociologist Christopher Jencks (1971) advocated vouchers as a way to break the bureaucratic indifference of city schools that many associated with their monopolistic position. A choice among schools might amplify the criticisms of low-income and minority parents. To support public goals such as desegregation and compensatory programs, Jencks proposed that low-income families receive a more valuable voucher. Then, schools would accept it as full payment, turn no one down as long as vacancies existed, and randomly fill half its slots if applicants exceeded places. In essence, those limits on what private schools could do in terms of racial balance, meeting special needs, and serving all students would require another bureaucracy. Otherwise, some schools would "skim the cream" of able students, reject high-cost students, and thereby perpetuate class and racial disparities.

> **Devise a voucher plan for a school lunch program that meets the needs of different metabolisms, cultural and religious preferences, as well as personal tastes.**
>
> **Is a meal ticket for a cafeteria (whose costs rise for special orders) fair to athletes, dieters, and junk food junkies?**

Although the idea of school choice is popular, any particular plan involves issues that reduce its support. For example, California has voted twice on statewide choice proposals and rejected both. In 1978, a constitutional amendment proposed vouchers equal to 90% of current costs except for transportation and "such factors as grade level, curriculum, bilingualism, special needs and handicaps, variations in local cost, need to encourage racial desegregation, and any other factor deemed appropriate by the Legislature so long as the right of every child to enroll in any school remains unaffected by his or her family's capacity to purchase education" (*Update on State Legislation*, 1979). It called for nondiscrimination and a right to teach values (and religion in family choice schools). It set rules for governance in independent public schools; rights of students, parents and teachers; and minimum standards for physical facilities and curriculum. Independent or choice schools could not charge extra fees, though they might accept donations or grants.

Chubb and Moe (1990, pp. 23, 38) urged a thoroughgoing destruction of public governance of districts. They contrasted flexibility in market-driven organizations with unresponsive public bureaucracies. Based on extensive analyses of data about student academic achievement, they argued that better schools had "clear goals, an ambitious academic program, strong educational leadership, and high levels of teacher professionalism." Those features were associated with "school autonomy, especially from external bureaucratic influence," which the authors blamed on public authorities imposing control from the top in order to cope with uncertainty. Indeed, they insisted, "the raison d'être of democratic control is to impose higher-order values on schools, and thus to limit their autonomy."

Private and public schools meeting minimal standards would compete for students with virtually no district oversight. A state-run choice office would keep records of school-age children and pay schools the "scholarship" allocated to each child based on his or her need. Although supporting equalization formulas to compensate poor districts, Chubb and Moe (1990, p. 220) feared that parental supplements would "produce too many disparities and inequalities within the public system, and many citizens would regard them as unfair and burdensome." Presumably "at-risk students would then be empowered with bigger scholarships than the others, making them attractive clients to all schools (and stimulating the emergence of new specialty schools)."

Then, "each student will be free to attend any public school in the state, regardless of district." State-funded parent information centers will provide "comprehensive information on each school in the district" and assist parents and students in applying to a school. "Schools will make their own admissions decisions, subject only to nondiscrimination requirements" (Chubb & Moe, 1990, pp. 221, 223). A sequence of application and acceptance cycles would match student preferences with an appropriate educational program. Schools could expel or deny readmission to students as long as they were not "arbitrary and capricious." Schools would set their own governance and operating procedures. Requirements for teacher certification would be minimized and tenure eliminated. Chubb and Moe relied on accountability from below—based on student and parent choices.

Advocates of vouchers and other choice plans depict parents or students as having a clear idea of what they want from education in distinction to current offerings or vague promises of excellence. They presume that teachers can control learning if freed from bureaucratic mandates. Additionally, they assume that academic knowledge is the crucial outcome of schooling and not a rank ordering of students as a way to sort adults into hierarchical occupations. Chubb and Moe (1990, pp. 224–225) charge parent information centers with a monumental task—to provide facts about each school's "mission, their staff and course offerings, parent and student satisfaction, staff opinions, standardized test scores (which we would make optional), and anything else that would promote informed choice among parents and students."

In the meantime, other experiences raise questions about how readily privatization improved efficiency. Some districts contracted for guaranteed test results with private firms who would operate schools in an entrepreneurial fashion. In Gary, Indiana, and elsewhere, contractors single-mindedly taught to the test that determined their success. As pupil growth slowed after 1970, many public school districts established open enrollment plans on a space available basis. Choices among public schools avoid constitutional issues about funding parochial education. Yet even magnet schools have trouble attracting participants. In an experiment with alternative elementary programs, most parents opted to send their children to a nearby building. Information about specific programmatic differences in other schools was hard to obtain and harder to assess.

## Public Purposes of Schooling

Advocates of privatization suggest that schools cannot get any worse, so why not try something else. We argue that market-oriented schools will not solve underlying issues of stagnant productivity or unequal life prospects. Learning depends on students' motivations as well as how effectively teachers make information accessible. Educational institutions are crucial sites for constructing social and personal meanings. Learning that contributes to a better future involves a curriculum that supports positive aspirations for all children, that opens discussions among teachers and citizens about educational purposes, and that builds on hope rather than alienation. It is a matter of collective choice about whether all children have prospects for a decent home, job and family. Personal safety and social security require public efforts. Ideally schools sustain ongoing reconstructions of community standards.

Many experts on markets and democracy emphasize the public interest in education. Elementary and secondary education bring benefits to society at large and assure future economic well-being. "We are all better off, both economically and otherwise, when our fellow citizens are literate, schooled in the fundamentals of civics, and partake to some degree of our common culture," as Donahue (1989, p. 189) noted. Political, social and economic relations are easier when people can assume others share basic literacies. Mandatory attendance and public support for schools support democracy and economic growth. In the United States, privatization would still have governments collect taxes for subsidizing individual choices but rely on profit-seeking or nonprofit agencies to deliver appropriate educational services. Privatization implies that government is coercive and inefficient, whereas public education symbolizes a positive view of collective endeavors.

There is little evidence that instruction can be reduced to techniques or that principal-agent communication can be clarified without explicit or implicit long-term contracts. Developing a contract between public officials and private providers is nearly impossible because not every worthy goal can be identified or measured. Educators sensibly adopt multiple missions that muddle responsibility and accountability. They encourage a diversity of programs and individualized instruction, although too often an emphasis on orderly behaviors and rank-ordered grades dominates. Teachers make hundreds of judgments every day about issues to cover, praise versus criticism, on whom to focus, and so on. They often succeed or fail without much idea about what activity actually led to learning.

Efforts to write outcomes for standards for certain grade levels and graduation are an interesting approach to holding a school staff and students accountable without specifying the means, but goals such as "distinguish fact from opinion, identify stereotyping and recognize bias" are difficult to translate into specific curriculum (Massachusetts Department of Education, 1994). Others such as "develop and present conclusions through speaking, writing, artistic and other means of expression" are not easy to monitor and assess. Although understanding principles of equality and justice is called for, there remains a contradiction between mandated outcome standards and democratic schools. Moreover, state or national standards raise profound issues around inequities in school finance as well as class, race and gender biases.

Three practical issues mitigate against choice or voucher plans achieving their advocates' promises. First, comprehensive schools enroll children from a reasonably broad geographic area, and travel time makes a difference for students and parents who must pick up a sick child or attend conferences and school events. Second, an initial advantage of new schools where beginning teachers earn lower salaries and bring fresh enthusiasm soon fades as private educational ventures either break an implicit contract of job security or come to resemble public schools. Third, after a time, a few public districts and large private corporations would predictably attract most students—less because parents choose wisely than because advertising and market dominance discourage potential competitors. For instance, a popular high school might induce enrollment in associated elementary schools by citing a compatible curriculum.

The logic of collective behavior suggests that private schools reinforce America's competitive individualism and discourage cooperation. A citizen may willingly pay a progressive tax in order to assist a public school and yet not voluntarily tutor or contribute to a fund drive. A student may prefer nonmaterialistic values and yet opt for a school that promises a competitive edge. A youth might flourish in an alternative program based on student responsibility, cooperative learning, ecological concerns, and peaceful negotiation and yet reject that option if it is perceived that success depends on attending an elite college that requires high Scholastic Aptitude Test scores.

If full-scale choice plans worked at all, they would destroy public schooling. Will taxpayers—who have surrendered their voice about what happens in schools—continue to fund private choices by parents? In *The School and Society*, Dewey (1956, p. 7) insisted that society should offer all children "what the best and wisest parent wants for his own child." That dialog, however contentious, is central to a democratic future. Perhaps current fissures—between fundamentalism and secular humanism, monoculturalism and multiculturalism, cooperative learning and norm-referenced tests, vocational training and civic values— can be neither compromised nor encompassed within a public school. Family choice schools seemingly shift those disagreements out of politics, but they predictably will reappear in debates over an appropriate curriculum or the value of a voucher.

## Financing Schools Fairly

Investing in future productivity requires a society to pay attention to children's access to decent education. No person between the ages of 3 and 21 should be denied a high-quality school based on economic factors outside that person's control. Children with similar needs, motivations and abilities should gain comparable educations regardless of their residence, family background, race, religion, sex, personality, appearance, or other extraneous issue. No person should receive a quality of education so low as to preclude useful participation in social, economic and political affairs. No one should find their home life or career opportunities so bleak that they destroy hope for a better future. Left alone, capitalism and free markets have not assured those rights.

Historically, state funding for schools recognized expenses that impact unequally on districts. For instance, states aided busing in sparsely settled rural areas, new building costs in burgeoning suburbs, and vocational programs. Formulas adjust payments to compensate for differences in taxable property per school-age child. Moreover, most compensate for extra costs in schools serving low-income neighborhoods, bilingual students, and children with special needs. These schedules for state aid require ongoing adjustments as costs and property values shift with economic developments. Their implementation depends on the state's share as a percentage of total expenditures. When rising school costs outpace state aid, disparities increase.

Educational costs and racial differences segment communities in ways that threaten public support for all schools. As Reich (1991, pp. 42, 44) noted, the "fortunate fifth is quietly seceding from the rest of the nation." He described three Boston suburbs, each with mainly White residents—Belmont, Somerville and Chelsea, in descending order of wealth. Belmont paid teachers an average salary of $36,100, and over 80% of high school graduates attended a four-year college. Somerville teachers earned $29,400, and more students left school without a diploma than went to college (about one-third in each group). Teachers in Chelsea, "facing tougher educational challenges than his or her counterparts in Belmont, earned $26,200 in 1988. . . . More than half of Chelsea's 18-year-olds did not graduate from high school, and only 10 percent planned to attend college."

Equalization of school finance is the single most important reform in education today, and it will take combined action by all branches and levels of government. Federal and state formulas should focus on equalizing resources, with sufficient local control (probably by individual schools) to facilitate meeting specific community needs and parent's wishes. As important as this reform is, it will not quickly raise retention rates, Scholastic Aptitude Test scores, or readiness for high-tech employment. If equitable distributions lowered spending in wealthy districts, average test scores might decline. Likewise, if lagging districts raised teachers' salaries to their state's average, there would be little short-run impact on the quality of teachers. After a time, equal resources would allow differences to reflect local educational leadership, not the wealth of the district. Over longer periods, decisions about locations for households and firms would be less influenced by variations in local taxes.

Ideally, public schools receive resources matched to the educational needs and goals of students so that different learning styles and goals do not determine their academic success. In practice, that means adjusting for high-cost students and state funding formulas that compensate for variations in taxable resources per school-age child. To date, however, no state successfully equalizes resources for districts even when under court orders. Federal supplements under Title I (formerly Chapter 1) or Head Start programs direct funds to districts serving low-income neighborhoods, but in inadequate amounts. Moreover, federal support for higher education goes primarily to those who are relatively well-off.

As an illustration about how to combine principles of equity and efficiency through local decisionmaking, we propose a change in federal compensatory aid. Assistance to low-income or low-achieving districts and schools should not reward their failure as existing eligibility seems to do. Instead, federal or state governments should fund school improvement plans based on the following principles:

(1) involve teachers, students, parents, and pertinent community groups;

(2) establish a policy advisory committee with a majority of its membership made up of parents with children in the affected schools;

(3) identify needs, possible solutions, and appropriate technical assistance;

(4) draft a three-year plan with goals, activities, and specific outcomes;

(5) submit proposal for evaluation of its feasibility; and

(6) report modifications and evaluations after each year to the local community and the funding agency.

Based on identified successes and problems, schools then would develop another three-year plan, thereby encouraging effective change strategies.

Individual and family differences in learning styles will persist. Therefore, districts should distribute resources among schools and teachers allocate their time and skills within classrooms in such a way that children are supported in equitable achievement. Federal and state laws and court decisions set forth minimum standards for racial balance, mainstreaming special needs, gender equity, and bilingual programs. They should be welcomed by educators as national standards of fairness, but the burden of implementation falls mainly on low-income, minority and urban districts. At the same time, important educational decisions should be left to students, their families, their schools, their local communities, and their states. Those choices make real the possibilities of creating a better future.

## UNCERTAINTIES AND ASPIRATIONS

Uncertainties cast a shadow between today's decisions and tomorrow's conditions and make information economically valuable. According to standard economic analysis, uninsurable risks usually create a downward bias for demand and supply schedules—though often a greater demand for information. In general, as Arrow (1962) demonstrated, uncertainties result in a higher discount rate for anticipated gains, that is, people normally will invest less in human or physical capital when social instability indicates an unpredictable future. Education is doubly plagued. First, its potential benefits are essentially unknowable before one has incurred the costs of learning. Second, its market values depend on future consumer preferences and technological developments—both continually being reshaped by current constructions of cultural standards and by research activities. During the 1970s, public opinion turned pessimistic, risk assessments flourished, and schools floundered without a common sense of purpose.

Projected labor demands obviously influence personal decisions about schooling as an investment in human capital. Economists depict a segmented market roughly divided between unskilled, temporary jobs and careers open to those with formal educations. Although personnel directors seek employees who will fit into the organization, communicate with others, and continue to learn, they have few clues about the productivity of future labor, especially in positions requiring knowledgeable judgments. By default, then, academic credentials carry great weight, as do records of employment, previous salary, military service, arrests, and health. Because degrees are a primary screening device, class, race and gender biases in schools have exaggerated impacts on individual prospects, with real social consequences.

Information gathering helps reduce uncertainties and justifies public support for much basic research. Because the United States encompasses a diversity of people and activities, that knowledge cannot be contextual or gathered through experience. The abstract concepts learned through school help enormously in aggregating data into salient conclusions that might enable citizens to comprehend feasible choices. Otherwise, uncertainty about risks and self-interests divides voters and encourages democratic gridlock. Moreover, ignorance induces partisan loyalties and persuasion rather than a discourse about a common good.

At the same time, uncertainties make information economically valuable. If organizations respond too slowly to changing conditions, they lose out to competitors. Firms focus research and development in areas of effective demand, that is, where people have money. Yet innovations also introduce personal risks for those citizens whose jobs are threatened. Individuals face diverse risks—from crime, nuclear holocaust, environmental degradation, or incurable disease. Fears of joblessness and underemployment discourage investing in job skills. Only collective action to limit risks based on adequate data can foster stable, healthy environments that encourage positive steps to improve oneself and one's community.

### Public Policies and Individual Rights

Although Americans have traditionally stressed individualistic decisions and competitive markets, modern industrial societies mandate rights that assure all individuals certain powers and privileges and otherwise compensate for market failures. Legislation and court decisions define areas of equality and choice independent of one's income or wealth. Most fundamental rights entail either relatively low costs—such as suffrage, habeas corpus, free speech, and religious toleration—or an inability to limit use as in access to city streets or to national defense. Education and health care are major exceptions, entailing high costs, especially for those in greatest need. During the past 30 years, increased spending, especially by governments, for health and education has served previously underserved groups without creating a sense of increased well-being for the majority of individuals.

Societies that avoided tyranny, which is always hierarchical, have devised overlapping as well as nested "spheres of justice," in a helpful phrase from political philosopher Michael Walzer (1983, p. 318). He envisioned the United States as "a decentralized democratic socialism; a strong welfare state run, in part at least, by local and amateur officials; a constrained market; an open and demystified civil service; independent public schools; the sharing of hard work and free time; the protection of religious and familial life; a system of public honoring and dishonoring free from all considerations of rank or class; workers' control of companies and factories; a politics of parties, movements, meetings, and public debate." Defining substantive and procedural rights for those subunits and their interconnections is an ongoing political responsibility, yet it is seldom addressed in the formal curriculum because it seems "political."

> **The challenge for democracy is to maintain both diversity of opinion and enough consensus for an active, yet stable, government authority.**
>
> What elements are essential for a just (fair and equitable) society that also sustains a reasonable diversity of political, cultural, religious, and philosophical viewpoints?

Because the United States has not achieved a sense of justice among its citizens, they are reluctant to approve increased funding to support programs for social equity. As Rawls (1971, pp. 133, 14–15) recognized, the "stability of social cooperation" depends largely on the rules of justice being known and accepted. Trade-offs between equality and efficiency are especially sharp when major costs are required to assure minimum standards for education, health and personal safety. Yet fairness to individuals must have priority over maximization for the group if a simpler, less risky world is to prevail. Or, in Rawls's terms, "social and economic inequalities, for example inequalities of wealth and authority, are just only if they result in compensating benefits for everyone, and in particular for the least advantaged members of society."

Equity requires group agreement on basic, common rights in an order of priority. But democratic decisionmaking is a peculiarly irrational process—subject to understatement of interest in public goods, indeterminate social preferences, and stakeholders who include children and future generations. Effective public actions require policy guidelines that reflect a mix of goals and yield unambiguous signals for action. We offer some historical examples that share those character-istics and point toward a world where assured minimums of security temper projections of current trends toward a global disaster. The following sketches are neither inclusive nor universally popular, but they suggest something of the nature and spirit of the tasks ahead.

During the New Deal era, a federal responsibility for maintaining full employment through appropriate monetary and fiscal policies satisfied humanitarian concerns and stimulated economic growth and investment in human capital. Full employment means a larger national income pie so that individual shares can grow and become more equal. Although women and people of color confront a dual labor market, discriminatory barriers usually fall during periods of rapid economic expansion. State and local governments as well as firms anticipate steady growth in aggregate income. Wage earners project steady work, which encourages home ownership and family planning. A strong demand for labor allows individuals to change firms or occupations—to avoid harassment, intimidation and unsafe conditions or to find a type of work more to their liking.

Later, civil rights legislation successfully reduced risks from discrimination. Previously, laws enforced segregation in much of the United States, and the justice system tolerated wholesale violations of minority rights. Although still far from achieving equality of income or opportunity, African Americans have moved a step or two from the precipice of apartheid because of the successes of voter registration, compensatory education, equal access to public accommodations, jobs programs, fairer law enforcement, and affirmative action. As a result, more Black students finish high school and continue with postsecond-ary education. The transformation in civil rights also encouraged other Americans to assert pride in various ethnic heritages and women to demand equality in legal terms and employment practices. By reducing threats of segregation or genocide for African Americans, the nation reduced pressure to conform on other citizens whose lifestyles differed from a dominant middle-class and Puritan culture.

An educational revolution may result from Public Law 94-142, which mandates identification of children with special needs and the development of individual educational plans in the "least restrictive" setting. When standardized test scores and deviations from strict behavioral standards categorize students from talented to retarded—and when equal educational opportunities means identical classrooms and texts, students learn that they should fit into a predetermined norm. Thus, traditional schools discredit individual interests, diverse life experiences, and special talents. By removing the punitive aspects of a "special needs" category, schools may help millions of learners who struggle to fit through the standardized "mesh" implicit in national texts and tests.

In these three illustrations, public actions removed previous punishments—loss of income, segregated and inferior facilities, or caretaker education—that were based on factors outside of an individual's control. In practice, these public policies extend equality of conditions. They enhance individual rights and freedoms without denying those rights to others. They are affirmative in tone, rather than relying on regulations and punishments. These government actions secure basic rights and reduce uncertainties without stultifying individual or group desires to excel. However, they do require experts and managers to balance public missions, clarify goals and means, and seek consensus on functional policies to enhance freedom. That understanding about positive government roles needs to be taught in schools both as a subject and through democratic practice.

## Fostering Equity in Schools

For better or worse, schools are one of the few institutional sites for public discourse about desirable futures. Moreover, governments invariably assign social purposes to schools—health and safety, literacy and computation, national ideologies and citizenship, and readiness for work. Asked about preparing students to change society, an assistant principal noted "*so many areas of deficiencies. We want students to find ways of eliminating poverty and ways of dealing with all of the pressing issues of the day. So we want change, and I think it is our responsibility to prepare them to make those changes and to encourage them to be diverse in their approach.*" Ideally, schools build public support when they demonstrate democratic fairness, effective public management, and a voice for students, parents and staff in their mission. When social inequalities stunt their students' aspirations and opportunities, teachers either acquiesce or criticize the taxpayers who provide their salary. Those conflicting values distort dialog toward technical solutions.

Schools for an information age will evolve through multiple phases linked together through holistic images of households, work, schools and society, as we shall explore in the next four chapters. An innovative teacher noted that his colleagues "*talk a lot about wanting to restructure and reorganize and revitalize schools, but yet there is not the political will to really provide the resources necessary to do the job.*" Despite his zeal for reform, he was skeptical about panaceas. He recognized that "*a school administrator or teachers in classrooms . . . have a vision for the kind of world that we would like to see our society develop into. And given that, we certainly need them to develop the kinds of critical-thinking, problem-solving, decisionmaking skills in our young people that may in fact help us to improve our society.*" Yet he feared "*that attempts at social engineering societal problems simply lead to more complex problems.*"

A first step is to encourage schools where all students cooperate in multicultural settings. As an administrator noted, mobility and international capitalism call for *"greater understanding of different cultures in order to work with people who are different."* A bilingual teacher commented on a need to cooperate across district and class lines: *"In the Bronx and Lowell the poverty is so bad that students are dropping out. I don't think the students are having problems but the school just does not provide them with a lot of support, or provide them with a lot of good teachers, for lack of money."* No other issue elicited as many spontaneous comments as working with culturally and linguistically diverse students.

Second, schools need to bring science and technology within public discourse so that transmitting academic knowledge is made problematic by situating it historically and socially. A beginning teacher wanted to introduce personal and political issues into sciences: *"When we're just limited to teaching kids what they need to get by, and make the money to survive and have a career, I think we are far too limited in scope. Of course that's what they're going to need. But . . . if we could bring in* [real] *issues . . . and discuss them in terms of society, they'll be so much better equipped once they're out in the world."* Typically, this issue arose in comments about computer literacy.

Third, in a rapidly changing world, the United States needs public policies to support lifelong learning for everyone—including educators. Innovations and inventions induce instability and exploitation by those in the know. Widespread low-cost dissemination of information enables people to cope with change and thus helps restore social equilibrium. A teacher feared future stagnation *"if curriculum is truly a powerful instrument, as we believe it is, in terms of getting people ready for the future and deciding what it is they've got to learn to prepare themselves for the future and what we are going to teach kids."* Schools should demonstrate civic responsibility and organizational effectiveness, yet she wondered about *"how we govern ourselves and who is in charge."* Site-based management meant *"figuring out who wants to be in on what decisions."*

Developing a multicultural curriculum, viewing science and technology as socially constructed, and exploring lifelong learning reframe educational purposes and democratic possibilities. Teachers may organize curriculum around common human values and varied personal interests. By using low-cost information technologies, they can acknowledge individual diversity without hierarchical groups. Defining equality in terms of a social insurance against conditions that stunt human development encourages diversity while emphasizing common rights. People reduce paralyzing risks that too often inhibit a sense of individual autonomy by acting in concert through democratic governance. Then, schools will promote liberating choices in private and communal spheres.

**RELATED READING**

For readable accounts of the connection between politics and the economy see Arthur M. Okun, *Equality and Efficiency: The Big Tradeoff* (Washington, DC: Brookings Institution, 1975); Kevin P. Phillips, *The Politics of the Rich and Poor: Wealth and the American Electorate in the Reagan Aftermath* (New York: Random House, 1990); and Lester C. Thurow, *The Zero-Sum Society: Distribution and the Possibilities of Economic Change* (Baltimore, MD: Penguin Books, 1980).

Useful accounts of the role for governments may be found in Margaret Weir, Ann Shola Orloff, and Theda Skocpol, eds., *The Politics of Social Policy in the United States* (Princeton, NJ: Princeton University Press, 1988); Forrest Chisman and Alan Pifer, *Government for the People: The Federal Social Role: What It Is, What It Should Be* (New York: W. W. Norton, 1987); and James Q. Wilson, *Bureaucracy: What Government Agencies Do and Why They Do It* (New York: Basic Books, 1989).

# 7

# Cooperating in Multicultural Settings

In our interviews, teachers and administrators struggled to make sense of class, race and gender in schools. *"The curriculum is geared—as everything in our country is—toward the White middle class,"* noted a reading specialist. *"Someday our curriculum has to include everyone because that is how our country is."* A student teacher wondered how to bridge the gap between her suburban background and her students' urban experiences: *"You often have students not becoming as literate as they are capable of, mainly because the teacher doesn't know how to approach the material so that they can best grasp and grow with it. So the idea is . . . using the student's first culture—be it their adolescent culture, their Hispanic culture, whatever it is, using their economic, social culture as the resource on which to build their skills."*

A multicultural specialist puzzled about how to teach the promise of democracy to students of color:

*Now in the schools it's obvious they are not preparing people for that because when you say liberty and justice for all, you're thinking about liberty and justice for all who are White—liberty and justice for all who have the power; liberty and justice for all who have economic means. If that was the goal of our forefathers, then that should be the goal of the nation right now and it should be in every aspect, not only in race and nationality, but also in technology, in social classes, in economics. All of it should go together if this is going to be the land of the free.*

Another teacher raised the dilemmas for women who face salary discrimination and a glass ceiling on promotions: *"At one point you are going to have to tell them that 'you are a woman, forget about being President.'"*

Educators are in the midst of contentious debates about ethnic diversity and multicultural education as the one in three students who come from regions other than Western Europe seek to establish social

identities and cultural roots. Moreover, racism, sexism, ethnic prejudices, and class status are now entangled with issues of empowerment
in current as well as future settings. Typically, dominant groups cite
impersonal factors—such as IQ scores, high grades and hard work—to
account for their privileges. Teachers recite historical, economic and
social "facts" to discuss the plight of women and minority groups without ever listening to their voices. A presumed superiority of White,
male, technological knowledge cheats many students of models for
positive self-identity.

As teachers acknowledge diverse cultural perspectives and historical
patterns of racial and ethnic subordination, they often subvert their
own authority. By focusing on liberal traditions and civic participation
in a largely Anglo-Protestant cultural milieu, the curriculum has presented a uniquely coherent national history in which newcomers were
successively acculturated—while each contributed a special flavoring to
the whole. People of color and feminists bring to the surface issues that
are "invisible" in those standard accounts of consensus and progress.
Students who speak different languages or dialects implicitly raise
questions about the formal canon of history and literature incorporated
in texts and tests.

In this chapter, we discuss ways to understand cultural diversity in
schools today. When African Americans, Latinos, Asians, and Native
Americans as well as females fail to achieve equally, teachers either
reinforce orthodox explanations for inequalities or they question the
goal of assisting *all* children in developing their potential. White
participants in teacher workshops on racism tend to ignore evidence of
discrimination in their schools and to offer one of two explanations:
Some assert that they treat everyone the same, while others ask why
African Americans cannot assimilate like European ethnic groups.
Multicultural advocates as well as critical theorists show how schools
value middle-class beliefs that advantage some children. "America is
like a melting pot," they quip, "people at the bottom get burned and the
scum floats to the top."

An underlying puzzle is how Americans reconcile their democratic
ideology with widely held assumptions embedded in race, gender and
ethnic categories. We describe typical interactions between dominant
and subordinate groups. Next, we contrast three approaches to teaching
across cultural boundaries—a compensatory model, naive multicultural
education, and mutual learning through dialog that is inclusive and
converging. Then, we present ways to foster such discussions among
diverse groups through whole language and cooperative learning
approaches. Finally, we consider how multicultural perspectives may
help internalize the multiple realities of postmodern societies.

## SOCIALLY CONSTRUCTED IDENTITIES

Culture consists of widely shared and long-lasting socially constructed frameworks that establish personal and group identities. Initially, culture is revealed in shared practices—foods, holidays, public and private ceremonies—and in public rhetoric that "interprets" events—political speeches, histories, social science studies, novels, sermons, and homilies. At a deeper level, cultural interpretations seek to reveal embedded meanings that offer plausible accounts of otherwise puzzling events. Culture evolves through interactions with others as new experiences reconstruct meanings. It may be viewed in three layers: taken-for-granted assumptions that facilitate unthinking responses in normal situations; ambivalences or endemic tensions where personal and social choices are incorporated within one's framework of understanding; and underlying webs of significance among these beliefs.

Family values, in-group lifestyles, academic disciplines, occupational norms, and national beliefs are constructed through repeated interactions. In turn, those categories shape our daily practices. Culture follows from a natural human activity of "making sense" of one's experiences. In anthropologist Ulf Hannerz's (1992, pp. 3, 7) words, "she literally produces sense through her experience, interpretation, contemplation, and imagination, and she cannot live in the world without it." In constructivist terms, culture "is the meanings which people create, and which create people, as members of societies." Persisting attitudes and activities gain authority from tradition; dysfunctional ones are abandoned. Consequently, in-group members remain largely unconscious of their own beliefs unless they conflict with views of others.

Culture is revealed only indirectly through articulated ideas, shared practices, and the ways those attitudes and behaviors affect diverse members of society. Hannerz (1992, p. 7) distinguished three facets:

1. *ideas and modes of thought* as entities and process of the mind—the entire array of concepts, propositions, values and the like which people within some social unit carry together, as well as their various ways of handling their ideas in characteristic modes of mental operation;

2. *forms of externalization,* the different ways in which meaning is made accessible to the senses, made public; and

3. *social distribution,* the ways in which the collective cultural inventory of meanings and meaningful external forms—that is, (1) and (2) together—is spread over a population and its social relationships.

Ordinarily, culture is viewed as a largely fixed set of attributes that generally characterize people (or at least dominant groups) living within a geographic area. Many commonsensically attribute in-group sentiments to familiarity and prejudice about outsiders to instinctive or natural fears of strangers. Some, arguing that selfishness is essential for Darwinian survival despite evidence of altruism among many species, insist that competition among groups is natural. A few cling to a notion of biological differences, although scientific definitions of race as a distinctive species or genotype have been amply discredited. We propose, instead, that cultures are learned beliefs that persist because they benefit the powerful. Historically, dominant Americans have used class, race and gender categories to justify inequalities in a democracy that promised liberty and justice for all.

Because beliefs are not always internally consistent, they raise characteristic tensions for members of a culture. For instance, Americans seek both individual autonomy to define themselves and a sense of belonging to a community. Through interactions with members of diverse groups, people recognize differences that help define their own cultural beliefs. That raises a question: How did White racism, patriarchy, and Anglo-Protestant values remain powerful in a nation where so many experienced discrimination based on some ascribed characteristic or national origin? As a partial answer, we present three illustrations: immigrants seeking identity as mainstream Americans; racism as socially constructed and consequential, although without biological validity; and schools reproducing gender differences.

## Immigrants and Ethnicity

A plausible historical approach suggests how power relations embodying economic and political forces became embedded at the outset in constructions of cultural differences in the United States. From the age of exploration to the present, growing world trade enhanced contact among formerly isolated groups. Europeans saw themselves as bringing civilization (and Christianity) to primitive peoples and cultures. A persistent racism, defined as a belief in the superiority of White Europeans, served as a central tenet of dominant beliefs and helped account for a legal system of chattel slavery in the English colonies more inhumane than any other in the New World. Manifest Destiny in the 19th century justified American expansion to the Pacific Coast as well as later imperialistic incursions in the Philippines and Central America. A widespread view that people of color lack a capacity for, or right to, self-determination made it easier to accept dropping atomic bombs on Japanese civilians as well as military interventions in Vietnam and Afghanistan.

With the important exception of African slaves and English prisoners, most immigrants came voluntarily in response to higher wages, greater freedom, and eligibility for citizenship. Though officially welcomed, most newcomers experienced a rejection of their language,

religion, customs, and values in a complex process of Americanization
or assimilation. As strangers in a new land, they simultaneously
reconstructed previous meaning systems and found their acculturation
into new ways limited by language, job discrimination, and a longing for
familiar customs. In that way, people who had identified with a family,
village or a tribe became "African" or "Italian" in the United States.

As a nation of immigrants, why have Americans embraced Anglo-
Protestant values of Puritans and the Founding Fathers? Americans
defined nationhood around democratic ideas and civic participation
more than an accretion of customs and traditions bound to place and
institutional settings. A restless, individualistic and materialistic
people, they preferred actions to words yet remain peculiarly idealistic
or moralistic in their self-expression. That openness to material progress and ideological commitment to democratic equality shaped the
ways by which immigrants could accommodate to dominant values and
habits. Attracted by a promise of freedom and abundance, immigrants
sought economic mobility. They found an opening in citizenship and
participation in voting and other civic activities, as well as a rapidly
expanding economy.

At the time of the Revolution, there were approximately 3 million
mainly English-speaking settlers and 600,000 Africans in the 13
colonies. During the 19th and 20th centuries, over 50 million people left
their homeland for the United States. Through 1960, some 35 million
immigrants came, primarily from Europe: 4.5 million from Ireland; 4
million from Great Britain; 6.7 million from principalities that formed
Germany; some 2.4 million from Scandinavia; nearly 5 million from the
Italian peninsula; some 8 million from Eastern Europe—Poles,
Hungarians, Bohemians, Slovaks, Ukrainians, Ruthenians—many of
whom were Jewish; and, finally, 3 million from the Balkans and Asia
Minor—Greeks and Macedonians, Croatians and Albanians, Syrians
and Armenians. Of the 12 million who have arrived since 1960, almost
10 million came from Central and South America, Asia or Africa.

Migration tore people away from their traditional customs and
language and placed them in unfamiliar settings, a phenomenon mov-
ingly depicted in Oscar Handlin's *The Uprooted* (1951, pp. 108, 109–
110). Emigrants left villages where they and their families had lived in
much the same way for generations; they arrived as individuals,
shocked by the voyage and fatigue and dependent on others for a job
and shelter: "Loneliness, separation from the community of the village,
and despair at the insignificance of their own human abilities, these
were the elements that, in America, colored the peasants' view of their
world." For these newcomers, self-improvement seemed beyond one's
control: "Their view of the American world led these immigrants to
conservatism, and to the acceptance of tradition and authority."

Life in the United States divided families. A job and earnings determined one's status, whereas European youth had established

relationships within a family and village: "The boys and girls were to be properly brought up, taught the skills necessary for their own adulthood and imbued with the beliefs necessary for continued membership in the community" (Handlin, 1951, pp. 241, 248). Children "were to obey their elders and particularly him who stood at the head of the family." American schools introduced a rival authority whose texts seldom spoke to immigrants' experiences: "it was better not to question the teacher's world. The wise fellow . . . came to believe in a universe, divided as it were into two realms, one for school and one for home, and each with rules and modes of behavior of its own." Most children of immigrants eagerly embraced the new and thereby dismissed their family's customs and values.

Many immigrants sought to maintain old ways through ethnic clubs, traditional churches, and holidays. For instance, in 1921 about two-thirds of Polish American children attended parochial schools. The first generation felt cut off from both old and new worlds:

The only adjustment they had been able to make to life in the United States had been one that involved the separateness of their group, one that increased their awareness of the differences between themselves and the rest of society. . . . The demand that they assimilate, that they surrender their separateness, condemned them always to be outsiders. In practice, the free structure of American life permitted them with few restraints to go their own way, but under the shadow of a consciousness that they would never belong. (Handlin, 1951, p. 285)

Despite a professed goal of assimilation, ethnicity persists in social and political relationships, along with some surprisingly permeable boundaries. Political campaigns often count on ethnic loyalties—for example, in 1968 Polish Americans turned out for the ticket of Hubert Humphrey and Edmund Muskie (originally Marciszewski). Categories such as Hispanic, Asian or Black treat a diversity of countries, languages, and traditions as one. For instance, the editors of the *Harvard Encyclopedia of American Ethnic Groups* decided on 106 entries by lumping together peoples who had felt little connection in their homeland. Native Americans were subsumed under one listing covering 1.5 million people from 107 officially recognized Indian nations. Meanwhile, Indian activists insist that "more than 400 indigenous peoples continue to exist within the borders of the 48 contiguous states" (Churchill, 1991, p. 5).

Most Americans applaud the struggles of immigrants to assimilate—after they gained income and access to mainstream institutions. Predominantly European groups blended into existing social patterns, although many families Anglicized their names and abandoned ethnic foods and holidays. Power induced acceptance, and then, educators celebrated the accomplishments and traditions of Irish, Italian or

Jewish Americans. Textbooks added representatives of people of color and ethnic Americans. If oppressed groups alluded to discrimination that marked their common lot, they avoided blaming those in power or analyzing the dynamics of social identity formation. Unsurprisingly, many children lack enthusiasm for classes where they can neither recover their past nor see their future.

## Realities of Racism

The major dilemma for dominant Americans has been a manifest contradiction between an ideological commitment to equal and free individuals and the treatment accorded African Americans. That inconsistency also applies to indigenous peoples who were decimated or displaced to reservations, to Asians denied a right to immigrate or own property, to non–English-speaking people from Latin America, to most immigrants at one time or another. Dominant groups explain the subordinate position of others as personal flaws (individuals are dumb, lazy, dishonest, criminal) or as institutional outcomes (segregated schools are unequal, Black families still suffer from a legacy of slavery).

From the outset of their arrival as indentured servants in Jamestown in 1619, African Americans were treated differently in practice. Reflecting prevailing attitudes of Elizabethan England, White colonists looked down on Africans and non-Christians, but they had no legal category of permanent servitude. In the context of slavery in Spanish colonies and their claims to land in the New World, they moved to legalize ownership of another person—enabling Whites to exploit Blacks' labor and person. Over time, "African" and "slave" became linked in practice. Racist reasoning provided ideological justifications for exploitation and debasement of other human beings. By the end of the 18th century, not even a rhetoric of equality set forth to justify the American Revolution could overcome a desire to subordinate Blacks (and a fear of what might happen if White domination ended).

In the new state of Virginia, where the author of the Declaration of Independence still lived, democratic legislatures limited the ability of slave owners to emancipate their chattels; and efforts were made to reenslave freed Blacks. Some members ably reiterated a commitment to equality and liberty for all men: "At the same moment, however, many of his most profound urges, especially his yearning to maintain the identity of his folk, his passion for domination, his sheer avarice, and his sexual desire, impelled him toward conceiving and treating the Negro as inferior to himself, as an American leper" (Jordon, 1969, p. 58). From the outset, that language of raw exploitation and debasement of Africans and native peoples was translated into rhetoric about retaining purity of (White) women and family and the importance of (European) civilized behaviors.

Six decades later, Americans fought a devastating Civil War to determine, as Lincoln said, whether this "new nation, conceived in Liberty, and dedicated to the proposition that all men are created equal . . . can long endure." That second American revolution eradicated slavery and declared equal rights for African Americans with the 13th, 14th and 15th amendments; it did not end a conviction that Blacks were inferior (a belief shared by many abolitionists who emphasized the sin of owning a person). A sharecropping system with crop liens kept Southern Blacks in debt to local landowners and attached to a place. Reconstruction gave way to Jim Crow segregation, which received Constitutional sanction in *Plessy v. Ferguson* (1896). Inferior schools, public accommodations, jobs, and civil rights combined with lynchings and cross burnings denied Blacks any semblance of liberty and equality.

Following Charles Darwin's *Origin of Species* (1859), racist ideologies hardened into scientific doctrine, with Social Darwinists condemning private charity for perpetuating the unfit. Eugenicists supported sterilization among those declared retarded, criminal or unable to support themselves. Many Americans used race as a convenient explanation for hierarchical classes, endemic poverty, and social dislocation that marked industrialism late in the 19th century. Social scientists assigned a genetic base for characteristics such as intelligence in support of popular movements to limit immigration, especially of those considered "degenerate." By doing so, they justified social status based on national origin as the unequal outcome of equal opportunities.

Academics used their prestige to advance a class and racist agenda. For instance, at Princeton University in the 1920s, Carl Brigham cited evidence of steadily rising IQ scores based on length of residence in the United States as proof of "a gradual deterioration in the class of immigrants examined in the army, who came to this country in each succeeding five year period since 1902" (quoted in Kamin, 1974, pp. 20–21). Brigham and others took the ordering of IQ scores from African Americans to Anglo-Saxon Protestants as proof that they had successfully measured real brain power. Nordics were superior ("rulers, organizers, and aristocrats . . . individualistic, self-reliant, and jealous of their personal freedom . . . as a result they are usually Protestants") while Alpines were "the perfect slave, the ideal serf." Mexicans and Blacks were clearly inferior to anyone from Europe, including Russian Jews. As secretary of the College Entrance Examination Board, Brigham helped design the Scholastic Aptitude Test.

Beginning with the Great Migration around World War I, Southern Blacks moved to Northern cities, where they found less overt segregation and better jobs—though plenty of aversion and discrimination. Outbreaks of civil disorders resulted in many deaths among Blacks, and overcrowded tenements and deteriorating urban schools marked their fate. Although the New Deal took some steps toward including African Americans in relief and public works projects as well as agricultural assistance, President Franklin D. Roosevelt never endorsed federal antilynching laws. With recovery and World War II, Blacks found more jobs and began slow progress toward dismantling segregation, as shown by dates of key executive orders, Supreme Court decisions, or legislation: the military (1948), higher education (1950), public schools (1954), public accommodations (1964), and voting rights (1957, 1965).

---

**All humans share a broad genetic inheritance. Viewed from outer space, we share one planet with a narrow range of viable environments. Yet people often exaggerate small differences.**

**What activities are common to all human cultures? In a parallel column, add some variations among those activities. For example, everyone eats, although ethnic groups may prefer customary foods. Are similarities or differences more significant?**

---

At first glance, African Americans seem to be making steady progress toward integration and acceptance since the Civil Rights Movement. Recording three decades of race relations, Bob Blauner (1989, p. 169) found progress and change overridden by powerful White racism. There is a growing Black middle class who have attended college and are succeeding in business and politics. Nevertheless, half of all Black children are growing up in poverty, fewer than two-thirds of Black men participate in the labor force, and unemployment rates for young Black men are double those for Whites. More than 12% of the population, African Americans hold less than 2% of elective offices, and those are mainly local. They are "more likely to be welcomed into formerly white worlds—if they meet white middle-class standards of acceptability," in other words, if they abandon fictive kinship and cultural roots with other African Americans.

Since 1900, Blacks have gained on Whites in their school enrollment, and much of the gap in years of schooling has disappeared. Nevertheless, in 1992, 68% of Black individuals 25 years or older had graduated from high school or college, compared with 81% of Whites; 12% of Blacks had Bachelor's degree or higher, compared with 22% of Whites. Even for comparably educated Blacks 25 years or older who work full-time, a disparity of earnings persists (see Table 7.1). This evidence of significant racism affecting all prospects for earning a living and enjoying civil liberties suggests a low ceiling on Black aspirations for education and their capacity to sustain families.

The sheer disparity of income and power between Black and White Americans effectively separated the groups. In response to their isolation, Blacks developed stories, music and religious practices that expressed and offered release from their oppression. A few imitated

**TABLE 7.1**
**Median Earnings by Education, Sex and Race, 1991**

|  | *Male* | *Female* |
|---|---|---|
| Black High School Graduate | 20,730 | 16,960 |
| White High School Graduate | 26,790 | 18,250 |
| Black Bachelor's Degree or Higher | 34,340 | 28,130 |
| White Bachelor's Degree or Higher | 43,690 | 30,520 |

*Source*: Figures from U.S. Census.

European middle-class and Puritanical values in a vain hope of gaining acceptance. Arrests, bombings, beatings, and murders marked White resistance to nonviolent demands for equal rights during the Civil Rights Movement in the 1960s. In a peculiar way, White American self-identity as a free, affluent and upright citizen came to depend on a contrast with Black Americans.

## Patriarchy in Schools

Following precedents from the Civil Rights Movement, women in the 1970s organized protests and political action against inequalities in jobs, legal rights and households. An important impact of that movement for women's liberation "lay in its capacity to stimulate such deep rethinking, to pose, *as a problem*, concepts such as femininity and motherhood and relationships previously taken for granted" (Evans, 1989, pp. 289, 290). This "reintroduced the personal experience of being female into the political discourse of the day, challenging the obsolete language that bifurcated public and private life along lines of gender." Nevertheless, patriarchal structures are continually reconstructed around responsibility for nurturing relationships in families or workplaces.

Political events in the 1980s mark a reversal of women's growing power, deflating aspirations for positions of authority and public responsibility. Women were the last to acquire a right to vote—for 125 years American democracy excluded half the adult population. First introduced in 1923 and passed by Congress in 1972, the Equal Rights Amendment to the Constitution appeared blandly self-evident: "Equality of rights under the law shall not be denied or abridged in the United States or by any State on account of sex." Thirty-five state legislatures approved, one short of the number needed for adoption. America's grudging support for childcare and early childhood education disproportionately affects women and allows employers an excuse for not promoting female workers.

Male domination of females is harder to account for than racism directed toward a weaker, or minority, segment of the population. It raises discomforting questions about families, sexual relationships, friendships, and values of empathy and love. Rape and abuse of women and children discredit the family as a central institution for nurturing the young. The presence of sex in personal relations provokes issues of the socialization, trustworthiness and fairness of men. Because women play a primary role in raising children in home and school, patriarchy is a troublesome issue: Has male power become so internalized that its victims, including most teachers, unwittingly model subordinate roles to young females?

Oppression of women receives a powerful impetus from schools that shortchange half their students, who are presumed less active, less ambitious, and less able at professions using mathematics and science. First, adult role models include a predominantly female instructional staff (70%) who report to mostly male administrators (90%). Second, texts deliver markedly different messages—in children's literature, for example, males usually appear as problem-solving heroes, while females are subservient or dependent. Histories largely omit women despite their importance in shaping family values, workplace norms, and social reforms. The effect is to marginalize females by downplaying empathy and nurturing roles.

Third, observations of classrooms reveal that teachers pose more complex questions to boys, allow more time for answers, and respond more positively. Girls are rewarded for following classroom directions with generally good, but seldom outstanding, grades. Boys are disproportionately evaluated for self-contained special education placements or recommended for advanced placement in math and science. African American females experience the least interaction and praise from adults. Neither the formal nor the informal curriculum supports an adolescent search for positive self-identity among girls, who typically lose self-confidence from ages 10 to 16.

Fourth, aspirations are "engendered" by schools. Inexperienced in forming hypotheses, designing experiments, and solving problems, girls are less likely to pursue math and science in college or technical careers. Females are directed toward "pink collar" service jobs as secretaries, beauticians and sales clerks or the caring professions of teaching, nursing and social work. Males are directed toward (formerly) physically demanding, well-paid industrial jobs or technical, professional and managerial positions. In 1970, women were 51% of the population, 9% of full professors in universities, 7.6% of doctors, and 2.8% of lawyers. Today, women remain locked into traditionally female occupations—holding 99% of jobs for kindergarten and preschool teachers, dental hygienists and secretaries, as compared with 17% of architects and 8% of engineers.

Fifth, attitudes toward athletics and sexuality further discriminate against females. Despite some progress under Title IX, sports programs are unequal, and attitudes linger that females should neither sweat nor become aroused sexually. Health issues—including pregnancy, sexually transmitted diseases, incest, rape, and physical violence—are discussed as problems for "responsible" females to avoid. Moreover, surveys indicate that more than one in ten high-school students experience same-sex attraction. For that significant group, little in the formal curriculum or implicit views expressed through school dances, depictions of family values, peer pressures about dating, or popular media offer guidance for gender identity or positive adult roles.

Sixth, gender enormously complicates cultural divisions in schools. Sex role differentiation characterizes most working-class families—not because they are locked in a traditional culture or immune to feminist views—but because specialized production is efficient. According to economist Amartya Sen (1990), over 100 million women in Asia, Africa and Latin America have died too soon because of inadequate health care in societies that devalue females. Recent immigrants bring traditions of male-dominated families. Machismo among Latinos and roles of priests, monks and imams reinforce patriarchal assumptions. Moreover, most research on human development focused on males. As Carol Gilligan (1982) pointed out, Lawrence Kohlberg's emphasis on abstract princi- ples in moral reasoning among males ignored female morality based on values of caring, concern and connection.

Gender relations in the United States remain dominated by men and oppressive for many women. Patriarchy cuts the pool of potential leaders in half. Positive steps toward gender fairness include substan- tively changing the way teachers respond to all children; curricular materials that respect women's roles; an emphasis on math and science for both sexes; cooperative learning that features mixed-gender group activities; sexuality education that includes family roles and issues facing females; and literature and history that celebrate the importance of caring and relating to others. If teachers and students acknowledge discrimination based on sex, they may start reconstructing key social institutions such as families and workplaces on a basis of equality.

Schools serve as a biased sorting machine and then legitimate those differences through their structures, staffing, courses of study, and extracurricular activities. Historically, most European immigrant groups were allowed to imitate some of the manners and mores of Anglo-Protestants, thereby reinforcing dominant norms. Other groups, notably African Americans, were kept subordinate, thereby motivating poor Whites to emphasize color over class. Industrialization peculiarly advantaged males in their earning and learning outside the household, thereby reinforcing their domestic dominance. Nevertheless, democratic ideologies always posed some contradiction to hierarchy, and many immigrants, Blacks and women have actively resisted by appealing to those cultural tensions.

## PATTERNS OF DOMINATION AND SUBORDINATION

Many who are comfortable with current distributions of wealth and knowledge either ignore other possibilities or accept a variety of explanations that treat such differences as necessary consequences of economic and social dynamics. Empirical descriptions of culture commonly reflect the views of dominant groups. Because any summary of group beliefs necessarily captures attitudes that are pervasive and persistent, it cannot also include alternatives that might have developed as resolutions to contradictions in personal or social thought. Ethnographic reports on subordinate groups may mistake behaviors that reflect accommodations to powerlessness as racial or ethnic characteristics. Unless oppressed groups raise their voices, cultural traits can substitute for racial ascriptions to make subordinate roles appear natural and inevitable.

Oppressed groups stand to gain from equality, so they have taken the lead in reminding more comfortable Americans of the commitments to equal rights embedded in the Declaration of Independence and the Constitution. Rather than challenging dominant groups with their differences, they have pointed to the tension between social inequities and an ideology of equality. In fact, democracy and markets are usually more flexible than autocratic controls, and Americans have gradually eliminated obvious contradictions in their ideology. Participation in setting political agendas was extended—to the middle class in the Progressive era, to labor during the New Deal, to African Americans after the 1960s, and to women in the 1990s.

Currently, however, negative cultural traits serve to stereotype others by ignoring distributions of knowledge and power among Americans. Group boundaries typically are described around differences rather than human similarities and individual diversity. All races, genders and ethnic groups use arms and legs, five senses, and words to interact with each other, yet in-groups focus on differences in location, skin color, or language. All people eat, sleep and procreate, yet texts depict differences in foods, living arrangements, and rituals for coming of age. Moreover, everyone's way of doing these things is determined largely by their history and their position of relative power in the society.

### Dominant Groups

Dominant and subordinate groups experience schools differently. As they develop intellectually and socially, children from advantaged groups move through a succession of generally harmonious, increasingly power-laden settings. They discover few discontinuities in family, neighborhood, mass media, school, consumers' roles, worlds of work, and citizenship. European American males whose everyday life pattern is seldom challenged may never become self-conscious about how cultural beliefs inform their responses. For instance, they may presume that all individuals can determine their income, lifestyle and values—unaware how their exceptionally favorable prospects depend on an ascribed status (or the powerlessness of others). Each stage prepares elites for the next; their accumulating cultural baggage serves them well in a class-structured, racist and patriarchal society.

Those who do well academically seldom question their belief that schools fairly reward those blessed with native intelligence, diligence and positive aspirations. Evidence that grades, test scores, and college attendance correlate more closely with family income than IQs measured in third grade seldom generates contradictory thoughts. White male predominance among political leaders and corporate directors raises no eyebrows. If questioned by outsiders about their privileges of class, race and gender, they dismiss such comments as the lame excuses of poor losers. Students in elite colleges resist suggestions that they are being socialized and trained to serve capitalists' interests, yet many talk glibly about alienation among workers.

White males trained for careers as technicians, professionals or managers and living in middle-class suburbs seldom need to ask how they should act in their daily lives. They may watch the Superbowl and regard the action and ads as natural. The game's violence interrupted for cheerful people to pour glasses of beer (that no one on-screen ever drinks) scarcely seems odd. Cultural tensions, such as individualism versus community, are reenacted in an announcer's presentation of the team's effort while praising superstars by name. The physical contest on the field followed by handshakes and a relaxing shower mirrors their own experiences. Avid competition on the job, both open and covert, contrasts with what they see as cooperation and altruism at home.

Dominant groups (usually majorities) act mainly on taken-for-granted assumptions within specialized occupations and communities that are increasingly isolated from common experiences. They attend prestigious universities, read the *New York Times*, identify with elites in other places, and lose contact with nearby subordinate groups. Economic and political power institutionalize their dominance in a web of organizational structures and governmental policies. Intellectuals in universities and media depict endemic tensions in ways that legitimate leadership roles. For instance, free-market economists justify owners' control over workers' income and prospects. Capitalists welcome images and rhetoric about material rewards for saving, individual responsibility for one's income and status, and "progress" through exploiting technological knowledge in hierarchical organizations.

Only by surfacing issues of oppression in a cultural context can educators uncover taken-for-granted beliefs about unequal rewards from competition, White superiority, and patriarchy that mold and reflect common behaviors. When Americans select leaders from among

White males who are rich and conventional in their attitudes and behaviors, they perpetuate misunderstandings about how public policies institutionalize inequalities. Apparently, voters trust only those who take every opportunity to advance their selfish interests: Can anyone name a leader who acted to equalize income and power? Few who enjoy upward mobility question the hierarchical system that keeps most people at the level of their parents.

Gradually, some oppressive behaviors have become unacceptable to dominant groups. Those who recited the Declaration of Independence on July 4 eventually concluded that slavery was inconsistent with rhetoric about equality. After 75 years of protest and marches, men acceded to women's suffrage. History texts described the United States as a free and equal society in contrast to the rest of the world, even as the Civil Rights Movement showed how odd that rhetoric of democracy sounded to African Americans. By listening to voices of outsiders, dominant groups may discover unchallenged prejudices that contradict their espoused principles. Predictably, in another 25 years some current inequities in schools and society will appear oppressive and unacceptable to most Americans.

## Subordinate Responses

Subordinate groups (often "minorities" or "newcomers," but also unskilled workers and women) typically act in settings where others define taken-for-granted assumptions, endemic tensions, and webs of significance. Although many low-income and minority parents provide their children with extraordinary support and affection, they cannot endow them with cultural values in harmony with a curriculum that sustains hierarchies based on class, race, national origin, or religion. Youth from subordinate groups learn that the outside world is not for them—that middle-class, White males block many positive options. Although a slight majority, women divide along class, race and ethnic lines. Likewise, class-based movements are hampered by race, ethnic and gender divisions.

Those who do not fit the mold of European, middle-class males with mainstream values bear a double burden in socially constructing their public identities. They operate in settings where power belongs to others. They need to learn a set of behavioral rules to communicate within the normal language of dominant groups. For instance, advertisements on television or in magazines symbolize a high-consumption economy, although they seem terribly misplaced to those who are hungry, homeless or poor. No wonder oppressed people welcome in-group interactions where communication can be taken for granted and self-esteem is not continually undermined. Extended fictive kinships among African Americans—symbolized by hailing friends as brothers and sisters—as well as occasional self-isolation from Whites make sense in that context.

Subordinate groups simply have a hard time making their voices heard by those in power. Mass media responds to corporate advertisers; teachers dismiss students' opinions as childish or immature; and a "glass curtain," in W.E.B. DuBois's memorable phrase, seems to separate Blacks from Whites. Usually, when members of dominant groups struggle to put themselves in someone else's shoes, it is to control them—not to respect them or to interact as equals. Teachers who seek multicultural techniques to enhance their "effectiveness" define diverse beliefs as problems—not opportunities to share interesting ideas. Many students earnestly seek to break through cultural barriers of race and gender, but they find that conventional roles interfere with positive and open dialog, no matter how sincerely desired. It requires patience and a willingness to feel awkward while initiating relationships across cultural boundaries.

> **Consider how a familiar text in history or literature represents African Americans or another minority. Watch a television newscast or show and observe its reliance on stereotyped roles and cultural groups.**
>
> **What strategies for protest and self-identity formation are expressed? Whose power shaped that discourse?**

Meanwhile, some members of oppressed groups seek to win favors from those with perceived power. Students psych out teachers to their own advantage; some act out their frustrations, while others become a "teacher's pet." Women sometimes use their presumed weakness to their own advantage. Minority speakers may appeal to their oppressors' better side. Similar fractures mark every oppressed group. Some seek an accommodation with those in power—Booker T. Washington spoke about being separate as the fingers of the hand socially while joined in economic progress in order to gain funds for Tuskegee Institute as well as a voice in appointments of Blacks to public office. Martin Luther King, Jr., demanded civil rights—integration of schools and public facilities, voting and jobs—but his strategy of nonviolent resistance minimized threats to Whites. Malcolm X insisted on equal rights and, perhaps, the superiority of Black values.

As a result, oppressed peoples struggle to conceal internal disagreements over strategy and tactics. Differences within and among powerless groups allow corporate owners to maintain their dominance. Elites who are in a numerical minority adopt conscious strategies to divide and conquer: Planters bought slaves from varied language groups so that communication had to be in English; Andrew Carnegie deliberately mixed European ethnics in steel plants to hinder union organizers; and conservative politicians rejuvenate racism to persuade poor Whites to oppose welfare because it might also assist Blacks. By identifying with others who are oppressed, subordinate group members separate themselves from powerful allies whose willingness to help entails a patronizing undertow.

Because denigrated groups are mostly poor, class biases invariably mix with ethnic or racial stereotyping. Moreover, patriarchal sensitivities are usually at stake. A common pattern of discourse about oppressed groups reiterates a lack of cleanliness and morals, then addresses a presumed lack of sexual control—with implications about numbers of children and about the safety of women in the dominant group (Van Dijlk, 1987). According to these repeated stories, contact necessarily leaves dominant group members soiled. These charges have nothing to do with observed behaviors of the groups described. No amount of soap, Christianity, and moral rectitude freed African Americans from charges of filth, paganism and licentiousness. Indeed, by ascribing negative traits to others, Whites implicitly proclaim their own virtues.

## Unrealities of Race

White oppression of Blacks serves as an underlying text for all subordinate groups because presumptions about fixed genetic (or cultural) traits remain strongest for African Americans. Socially defined races (as well as classes, ethnic groups, and genders) depend on the self-interest and power of those doing the labeling. When powerful groups discriminate on the basis of national origin, they treat ethnicity as a relatively fixed cluster of characteristics. Identifying pools of genotype and phenotype by geographic region offers a "scientific" justification for discrimination against Slavs, Italians or Appalachian mountaineers. All such reasoning is tainted by a presumption that differences are more important than similarities and that negative factors are largely unmodifiable through education or inclusive social settings.

Despite the manifest impact of White prejudice, race is "a social construct that relies on common understandings and self-definitions rather than scientific criteria" (Jaynes & Williams, 1989, p. 566). As anthropologist Franz Boas insisted over 70 years ago, no one can define a race such that observable differences are not vastly greater within the group than any that supposedly distinguish them from others. No set of stereotyped characteristics applies to all members of an ascribed group. Some labeled White have dark skin, while some Blacks are lighter than Europeans in summer, and no one has shown that melanin affects character or intelligence. Some anthropologists attempt to resurrect "race" as a pool of genotype and phenotype within ranges of probability, but sorting people into categories according to arbitrary criteria scarcely demonstrates that those distinctions are useful or a part of nature.

Racialists disagree over the number of races—3 to 37 or more—and how to define persons with "mixed" ancestry (certainly over half of the U. S. population). Racial ascription has little relation to phenotypic features (other than skin color) but has profound consequences for those defined as inferior. Oppression or relative deprivation affects income and status, setting limits to how much adults invest in their children. Nature and nurture overlap in ways that are logically indistinguishable. For example, if Whites learn to debase people with dark skins, but melanin is primarily a matter of genes, then prejudiced behavior results from an interaction of genetics and experience that cannot usefully be separated. Once groups are socially constructed, then features that distinguish them from others gain prominence—statistical portraits focus on differences in IQ, crime rates, teenage pregnancy, income, and life expectancy between White and Black Americans.

As long as contacts among groups are limited by reinforcing cycles of oppression and poverty, dominant individuals have little reason to change their initially negative attitudes. After wholesale exterminations of native tribal groups in the continental United States, few European Americans interacted with Indians—now about 0.6% of the population, but with legal claim to about 30% of the land (Churchill, 1991, p. 6). Following 200 years of chattel slavery, African Americans have been kept separate by legal and de facto segregation. Puerto Ricans in New York City, Mexican Americans along the Texas to California border, Cubans in southern Florida, and Asians in urban "Chinatowns" remain isolated from Whites. Whatever intergroup contacts occur usually involve parties of unequal status. Thus, negative stereotypes among White males seldom encounter a "reality check."

One of the persistent tensions of American life has been the contrast between a relatively open definition of citizenship and individual rights and a social construction of genetic effects that sets narrow boundaries around those groups and behaviors deemed acceptable or desirable. Ironically, influential White males created a legal and social system in which a single known African, Indian or Asian ancestor determines one's identity—as though European lineage were a recessive gene. The result for people of color is that they are invited in by democratic rhetoric but—no matter how much they adopt and imitate European middle-class ideas and values—are still regarded as different. That puzzle is revealed by reactions to Blacks who conduct or play classical European music or the reluctance to cast Black actors in roles where race is unspecified.

Instead of racial characteristics fixed in genes or transmitted as cultural beliefs in some mysterious way, we account for continuities in dominant group responses to people of color through self-fulfilling prophecies (Myrdal, 1944, Chap. 17). In brief, a society that treats

African Americans as cognitively limited does little to support schools that foster high expectations for students. Lacking academic skills, young Blacks are unemployed or shunted into unskilled jobs. They earn little and are crowded into decaying housing with inadequate public services. In turn, their children are denied decent jobs and neighborhoods, and the pattern repeats. Related cycles affect Whites who have little direct contact with Blacks but whose prejudices are reinforced by media reports of low test scores in urban schools, ghetto violence, broken families, and drug abuse.

This institutionalization of racism allows Whites to use euphemisms that conceal their unwillingness to accord equality to people of color. They use code words such as "low scores on IQ tests," "dropouts," "violence," "drugs and crime," "dysfunctional families," and "welfare cheats." From a Black and Latino perspective, these issues are not rationalizations for inequality but all-too-real conditions that deny a fair chance for their children to participate in the American dream. The impact of poverty affecting half of all Black children and of inadequate urban schools will last for the next half century. The 50% unemployment rate among young Black men affects not only their investment in learning job skills but also their ability to form and support a family.

## Learning Prejudice

Today's students report recurring incidents of White hostility to Blacks without knowing how to react. When we asked a class to "describe a time when you acted in a racist way," the collective responses were startling.

*I witnessed racial incidents in my high school everyday. There was fighting on a regular basis after school.*

*As we sat around my floormates' room, the topic of conversation turned to another woman on our floor not present. We were sitting in her room with her roommate looking at all of her pictures, posters and other objects that reflected her African American heritage. They began making fun of her and what she believed in. Even though I knew better, I did laugh; but I remained basically silent.*

*I remember a Black janitor whom one particular teacher referred to as "boy" or "Bucky." The teacher always complained in a derogatory manner about the poor quality of his work and said he was lazy and slow.*

Because racism has been persistent, pervasive and powerful, we conclude that it is functional for most Whites in the United States. Attitudes—or "a learned predisposition to behave in a consistent way, usually favorably or unfavorably, toward a particular class of objects"— affect how any individual 1) adapts to the real world, 2) interacts with others, 3) copes with personal psychological needs, and 4) expresses one's values (Elms, 1972, pp. 83–85). Typically, strongly held views serve one or more of these roles better than another but are seldom seriously dysfunctional in any arena. Racist beliefs thus help in *"object appraisal"* about ordinary material features, *"social adjustment"* or establishing functional relationships with others, *"externalization"* or projections and displacements that release inner hostilities and fears, and value expressions that define who we are or want to be.

In terms of adapting to the real world, racial discrimination offered few material rewards to most Whites, but neither did it cost them much. Historically, anti-Black attitudes raised few problems for Whites in the real world of getting and spending. African Americans were locked into poverty, isolated, and denied equal education. As long as those vicious cycles affected most Blacks, few Whites interacted with them as equals at work or in public places. In the South, where most Blacks lived prior to 1960, separate schools, drinking fountains, public accommodations, and transportation prevailed. Except during wartime or labor strikes, Northern employers seldom hired Blacks. Few businesses marketed to them. These practical factors dramatically affected African Americans because poverty and miseducation burdened their participation in a modern industrial society.

Psychologists suggested that people fear strangers and define others as different in order to solidify their standing as members of an in-group. In a pathbreaking study, *The Nature of Prejudice*, Gordon Allport (1958) contended that people who discriminate vent frustrations on convenient scapegoats. He traced an escalating pattern from slurs and avoidance to lynchings and programs of mass relocation or extermination. In a racist context, intergroup contacts often fostered expressions of hostility—unless reframed to build understanding. Many social psychologists associated extremes of prejudice with an "authoritarian personality," as described by Theodor W. Adorno and others. Using a test that focused on anti-Semitic views, this work offered a certain comfort to academicians and political leaders. In general, educated, middle-class Whites in the North scored as more tolerant. That outcome suggested that schooling helped but that prejudice based on presumably stable personality traits would not change through forced integration.

Emphasizing psychological explanations created a puzzle. If Blacks were merely a scapegoat for repressed hostilities or fears, how could society combat prejudice? If intolerant persons felt threatened, hostility might escalate into violence, as seemingly happened in response to civil rights protests. On the other hand, if public leaders supported their racist fears, they might feel reaffirmed in categorizing African Americans as inferior. President Dwight Eisenhower exemplified these views in his reluctant response to court-ordered integration of Little Rock's Central High School in 1957. After the Arkansas governor led the resistance to a Supreme Court order, the President still insisted that "you cannot change people's hearts merely by laws." After contacts in desegregated classes, some White students acknowledged their previous ignorance about Blacks and asserted that "we're going to change our mind" (quoted in Lewis, 1965, p. 56).

In many cases, African Americans served as useful scapegoats because they were relatively powerless to resist. Yet the distribution of authoritarian personalities, or those seeking moral sanction for dividing behaviors into good and bad, scarcely accounted for historical or situational variations, such as racial incidents in Northern cities and universities. Isolated individuals who commit violent acts in the Ku Klux Klan or contemporary White supremacist groups fit the model, but personality alone fails to explain why many others join or tacitly support organizations resisting integration of neighborhoods and schools. Scapegoating provides little understanding of Eisenhower's reluctance to enforce constitutional law or of White students whose views changed after contacts with Black classmates.

Functionalist approaches today emphasize social adjustment as a key factor for perpetuating racism and other stereotypes. Dominant Whites use a vocabulary of prejudice as a way to establish rapport with others. Friendly words about the weather or a local sports team serve to open relationships based on tacit agreements. Stereotypes incorporated in jokes or complaints about outsiders often build a feeling that those present are members of a group that is superior to those who are presumed different. For instance, adolescent males boast about "scoring" and often repeat homophobic epithets to emphasize their masculinity. Accustomed to racial isolation, Whites in newly integrated groups may feel self-conscious about how their friends and neighbors view their behavior.

Once social conventions are established, those who are in the public eye fear to contradict them. Literally hundreds of surveys revealed that people regarded others as more prejudiced than themselves (Williams, 1964). For instance, soldiers indicated they would not mind serving under Black officers, but they thought others would object. Restaurants misplaced or delayed reservations for parties known to include Blacks but accommodated biracial parties that arrived unannounced. Apparently, an anticipated immediate objection carried more weight than the possibility of someone later complaining. White educators whose own status is uncertain worry that teaching a predominantly Black or Latino class will reduce their social standing.

Growing economic and political power now makes it costly for many Whites to dismiss or ignore Blacks. Advertisements increasingly include African American models, and few politicians consciously offend Black voters. When middle-class professionals are stopped by police or ignored by salespersons based on their skin color, their objections are heard. Demeaning, insensitive remarks as well as discriminatory behaviors are still common, but the public climate has shifted enough so that aggressive resistance usually raises the costs of thoughtless bigotry. Many voices are nevertheless silenced or distorted by an effort to communicate some resentment or positive feelings, given the misrepresentations shared by dominant group members.

Presumed peer pressures affect not only mobs but also bystanders who fear getting involved in defending outsiders. One student offered a typical reaction to a racist incident in a dorm: *"I did nothing because I was one person who felt nothing could be done."* She walked down a different corridor so as to *"not confront the situation."* Students and other relatively powerless people find it difficult to break with social patterns, even though they might benefit from equality. Powerful figures, including teachers in their classrooms, can make class, race and gender stereotyping dysfunctional for those who are simply trying to build in-group rapport. One can object to humor that stereotypes someone else's subordinate position. One can report achievements by outsiders that affirm positive role models. One can demonstrate friendships across cultural boundaries.

Those in powerful positions can change the social context by demonstrating contact, cooperation and respect for members of oppressed groups. Role models and pioneers break those social barriers and raise aspirations and expectations within subordinate groups. Black educators, business leaders, generals, entertainers, outstanding athletes, writers, and intellectuals inspire youth and establish a social pattern of accomplishment and acceptance. When television news is presented by women or people of color, it takes on fresh meanings. The first Italian, Cambodian, or Puerto Rican to serve as judge or university head visibly contradicts assumptions about group capacities and, more critically, about what society as a whole views as normal and acceptable.

As a result of social conventions and institutional continuities, learned biases may persist as oppression is reconstructed to fit new conditions. Manifestations of prejudice shift from generation to generation, allowing people to claim they are not bigoted like their parents. Today, class, race and gender differences are sustained through academic credentials that screen people into or out of power positions. A second generation of discrimination has replaced dual school systems: Systematically unequal education now occurs primarily through tracking but also through differential assignments to special education, to bilingual programs, and to disciplinary treatment, especially suspension (Meier, Stewart, & England, 1989). It also occurs through a curriculum that rewards docile students and ignores cultural insights among oppressed groups.

## TEACHING ACROSS BOUNDARIES

Most White, middle-class male Americans appear puzzled by issues of oppression in schools and society. They assume individuals are primarily responsible for what happens in their lives. That theme is deeply imbued in U.S. history and myths as well as religious themes of personal redemption. Individualism—whether presented in modern variants of Benjamin Franklin's advice about self-help or William Graham Sumner's Social Darwinism—is particularly comforting to those who enjoy relative success in school and in later life. Well-to-do men and women like to recall their striving to learn and achieve. It is easy to forget that others also studied (but found the curriculum contradicting their experiences), worked hard (but at jobs that offered few opportunities for promotion), and aspired for advancement (but without reward).

Those who empathetically recognize that many others do not have a fair opportunity to learn and earn usually frame their understandings within that dominant ideology. Assuming that others would like to get ahead, they look for obvious barriers and seek to reduce them or to compensate for previous handicapping factors. Charity—whether personal, foundation-supported, or publicly funded programs—offers direct assistance to those with visible needs. Yet the resulting interactions often establish a self-defeating dynamic: To get tangible help, people stress their poverty, pathologies and powerlessness. Often they imply a wish to become like those who represent success—by scoring higher on standardized tests, moving out of old neighborhoods, or abandoning traditional customs. This approach assumes that teachers provide knowledge needed to function as a productive citizen while students passively adopt mainstream attitudes (Figure 7.1).

**FIGURE 7.1**
**Compensatory Model**

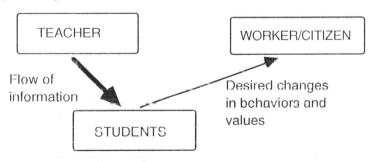

Critical thinkers start with a well-developed critique of compensatory programs for fighting poverty, especially among people of color. Logically, they argue, oppression should not be blamed on its victims but on those who hold power. Various villains are indicted—capitalists, "poverty pimps," teachers who perpetuate a middle-class or Eurocentric hegemony, White racists, a military-industrial complex, or male chauvinists. Such reasoning emphasizes that persistent, pervasive and powerful oppression by class, race and gender is now institutionalized in the United States. Unfortunately, this critique leads to remarkably little social action among relatively advantaged groups (such as college students), who are unwilling to jeopardize their future prospects by attacking bigotry in education and business.

### Naive Multiculturalism

In partial response to that critique, as well as to growing numbers of self-assertive people of color in schools, educators respond with what we identify as a naive or first-stage multiculturalism (Figure 7.2). It dismisses overt racism as socially unacceptable and elevates ethnic groups into a key category with an emphasis on learned behaviors as a source of difference, but it ignores denial of civil rights and dismal economic prospects that underlie students' cultures. Seeking to avoid patronizing others by assuming that everyone wants to join the mainstream, it praises tolerance and respect for differences. Many districts serving "diverse" students have instituted a multicultural curriculum that includes "contributions" of women and people of color.

**FIGURE 7.2**
**First-stage Multiculturalism**

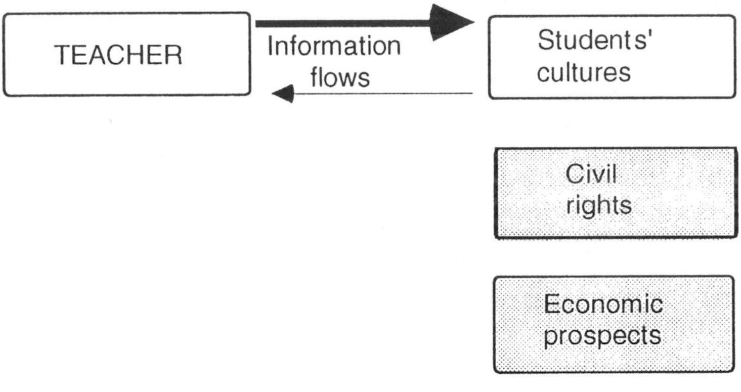

This first-stage multiculturalism urges teachers and students to celebrate diversity and sponsors ethnic "potlucks" meals as well as music and dance programs from around the world. Its curriculum includes writings by African Americans, women, Asians, and sometimes South American or Middle Eastern authors. Pictures of Black achievers adorn texts and corridors. At times, naive multiculturalism parodies a two-week tour of the world with pizza, polka and piñatas. Superficial and exotic details displace efforts to understand enduring values. Its affirmation that everyone should know and take pride in her or his ethnic roots appears feasible as a curriculum goal and politically correct; yet it omits serious discussions of prevailing institutional practices that embody patriarchy, racism and class discrimination.

Objections to naive multiculturalism in schools come from traditionalists who insist that the canon of Western literature is essential to transfer "American" (sometimes "Judeo-Christian") values and beliefs to succeeding generations. Bilingualism is criticized on the grounds that everyone needs to read and write English. Celebrating diversity makes everything seem equally acceptable. Traditionalists on the right object to tolerance for gay, lesbian and bisexual lifestyles. Those on the left seek to elevate liberal virtues of freedom of speech and religion, democracy and equality over other values—lest schools mindlessly sanction such customs as traditional subordination of Chinese women or violence among Cossacks and Mafiosi.

## Interactive Multiple Realities

Constructivists join this debate on three levels. First, they question whether ethnocentric cultural boundaries are a primary category. Americans belong to multiple groups—some by virtue of birth and others by choice. Many, perhaps most, categories that raise educational debates are labels attached to subordinate groups by dominant groups. There is something patronizing about designating February for Black history and March for women's rights. Too often, multiculturalism serves as a euphemism for a curriculum about oppressed people but without asking how they would describe their lives. In modern societies, acquired identities often supersede ascribed characteristics. For instance, a Jewish grandmother may identify herself primarily as runner and a teacher.

Second, dialog across boundaries, although often painful and divisive, usefully clarifies thinking about future societies. Logically, no school can offer everything for everyone—feminist, ethnic and popular literatures can be endlessly subdivided in a vain attempt to satisfy all viewpoints. There always will be someone whose background or aspiration is ignored, but the debate needs to be joined because whatever ends up in the curriculum becomes a new canon. There is much to be learned from other cultures, and the meaning of any selection of important lessons continuously evolves. Segmentation by racial or ethnic groups may avoid overt conflict, but it stifles discourse about what parents want for their children.

Third, from a constructivist point of view, acculturation to cultural differences requires dialog and a dominant group that listens and learns from those interchanges (Figure 7.3). White Americans can equalize schooling and jobs for African Americans *and* appreciate jazz,

**FIGURE 7.3**
**Constructing Multiculturalism**

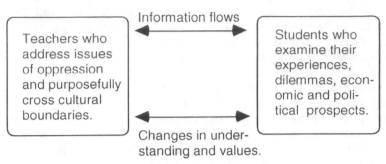

the blues, and rap music. Tolerance without allowing acculturation *and* learning from oppressed groups is a sham. Ideally, cultural differences create occasions for melding beliefs and lifestyles while gaining insights into one's own self-identity and cultural beliefs.

By contrast, naive multiculturalism focuses attention on personal, family and religious differences where tolerance has long been part of America's tradition (despite many notorious exceptions). In that sphere, differences need not foster significant inequalities. Access to citizenship, suffrage, a Bill of Rights, and the 14th Amendment are regarded as the important areas where equality prevails. By omitting issues of class or income that allow one to obtain decent schooling, housing, and personal safety as well as to exercise political rights, this discussion is incomplete. For example, Black youth who have grown up with poverty, unequal schools, and violence adopt a different slant on life than those raised in a more favorable environment, so that desegregation may not promote positive interactions among classmates.

Consciousness of multiple realities lies at the heart of postmodern thinking; schools must incorporate diverse voices into its curriculum, with particular attention to those who have been silenced. Understanding others requires listening to their stories for themes that enable them to make sense of their lives. Teachers should encourage students to explore their identities and histories through comparisons and contrasts. Although no interpretation fully captures another's framework, communication across boundaries of time, space and status enrich multicultural approaches in literature, social studies and the arts by establishing intra- and intergroup meaning systems. Finding a way to achieve multicultural awareness among all students while combating oppression and discrimination is a goal worth pursuing.

## EDUCATION FOR CULTURAL UNDERSTANDING

Basically, no one can "teach" cultural understanding in a traditional classroom setting because those with a small advantage will build on existing differences in power. Students compete with each other for grades, reflecting the individualistic and competitive aspects of American culture. Many interracial contacts in classrooms engage individuals who are equally eager to learn but unequally prepared for the curriculum. Nor is multiculturalism a simple matter of learning facts about the consequences of discrimination or different cultural beliefs and behaviors, though knowledge about people and instructional tactics are important. On the other hand, there are ways to break down racial, ethnic, religious, language, class, and gender stereotypes.

Cultural barriers erode when members from different groups come in contact with each other and must work together in order to accomplish a common process or purpose. According to social psychologist Thomas Pettigrew (1971, pp. 315, 311), "isolation between two contiguous groups generally leads to: (1) the development of diverse values, (2) reduced intergroup communication, (3) uncorrected perceptual distortions of each other, and (4) the growth of vested interests within both groups for continued separation." Intergroup contacts under the conditions spelled out by Allport's great study break down negative stereotypes when both groups "(1) possess equal status in the situation, (2) seek common goals, (3) are cooperatively dependent upon each other, and (4) interact with the positive support of authorities, laws, or customs." Anxieties about strangers inhibit interactions and competitive pressures block shared processes and goals; yet Allport's conditions apply in many situations today.

> Suppose schools were meritocratic—no one faced low or different expectations because of sex, racial label, or parent's income and status; no student was handicapped by learning styles, language, dialect or cultural beliefs; no one lacked appropriate instructional resources—but that job hierarchies and divided communities persisted.
>
> Desirable careers would be open to people of color, women, as well as children of poor and working-class parents based on their motivation and knowledge. Some of today's elites would lose, and some outsiders would gain.
>
> Would those new insiders try to pass advantages on to their children?

Insiders and outsiders know different things, and crossing those boundaries establishes a new perspective. A sociologist of science, Robert Merton (1973b, p. 129) concluded:

The actual intellectual interchange between Insiders and Outsiders—in which each adopts perspectives from the other—is often obscured by the rhetoric that commonly attends intergroup conflict. Listening only to that rhetoric, we may be brought to believe that there really is something like "black knowledge" and "white knowledge," "man's knowledge" and "woman's knowledge" which somehow manage to be both incommensurable and antithetical. Yet the boundaries between Insiders and Outsiders are far more permeable than this allows.

Each group borrows ideas from others, in part to understand each other and in part to serve their own purposes. When Whites express disagreement with Black nationalist arguments, for instance, they necessarily consider those viewpoints.

Too often in academic discourse the temptation is to omit the raw, personal experience of oppression based on race or gender. As Black psychologist Kenneth Clark (1965, p. 75) expostulated: "The tendency to discuss disturbing social issues such as racial discrimination, segregation, and economic exploitation in detached, legal, political, socioeconomic, or psychological terms as if these persistent problems did not involve the suffering of actual human beings is so contrary to empirical evidence that it must be interpreted as a protective device." Social scientists' detachment and statistical analyses reveal measurable differences, but they also conceal important truths. How people feel about oppression and being silenced often determines their readiness to learn and to participate in democratic discussions.

Unless teachers break through that critical and somewhat negative stance toward America's problems, they can scarcely establish a level of rapport with victims of bias or recognize their own blinders. When teachers instill competition for grades within a Eurocentric and middle-class curriculum, they silence many students. Powerless youth must feel safe to describe their personal experiences. We consider two curricular approaches for children to build a sense of themselves as purposeful actors: writing for self-expression and cooperative learning. Ideally, teachers facilitate self-expression and interaction rather than offering separate curricular units about other cultures.

### Writing for Self-identity

When encouraged to write in supportive settings, children and youth reveal amazing insights into their sense of self as well as their appreciation for a nonjudgmental audience. At a voluntary afterschool writing club, an eight year old used invented spelling and drawing as well as print to urge others to join because *"we write and no matter what religan, shape, size, color or gender you can still come here."* Invited to share ideas through writing, urban youth at a summer camp revealed intense interests in family issues, relationships with peers, and their hopes about doing things with their lives. An 11-year-old girl contributed a help-wanted ad to the camp newspaper: *"Social worker to work as an integral member of helping kids keep out of the streets."* After two prisoners addressed the campers, she wrote, *"even if you don't have freedome at home but it is better than jail."*

Self-expression and reflection are essential to overcome the barriers of cultural boundaries. Children begin to make sense of their experiences as they express them in images and words. This is a natural activity that usually starts at home where young children learn to speak by listening, observing and gradually acquiring vocabulary and grammar. Parents and other adults support development by praising children's efforts, answering their questions, stimulating their curiosity, and modeling speech. Whole language approaches to writing begin with personal experiences of young authors rather than academic information or adult topics. Teachers value each student's experiences and vocabulary, emphasizing meaning rather than spelling and punctuation.

Writing precedes or accompanies reading. Putting thoughts on paper, or encoding, is a natural ability that all children possess; too often it is squelched by a focus on handwriting, spelling, grammar and other conventional rules. Traditionally, children in elementary school were expected to commit to memory separate skills—the sounds of letters, punctuation, capitalization, complete sentence formation—that are later applied in reading and writing. By trying to communicate to an audience something of importance to the author, children learn skills while clarifying their own views and values. Being able to express oneself clearly is empowering, particularly for young people whose identities are omitted or represented inaccurately by the media.

Whole language teachers recognize that children know an enormous amount before entering school and that they will continue to learn, not only in school but in every setting. Many children find no expression of their deepest concerns in popular media or publications, and that is most true for those who are unhappy, brutalized or stigmatized. When encouraged, children freely express themselves about meaningful experiences. Their audience's reaction generates further thinking and writing. Racial and gender stereotypes as well as violent themes may appear in children's writing. Yet fears lose their power when they are expressed and discussed by children and adults together. Writing against the grain of dominant experiences helps build a sense of self as an actor.

Self-expression promotes positive self-images and is particularly important for powerless groups who are either ignored or depicted in cruel stereotypes. Notable African American authors create a positive meaning of Black culture and history. In particular, they emphasize "(3) a sense of community among Blacks; (4) the importance of warm and loving human relationships, particularly within families; (5) a sense of continuity; and, above all, (6) the will and strength and determination to cope and survive" (Sims, 1982, pp. 96, 99). These writers are "witnesses to Afro-American experience," thereby enabling "Afro-American children to find themselves and their experiences mirrored in this fiction" and "to understand 'how we got over' in the past and to recognize and develop the inner strengths that will enable them to 'get over' in their own times."

Speech and writing are not the only ways to establish a sense of personal identity, but they are key in a postmodern society that invites each person to define themselves and present that self to others. Most of us have experienced surprise about what we have just said or written—as though the thought gained force through its expression. Likewise, reflection and rewriting ordinarily clarify beliefs and help sort out redundant or inconsistent views. Those opportunities are doubly valued by people whose voices are seldom heard or respected. Literature about growing up by many different groups, especially those whose lives are unfamiliar or seldom heard, both defines and reveals what it means to be Black or Asian or female or handicapped in an unequal society.

## Cooperative Learning

Many educators advocate cooperative learning as a way to motivate students and improve overall school performance. Teachers in our interviews repeatedly linked cooperation to increased school effectiveness. *"This is what I get excited about—cooperative learning,"* said one intern. After his school instituted team teaching and cluster scheduling, a middle-grade principal commented: *"We need to be moving much further along in terms of having them work through problems to solutions—and helping them to learn also how to work in a team, how to work with other people, which means certainly going away from homogeneous grouping and looking at instructional techniques such as cooperative learning and helping kids to learn how to work in a group."*

Cooperative learning has been slow to emerge as an alternative to the widespread use of "ability grouping" or "tracking" by school districts. Part of this reluctance stems from the centrality of competition in American culture. Teachers and parents see cooperation as a distraction from the job of the school to prepare students to seek their own advantage. A suburban principal noted: *"Because of the placement of my particular school which is in a highly competitive, affluent community, we are having a lot of negative feedback from parents around cooperative learning. They are very concerned that their children, as one woman said, 'will only know how to cooperate and what good is that?' They are afraid that in our teaching kids how to cooperate, they will lose that competitive edge."*

In cooperative settings, desks and rows give way to open spaces and tables where small groups work together. Students ask questions of one another, listen to peers, explain materials to classmates, and help set rules of conduct in the room. Teamwork is continually reinforced with messages about group interdependence. Students are asked to take on different roles—for example, researcher, observer, recorder, facilitator, or summarizer. Investigating the ecological consequences of a polluted river or a toxic waste dump requires group members to use brainstorming, library searches, data compilation, critical assessments of multiple views, and presentation skills. Students tend to stay on task, care about other members of the group, and learn as effectively as in traditional settings.

Cooperative learning, though difficult to implement among students acculturated to individual competition, fosters dramatic changes within classroom environments. Working in small groups serves some goals particularly well: analytical and creative thinking, communicating with others, and active engagement in learning. Small-group activities respond to the developmental needs of children, particularly young adolescents. Youth establish a sense of identity in relation to their peers by working together, learning to resolve conflicts, trying out new roles, and clarifying personal values in school. At the same time, students learn that disagreements are often legitimate and appropriate without labeling others in negative terms. Children who do not interact with one another only know what they have heard from adults, media and other sources.

As an urban administrator noted, White and minority students in academic tracks *"don't know each other in classes so they never eat together, they don't talk to each other in the corridors and if they are in a study hall together there is no exchange because in studies there is no talking."* By contrast, cooperative learning fosters *"kids working with kids. There is going to be some relationship there that will tear down some walls of ignorance and prejudice. Projects, for example, that are assigned to groups of kids where . . . you make sure it is a multi-ethnic group . . . will go a long way to helping kids in an informal way get to know each other and understand each other."*

Common school experiences, especially court-mandated desegregation, have changed some behaviors, but the results have been disappointing for those who believed that ignorance would quickly disappear following interracial contacts. As educational researcher Robert Slavin (1985, p. 47) noted, school interaction "between students of different ethnicities is typically superficial and often competitive." Only in sports do "different" groups share goals and cooperate as a team. Accordingly, he and others strive to induce cooperative behaviors in classrooms with the explicit goal of reducing negative stereotypes. That goal, of course, is easier when classrooms include diversity along racial/ethnic lines.

Slavin (1985, pp. 48–53) offered seven practical methods that may be applied across grade levels to improve academic performance:

- Heterogeneous groups of four receive instruction but are graded as a team, based on combined gains in test scores.
- Teams compete in "academic game tournaments."
- In some teams, students incorporate considerable responsibility for helping each other.
- Each team member researches a topic and teaches it to others, with test scores being summed.
- Smaller groups work together to complete a common assignment.
- Teams present a collective report to the class based on their research.
- Intergroup interactions become the explicit purpose and topic for team activities.

In 16 of 19 studies, "some aspect of friendship between students of different ethnicities improves."

If cooperative learning merely reinforces curricular patterns of inequality in classrooms, then its potential as a school improvement strategy will go largely untapped. Prevailing White racism might induce students to view Black and Latino classmates as less able. On the other hand, a natural range of student abilities moderates those views, particularly where individual gains rather than final scores are summed to assess each team's effort. As for institutional norms, typically educators remain "uncomfortable about the issue of race," usually choosing to ignore it (Slavin, 1985, pp. 57, 59). Cooperative learning teams with explicit diversity indicate "approval of interracial interaction" whereas self-selected or homogeneous teams convey the opposite message. In conclusion, four of seven methods brought academic gains, and the effects on friendship choices were "strong and long-lasting."

Group activities break with industrial-era patterns of a passive, adult-directed curriculum. Children who have used computers at home for games and education, who are linked to the world through movies, television and the Internet, and who are accustomed to planning many activities are not motivated by fragmentary facts and definitions presented in texts and lectures. Effective teams accommodate individual differences in learning styles and background among students without a teacher individualizing instruction. Moreover, small groups are natural for community service learning that links youth to adults in businesses or public agencies. Team leaders who gain confidence in their own voices may openly share their ideas about the curriculum, school and community.

## ENVISIONING MULTICULTURAL FUTURES

Thinking about future schools is constrained by the difficulties of imagining a multicultural and nonhierarchical society. How can educators create innovative strategies and structures when adults are rank ordered into income classes, divided by racism, and socialized into gender roles? Males of European descent have controlled production of things, access to decisionmaking and managerial positions, military or police forces, and most families. When social scientists observe and measure material outcomes, they reinforce the importance of White male domains. Values of caring, concern and connection across class, race and gender boundaries are less easily assessed or appreciated. Validating diverse topics as worthy of dialog and meaningful activities helps teachers and students become more self-aware about how embedded cultural beliefs frame perceived options for individuals, groups and society.

Positive steps toward building a multicultural school begin with a recognition of how schools reinforce dominant cultural assumptions. First, schools legitimate and delegitimate students based on the cultural beliefs they bring to the classroom. In so doing, schools privilege cultural values associated with White, middle-class Americans seeking professional, managerial and technical careers. Second, educators take it as a primary responsibility to prepare youths for hierarchical job slots in an industrial economy. Ethnic, racial and gender biases simplify that rank ordering. Moreover, norm-referenced tests serve that purpose even when school-based knowledge has little real connection to work-related competencies. Finally, institutional arrangements of tracking and school finance inequitably allocate opportunities—without anyone's conscious complicity.

### Oppressive Forces

If teachers assume that their values represent the right and best way, then the message conveyed is that anyone else's ideas and beliefs are inadequate, irrational or even harmful. Many educators have countered by urging a "balanced" curriculum, covering each ethnicity in turn. That naive multiculturalism accepts existing social constructs in defining groups; it ignores the practical reality that in contemporary society, people affiliate with multiple groups—both ascribed and acquired. In so doing, educators stereotype others in terms of specific characteristics or beliefs that do not apply to many in the group. Individuals might act differently if they had more opportunities to present themselves as they might like to become in mainstream settings. Unless oppression and power are openly discussed, multiculturalism effectively reinforces a sense of "Otherness."

Extending the range of oppressions to include class, race, gender, sexual orientation, age, and disabling conditions has aided understanding that racially separate schools are only one piece in a pattern of educational inequities. Voices of African Americans, feminists, lesbians, gays, and people with disabilities have joined critical theorists to reveal Eurocentric and patriarchal presumptions underlying mainstream cultural attitudes. By showing how they privilege academically credentialed White males, oppressed groups have raised questions about the taken-for-granted curriculum in most schools. They have defined and celebrated their subjectivity apart from the stereotypes or assimilationist assumptions of dominant groups.

An initial response to oppression as social injustice is to identify the repressive forces in a particular situation (Young, 1990, pp. 48–64):

- First, there remains a persistent *exploitation* that allows the labor of some to benefit others.
- Second, a growing *marginalization* denies many people a useful and purposeful role in the economy and civic decisionmaking.
- Third, *powerlessness* marks those who lack capital or professional status, authority and respectability, thereby limiting their opportunities to develop functional capacities over a lifetime.
- Fourth, *cultural imperialism*, or the stereotyping of oppressed groups as deviant and inferior by dominant groups who assume their norms are unquestionable, affects all oppressed groups in the United States today.
- Finally, *systematic violence* is directed particularly against groups such as women, gays, lesbians, and many people of color who lack power.

Systemic forces affect various oppressed groups in different ways and suggest that effecting change will require multiple efforts along many different fronts. Class, race and gender issues are intertwined and reinforced in the dominant culture and need to be examined in that light. For instance, unskilled workers are paid low salaries and subjected to periodic unemployment, and their unstable home life contributes to their being silenced in voting or influencing working conditions. Attacking any specific oppressive mechanism or outcome is likely to allow other forms of oppression to generate resistance to change. Thus, social welfare programs and compensatory education help meet basic needs among people who are exploited or marginalized, but narrowly targeted programs also contribute to stereotyping some groups as inferior.

In *Affirming Diversity*, Sonia Nieto (1992, p. 208) connected multicultural education to larger issues of school reform and social justice. Celebrating different ethnic traditions or applying human relations training is only a first step. A multicultural perspective, she held, "challenges and rejects racism and other forms of discrimination in schools and society and accepts and affirms the pluralism (ethnic, racial, linguistic, religious, economic, and gender, among others) that students, their communities, and teachers represent." She proposed seven characteristics to ascertain if a teacher is fostering mutual understanding. Multiculturalism is *"antiracist, basic, important,"* and central to the entire curriculum. It forms the basis of *"education for social justice"* when taught as a *"process"* involving a *"critical pedagogy."*

Elite monoculturalism is dangerous in a changing world. Adults who never had reason to question their taken-for-granted assumptions (or who have unconsciously adopted the views of dominant elites) presume that their stock of knowledge is sufficient to cope with whatever situations develop. Can the United States sustain equality of political rights with permanent inequities of economic outcomes? Without common beliefs and interests, voters cannot agree on how to manage ecological concerns or public programs for health, education and recreation. Outsiders feel the costs of being excluded, and leadership voices from women and culturally and linguistically diverse individuals are needed to enlarge a sense of commonalities around the world.

## Affirming Differences

Unless the curriculum is open to dialog among multiple voices, it perpetuates a single standard that draws its vocabulary and icons from an Anglo-Protestant past. Students may ignore it or resist it, but they lack resources to construct an alternative and inclusive definition of their own beliefs. Typically, children from subordinate groups—whether workers, immigrants, Blacks, or women—struggle to gain acceptance by adopting the school's underlying norms. Individually, they negotiate for a place in American society; once this is achieved, they want to forget their earlier frustration or any assistance needed to get ahead. Instead, they recall their hard work and pain, often insisting that others be similarly challenged. In that way, previous initiates reinforce traditional standards.

Growing doubts among youth about the values of modernization creates an opportunity for educators to introduce alternative views and to deconstruct dominant discourses as self-serving. Critics of materialism have gained force as people question progress under capitalist, market economies. Ecologists and feminists, as well as technophobes and anti-intellectuals more generally, are establishing cultural perspectives from which to critique modernist assumptions. Postmodernist educators "encourage the multiplicity of as many voices and perspectives as possible, without seeking to reconcile them or combine them into a single, consistent, unified account." Indeed, Burbules and Rice (1991, pp. 394, 395) saw a tendency to raise *"difference* as a value that is in opposition to such traditional values as consensus and inter-subjectivity."

Although White racism is a central theme in U.S. history, many European Americans work toward equality, and many Blacks enjoy productive and creative lives. Not all families are patriarchal or dys-functional; millions have married and sustained caring families across racial, religious or ethnic boundaries. Critical theorists who reduce relationships to power like those who mindlessly approve of differences leave little ground for establishing common understanding through dialog. Any categorization by culture or race fails to acknowledge the mix of lived experiences that include loneliness and intimacy, pain and pleasure, despair and hope. Sharing conflicting personal experiences with others creates opportunities for understanding what it means to be human.

Multicultural interactions among equal groups bring three potential benefits: fostering a sense of personal identity within diverse subcom-munities, challenging ethnocentric views, and strengthening demo-cratic practices (Burbules & Rice, 1991, pp. 404, 405, 409). Persons who identify with diverse groups facilitate "the establishment of relations of negotiation, cooperation, and pursuit of common interests (where they exist), which tends to promote mutual tolerance and the nonviolent resolution of conflicts." By validating outsiders' perspectives, insiders gain insights into their own taken-for-granted assumptions. As a result, multiculturalism builds "such 'communicative virtues' as tolerance, patience, and a willingness to listen." Nevertheless, *understanding and misunderstanding always occur together.*"

Through dialog, educators come to recognize how social and histor-ical backgrounds of participants, including themselves, distort com-munications and often foster stereotypes or typifications with negative connotations. When dominant views are challenged, many advantaged people experience cognitive dissonance and seek to dismiss contra-dictory views by blaming victims for ineffective tactics. For example, many agree that urban youth are caught in a no-win situation, yet they condemn riots as an ineffective protest. Open dialog in a classroom where class, race and gender hierarchies have shaped experiences raise uncomfortable issues that temporarily heighten awareness of differ-ences. Because no one is comfortable in that discussion, teachers intentionally must listen to and validate previously silenced voices.

Dialog open to multiple realities requires a modification of academic norms that reward "an aggressive style of communication" as well as certainty in right answers based on faith in progress and citation of experts (Burbules & Rice, 1991, pp. 412, 413). Controversial issues raise puzzles for teachers that threaten their role as dispensers of knowledge. Honest discussions about alcohol and drugs, sexual identity and behav-iors, and the discriminatory nature of tests are first steps toward restor-ing trustworthy communications. As Burbules and Rice concluded, "developing as a person involves incorporating painful lessons, failures, and frustrations, without being paralyzed by them; it involves living with tensions, rather than striving to mask them with oversimplifications that might make the world seem more palatable."

Teachers should start from where their students are, drawing on their concerns, their language, and their values to connect with a formal curriculum in order to address issues of power and self-identities. In the next chapter, we address some puzzles about the authority of teachers and texts that are raised by multiple perspectives. Presumably, the law of gravity applies among the remote Tasaday as well as among physicists—regardless of their interpretive frameworks. If multiculturalism suggests where instruction begins, will the curriculum converge on modern, scientific frameworks as youngsters prepare to function in an increasingly interdependent economy? Where can postmodern people find a source for authoritative knowledge as disciplinary boundaries begin to break down?

## RELATED READING

A number of ethnographic studies depict life on city streets or in urban schools with an appreciation for the ways children and adults make sense of those situations. For illustrations, see Shirley Brice Heath, *Ways with Words* (New York: Cambridge University Press, 1983); Denny Taylor and Catherine Dorsey-Gaines, *Growing Up Literate: Learning from Inner-City Families* (Portsmouth, NH: Heinemann, 1988); and Elijah Anderson, *Streetwise: Race, Class, and Change in an Urban Community* (Chicago: University of Chicago Press, 1990). For academic accounts, see Cameron McCarthy and Warren Crichlow, eds., *Race, Identity, and Representation in Education* (New York: Routledge, 1993) and Ronald Takaki, *A Different Mirror: A History of Multicultural America* (Boston: Little, Brown, 1993).

For curricular suggestions, see Sharon A. Edwards and Robert W. Maloy, *Kids Have All the Write Stuff: Inspiring Your Children to Put Pencil* to Paper (New York: Penguin Books, 1992); Carl A. Grant and Christine E. Sleeter, *Turning on Learning: Five Approaches for Multicultural Teaching Plans for Race, Class, Gender, and Disability* (Columbus, OH: Merrill Publishing, 1989); and Myra and David Sadker, *Failing at Fairness: How America's Schools Cheat Girls* (New York: Charles Scribner's Sons, 1994).

# 8

# Transmitting Constructed Knowledge

For centuries, a dominant narrative in Western societies attributed progress to science and technology. Compasses and guns, microscopes and watches, steam engines and airplanes, computers and nuclear reactors were visible signs of cultural values. Industrial societies honored scholarship that exploited nature or promoted social control. Universities organized academic disciplines and professional training to serve commercial and industrial needs. In turn, material progress validated fortunate discoverers, successful inventors, property owners, and political leaders as well as a way of thinking—namely, empirical research that linked reactions to stimuli, outcomes to causes. That framework shaped what knowledge should be transmitted and in what form in 20th-century America.

From the outset, some resisted industrialization. Those left behind blamed machines for the destruction of jobs and an agrarian way of life. Social critics in a Marxian vein predicted an ultimate collapse because of the overreaching control exercised by capitalists and military-industrial interests. Today, diverse critiques question the long-run viability of modern societies that overvalue science and technology. The benefits of science are weighed against possible nuclear destruction, genetic manipulations, electronic controls or surveillance, and a diminished sense of play as our lives are rationalized by machines and bureaucracies. Industrialization on a worldwide scale threatens nonrenewable resources, ecological balances, and indeed all human life. Afrocentric philosophies and Eastern religions as well as feminist viewpoints demonstrate that Western science is neither universal nor objective.

Although philosophers and commentators raise questions about socially constructed frameworks for conveying information to others, the school curriculum reinforces a view of technology as an independent, external force. In our interviews, a first-year teacher who had majored in science regretted how his high school *"totally isolated the disciplines."* Some students *"who don't like any math or anything, who just like to read and memorize biological terms, they love biology, and they all got As."* There were few interdisciplinary courses, even though *"the majority of the groundbreaking is taking place in molecular biology and biochemistry."* Nor were social, historical or economic issues discussed in beginning science courses: *"You don't even talk about say, nuclear chemistry anymore. Nuclear reaction, nuclear waste and what that's about. You don't talk about acid rain, you don't talk about greenhouse effect and many of those issues, which the kids are interested in."*

Educators displayed a mix of positive and negative attitudes toward information technologies. Teachers repeatedly cited the importance of computers for their students' future jobs; for instance, *"everybody must be computer literate in a most limited sense."* Few talked about modifying their own approach to instruction, however. Those who did so noted their colleagues' reluctance to utilize new software or a scarcity of equipment in their classrooms. Educators wondered about how information technologies might alter their responsibilities, reallocate school resources, and reshape student roles, but those decisions appeared beyond their control.

Over time, scientific research has become a model for ascertaining truth and for determining what should be done about issues that are regarded as "problems." By abstracting from messy phenomena and nesting subsystems in hierarchies of generalization, the accumulated knowledge of the past can be efficiently transmitted to the young as a set of heuristics or guidelines for solving problems. Textbooks and classroom instruction structure knowledge into a handful of principles that explain multiple natural events. Other categories and central narratives structure national histories and creative arts. The curriculum, thus, reinforces a view of knowledge as facts to be acquired by the young and used later in life—not as cognitive frameworks that are continuously being reconstructed by fresh experiences and purposes.

This chapter starts by raising questions about why, what and how knowledge is transmitted in schools. Abstract categories and relationships allow complex phenomena to flow from simple causes. In describing science and technology in that way, we seek to gain perspective on their strengths so that teachers and students may use them rather than being controlled by their authority. Next, we describe some ways scientists and engineers have used class, race and gender to gain power by privileging insiders. We detail how feminist perspectives enlarge the sphere of inquiry to include historical developments and social distributions of knowledge. Then, we examine computers in schools and the issues they raise around how instructional modes shape what knowledge is transmitted to others. Finally, we argue that opening the curriculum to multiple ways of knowing allows discourse about identity and purpose to include science and technology.

## UNDERSTANDING A COMPLEX WORLD

Why should most students acquire an expert's information? If knowledge is merely a means to some end, then efficient people would learn only what helps them achieve their goals. Indeed, hierarchical command systems, bureaucratic procedures, and mutual equivalence structures minimize a need for learning by regularizing specialized, interdependent roles. In a segmented world, everyone remains ignorant about most things—how planes fly, Congress passes a law, Japanese factories arrange production, banks extend credit, or computers adjust gasoline and air in carburetors. Presumably, specialists know these things and can explain the mysteries to others. If knowledge is neutral, abstracted from social contexts, then one can always consult a text to learn how to apply a technique to fit one's purposes.

From Francis Bacon through Auguste Comte to most educators today, knowledge has been regarded as empowering. The dream of organizing information to conquer nature and control human societies in order to increase well-being is attractive to most of us. In *The Quest for Certainty*, Dewey (1929, pp. 250, 251) noted that sciences were treated as the epitome of knowledge: "The selection is justified because the operations of physical knowledge are so perfected and its scheme of symbols so well devised." There were other ways to learn, but science best served "deliberately to transform doubtful situations into resolved ones." Traditional beliefs prevailed in politics and religion because there seemed no other authority for values. In these areas, people avoided serious investigation, choosing "to accept what is and muddle along."

Education, Dewey (1929, p. 252) argued, "holds the key to orderly social reconstruction." Schools, however, emphasized the "inculcation of fixed conclusions rather than development of intelligence as a method of action." Then and now, schools separate knowledge from activities that give it meaning. The key for education lies in "the realization that intelligent action is the sole ultimate resource of mankind in every field whatsoever." Today, a lot of learning seems devoted to defensive purposes—to avoid being fooled by sales persons, by media, by propagandists, by politicians, by professionals. Persuasive explanations may induce decisions contrary to one's long-term interest. Recent revelations about testing of radioactive materials sanctioned by the government in the 1950s or toxic chemicals in workplaces suggest the dangers of trusting experts, public officials, and the press.

To make sense of the complexities of everyday life, Western scholars developed two institutional responses: structuring academic disciplines in hierarchical subsystems and encompassing many events in a single grand explanation. Modern societies rely on artificial codes and general principles learned in schools. Contemporary communication depends on formal training and abstract concepts. Publicly available speech, print, images, and multimedia mark a growing interdependence across space and time among functional units. Facts and frameworks sometimes make it seem as though rational individuals must adapt to existing economic, political and social conditions.

### Simplicity in Complexity

Discipline-based inquiry allows humans to subordinate innumerable observations under manageable numbers of basic principles. Students learn to "see" gravity in planetary orbits or an inclined plane in an ordinary screw. Arranged in nested subunits according to a level of generalization, scientific information can be recalled or transmitted to others as mathematical laws or convenient rules. In the last quarter of the 19th century, academic disciplines became specialized in research universities, allowing modern scholarship to flourish. A century later, researchers discuss narrow answers to remote problems at professional meetings. Academics complain (or boast) that they lack time to read major publications in their field because specialized journals require their attention.

For a century after 1875, segmentation of knowledge seemed to benefit both scientists and laypeople: Specialists pursued their interests without justifying costs or purposes to outsiders—who, in turn, felt no need to understand the mathematics or import of scientific research. Faith that science brought progress served insiders and outsiders: It justified discipline-based faculties and legitimated a hierarchical educational system. Academic tracks in high school fed an elite into narrowly focused majors in college. By graduate school, economists seldom took courses with political scientists or physicists with chemists. Today's knowledge workers, who are adept within their own research program, find it hard to communicate with the lay public. No longer confident of human progress, people fear what they do not understand and distrust those who claim scientific authority or technological necessity.

Those disciplinary divisions and occupational categories grew within a particular stage of industrialization. As an efficient way to arrange specialized knowledge for transmission, sci-tech adopted categories and relationships that then shaped how people interpreted natural phenomena. It separated experts—increasingly trained in academic disciplines—from laypersons. Sci-tech's materialistic and patriarchal presumptions stand out, along with its ability to exploit natural resources for military and industrial powers. For instance, scientists search for new energy sources rather than ways to conserve petroleum. Medical researchers seek cures for neoplasms or blame genetics for diseases and deviant behaviors, generally ignoring prevention through diet, exercise and lifestyles that are relevant to individual beliefs within diverse cultures.

Social scientists emphasized social order or control, often favoring a crude behaviorism that reduced complex phenomena to a single cause and downplayed personal volition and interactive dialog. Dynamic human processes, however, suggest probabilities and choices, not predictability and objectivity. Information systems struggle to provide ever more data to decisionmakers—whereas, their problem is less ignorance than continual distractions. Attention to relevant issues, however, depends on understanding how things function and people interact in distant places and over time. "As the web of cause and effect is woven tighter, we put severe loads upon our planning and decision-making procedures to deal with these remote effects" (Simon, 1981, p. 183). Pessimism about knowledge follows "because we have learned to look farther than our arms can reach."

As economist and organizational theorist Herbert Simon (1981, pp. 126–127) reiterated, human behaviors appear enormously varied and complex because individuals' environments include their socially constructed knowledge:

That information, stored both as data and as procedures and richly indexed for access in the presence of appropriate stimuli, enables the simple basic information processes to draw upon a very large repertory of information and strategies, and accounts for the appearance of complexity in their behavior. The inner environment, the hardware, is simple. Complexity emerges from the richness of the outer environment, both the world apprehended through the senses and the information about the world stored in long-term memory.

People are much alike in seeking to ease their daily existence and plan for a better future; but rich and poor, Black and White, male and female have different experiences and face different opportunities.

Despite billions of gigabytes of electronic data and libraries filled with millions of books, much about the world remains bafflingly inexplicable. Complexities multiply, as E. B. White once prophesied, "what with one thing always leading to another." To suggest why people sense an information overload today, we distinguish three levels of knowledge: *data* or definitions (e.g., house, 27, honesty), *relationships* between two things (a cow is in the lower pasture), and their pragmatic *significance*. If one's worldview includes few causes or purposes, then connections and their potential implications are limited, even though sensory inputs flood one's mind with local or transient information. For instance, a forester might mentally identify trees but never speculate about their causes or consequences. By contrast, medical researchers' "ignorance" about possible carcinogenic relationships grows exponentially: a new compound (or impurity) may cause (or inhibit) many neoplasms and cast doubt on previous research results.

Although experienced personally, complex technologies and organizations are usually described in abstractions—scientific laws, mechanical principles, blueprints, tables of organization. Nevertheless, virtually an infinite number of facts and theories might be taught. Bell

(1973, pp. 165–168) depicted the "dimensions of knowledge and technology" through Jorge Luis Borges's metaphor of an endless library filled with all the world's information (and misinformation) so vast that it could never be read, cataloged, destroyed, or significantly enlarged. As subdisciplines and interdisciplinary studies proliferate, students find their choices confusing and disconnected. In their focus on narrowly answerable questions, academic disciplines fail to address many social and personal issues that concern youth today.

### Singular Explanations

In the past, cultural narratives posited a dominant force or cause to "explain" events and clarify what needed to be done. For many, perhaps most people, religion has served that purpose; but in modern secular societies, empirical sciences have provided a basic explanation for observable progress. In the 18th century, many commentators argued against hereditary rulers and arbitrary government. Fearing the unbounded passions of the masses, some looked for self-regulating systems akin to Isaac Newton's "clockwork" physical world. Adam Smith identified an "invisible hand" in competitive markets. The framers of the U.S. Constitution devised a series of checks and balances for a federal system. They explained how rational individuals might interact in markets and politics to achieve a stable, yet progressive, equilibrium.

Social scientists imitated physicists, first looking for an analog to the law of gravity, a grand explanation underlying complexities of human development. In the 19th century, two major intellectual systems accounted for conflict and historical change in industrial nations. Marxists attributed the misery of workers as evidence of a class struggle that would inevitably dominate a political contest for the State as an instrument of social control. Progress came with the triumph of workers and the withering away of the State into a community without exploitation. Darwinians argued that evolution depended on tooth and claw competition resulting in the elimination of the weak. Progress followed from encouraging entrepreneurs to make money, thereby generating economic growth. Both Marxists and Darwinians claimed to have a scientific explanation for historical change.

In a contemporary metanarrative, science and technology promise social benefits, only to reveal unanticipated threats. Variations of Frankenstein live on in many futurist accounts. Individuals acquire material goods or security; collectively, their actions court ecological calamity. On the one hand, scientists, engineers and economists contribute to economic growth by applying rational approaches instead of customs, traditions, and a belief in the sacred. On the other hand, modern thinking has destroyed community, human scale, and a sense of awe. A shift from relationships based in a community to functional roles in impersonal structures (or from *gemeinschaft* to *gesellschaft*, as described by Ferdinand Tönnies over a century ago) has become a commonplace. Since World War II, there have been two scenarios for disaster—one sudden and swift, the other slow and sure.

Governments have applied sci-tech to armed force in an upward spiral of destructive potential. New weapons justify more spending for arms and enhance a willingness to use them. At different times in the 20th century, political leaders and military strategists have proclaimed a "war to end all wars," peace through defense, or mutual assured destruction as a strategy for nuclear stalemate. For 40 years following World War II, military purposes dominated federal support for research, and industries with links to the Pentagon shaped strategic decisions. In the 1990s, the collapse of the Soviet Union opened a debate over a "peace dividend." Should research spending go for industrial competitiveness or for human needs such as decent housing and health care?

For a half century, a nuclear holocaust has threatened global annihilation. Jonathan Schell (1982, pp. 3, 93) eloquently warned of catastrophe:

The blinding of insects, birds, and beasts all over the world; the extinction of many ocean species, among them some at the base of the food chain; the temporary or permanent alteration of the climate of the globe, with the outside chance of "dramatic" and "major" alterations in the structure of the atmosphere; the pollution of the whole ecosphere with oxides of nitrogen; the incapacitation in ten minutes of unprotected people who go out into the sunlight; the blinding of people who go out into the sunlight; a significant decrease in photosynthesis in plants around the world; the scalding and killing of many crops; the increase in rates of cancer and mutation around the world, but especially in the targeted zones, and the attendant risk of global epidemics; the possible poisoning of all vertebrates by sharply increased levels of Vitamin D in their skin as a result of increased ultraviolet light; and the outright slaughter on all targeted continents of most human beings and other living things by the initial nuclear radiation, the fireballs, the thermal pulses, the blast waves, the mass fires, and the fallout from the explosions . . . lead[ing] to the extinction of mankind.

In terms of costs and benefits, atomic warfare is an absurdity. Mutual assured destruction can make sense only if it is never used. For years, machines were programmed to unleash global destruction in the event of an atomic attack. An ever-present potential for nuclear weapons threatens each nation's preference for peace, leading to defensive measures that induce other nations to build more bombs and missiles. Moreover, industrial uses of atomic power justify a secretive, bureaucratic State that fosters paranoid fears about a reactor meltdown or release of radioactivity into the atmosphere. Meanwhile, poisonous wastes pile up without safe disposal. Atomic energy that once promised free power to everyone has come to symbolize science and technology run amok.

Upward trends sooner or later bring absurd or calamitous results. The Club of Rome based its predictions on computer simulations: "If the present growth trends in world population, industrialization, pollution, food production, and resource depletion continue unchanged, the limits to growth on this planet will be reached sometime within the next one hundred years" (Meadows, Meadows, Randers, & Behrens, 1972, pp. 29, 186). Its report concluded: "As soon as a society recognizes that it cannot maximize everything for everyone, it must begin to make choices. Should there be more people or more wealth, more wilderness or more automobiles, more food for the poor or more services for the rich? Establishing the societal answers to questions like these and translating those answers into policy is the essence of the political process." Yet democratic governments seldom put these issues on their agenda. Nor can future generations vote on current policies!

Environmentalists argue that ecological awareness will lead to less waste and destruction, more family planning, and simpler lifestyles. The *Global 2000 Report* predicted a world "more crowded, more polluted, less stable ecologically, and more vulnerable to disruption." To cope with resource depletion, people will produce more and yet "be poorer in many ways than they are today" (Council on Environmental Quality and Department of State, 1982, p. 1). Regional differences, notably a north-south dichotomy on the planet, reflect a dilemma: Poor nations with growing populations must industrialize to achieve a decent standard of living, yet they control few resources to invest in physical or human capital. Moreover, state support for commercial development usually destroys traditional village economies and cultures.

One way to describe modern tensions is through a historical narrative that blames technology in the service of capitalists. During an industrial era, information technologies developed to control machines and workers. Schooling served a dual purpose of preparing workers to follow orders while an elite learned to design and implement technologies of control. Later, electronic media provided distractions for people whose lives were dulled by routines and rationalized functions. Human competencies that facilitated interactions with machines and things were regarded as more important than aesthetic, creative or spiritual knowledge. During a period of marked success in extending life and well-being for most people in industrial economies, science served rationalizing purposes in dominating nature and organizational structures.

This counternarrative, however, converts science, technology and the State from the solution to the problem. Neither account leaves much space for resistance—for people to construct identities around cooperation and creativity. Moreover, a blanket acceptance or rejection of modernism may feed personal apathy and alienation that devalues a liberating education. Today's learners have access to ample information but must determine what is meaningful or useful in arrays of media, publications, software, and everyday interactions. Their challenge is to see both strengths and limitations in the way science finds simplicity in complexity and in disciplinary knowledge bases. That cognitive framework also should incorporate a purposive self and multicultural perspectives.

## SCIENCE AND TECHNOLOGY

To act effectively in industrial America, people need to predict how individuals and things will behave, to use physical and organizational devices, and to operate within stable, specialized social systems. Useful knowledge is "formatted" in cognitive frameworks of language—in origin stories or academic disciplines, in technologies or techniques, and in productive organizations or political institutions. Abstract information gains its context from paradigms expressed in verbal, mathematical, or logical relationships, making it easier to recall or to convey to others through sequential courses. Technologies—tools, machines, engines, and electronic controls—extend human capacities and embody skills in designs, thereby simplifying many competencies and facilitating learning by doing. Organizations structure predictable interactions among households, firms and governments.

Although technological developments often precede scientific advances, today science is credited with the primary role. In part, that reflects a higher status accorded abstract ideas over practical applications. Yet technology and science are closely entangled with each other as well as with education, corporations and the nation-state. From 1750 to 1850, farmers improved animal husbandry and untrained workers made small adaptations in mechanical devices, but thereafter formal education has become increasingly necessary for invention. Telescopes, microscopes, clocks, compasses and scales enabled measurements that revealed underlying relationships in natural phenomena. Today, science depends on government and corporate support for experiments in costly laboratories.

Sci-tech raises a core issue of all socially shared cognition: "how it is that actors (people, organizations) are both shaped by, but yet help to shape, the context in or with which they are recursively implicated" (Bijker & Law, 1992, pp. 10, 9, 10). Technologies do not develop in a black box or function simply in response to their internal logic or scientific laws. They "are born out of *conflict, difference, or resistance.*" They have advocates and opponents, each with their political and economic strategies. Some resolution is reached (or a technology is stabilized) when "the network of relations in which they are involved—together with the various strategies that drive and give shape to the network—reach some kind of accommodation." Social structures influence strategies for technological advances, which then extend or modify those formats so that new opportunities and allocations become possible.

## Understanding Technology

Hand tools and regular activities encourage disciplined thinking about how things work. Through technology, humans try "to organize the world for problem solving so that goods and services can be invented, developed, produced, and used" (Hughes, 1989, p. 6). Over time, certain usages become unproblematic, such as the advantages of factories, automobiles and computers. Those artifacts, in turn, define a range of other social relationships and create fresh concerns. Each advance leads to new "reverse salients"—areas where flows are constricted or scarcities appear most remediable. Technological "problems" are thus defined by what is known, by what people wish to accomplish, and by what appears possible. For 500 years in the West, those areas revolved around obtaining material plenty by exploiting natural and human resources.

Technology has organizational, technical and cultural dimensions. Organizationally, there are "many facets of administration, and public policy; it relates to the activities of designers, engineers, technicians, and production workers, and also concerns the users and consumers of whatever is produced" (Pacey, 1983, pp. 5, 6). Then, there is a physical side "that has to do with machines, techniques, knowledge and the essential activity of making things work." Finally, there are "values, ideas and creative activity" connected with a culture of technology. For Pacey, "technology-practice is thus *the application of scientific and other knowledge to practical tasks by ordered systems that involve people and organizations, living things and machines.*"

Separated from their social contexts, complex technologies simply combine various components embodying principles of mechanics or electronics. For example, machines draw on a handful of simple devices—"levers, gears, belts, wheels, cams, cranks, and springs"—to control complicated movements and forces. In *The Way Things Work,* David Macaulay (1988, p. 10) marvelously illustrates the principle of inclined planes in wedges, Yale locks, axes, scissors, plows, and zippers. Levers are incorporated in wheelbarrows, nutcrackers, fishing rods, balance scales, and pianos. Wheels and axles combine in wrenches, faucets, and turbines, while gears and belts transfer the direction, location and speed of movement to drive a lawn mower. Cams and cranks that transform rotary motion into back-and-forth actions control windshield wipers or sewing machines. Pulleys reverse directions and amplify force to lift elevators. Rotating wheels bring into play a variety of factors: precession to keep a bicycle upright, inertia in a flywheel, or centrifugal force to spin clothes dry. Elasticity and friction complete Macaulay's list.

Explaining complex machines such as a bicycle would make engineering instruction horrendously complex. Each principle serves multiple purposes—for instance, an inclined plane fastens two objects together in a screw or augments force in a faucet. A parking meter uses dozens of devices that respond to a coin's weight. By identifying simple principles underlying many possible applications, ideas can be recombined in new ways. At first, people who worked with machines proved most adept at making adjustments and adding improvements. Gradually, industrial processes required formal training in chemistry to make steel or photographs, in electromagnetics for telegraphs and telephones, in physics for energy sources or wireless transmission, in biology for medicine. Scientific principles were embodied in equipment and processes.

One way to understand technology is as a method for acquiring, storing and conveying information. People look for reliability and stability in their purposive interactions that do not require "immediate attention" (Law & Bijker, 1992, p. 294): "That is, they try to find ways of ensuring that things will stay in one place once those who initiated them have gone away and started to do something else." Characteristically, once a device works, it is taken for granted by both designers and users. Bruno Latour (1992, p. 229) recounted the function of a door as a technology that enables a wall to protect people or things without denying access. Then, he generalized, "every time you want to know what a non-human does, simply imagine what other humans or other non-humans would have to do were this character not present." In essence, "we have delegated (or translated or displaced or shifted down) to the hinge the work of reversibly solving the wall-hole dilemma."

To take advantage of the repetitive actions of machinery, people learned new skills and competencies. Technicians visualize novel combinations of simple devices, mentally rearrange flows, and conceive of questions to resolve puzzling events. Programmers for microprocessors "see" the flow of an electron through their millions of switches. Economists reify elasticity of supply and demand curves. Scientists become so familiar with subatomic particles and "big bang" cosmology that both appear to follow the same rules. That level of abstraction enables people who have time and training to perform cognitive operations beyond the here and now of observable objects and interactions.

Those who could envision new combinations of mechanical devices gained an economic advantage similar to that earlier held by good judges of seeds, animals and soil. No longer dependent on weather or the vagaries of diseases, people attributed progress to rationalizing processes (urbanization, industrialization and bureaucratization). In turn, that belief privileged rationalism (secular, empirical and pragmatic thinking). Those ways of thinking served a rising bourgeoisie who were eager to extend their control over things as well as people. Business and government employed technology for their own ends. Sci-tech's authority was not to be questioned, no matter what its consequences for ordinary people—or the future.

## Modern Science

From a layperson's perspective, science uses a remote and cryptic vocabulary unconnected to everyday uses or personal curiosity. Indeed, an introductory biology course may introduce more new terms than a beginning French class. Accessible mainly to trained elites, sciences are embedded in textbook summaries of past discoveries that ignore ill-structured puzzles and alternative research programs. By attributing discovery to individual genius, scientists lend an aura of mystery to their claim of authority. Major corporations and governments gain credibility from experts in laboratories who legitimate products and policies. Elementary teachers often shy away from arithmetic and science, while mathematics, chemistry and physics instructors at the secondary level assert the importance of their subject matter for admission to college.

Western societies privilege science as objective, positive and authoritative knowledge verified by a community of scholars. Its great accomplishments depend on a level of abstraction and a hierarchy of subsystems that incorporate an infinitude of phenomena in a few simple laws. As commonly defined, scientists apply empirical thinking to organize knowledge about the physical world. At the heart of science lies a method—information gathering followed by testing and retesting of hypotheses that constitute a tentative set of principles or laws. Most Americans assume that "science" is possible—that experimentation checked by other scientists clarifies "truths" that are universal, accessible to others, and useful.

As a scientist, Richard Feynman (1967, pp. 14, 23) related abstract theory to observed phenomena, and vice versa. He introduced the law of gravitation—"two bodies exert a force upon each other which varies inversely as the square of the distance between them, and varies directly as the product of their masses." Science's first giant step was observation in response to a hypothesis. Once confirmed in a general way, gravity explained planetary orbits, while raising questions or anomalies. As the Nobel Prize–winning physicist explained, "if we had not known the Law of Gravitation we would have taken much longer to find the speed of light, because we would not have known what to expect of Jupiter's satellites."

At end of his first lecture, Feynman (1967, pp. 33, 34) noted that physical laws are ordinarily expressed in mathematics yet are inexact ("There is always an edge of mystery"). Simplicity seemed the key: "I do not mean it is simple in its action—the motions of the various planets and the perturbations of one on the other can be quite complicated to work out, and to follow how all those stars in a globular cluster move is quite beyond our ability. It is complicated in its actions, but the basic pattern or the system beneath the whole thing is simple." Character-istically, laws of physics apply comprehensively: "Nature uses only the longest threads to weave her patterns, so each small piece of her fabric reveals the organization of the entire tapestry."

Some phenomena remain unexplained, although mathematical laws presumably apply to everything from atomic structures to galaxies. Feynman (1967, pp. 55, 59) noted the importance of expressing axioms and reasoning in several ways: "I always find that mysterious, and I do not understand the reason why it is that the correct laws of physics seem to be expressible in such a tremendous variety of ways. They seem to be able to get through several wickets at the same time." Underlying the many complicated laws governing electricity, magnetism, nuclear interactions, and so on, he identified a handful of general principles: "conservation, certain qualities of symmetry, the general form of quantum mechanical principles, and unhappily, or happily, . . . the fact that all the laws are mathematical."

At different levels of observations, scientists describe behaviors without tracing everything back to subatomic structures. Waves and rainbows are typically explained without relating surface tension of water or refractive indices to atomic operations. Something like a storm or a frog combines various physical forces, each of which might be "explained," though each link is "a little weak." Feynman (1967, p. 125) then asked about humans and history, good and evil:

> Which end is nearer to God; if I may use a religious metaphor. Beauty and hope, or the fundamental laws? . . . All the sciences, and not just the sciences but all the efforts of intellectual kinds, are an endeavor to see the connections of the hierarchies, to connect beauty to history, to connect history to man's psychology, man's psychology to the working of the brain, the brain to the neural impulse, the neural impulse to the chemistry, and so forth, up and down, both ways. And today we cannot, and it is no use making believe that we can, draw carefully a line all the way from one end of this thing to the other, because we have only just begun to see that there is this relative hierarchy.

Quantum physics suggests elements of unpredictability quite aside from a question about whether tracing effects from subatomic matter to aesthetic responses results in a deterministic universe. An issue remains about how much information, at what costs, would be required to describe such a world—or whether one description can serve many purposes. Even for physics, as Feynman (1967, p. 168) noted, some phenomena require two different though equally effective ways of explaining the underlying principles: "Therefore psychologically we must keep all the theories in our heads, and every theoretical physicist who is any good knows six or seven different theoretical representations for exactly the same physics." Paradoxically, most citizens usually regard physics as an esoteric way to explain daily experiences that they account for in other terms.

Knowledge about the natural world and human behavior is structured in artificial systems or academic disciplines in order to facilitate its transmission to others. Since Newton, scientists have searched for basic, underlying "laws" that give mathematical certainty to natural phenomena and, thus, convey authority to scientists. That approach has been remarkably successful in enabling people to exploit nature. It underlies the formal operations of cognition that enable us to abstract qualities and consider them in different contexts or in different uses. Courses are reduced to memorization of definitions and laws in an effort to convey the accumulation of knowledge. They omit the excitement of exploring uncertainties that is so richly conveyed by Feynman and many teachers of science today.

## Multiple Paradigms

From a constructivist perspective, scientific knowledge is socially assembled by practitioners located within organizations that have economic and political relationships to the rest of society. Three decades ago, T. S. Kuhn (1970a) argued that each science structures a body of answerable questions, complete with methods for determining their "truth." Occasionally, a revolution establishes a new paradigm or structure. Kuhn's description of a paradigm generated fruitful controversy and discussion. In naive terms, that debate hinged on the importance of socially constructed cultural meanings attached to particular truths. Karl Popper's work in spelling out the role of successive falsification of hypotheses as the key to scientific advance provided a foil to Kuhn's sense that even scientific skepticism occurs within boundaries determined by group norms of that time and place.

In arguing his case, Popper (1962, p. 51) set forth a hypothesis about how best to learn about the world:

Assume that we have deliberately made it our task to live in this unknown world of ours; to adjust ourselves to it as well as we can; . . . and to explain it, *if* possible (we need not assume that it is), and as far as possible, with the help of laws and explanatory theories. *If we have made this our task, then there is no more rational procedure than the method of . . . conjecture and refutation:* of boldly proposing theories; of trying our best to show that these are erroneous; and of accepting them tentatively if our critical efforts are unsuccessful.

Kuhn (1970b, pp. 22, 20) countered by emphasizing "the social-psychological imperatives" that define the "problems" considered by a scientific community. He noted a worsening of "communication across the boundaries between scientific specialties." Paradigms address the issues of their time and place, and a revolutionary hypothesis has no claim to be universally better.

Because paradigm shifts have fuzzy borders at best, historians and philosophers of knowledge often talk of "scientific research programs" as a clearer description for normal science. It captures the sense of a framework for asking questions, together with methods for resolving them. Also, it suggests that many communities of scholars now flourish—in keeping with multiplying subdisciplines that engage researchers. But underneath lies a question about reality. If scientific puzzles are an intellectual game for describing observations that are partially determined by one's preferred research program, then there is no reassurance that we are approaching a fundamental understanding of objects, energy or time.

From a sociological perspective, science backed by technology becomes a way to strengthen rhetoric (or belief) through research, publications, experiments, and chains of allies who support particular claims to truth (Latour, 1987, pp. 108, 142, 179, 180). A fact builder seeks to "spread out in time and space." To do that requires two contradictory actions: "to enrol others so that they participate in the construction of the fact; to control their behaviour in order to make their actions predictable." In a constructivist frame, neither scientists nor engineers "know what society is made of, any more than they know the nature of Nature beforehand." Technoscience is both "a demiurgic enterprise" to recruit supporters and "a rare and fragile achievement" recognizable only after it controls its version of what is taken as real.

Scientists discovered that mobilization of resources is easier if applications have military or medical uses. In many other areas, "scientific" approaches of observation, hypothesis building, and testing go on, but potential supporters are relatively independent and modify the conclusions to suit their needs. As a result, no authority accrues to the person(s) or place(s) claiming originality. In Latour's analysis, soft facts are those readily adopted and adapted, while hard science is "the only solution if one wants to make others believe something uncommon" (1987, p. 209). Widely accepted beliefs do not require extensive networks of control and thus require little power to implement. "Harder facts are not the rule but the exception, since they are needed only in a very few cases to displace others on a large scale out of their usual ways."

In this context, science and technology had a dramatic impact on historical development by answering a simple question (Latour, 1987, p. 223): "how to act at a distance on unfamiliar events, places and people?" During an age of exploration, discovery, map making, and classification of the world's flora and fauna, Europeans learned to collect and categorize facts that then could be applied in commerce. English or Spanish sailors navigated and traded as successfully as native peoples. Capitalists could sit in Paris or Boston, arrange to mine ore in Chile, refine it, and transport copper for telephone lines in New Orleans. Exercising control over large spaces and long time frames expanded the mental framework, requiring more subdisciplines.

> **Consider a common historical metanarrative in light of today's curriculum:**
>
> American progress flowed from individualism, rationalism, capitalism, and democracy—propelled by science and technology. People came to a new land seeking freedom and material plenty. The Founding Fathers institutionalized democracy with a Bill of Rights and private ownership guided by competitive markets. Technological advances in machines, energy, transportation, and communication led to expanding output for a growing population. In the 20th century, American industrial and military power has protected democracies from totalitarian threats.
>
> How does that mainstream account shape the science and technology curriculum? Does it affect attitudes toward class, race and gender?

Most schools emphasize science and technology by making it a central part of the required curriculum. At every grade level, students are expected to learn science—how plants grow, the order of planets in the solar system, names of rocks and minerals, parts of the human body, mathematical laws governing motion. They encounter abstract and decontextualized definitions. Many students, especially females, resist learning how things work in technical terms. Largely omitted from these discussions are the historical, social and economic contexts of sci-tech—how certain technologies came to dominate the market, how some inventors became successful entrepreneurs, or how classification systems privileged the experiences of White males.

For centuries, science as a search for simple explanations underlying complex phenomena appeared remarkably useful. Now, uncertainty—variously attributed to the Heisenberg principle, quantum physics, Kuhn's paradigms, or, more broadly, constructivism—undercuts embedded beliefs about nature and human understanding as objectively knowable. A cognitive psychologist described the transformation during his lifetime:

Today, instead of regarding nature as a forest full of hidden treasures to be discovered through clever use of the proper techniques, it has become a series of brief memoranda written in different languages, delivered on an irregular schedule, telling the scientist where next to search. Upon arriving at each new secret location, the investigator finds only another note. It took me too long to realize that the treasures did not easily fit into the small box that I had brought, although the pile of notes fit perfectly. (Kagan, 1989, p. 2)

In developmental terms, most science is described at the level of durable categories and formal operations of cognition. Few individuals demonstrate Feynman's ease in shifting from physical phenomena to mathematical relationships to multiple ways to illustrate a point. Moreover, in their desire to appear objective, scientists seem reluctant to acknowledge their economic dependency on universities, foundations, corporations, and government sponsors. When the threat of nuclear disaster or the spread of AIDS breaks that pattern, scientists appear uncomfortable in a visibly political role. By recognizing the large system of knowledge and power of which they are a part, however, scientists and engineers might responsibly communicate with a segmented society—while providing students a clearer sense of why sci-tech is worth learning.

## SOCIAL CONTEXTS OF SCI-TECH

Paradoxically, science claims to be universally true, while scientists erect barriers around their discipline and their membership. Insiders who have learned a basic paradigm with its research methodology either criticize the findings of others or line up in support of accepted laws and conclusions. Outsiders are expected to fall into line, especially when scientific findings violate commonsensical views or the self-interests of others. Insiders in academic institutions or industrial laboratories compete for the honor of discovery against their peers, and they can scarcely comprehend the resentment and apparent prejudices of outsiders. They often have succumbed to a temptation to use class, race and gender biases to strengthen their insider's status and claims to truth.

As scientists seek to extend validated knowledge, they adopt a method for testing truth and make claims to "universalism, communism, disinterestedness, organized skepticism" (Merton, 1973a, pp. 270, 273):

The technical methods employed toward this end provide the relevant definition of knowledge: empirically confirmed and logically consistent statements of regularities (which are, in effect, predictions). The institutional imperatives (mores) derive from the goal and the methods. . . . The technical norm of empirical evidence, adequate and reliable, is a prerequisite for sustained true prediction; the technical norm of logical consistency, a prerequisite for systematic and valid prediction.

Writing in 1942, Merton intended a contrast to Nazi Germany's exclusion of Albert Einstein from "Aryan" physics. By communism, he meant quite literally that "the substantive findings of science are a product of social collaboration and are assigned to the community."

Stimulated by Black nationalists' critique of American education, Merton (1973b, pp. 99, 101) revisited epistemological issues raised by insiders versus outsiders. Questions about how to determine valid truths recur "in times of great social change, precipitated by acute social conflict and attended by much cultural disorganization." Not even total access would enable people to master all available truths:

As cleavages deepen between groups, social strata, or collectivities of whatever kind, the social network of mutual reliance is at best strained and at worst broken. In place of the vigorous but cognitively disciplined mutual checking and rechecking that operates to a significant extent, though never of course totally, within the social institutions of science and scholarship, there develops a strain toward separatism, in the domain of the intellect as in the domain of society.

On the other hand, oppressed groups need to assert knowledge based on their own experiences in order to establish their identity and self-worth.

Social realities include the differences raised by insiders' and outsiders' perspectives into their taken-for-granted assumptions. Otherwise, as Merton (1973b, p. 104) wryly suggested, "it would then plainly follow that only sociologists can possibly understand their fellow sociologists." For a century, educated elites sought to define particular authority for themselves by segmenting knowledge, using specialized vocabularies, and answering questions of limited social importance. Moreover, their judgments, expressed in the guise of science, reinforced social divisions by class, race and gender in ways that violated their own rules for objectivity. Today, learning communities depend on people sharing ideas and insights across as well as within disciplinary boundaries.

### Race and Gender Barriers

Scientific scholarship serves as a source of authority, a means to legitimate knowledge. It enables scientists and engineers to obtain resources for themselves and their organizations, which are bastions of White, male, middle-class power. Working-class children learn that sci-tech entails complex mysteries beyond their desire to learn. People of color have few role models to encourage career choices in those areas and, if so motivated, typically focus on medicine or social sciences. Many females fear mathematics and, if they show an interest in science, are often directed toward biology. Thus, schools simultaneously screen out girls and students of color while preserving an aura of authority and selectivity for technicians, professionals and managers.

Systematic exclusion has been a partially conscious strategy by male workers seeking to gain professional status, income and authority for their particular competency. As Carolyn Marvin (1988, p. 15) documented in a history of communications, "electricians were wont to indulge a powerful impulse to identify aliens and enemies, those suspect in electrical culture and perhaps dangerous to it, in terms of their textual competence." Existing prejudices reinforced hierarchy: "By a supplemental logic of explicit social control, any additional marginality of race, class, gender, or lifestyle was taken as confirming alien status." Trade journals printed jokes in which female effusiveness violated telegraphic terseness, African Americans huffed and puffed at Edison's lamps when ready for bed, and rural bumpkins shouted at a telephone hanging on the wall. "The professional literature exhibited scant interest in whatever ethical questions might be involved in deceptive manipulations to achieve power over the less expertly informed." Today, computer buffs speak knowingly of RAM, ROM, WYSIWYG, gophers, processor speeds, and network protocols.

In the late 19th century, academics took a leading role in anti-immigration agitation. For example, Francis Amasa Walker, a noted statistician who served as head of the American Economic Association, asserted that "so long as the least reason appears for the miserable, the broken, the corrupt, the abject, to think that they might be better off here than there, if not in the workshop, then in the workhouse, these Huns, and Poles, and Bohemians, and Russian Jews, and South Italians will continue to come, and to come by the millions." Although other social scientists then and later contradicted Walker's ethnic slurs and his use of statistics, racist biases were openly expressed by many "objective" scholars (Walker and contrary evidence are conveniently located in Handlin [1959, pp. 71–75]).

> Do you think it would have made a difference in terms of the research and outcomes if half of the scientists and engineers had been women? Are there examples that illustrate your view? What about public bathrooms or lighting of parking lots?
>
> Consider the same questions if people of color in the United States had been represented in proportion to their numbers in the population.

From 1870 through 1920, the denigration of women and people of color was a common part of scientific knowledge among leading scientists. Historian Cynthia Russett (1989, pp. 188, 203) concluded that misogyny among scientists violated three out of four of their methodological rules: "Their work was neither scrupulously empirical, nor skeptical, nor objective." Perhaps scientists were more antifeminist than other middle-class males because they were accustomed to categorizing individuals and then generalizing about group differences. Science seemed to validate specialized roles, and educated men presumed that discontent followed from trying to overreach one's proper place: "Scientists became the prophets of an updated Calvinism, ordaining some—the white, the civilized, the European, the male—to evolutionary maturity, and others—the dark-skinned, the primitive, the female—to perpetual infancy."

When experts attributed criminal behavior, low IQ, or diseases to genetics while ignoring environmental factors, it was little wonder that targeted groups came to resent such "science." Scientists mismeasured cranial capacity, intelligence, and genes in order to "demonstrate" the superiority of northern European ethnic groups. Despite refutations and recantations of racist conclusions by most scientists, some educators and psychologists reiterated fundamental errors in reasoning in order to raise questions about the efficacy of education for Black children. As Stephen Jay Gould (1981, pp. 318, 323) charged about Arthur Jensen, a "caricature of evolution exposes his preference for unilinear ranking by implied worth." Jensen and many others focused on small, external distinctions to make "subjective judgment of important differ-ences. But biologists have recently affirmed—as long suspected—that the overall genetic differences among human races are astonishingly small."

In 1994, these issues reappeared in *The Bell Curve: Intelligence and Class Structure in American Life*, which generated considerable publicity and public reaction. At best, Richard J. Herrnstein and Charles Murray mix bad science with an ugly political message, and their antagonism to compensatory education programs, welfare, immigration, nontraditional families, and lax school standards motivated the burst of commentary about the book. Aware of the serious critiques of their use of IQ scores, genetic trends, correlations of intelligence with welfare and crime, and various other matters, the authors start by hedging their predictions of dysgenic disaster, only to later write as though it were an established fact. They ignored dozens of more plausible cultural and environmental factors that would account for the outcome with fewer inconsistencies than genetic causes. Perhaps most important is their heedlessness about the social and political consequences for those they labeled as doomed by their presumed IQ. In that context, how can Black Americans respect educators who view them as capable of little more than memorization?

Elitism among practicing scientists served their professional interests. Historically, they gained public notice, funds, and national influence during wars; and now the State funds most basic research. By the 1970s, a dependence on public allocations raised doubts about the disinterestedness of scientists: "Now, the capacity of physicists to comprehend the universe far beyond the ordinary ken, their power to master nature yet unleash terrifying forces, their command of a body of esoteric knowledge essential to public decisionmaking, and their simultaneous dependence upon a political process of public choice—all promised to keep the dilemmas alive indefinitely" (Kevles, 1978, p. 426). Scientific elites seek financing for enormous projects—such as a supercollider (now unfunded), a catalog of human genes, or a telescope in space—without much accountability to voters' needs or preferences.

Moreover, public research budgets support medical and military establishments rather than ecology and the arts. At the onset of the 1990s, the *New York Times* (Pollack et al., 1991, pp. 35, 38–39) projected ten new technologies in the upcoming decade: micromotors, supercomputers with parallel processing, genetic engineering for food and medicine, superconductors for transportation and sensors, digital imaging in high-definition television (HDTV), computer-designed silicon circuits to speed complex calculations for image and speech recognition, photovoltaic cells and batteries, fiber optics, ceramic composite materials to withstand heat, and software developments. These choices were justified based on energy, speed, and above all military applications. For example, HDTV would support a silicon chip industry and "we've decided that the semiconductor industry is vital to national security."

In the 1990s, some commentators described America as a cynical society. No one's expertise seemed trustworthy. African Americans learned that Black syphilis patients in an experiment never received penicillin even after its efficacy was established. Women increasingly recognized that their typical occupations as secretaries, teachers and nurses brought lower status and income. Citizens discovered that the government had tested radioactive materials on the public without informed consent. Yet democratic debate based on the best scholarship also offers a responsible way to counter self-interested ideologies and hierarchical structures. Rather than abandoning science, teachers and students should apply its skepticism and inquiry to its own presumptions and methods.

## Feminist Perspectives on Knowing

Over the past 25 years, radical critiques have shaken a dominant faith in progress based on science, technology, democracy, and capitalist competition. A deep ecology, or Gaia, movement questions a presumed right of humans to exploit the planet and destroy other species. Others challenge Western ways of knowing through rational empiricism by raising Asian, Native American or Afrocentric beliefs about the meaning of life. Feminist critiques of science profoundly question its objectivity and universalism. These perspectives undercut a widespread faith in sci-tech without generating a new consensus. Indeed, they partially contradict each other about how to redirect knowledge now embedded in technologies, organizational structures, and democratic institutions.

Feminists started with a critique of "the social structure and uses of science" and then questioned "the origins, problematics, social meanings, agendas, and theories of scientific knowledge-seeking" (Harding, 1991, pp. vii, 47–48). "We can begin to sense the contradictions when we note that conventionally, what it means to be scientific is to be dispassionate, disinterested, impartial, concerned with abstract principles and rules; but what it means to be a woman is to be emotional, interested in and partial to the welfare of family and friends, concerned with concrete practices and contextual relations." Those concerns arose not from genes but from the roles allotted them: "the care of all bodies, including men's, and the local places where bodies exist (houses, offices, and so on), the care of young children, and 'emotional work'—the processing of men's and everyone else's feelings." Philosopher Sandra Harding asked why women should "renounce what they can know about nature and social relations from the perspective of their daily lives in order to produce what the culture is able to recognize as knowledge?"

A critical stance might strengthen science's validity. Women scientists and feminist perspectives contribute in multiple ways to seeing science as a product of its time and social history. Some aspects of sci-tech are visible only when examined "systematically over large sweeps of history" (Harding, 1991, pp. 94, 95). Elite researchers depend on powerful business and governmental interests: "Science generates capital in the form of information, ideas, and technologies that are used to administer, manage, and control the physical world and social relations." Moreover, "in modern Western cultures, middle-class white men tend more than other groups to believe in the ability of their individual minds to mirror nature, their faculties of judgment to make rational choices, and the power of their wills to bring about their choices."

Paradoxically, women and other oppressed groups have a particular advantage in understanding how dominant ideologies constrict choices, thereby inhibiting learning. As Harding (1991, pp. 125–126) noted, "women's oppression, exploitation, and domination are grounds for transvaluing women's differences because members of oppressed groups have fewer interests in ignorance about the social order and fewer reasons to invest in maintaining or justifying the status quo than do dominant groups. They have less to lose by distancing themselves from the social order; thus, the perspective from their lives can more easily generate fresh and critical analyses." Feminist perspectives strengthen scholarly objectivity by including an awareness of the observer's role.

Good science incorporates feminist insights and recognizes its previous limitations: "First, we must say of science that it is politics by other means but also that it can produce reliable empirical information; it can do so as, for better or worse, it participates in politics" (Harding, 1991, pp. 308, 312). Second, science lends itself to positive and negative purposes, "and it leaves itself open to manipulation by regressive social forces to the extent that its institutions do not acknowledge and grapple with these contradictory internal features." Third, there is no distinction between observers and objects. Science "can appear to us only as already socially constituted, and it is socially reconstituted through scientific processes, among others." Fourth, claims to truth necessarily imply both epistemological theories and a sociology of knowledge, but current academic views are generally "archaic" and "excessively narrow." Critical approaches break through the ignorance of privileged groups and make knowledge available to majorities who can "gain democratic control over the conditions of their lives."

Whether seen through feminist critiques, Afrocentric values, Eastern religions, or ecological concerns, the issue of transmitting knowledge raises the question posed in Harding's title: "Whose Science, Whose Knowledge?" Many females and students of color recognize that mathematics and science as usually taught in schools have excluded their experiences and knowledge. A holistic view of the world contains networks of interrelated processes, not just linear cause and effect relationships. In order to gain technical, professional or managerial authority, females have been forced to ignore or devalue their cultural knowledge—their caring, concern, and commitment. Ecologists have to think globally while seeking local economies to relieve environmental stress. Only elites find that "empiricism" supports their knowledge and power.

## RETHINKING COMPUTERS IN SCHOOLS

Powerful electronic machines linked to sophisticated software already have transformed many classrooms. In our observations of schools, teachers divide into a small number of computer buffs who enjoy technical mysteries of disk operating systems, a larger number of computer phobes who delight in tales of balky software and system crashes, and perhaps a majority of bystanders who would welcome assistance with routine tasks. They hope word processing will ease rewriting, check spelling, and review grammar; that spreadsheets will simplify their grade book; and that a machine will keep attendance records. For most teachers  who lack a telephone in their room or ready access to a photocopier—multimedia seems a distant dream.

Although today's students "use" computers in schools, levels of capability and access vary widely. Although over half of students in public schools have access to computers, the pace of innovation means that poorer districts are soon left with outdated equipment and software. In 1995, 15% of families earning under $20,000 had a computer at home, compared with 74% of those making $75,000 or more. Black and Latino families reported that less than 16% had home computers, compared with 43% of Whites. Educators express concern that unequal access to computers in homes and schools reinforces disparate outcomes, but they lack a solution.

Some technological enthusiasts predict that microcomputers will soon replace teachers and other experts in transmitting formal knowledge. At first glance, such a scenario is plausible and attractive. Information can be transmitted easily and quickly to large numbers of students, who learn at their own pace. Expert systems mimic interactions of exceptionally fair and effective teachers. Computer printouts on student progress or other administrative data facilitate individualization of curriculum. Principals monitor activities and resolve conflicts though dialog without rigid bureaucratic rules. Networked classrooms can connect learners and instructors throughout the world.

At their best, computers support flexible and interactive explorations among students and teachers rather than repeating drill and practice exercises. Word processing eases revising and "publishing," thereby encouraging self-expression. LOGO and the Geometric Supposer invite students to create and solve mathematics problems. Electronic bulletin boards facilitate communication without concern for distance or geographic and social boundaries. Graphic microworlds can illuminate scientific principles (gravity affecting a baseball on the moon or on Jupiter) or history (monasteries to explore). Hypermedia allows ideas and graphics to link across passages in a text file or a database. A student exploring the Civil Rights Movement might read key documents, study a time line of events, hear Martin Luther King, Jr., deliver a sermon, and view newscasts of marches in Birmingham.

### Technologies versus School Cultures

Reviewing the introduction of computers in schools, Larry Cuban (1993, pp. 198, 206) found three impetuses for reform. First, educators express a goal of preparing students for jobs using information technologies. Second, reformers seek to facilitate problem-solving and creativity-building experiences through appropriate software. Third, computers seem an effective way to improve productivity in schools and workplaces. To the extent they resemble other technological innovations accepted by schools, personal computers will not upset longstanding behavioral norms—"that teaching is telling, learning is listening, knowledge is subject matter taught by teachers and books, and the teacher-student relationship is crucial to any learning." In the struggle for a computer revolution in schools, the "classroom wins—for now."

Current inequities in classroom uses of computers aggravate biases in information technologies toward elite control over "dumbed down" workers. As C. A. Bowers (1988, pp. 5, 6) observed, students absorb a way of "thinking, status systems, social norms, and an economic-political orientation" from deep-seated patterns of schooling. Teachers "transmit them as part of the unexamined beliefs they share with students." In general, schools support "the technological consumer domain of society: attitudes toward technological innovation, the progressive nature of change, measurement and planning as sources of authority, a conceptual hierarchy that places abstract-theoretical thought at the highest, a competitive-remissive form of individualism, and the definition of human needs in terms of what can be supplied by a commodity culture." Computers reinforce an "emphasis on facts (objective knowledge) that can be rationally manipulated in order to provide the authority for decision making."

Modern schooling assumes that personal autonomy depends on knowing how to anticipate and coordinate interactions to resolve problems rationally through technical means. A sci-tech worldview promotes experimentation over intuition, theory over emotion, individuals over groups, and materialism over oneness with nature. Despite their rhetoric about developing human potential, teachers use technology to perpetuate adult control—confirming "that surveillance is essential to the development of the socially responsible citizen, and thus could be expected to view it as a normal, even necessary, aspect of adult life" (Bowers, 1988, p. 19). They presume that rational and well-socialized students and workers have nothing to fear from supervision.

> Consider children's fascination with, and proficiency at, video games. What lessons are implicit in popular programs in which male heroes must find their way though dungeons, castles, mazes, or outer space while destroying alien enemies?
>
> Can educational software similarly engage students' learning? Are speed, chance, discovery, and conquest essential to hold attention?

Computers reinforce thinking in binary terms—yes or no responses but those patterns were rooted in modern cultures where yes-or-no logical choices were long established. Instead, teachers might investigate the origin and development of ideas, along with their impact on language. Otherwise, computer-based "education for the Information Age fosters an egocentric universe in which decontextualized information is seen as the source of intellectual empowerment and connectedness among individuals." Bowers (1988, pp. 78, 99) insisted, "when individuals lack the language (vocabulary, including the generative metaphors that provide the conceptual frameworks necessary for organizing ideas in a coherent way) to make this knowledge explicit, there is little possibility that communication with others will lead to negotiating new meanings and relationships—which is the essence of the political process."

By structuring information for tests, educators encourage memorization of isolated facts. Ideas are treated like industrial production, that
is, standardized facts learned in sequence are later assembled to form
functional competencies for adults. Mastered competencies such as
letters, sounds, or definitions of biological terms are combined into
disciplines, much as a bicycle applies a few simple mechanical principles. Tightly coupled linkages of subunits are marvelously efficient
ways to recall details, but they reduce consequences to underlying
causes and leave little space for human volition. If that is the crucial
function of schools, however, computers are reasonable substitutes, and
Bowers's critical analysis applies to teachers and texts as well as to
educational technologies.

Computers, like most innovations, raise old dilemmas in new
contexts: Should teachers push students through a "foolproof" curriculum prepared by specialists, or should they be trusted to create
curricula through interactions with their students? Most instructional
programs are "characterized by a high degree of standardization,
fragmentation of learning into small and often unconnected parts, and
presentation of material through the pedagogical method of drill and
practice" (Budin, 1991, pp. 19, 21). On the other hand, informational
technologies may revolutionize schools "by offering tremendously
enhanced sources of information to students; by helping the teacher
become facilitator of learning rather than dispenser of information; by
helping students instigate long-term and actively involving projects; by
demanding changes in spatial arrangement of classrooms and other
learning environments; by promoting an open-ended and never-ending
attitude toward learning; and by prompting students to collaborate in
work and research."

## Computing Possibilities

Every month we receive magazines filled with stories about what
computers can do for schools and workplaces. Recent articles, for
example, described interactive approaches for a videodisc-based course,
distance education in Montana, automating university teaching, satel-
lite delivery of special education programs, auto racing and physics,
using Musical Instrument Digital Interface for teaching math, video-
conferencing in North Carolina, an expert system for accounting,
Networked Testbeds, and plans to implement technology in school
systems. Advertisements, which largely pay for these publications,
promise excitement, enhanced personal and organizational performance, ease of use, unlimited data, and multimedia at the touch of a
mouse.

Assuming that more information is better and that individuals want
to learn, computer advocates anticipate radical changes. Currently
available software can teach practically anyone to read, write and

compute at the level of a high school graduate. Learners who set their own pace surely will master the material in less than 13 years. Networked terminals in each household provide access to any other person, as well as entertainment, news and the world's databases. Workers design software, rearrange information, and monitor robotic output from their home. Consumers search through warehouses of products and order and pay for them with a keystroke. Software programs simplify "painting" pictures, composing and performing music, or writing a great American novel.

Although computers process data in a linear fashion, their speed generates multiple connections that are imitative of flexible, intuitive thinking. Dreamers envision "properly humanistic machines" (Brand, 1988, pp. 264, 251). Anything is possible: interactive television, holographic images for simulated experiences, animated "virtual realities" for educational environments, supercomputers with access to all the information in the world. Enthusiasts "would cure the pathologies of communications technology not with economics or politics, but with technology."

Computing systems might replace managers, professionals and technicians, whose current status is legitimated by a concentration of knowledge in college graduates. Adults would schedule their work time, draw on relevant engineering studies to design products or processes, and monitor their output. Expert systems help doctors diagnose problem illnesses; why not make that information available to everyone? With machine-read verification of immediate symptoms combined with personal data about other conditions that might have adverse effects, why not let everyone prescribe their own medicine from a low-cost terminal in one's home? Democracies might restore a town-meeting form of government—letting anyone express an opinion on any concern, inviting everyone to vote on daily issues. An executive branch would administer the laws, while a national leader, selected to represent the nation in international affairs, could be changed whenever a majority wanted a new election.

People use computers as an image for raising questions about their own role in the future. With multimedia and virtual reality simulations, plausible technologies may significantly alter how people work, think and play. Only installing, cleaning and repairing services combine physical actions with on-site decisions in familiar patterns of useful labor. Metaphorically, industrial workers were "chained" to machines, and information workers' eyes are "glued" to video display terminals. Yet if everyone can communicate with anyone anytime on any subject, how can anyone determine what is relevant in a jumble of words, numbers and images in a postmodern tower of Babel?

As old occupations fade away, learners, teachers, artists, planners, health maintainers, and leaders need new job descriptions. Over the past decade, many educators deemphasized memorization of facts and urged more critical thinking and cooperative learning. Professional organizations supported curricular reforms, such as whole language approaches in reading and writing, problem-solving strategies in mathematics, and hands-on activities in science. As the National Council of Teachers of Mathematics (1989, pp. 4–5) observed, an electorate informed about "current issues—such as environmental protection, nuclear energy, defense spending, space exploration, and taxation—. . . requires technological knowledge and understanding." These recommendations relate goals to educational requirements for the 21st century in an intuitive, rather than a behaviorist, fashion.

Constructivist educators consistently seek certain features in their classrooms. To allow students to take control of their own learning about the world, classes are learner centered and interactive, with an emphasis on inquiry and exploration of multiple texts. Assessment is criterion referenced, with portfolios and performances. Obviously, Internet connections, the wealth of material available on CD-ROMs, and interactive software in areas of mathematics and science makes that classroom more feasible. With rich resources and basic software to produce texts and multimedia, students can work with each other and with teachers to enrich a portfolio and to demonstrate their proficiency through "publications."

By examining how computers perform different functions, educators may gain insights into how humans think and apply their knowledge. Brains suffer glitches and inaccurately recall disparate items over time. Computers are inept at integrating ideas, synthesizing conflicting data, or forging new solutions to ill-structured problems. They lack key features of human thinking—"real intelligence depends on the ability to learn, to reason from experience, to *shoot from the hip*, to use general knowledge, to make inferences using gut-level intuition" (Shank, 1984, p. 34). Pondering how humans adapt to smart machines offers insights into social allocations of knowledge. For instance, the popularity of personal computers over mainframes relates to social organization of work and how people value privacy and openness.

If socially shared cognition is shaped primarily through interactions with machines and media, then knowledge itself acquires new meanings. Searching through Internet for an interesting message need not connect with a productive purpose. Widespread fascination with electronic games, television, or creative writing raises old questions about how technology affects our way of making sense of experience. Without human contact, people miss roles of caring and intimacy. Nature itself appears distant and disembodied when explored primarily through texts and video monitors. Producers of electronic images draw on self-referential scenes—repeating, or flouting, their own conventions. Technologies may remain black boxes for conveying facts and norms or become transparent systems that encourage self-awareness about using information for new purposes.

## MULTIPLE WAYS OF KNOWING

By assuming both social contexts and established procedures, schools foster a belief that questions have right answers. Moreover, well-structured problems fit neatly into disciplinary fields that specify relevant facts and methods for determining acceptable answers that are summarized in textbooks. When sci-tech is treated as an external force to which people must adapt, individuals often feel helpless to determine their own fate. Yet many social problems are ill-structured, complex situations. Only in textbooks and tests are problems presumed to hold the same meaning for all those with a stake in the outcome. "In the real world, there are either too many or too few data, never exactly the right amount of the right kind" (Mitroff, 1983, p. 166).

If "objective" knowledge varies by discipline and perspective, then how can we assume that science advances toward some core of ultimate truth? If science and technology have no independent standing as fixed entities, teachers and test makers lose some of their authority. When students think critically, they may question outmoded origin stories that support ethnocentric excesses or patriotic generalizations. After discovering that answers often follow from the categories already established in language and thought, however, we may imagine new questions. By applying more than one or two of the seven or more human intelligences, we may unblock other solutions.

Without meaning-making interactions, people may function as clever analog robots responding to unambiguous sensory signals. Historian Isaiah Berlin argued that "people can't develop unless they belong to a culture. Even if they rebel against it and transform it entirely, they still belong to a stream of tradition" (in Gardels, 1991, p. 22). Moreover, just as people voluntarily perform many tasks—tending a garden, attending art museums, testing new recipes, or visiting in hospices—they also learn many things unrelated to immediate practical goals. Such engagements help define one's values and meaning as a human being in relation to nature and to others. Voluntary acts convey signals about what kind of society is desirable and what "knowledge" is of value.

Thinking about all the parts of society in relation to every other part is difficult at best and starts by deconstructing some powerful images of modernism. As Adas (1989, p. 413) commented, "modernity is associated with rationality, empiricism, efficiency, and change; tradition connotes fatalism, veneration for custom and the sacred, undiscipline, and stagnation." Knowledge gave power to scientists and professionals; statistical methods and systems approaches rationalized decisions in corporations and governments. Yet people do not appear happy or at peace with themselves. Unless information technologies enable schools, media and governments to engage in interactive learning, scientific knowledge may be condemned as a source of social problems.

### Envisioning Alternatives

Social scientists seldom consider what might have happened—with only a small change in overall outcomes—if alternative technologies gained economies of scale and become elements in larger systems of productive activities. Asking why refrigerators hum, Ruth Cowan (1985, p. 215) noted how close gas and electric techniques initially were in costs, with perhaps a slight advantage for silent gas models. Refrigerators hum "because General Electric, General Motors, Kelvinator, and Westinghouse were very large, very powerful, very aggressive, and very resourceful companies, while Servel and SORCO were not." Refrigerators with compressors gained the advantage of familiarity and availability. After a time, compressor technologies were embedded in support systems of ubiquitous power lines and service centers.

Ordinarily, historical events are explained as understandable responses to previous technologies, cultural understandings, and political conditions. It appears as though no other outcomes were possible. In a pioneering econometric study, Robert Fogel (1964) questioned how essential railroads were to American economic development. He proposed a counterfactual case: A system of waterways to carry freight would have reshaped the geography of cities and factories without necessarily inhibiting growth. Other historians recall a pattern of light rail interurban lines that could have supported extensive travel without polluting the air or paving so much land. Before privately owned radio networks dominated the airwaves, telephone lines carried musical programs in Vienna, and multiple amateur wireless operators in the United States organized interactive broadcasts as well as emergency communications.

Technological problems are defined by historical developments and interactions with other parts of the entire society. Historian Thomas Hughes (1987, pp. 56, 57) proposed that "the history of evolving, or expanding, systems can be presented in the phases in which the activity named predominates: invention, development, innovation, transfer, growth, competition, and consolidation." Stages overlap and backtrack within a typical pattern: "During invention and development inventor-entrepreneurs solve critical problems; during innovation, competition, and growth manager-entrepreneurs make crucial decisions; and during consolidation and rationalization financier-entrepreneurs and consulting engineers, especially those with political influence, often solve the critical problems associated with growth and momentum." During each phase, a particular "reverse salient" engages widespread thought and energy, often richly rewarding those inventors or entrepreneurs who first solve the immediate stumbling block in various subsystems.

Over a century of industrialization, technological systems have grown and rigidified in artifacts, organizations, and "components usually labeled scientific, such as books, articles, and university teaching and research programs. Legislative artifacts, such as regulatory laws, can also be part of technological systems" (Hughes, 1987, pp. 51, 55). Seeking control over their innovations, "inventors, organizers, and managers of technological systems mostly prefer hierarchy, so the systems over time tend toward a hierarchical structure." Previous accumulations of physical and human capital make some continuities easier, thereby routinizing how persons and institutions interact. For instance, the United States has invested so much in streets and highways that light rail mass transit predictably will remain noncompetitive with buses for over a decade after any system is built.

By separating engineering applications from "science," popular thought has arrived at a peculiar conclusion: People adapt to sci-tech by imposing yet more institutions of control on themselves, although technology claims to benefit everyone. When critical thinkers point to powerful interests—capitalists and military powers—that are served by sci-tech, they appear "political." They threaten the underpinnings of a traditional curriculum. Hierarchical controls over sci-tech are concealed by assuming that corporations efficiently produce and distribute goods, devise commercial and transportation networks, and employ people (or not). Outcomes are presented as unchallengeable facts without attempts to see how science, engineering, management, social structures, and political institutions shape and reinforce each other.

Holistic thinking offers some advantages over componential logic. Current interest in fractals and chaos theory suggests a fascination with "random" factors and chance outcomes. As a molecular biologist noted, bacteria behave differently in clusters, that is, component parts often adapt new behaviors or have different effects when found in certain numbers or structures. "For 300 years or more, scientists have searched for the simplest unit that they could take apart, dissect and use to study the system"; now, "we need to understand more about how the properties of the whole arise" (Kolata, 1992). That insight drawn from bacteria applies also to social sciences, where explanatory factors between rational self-interest and folk myths, individual behaviorism and group dynamics, micro- and macroeconomics, Eurocentric and Third World perspectives all mark fragmentations of previous research programs.

## Reconnecting Postindustrial Communities

The pace of change in modern societies introduces a source of disorder. At the outset of the 20th century, Henry Adams (1931, p. 498) looked back on 700 years of technological and social developments, accelerating at an exponential rate "from unity into multiplicity." From the "virgin to the dynamo" provided images of a transformation from feudalism to industrialism. Adams foresaw a new worldview in response to the "violently coercive" educational force of technology, but

the human mind "would need to jump." In *Future Shock*, Alvin Toffler
(1970, pp. 2, 428) described a "shattering stress and disorientation that
we induce in individuals by subjecting them to too much change in too
short a time." Although "population growth, urbanization, the shifting
proportions of young and old" were associated with ongoing transitions,
he regarded technology as "a critical node in the network of causes."

In a cross-national study, Inkeles (1983, p. 101) depicted a coherent
"set of personal qualities" that characterize modern attitudes:

(1) openness to new experience, both with people and with new ways of doing
things such as attempting to control births; (2) the assertion of increasing
independence from the authority of traditional figures, such as parents and
priests, and a shift of allegiance to leaders of government, public affairs, trade
unions, cooperatives, and the like; (3) belief in the efficacy of science and
medicine, and a general abandonment of passivity and fatalism in the face of
life's difficulties; and (4) ambition for oneself and one's children to achieve high
occupational and educational goals.

Modernized people plan their schedules and check their watches. They
pay less attention to family or local matters and more to public affairs.

Linking sociology and economics, Bell (1968; 1973; 1987) documented organizational, political and cultural changes associated with a
postindustrial society. In an information age, human capital or
knowledge displaces physical property as the basis for class distinctions. Computers become the driving innovation and knowledge-based
services the key work. Bell (1968, pp. 4-6) charted four sources of
change in society:

- technology, notably biomedical engineering and computers;
- *"diffusion* of existing goods and privileges";
- "structural developments," including the "centralization of the
  American political system" and "the transformation of the
  economy"; and
- "the relationship of the United States to the rest of the world."

Bell (1968, pp. 8, 6, 7) concluded that "the society of the year 2000,
so quickly and schematically outlined, will be more fragile, more
susceptible to hostilities and to polarization." Fads, gadgets and
fashions are inconsequential in view of questions about "the kinds of
social arrangements that can deal adequately with the problems we
shall confront." Those problems include how to "reconcile conflicting
individual desires through the political mechanism rather than the
market"; "allow the citizenry greater participation in making decisions";
"reorganize the older bureaucratic patterns of hierarchy and detailed
specialization"; establish lifelong education; socialize the young by

schools rather than families; adjudicate "problems of privacy and
stress"; control "new densities and 'communications overload'" to reduce
"the potentiality for irrational outbursts in our society"; and adjust the
"growing disjunction between the 'culture' and the 'social structure.'"

In Bell's rich analyses, interdependency among key factors is a
source of continuity. Speculating about the United States and the world
in 2013, he argued "the key variable is *scale*. Societies work . . . when
the scales of institutions match—particularly economic and political
institutions. Increasingly, these are out of sync" (1987, pp. 29, 30–31).
He urged a "move away from bigness and bureaucracy. If there is a
universal consensus in Western societies, it is on the idea that individual and local community choice in as many matters as possible is a
desirable value." Low-cost communication makes possible an "artisan-
entrepreneur system exploiting niche technologies and specialized
markets."

Paradoxically, the more individuals strive to determine their future,
the less in control they feel. Following Max Weber, most social scientists
describe modernity in terms of individual alienation, disenchantment,
fragmentation, and anomie. Impersonal bureaucracies using informational technologies enable systems to control multistage, multiprocess
production and to coordinate global distribution and sales. Expectations
of progressive change carry a high price: "It is difficult to preserve
wholeness in a world that disallows contentment and demands that we
constantly seek improvement" (Kolb, 1986, p. 8).

For 200 years, Americans separated economic, political and personal
spheres. Industrialism applied linear, componential and functional
relationships to expand production. Information about causal connections was packaged in distinct academic disciplines and embodied in
technologies or institutional arrangements to facilitate the transmittal
of facts and skills. Unanticipated consequences appeared external to a
generally rational system of competitive markets and democracy. To
deconstruct prevailing assumptions, critics introduce considerations of
social justice, ecology, multiculturalism, feminism, or critical thinking
that evoke a sense of community values and offer alternatives to material affluence. We propose, instead, that less hierarchical structures of
production and information can facilitate individual security, environmental protection, peaceful international relations, and democratic
governance.

## Sustaining Multiple Frames

Communication in a high-technology world requires some grasp of
experts' language. Noting that shifts continually take place between
what is taken for granted and what is problematic, Collins (1990, pp.
106, 109) chose to "divide up our knowledge and abilities in a commonsensical way into four main categories: facts and formal rules,

heuristics, manual and perceptual skills, and cultural skills." Heuristics or rules of thumb and facts can be presented in an algorithm for solving problems, but other knowledge requires doing it (or simulating it) in order to build physical skills and ways of translating sensory inputs into appropriate responses. Moreover, all languages rest on embedded meaning systems: "It is our common culture that makes it possible to come to these agreements, and it is our means of making these agreements that comprises our culture."

Local or small-scale societies achieved congruency of meaning systems largely through redundancy. Most people shared similar experiences at some stage of their lifetime. Modern industrial societies achieve efficiency of knowledge by segmenting experiences in occupational and functional roles that are coordinated through hierarchies. Interactions are short and role dependent, with many responses based on implicit assumptions. "There is action without commentary, as well as commentary without observable action" (Hannerz, 1992, pp. 44, 45). Actors cannot always rely on unspoken assumptions. Instead, one's information exists within a bed of "metacultural knowledge: knowing one's own ignorance, knowing that others know something else, knowing whom to believe, developing a notion of the potentially knowable."

Constructivists view knowledge from several perspectives, suggesting that sci-tech or abstract, analytic ways of depicting "facts" are useful for advancing and applying knowledge but have less value for representing and integrating knowledge for concrete and purposive ways of knowing (see Figure 8.1). To resolve the dilemmas of postmodern thought, we need to reflect on our experiences and to integrate knowledge with values in order to reconstruct appropriate frameworks for interpreting events.

Given partial and contingent knowledge, redundant processes for discovering information are a source of congruency. Many experiences are initiated or simulated as conscious explorations of a perspective or scientific generalization. Experiments are rerun, courses are taken, novels read, and other cultures visited in order to gain insights into the experience of others. Media in all its variations facilitates that process of storing information and then making those experiences accessible in other contexts. Pictures, especially in motion and with sound, allow everyone to witness significant moments. As a result, postmodern adults find learning less a slow accretion of things that can be done without thinking and more a rapid oscillation between familiar activities and problematic moments.

Because the creation of coherence or an orderly paradigm in one area of knowledge raises incoherence or anomalies in other areas, complex cultures may model themselves after octopuses, as Clifford Geertz has suggested. They are neither highly integrated nor fast moving, yet their structural arrangements allow for adaptation to different environmental challenges. In Hannerz's (1992, pp. 168–169) paraphrase,

**FIGURE 8.1**
**Perspectives on Knowledge**

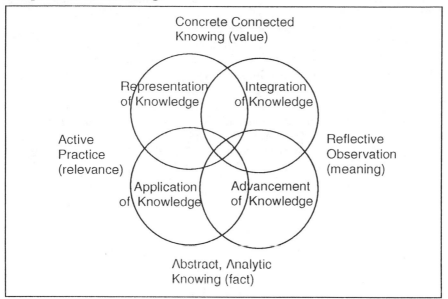

*Source*: Rice, R. E. (Winter/Spring 1990). Rethinking What It Means to Be a Scholar."
*Teaching Excellence: Toward the Best in the Academy*. p. 1.

"various segments of a complex culture may more generally serve as laboratories and reservoirs for the culture in its entirety, to be retrieved and put into new uses if opportunity or need arises."

Schools should represent diverse ways of knowing without privileging any. Science and technology then become open territory to be explored afresh with an awareness of the perspective and stake of the researcher. Only in that way can sci-tech knowledge serve as a basis for reconstructing holistic frameworks that include self and goals together with other persons and their goals, each in relationship with the other. To function effectively, people need to know about sci-tech and about social relations. Multiple lenses need not preclude setting priorities to actualize one's own values. It is perhaps the only way to meet the contradictory demands that are placed on people today in their various roles as family member, producer, citizen, and autonomous self.

**RELATED READING**

An introduction to sci-tech as socially constructed systems is Wiebe E. Bijker, Thomas P. Hughes, and Trevor J. Pinch, eds., *The Social Construction of Technological Systems: New Directions in the Sociology and History of Technology* (Cambridge: MIT Press, 1987). For educational uses of computers, see Seymour Papert, *The Children's Machine: Rethinking School in the Age of the Computer* (New York: Basic Books, 1993).

For more on alternative perspectives, see C. A. Bowers, *Education, Cultural Myths, and the Ecological Crisis: Toward Deep Changes* (Albany: State University of New York Press, 1993); Molefi K. Asante, *The Afrocentric Idea* (Philadelphia: Temple University Press, 1987); Paul R. Ehrlich and Anne H. Ehrlich, *Healing the Planet: Strategies for Resolving the Environmental Crisis* (Reading, MA: Addison-Wesley Publishing, 1991); Miriam Schneir, ed., *Feminism in Our Time: The Essential Writings, World War II to the Present* (New York: Vintage Books, 1994); and Langdon Winner, *The Whale and the Reactor* (Chicago: University of Chicago Press, 1986).

# 9

# Transforming Schools and Workplaces

In our interviews, we asked teachers and administrators to imagine life in the 21st century and then decide whether school improvement should start by changing instructional goals or restructuring organizations. Typically, they speculated about their work lives: *"New roles for teachers in restructured schools would build curricular reforms, and curricular reforms would hopefully ensure new roles for teachers in restructured schools."* Many advocated teacher empowerment and site-based management. A building administrator greatly valued voluntary study groups among teachers: *"the more we can do in school to make the life of the adults higher quality, the better off things are going to be in the long run for children."* Insightfully, educators thought about their activities and responsibilities—not a formal curriculum or a table of organization. Improving education entails new job descriptions for teachers and students.

Transforming schools requires modifications in tables of organization, staff development, political dynamics, and cultural values in order to change behavioral regularities for students. As one educator astutely asked: *"What good would changing the curriculum be—with more interdisciplinary projects, cooperative learning, etc.—unless the role of the teacher changed—unless emphasis went from teachers being information-givers to assisting students become information-seekers?"* Political mandates for structural innovations and instructional accountability have little direct impact on teacher performance or student achievement. Moreover, the success or failure of schooling is gradually revealed over a person's lifetime, and it is manifestly affected by class, race and gender inequalities in households, schools and workplaces.

This chapter suggests some ways to reenvision organizational strategies and structures of schools in light of information technologies, demographic shifts, and slow economic growth. Education is undergoing dramatic changes; by 2001, half the current teachers will have less than ten years' experience. One student in three will come to school with an

African, Asian, or Latin American heritage. Students and adults with access to computers and electronic networks will have anonymous connections to databases and bulletin boards of like-minded people. Organized activities will be more pervasive, yet participants will be expected to act more autonomously and cooperatively with coworkers.

Envisioning ways to reorganize schools to yield better outcomes is harder than adding multicultural perspectives or the social implications of technology to the curriculum. Most popular reforms reassert adult control and offer little chance for unleashing student interest. For instance, holding students to higher standards by making schools more accountable and efficient through computer technologies does not upset hierarchical power relationships. We propose, instead, various ways to move toward more democratic schools and workplaces because they are potentially more productive and humane. Low-cost gathering, processing, storing, and transmitting information allows for cooperation around shared purposes among relatively autonomous students and coworkers. That possibility, in turn, complements open and flexible organizations.

Transitions are difficult, however. Moving rapidly threatens chaos, but taking small steps allows old ways of thinking and customs to reassert themselves so that positive impacts are eroded. We begin this chapter by reviewing why entrenched ways of working together sustain divisions and hierarchies. Then, we proceed along four tracks—raising criticisms of current educational reforms, reenvisioning schools and workplaces, suggesting some plausible next steps for lifelong learning, and proposing multiple ways of looking at organizations and their functions in order to foster trust and cooperation. From multiple cognitive frames emerges a postmodern consciousness.

## ORGANIZATIONAL STRATEGIES AND STRUCTURES

What images or references help make sense of schools and workplaces today? At the outset of industrialism, observers described workplaces as schools—suggesting by metaphor that jobs should teach self-control and orderly behaviors. Early in the 19th century, capitalists argued that "a cotton factory is a school for the improvement of ingenuity and industry." Owners asserted that workers were "reclaimed, civilized, Christianized" by industrial discipline. Regular work enforced "punctuality, temperance, 'industriousness,' 'steadiness,' and obedience to mill authorities" (Prude, 1983, pp. 113, 112). Southerners depicted antebellum plantations as classrooms for slaves, who presumably learned European agricultural skills and cultural values.

Later, mandatory schooling appeared as a substitute for labor by youth on farms or in factories. Business leaders justified universal secondary education as preparation for supervised, time-scheduled workplaces. With their "cells and bells," schools resembled factories, and educators proclaimed their efficiency. Superintendents adopted structures of bureaucracy and staff command with teachers transmitting an unproblematic curriculum to age-segregated students as they moved from class to class. Principals consciously imitated business practices in managing schools. Periodic tests assured quality and sorted students into vocational, technical, commercial or college preparatory tracks. A few completed higher education, which legitimated professionals, scientists and engineers, or managers as a meritocratic, mainly male elite in a hierarchical, industrial economy.

An emerging knowledge society generates fresh metaphors for linking learning and earning. Given low-cost information exchanges based on electronic technologies, futurists anticipate support for lifelong education among employees and customers. Informated organizations will become learning communities. Postindustrial workers "must learn and learn to learn" in order to exercise discretionary judgments in sociotechnical organizations (Hirschhorn, 1984, p. 150). This implicit model, however, refers to universities with their libraries, laboratories, seminars, computers, and a campus setting. It also may resemble higher education in the relative invisibility of service workers who clean buildings, maintain equipment, or assist professionals.

Despite the growing inefficiency of hierarchy in coordinating activities and anticipating future needs, old metaphors and job descriptions linger on in most people's thinking. Calls for flatter structures and more autonomy are attractive but not easily implemented. Although many firms and agencies create a period of excitement around efforts to involve frontline workers in improving efficiency and quality, they soon discover that open participation in decisions takes time and that hierarchies often reappear in other guises. Predictably, the largest gains from democratic decisionmaking will not occur until people gain experience in many settings from classrooms to factories.

## Reflecting on Industrial Organizations

For a century, huge industrial corporations and public bureaucracies were remarkably efficient producers of goods and of social stability. To acquire an abundance of possessions, people moved to urban centers; accommodated to large-scale private and public organizations; conceded authority to scientists, engineers and professionals; and compromised on political equality in return for a promise of economic growth. Families, schools, mass media, productive workplaces, voluntary associations, and government agencies transmitted technical and social competencies to the young. Elites used class, ethnic and gender segmentation to divide workers and thereby enhance their control. Increasingly, they relied on educational credentials as well as attitudes conveyed by mass media to legitimize their power. Except for periodic depressions, their dominance paid off in general economic growth until 1973.

Specialization segmented knowledge so that coordination required command structures. Over time, feedback mechanisms, bureaucracies, and electronic information systems intended to direct machinery and people began to transform the nature of work—or what humans contributed to production. Technological and managerial concerns dominated as employees adjusted their thinking to interact effectively with machinery. Yet laborers also resented limits on their autonomy. They, like many students, resisted passively by acting "dumb," disengaging, and blaming outsiders for negative outcomes. Perversely, such reactions confirmed a belief among elites that they should tighten supervision.

Industrial-era hierarchies of control motivate individuals to conceal their self-interests in negotiating within, as well as between, organizations. Market exchanges and principal-agent communications raise increasingly troublesome issues; misinformation and information are often indistinguishable without shared contexts and situational details. As basic needs are satisfied, more goods incorporate scarcely visible technical qualities and more productive endeavors involve abstract as well as experiential knowledge. Furthermore, without productivity gains, business interests can no longer deliver higher wages in return for acquiescing to corporate domination. Specialized knowledge blocks cooperation unless both parties share pertinent data based on an implicit agreement of future exchanges.

What does this imply for the social efficiency? Individuals gradually learn to use (or to misuse) stable institutional patterns to serve their own ends. If elites seek to divide and control workers and consumers, structural innovations will generate only a temporary advantage. A current litany of advice for corporations and government agencies— such as fewer layers of supervision, flexible goals, worker participation and profit-sharing, total quality management, quality of work life, and trust—hint at open structures or communication networks that avoid the problems associated with a prisoner's dilemma. Yet without a measure of equality, perspectives soon will differ no matter how much leaders talk about shared ideas and values.

Innovative programs that modify behavioral regularities in schools generate resistance from those comfortable with old ways, as well as those perceiving themselves in charge. Most proposed reforms affect only small parts of what happens organizationally: "Any attempt to introduce an important change in the school culture requires changing existing regularities to produce new intended outcomes. In practice, the regularities tend not to be changed and the intended outcomes, therefore, cannot occur; that is, the more things change the more they remain the same" (Sarason, 1982, p. 116). As long as hierarchical control is embedded in organizational structures, teachers invariably see their role as rank-ordering youth, and academic achievement becomes a win-lose situation for students.

Although educators praise collegiality and feel themselves relatively powerless, their relationships are intensely political. Over time, most staff uneasily adjust to a complex setting and its perceived distribution of clout and respect. Current distributions of authority and status within educational organizations weaken feedback between the adult-determined curriculum and the next generation's roles and responsibilities. Issues of power—and issues of control over one's life—are intimately connected with definitions of teachers as professionals who establish minimum standards of acceptable behavior for students. When teachers' job descriptions impose subordinate roles on their students, they scarcely can serve as a "witness" for equality or liberate youth from subordinate roles.

By drawing on the dynamics of organizations and politics, it is possible mentally to rehearse alternative arrangements for productive interactions among groups. Moreover, by examining relatively effective organizations and proposals that seem responsive to current problems, we can form a sense about useful characteristics of future structures. Students may lack maturity to understand how self fits with dilemmas raised by hierarchical structures, but experience with open, flexible and innovative classrooms that encourage communication across class, race and gender boundaries will prepare them for work and citizenship in an information age.

## Educational Leadership

In our interviews, school leaders sketchily described new philosophies and emerging structures for educational organizations. An associate superintendent in an urban district stated her belief that curriculum must stress *"direct contact with individuals from different ethnic groups and races," "self-esteem," "technological preparation,"* and opportunities for students to *"make decisions and to work collaboratively."* An administrator in a suburban community urged professional pay and status for teachers, collaborations between schools and outside organizations, and more support for teachers to coach students' learning. A middle school principal wanted teachers *"to be more facilitators in the classroom, helping students explore alternatives as they try to solve problems within curriculum content contexts."* Classrooms should promote *"coping skills, learning skills, study skills, and working-with-each-other skills."*

Because learning is situational and interactive, successful leaders cannot simply impose curricular goals or instructional packages. Multiple goals and diverse viewpoints conflict with control and accountability in organizations. Ethnographic studies of administrators reveal an unending stream of decisions from budgets to bus schedules.

Principals manage through "face-to-face interaction among students and teachers and between principals, teachers, and members of the larger school community" (Blumberg & Greenfield, 1986, pp. 230, 239). They rely on interpersonal skills because "a climate of trust and open exchange of ideas are both critical to engaging teachers and others in an ongoing dialogue about the possibilities of good practice." At the core lies "value leadership, vision, and the capacity to exercise 'moral' imagination."

To manage their building, principals develop diverse but identifiable leadership styles: "organizer, value-based juggler, authentic helper, broker, humanist, catalyst, rationalist, or politician" (Blumberg & Greenfield, 1986, pp. 189–211, 239). Successful leaders find a style that is comfortable for them and gradually build a self-definition around those strengths but often find themselves less able to function in other areas. For many, it is "a position whose effect is to grind people down, particularly people who wish to make a difference in the life of schools; or at least to create in them a sense of having been dulled." The key is "the significance of school culture, the ethos of teachers as a group, and the larger social and political context within which the school is embedded."

As chief executive officers, school superintendents operate politically, using public relations and democratic forums to guide policy on the inside and to sustain external support. Nominally in charge, they spend their time attending school and community meetings and events. He or she acts "as decision maker, mediator, or simply as a human lightning rod who attracts controversy" (Blumberg & Blumberg, 1985, pp. 1, 203). Superintendents have responsibility for budgeting, hiring personnel, establishing district goals for curriculum and instruction, and evaluating staff to assure accountability. Yet "power to influence matters directly is frequently circumscribed, particularly if the focus of his attention is the normative structure or curricular patterns of a school."

Superintendents who survive adopt informal guidelines to aid them in sorting out competing demands and controversies that punctuate their work lives: "Defuse things as quickly as you can, avoid conflict when you can, but learn when it's appropriate to join battle, and anticipate and plan for problems you see coming up" (Blumberg & Blumberg, 1985, pp. 205, 208). Educational leaders face perplexing dilemmas: "In order to maintain the system so that the school board is pleased with its peacefulness, conflict must be anticipated, confronted, and diminished. However, in addition to reacting to potential or actual conflict and dealing with it in his organizational maintenance role, the *superintendent who would lead* must seek conflict out and occasionally promote it." Innovative superintendents assert priorities that often provoke disagreements from teachers, parents or the school board.

These descriptions of leadership roles suggest the importance of cultural beliefs in schools—and the degree to which they are socially constructed. Often charisma helps to bridge perspectives among a diverse audience. Perhaps the largest stumbling block is a temptation among educators to enhance their authority by using the jargon of researchers and referring to legal requirements or statistical studies. Although many adults still think in terms of a "best system" that is ascertainable through research, a diagnostic-prescriptive approach to educational expertise stifles democratic dialog. Moreover, because social norms silence oppressed groups, it is important for leadership to validate their voices and begin to translate their concerns into behavioral norms for classrooms and corridors.

Commentary by teachers and administrators suggests how institutional patterns severely constrain their thinking about change. Even when organizations appear dysfunctional, people have difficulty envisioning alternative missions and structures. The starting point for dialog is purpose related to quality of life for all citizens, not management techniques. In the assessment of innovative educator Dwight Allen (1992, p. 6), "as a society we have lost trust in many of our institutions. Regaining it will be a long and difficult process that must address the core values of the society." Unless those values are expressed through productive households, schools, workplaces, voluntary associations, and governments, we scarcely can build cooperative and collaborative communities.

## PARADOXES OF EDUCATIONAL REFORMS

Fundamental tensions characterize education. Students seek to expand their competence to act, while teachers enforce docility. Teachers intend to help everyone learn, yet they cannot individualize instruction for a class of curious, active thinkers. Administrators allocate resources to support instruction, but they face conflicting parental and community pressures. As superintendents, principals, teachers, and students recognize the frustrations of growing up today, they often ignore controversies or postpone decisions by reiterating familiar scripts. Mostly, they muddle through, speaking in vague and idealistic phrases because they lack a vocabulary to build consensus around a more flexible, fair and innovative organization.

A goal of strengthening basic skills has dominated reform rhetoric for more than a decade. During the 1980s, most business and political leaders stressed learning skills to prepare students for organizations where workers follow orders with accuracy, despite tedium. Educational reform reports echoed those concerns and called for longer days, shorter vacations, more courses, tougher tests, greater accountability, and less concern for those with special needs or limited English proficiency. They recited a litany of charges against schools for violence, low test scores, and ignorance of Eurocentric cultural traditions and values. Seeking additional funds, educators emphasized their shortcomings and needs, thereby fostering images of inefficiency or incompetence. An overriding purpose of producing more with less went without saying.

Implicit in this version of school reform lay a belief in a single best system. Presumably, experts in consultation with powerful members of society (mostly business leaders) should determine what skills and experiences are essential for productive workers. Then, they set goals and ask educators to design a production line from kindergarten to graduation that will mold five-year olds into young adults ready for work and citizenship. Imbued by this mindset, state and local educational reforms gave top priority to academic standards, second to modest increases in funding, and last to equity concerns. At the same time, a national commitment to equitable education (at least rhetorically) conflicted with local political factors that supported better schools in advantaged suburbs.

## Professional Autonomy

Many educators, resentful of outside criticisms, seek self-empowerment and higher status in imitation of professional roles earlier staked out by lawyers and doctors. Measuring pedagogical competence by national tests would force universities into "imbuing prospective teachers with the principles of acceptable professional practice" and districts to offer incentives for staff development (Labaree, 1992, p. 148). "This cuts to the essence of the exchange that a profession offers to the rest of society—a guarantee of collective competence in return for workplace autonomy." Professionalization "pushes technical questions into the foreground and political questions into the background as either unscientific or unproblematic." Good teaching, however, involves caring and building trust, in addition to offering rich resources that engage students in individual and group projects.

A theme of empowerment has a pronounced resonance among teachers, as well as in current literature about their work (Lieberman, 1988, 1994). They feel submerged in organizations that constrain their autonomy. Yet, their central responsibility is to make knowledge accessible to others, thereby breaking down barriers between experts and novices. What does professionalism entail? Is it discretionary judgments by frontline workers, tougher certification requirements, or mainly a positive attitude based on a decent salary and public respect? Optimists suggest that teachers can be "empowered" without upsetting behavioral regularities, bureaucratic procedures, or hierarchical school structures. Effective teachers who isolate themselves in order to implement positive improvements in their classrooms, however, seldom influence their colleagues.

A second plausible meaning of empowerment flows from a common perception that one's supervisors make the important decisions. Typically, those perceptions of being controlled from above extend from students to teachers to principals to superintendents to school boards to legislators and then to voters who determine budgetary constraints. Oddly, voters feel that they have no voice in school policies. Powerlessness is reinforced as individuals focus on immediate roadblocks to a preferred course of action. Someone else appears to hold a resource or to deny an approval needed to complete a desirable action. From this perspective, sharing power would open the way to significant progress. Those with authority, however, may see a political struggle over who gets what.

Bureaucratic controls that earlier enforced impersonal standards and allowed coordination of many specialized functions for an uneducated workforce now seem unfair because they maintain subordination of knowledge and control. Efficient producers of goods and services in a knowledge society will rely on new skills from all their employees: scanning quantities of public information, thinking holistically about ill-structured problems, communicating ideas and facts across disciplinary and organizational boundaries, cooperating in groups, and expressing personal and social values. When information technologies and automated machines handle the routine, people should explore the new, the ambiguous and the exceptional.

An overt struggle for empowerment raises two related fears. If power is limited, then reallocating authority from principals to teachers or to students fails to expand the capacity of the educational enterprise. The issue narrows to a question of whether teachers (or students) are more qualified to decide on a curriculum or the length of a school day than principals, superintendents or voters. If power is not limited, then how can society contain newly energized groups? Imagine what might happen if Freire's liberationist approach succeeded and those students who are now ranked in the bottom half on standardized tests engaged in analyses of class, race and gender biases. Empowerment without a vision of equitable communities mainly reallocates formal control, raising fears of abuses of power by those unaccustomed to its exercise.

## School Collaborations

On the surface, voluntary partnerships between schools and outside organizations make sense. Outsiders bring fresh perspectives and additional political support for public education. Parents and community groups benefit from what educators know about child raising, leisure time activities, and community concerns such as drug abuse or conflict mediation. Museums, libraries, theater groups, and recreation leagues can utilize instructional practices or share media resources with schools. Teachers can offer businesses their knowledge about appropriate curriculum for adult learners who seek new skills, career training, or counseling. Universities can help educators use and disseminate innovations or research results.

In practice, partnerships between schools and outside organizations involve conflicting interests, dynamics and cultures. At the outset of joint activities, partners routinely see benefits both in cooperating and in mainly pretending to work together. Each seeks to protect key interests and to avoid identifying their weaknesses, vulnerabilities and uncertainties. For example, firms volunteer time and some surplus materials or space in return for positive publicity. Many business leaders challenge educators to improve basic skills for job readiness, although personnel managers seek employees who can communicate effectively, work together in teams, solve problems, function independently, and continue to learn. Such misleading signals complicate collaborative interactions.

Leaders who seek quick and visible payoffs to interorganizational collaborations limit their potential. Hard data seemingly provide an equivalent to a firm's bottom line of profit and loss so that efficient programs can be replicated. Assessments of short-term results, however, ill serve projects with long-term or multiple goals. Clear results measured by standardized tests discourage significant innovations and other, perhaps more appropriate, goals. Education is a lifelong endeavor and positive or negative outcomes may not appear for decades. Pressures for accountability contradict a strength of school partnerships—namely, their exploratory interactions among individuals from different organizations that bridge varied cultural viewpoints.

Although their means of implementation vary, successful collaborative projects that foster long-term teacher development and school improvement efforts typically incorporate a number of lessons (Jones & Maloy, 1988):

- Outside change agents or potential partners respect each setting's culture while helping insiders clarify and articulate their situation.

- Goals and measures of success recognize the importance of small steps that allow teachers to participate in limited ways, to draw on resources that support their professional competency, and to have their successes recognized.

- Teachers (and other frontline workers) who have crucial clinical expertise are responsible for designing new curriculum, implementing it, and assessing its value.

- Project personnel share effective strategies and curriculum because that dialog helps change a school's ethos toward positive purposes.

- Documenting, evaluating and distributing information about successful processes, practices and products helps to institutionalize change.

Many schools foster hospitable climates, open bureaucratic structures, and flexible personnel policies to encourage multiple interorganizational linkages. Involved outsiders, extra resources, and multipurpose activities ease the way for other partners to join school improvement efforts. Voluntary collaborations provide occasions for experimentation and innovation that reduce teacher isolation and encourage greater understanding of the endemic dilemmas facing teachers in a classroom. Partnerships that flourish over many years may serve as a "holding company" for innovative activities. As subunits, they allow power to grow by trusting others with decisions and act as a scouting party to explore effective practices and structures.

Ideally, interactive partnerships support ongoing learning, community development and democratic processes. First, school partners discuss the skills, competencies and experiences that will prepare today's youth for jobs. Second, knowledge workers in many organizations also have experienced the dynamics of building consensus around ambitious common goals. Third, outsiders acknowledge teachers' endemic dilemmas and value their successes, thereby recognizing both shared interests and competing roles. Fourth, they may regard schools as microcosms of information-saturated societies that link knowledge to decisionmakers. Finally, partners gain insights into working together within a context of youth values, group processes, and uncertain futures.

As reform initiatives, professionalism and school partnerships emphasize a partial vision of positive developments while also drawing on past linkages between schools and industrial workplaces. Demands for minimum competencies involve a fallacy of composition: Some students, a handful of schools, or a few nations can gain by sharpening their competitive position, but not everyone gains unless current social hierarchies become more equal. Professional status depends on limiting access through degrees and exams, yet autonomy and discretionary judgments are crucial for all workers in an information age. Interactive partnerships can substantially improve two-way exchanges of trustworthy information between productive schools and workplaces, but their ultimate success depends on doing more than merely transferring resources to "needy" schools. They should open dialog connecting educational and social purposes.

## Thinking about Change

Beginning teachers bring a focus on students and an idealism about equitable outcomes to their classrooms, although many seem to lose their enthusiasm over the ensuing years of teaching. Interns and beginning teachers in schools serving low-income neighborhoods are shocked at the disrespect for students expressed by many veteran teachers. Next, they recognize that developing trusting relationships as a step toward effective instruction requires a lot of hard work in responding to student needs and developing new curriculum. Then, they express dismay at an emphasis on order and standardized tests by administrators, despite evidence that strict control only feeds resentment and that test scores poorly measure what students retain from their schooling.

As we have advocated the ideas expressed in this book to our students, we have found it difficult to offer practical advice to new teachers who have tried to implement hands-on activities, process writing, cooperative learning, multicultural perspectives, student use of computers, and more personable interactions with young people. Although our advice necessarily is tailored to specific situations and personalities, we find ourselves reiterating variations on the following points:

- Keep in mind that teachers and administrators are ambivalent about innovations. They expect and want new teachers to try new approaches, although they often appear skeptical and reluctant to allow any adjustment of established routines.
- It is not easy to change an institutional trajectory or an organizational culture, so one must emphasize small victories and avoid discouragement.
- Try to identify goals and strategies that have administrative support (often because of funding opportunities) that are complementary to one's own curricular goals and strengths.
- Avoid confrontation over minor issues by planning various alternative approaches to achieve one's primary goal.
- Establish and sustain supportive relationships with other new teachers and sympathetic experienced teachers. A support group can offer ideas, reaffirm values, and create a political force within the building.
- Practice and use dialog that builds consensus. Speak up to set agendas around positive topics. Note: discussions concerning violence, discipline codes, absenteeism, grading policies, or student deficits seldom yield positive outcomes; instead, they encourage a blaming game.
- Take students into your confidence at an appropriate level. Share some of your personal views about your subject and instructional approaches. Recognize that too much distance from school norms will raise dissonance for your students. You do not have to

accomplish the ideal classroom immediately as long as you continue progress in that direction.

- Focus on reaching and teaching students who have been left behind under traditional approaches. Those students who are prepared and ready to learn will proceed without much help. Knowledge that liberates is crucial—not scores on standardized tests.

- Use multiple voices in teaching, including student writing, primary sources, first person narratives, literature by women and people of color, video and audio recordings, and cultural artifacts to open discussions about class, race and gender.

The most important thing is to recognize the school's culture with its taken-for-granted assumptions and endemic tensions. Common metaphors and symbols are more revealing than organizational tables and mission statements. Increasingly, experts in school change are recognizing that recipes for reform and extensive planning processes are less useful than moving forward once a school improvement project has sufficient support. After the fact, then, teachers can reflect on what has changed or remained the same. Meaningful reform affects not only behavioral patterns but also the vocabulary and cultural frameworks used to describe roles of students and teachers.

Our answers to the questions posed throughout the book sound paradoxical because they do not use empirical evidence to propose technological solutions. We attempt to summarize the central theme of each chapter in the following dialog:

- What will schools be like in 2020? They will be nothing like we expect them to be.
- How can we prepare workers for tomorrow's jobs? By teaching democratic citizenship.
- How can teachers become more effective? By engaging students as independent learners and cooperative teachers.
- How can work and family life become satisfying and productive? By ensuring that everyone has a decent job, housing, and education so people can focus on their own creativity and preferences for the future.
- How can groups and organizations be more successful? By seeing organizations as sites for construction of evolving social meanings.
- How can people achieve social justice in a new century? By talking to each other about things that matter in a multicultural society.

- How can we teach children to get along with one another? By assisting them to learn how their own self-identities are structured through diverse interactions.

- How can we make sense of science and technology? By treating it as a product of past thinking and imagining different futures.

- How can the best of the present become part of the future? By engaging in new collaborative arrangements for change.

## CONSTRUCTING NEW VISIONS

A possible future is visible today in innovative and exciting schools that flourish in all kinds of communities. Teachers, students, administrators, parents, and members of public and private organizations are redefining the practices of industrial-era schools. They are implementing active, cooperative, nongraded, multicultural, gender-fair, flexible, technology-rich, student-centered, and democratic programs that are open to affective concerns. They are blurring student-teacher and teacher-administrator roles, linking insiders and outsiders in curriculum and instruction, and facilitating collective decisions by appropriate stakeholders. Classrooms, collaboratives, and alternatives facilitate processes for every student and teacher to actualize personal values and to explore creativity in safe, respectful and friendly settings. As schools engage in making knowledge accessible to others and building competencies for interacting in future settings, cognitive frameworks are being reconstructed.

Alternatively, we might list negatives about schools today. There is boredom, discrimination, drug abuse, and violence. Too many teachers are unprepared, hostile to students, authoritarian, and disinterested in instruction or guidance. Tests focus on narrow, irrelevant facts. Computers are outdated, damaged or locked in a closet. Buildings have exposed asbestos and broken desks. Interestingly, fixing up these flaws seldom inspires effective instruction. A clean, safe, orderly climate may be necessary for learning, but it is not sufficient. We suggest, however, that praising strengths in students, staffs and schools induces a greater readiness for change than criticism.

Constructing new visions of learning for tomorrow upsets familiar notions of education as six hours a day, 180 days a year, kindergarten through graduation, in buildings called schools. Consider what might happen if schools were open from 7:00 A.M. to 10:00 P.M. with creative daycare programs and extracurricular options. Year-long schedules might include periodic, brief vacations without interrupting the accumulation of knowledge. Students could demonstrate competencies at their own pace with cumulative records easily available from a computer. Rather than norm-referenced tests condemning most students to less than an A grade, everyone would master basic skills in order to meet their developmental and personal goals for a productive and satisfying life.

## Rethinking Schools

In many preschools and kindergartens, teachers place children's questions and discoveries at the center of educational processes, thereby actively supporting risk taking, questioning and decision-making. Adults see their roles as encouragers of youngsters' natural curiosity and interest in how things work. Open-space classrooms enable hands-on learning as students freely move about to find printed matter, use computers, get writing materials, conduct experiments, or play with blocks. Reading, writing, math and science are embedded in the processes used to generate questions and explore answers. Supported by adults, children engage in activities they find enjoyable and personally meaningful.

Ideally, middle-grade schools become centers of personal and intellectual transition for young adolescents. Rather than reproducing a scaled-down version of a traditional secondary curriculum, teachers focus on developmental concerns facing youths. Gender roles (including sexual activity, safety and orientation), ethnic and racist stereotypes, moral codes (including illegal substances, vandalism and violence), and personal aspirations are topics for formal and informal discussions. Well staged presentations using computers and other media efficiently transmit basic academic subjects to hundreds of learners. Large-group lectures complement small-group discussions with hands-on activities.

Project-oriented teams of students and teachers might conduct interdisciplinary activities that last several weeks. Instructional goals and objectives from various academic content areas are systematically incorporated into these student-teacher activities. Everyone participates in community service—volunteering in a hospital or homeless shelter, performing for a neighborhood group or senior center, writing a handbook or guide for younger students. Small groups and tutoring support those who need additional time to master particular skills. Democratic values, peer counseling, and conflict mediation are practiced in classrooms and corridors. Finally, students reflect on the meaning their experiences hold for their own identities and relationships with others.

In many high schools, students are engaged in productive roles in their communities. Adolescents explore careers by apprenticing in businesses, not-for-profit agencies, educational facilities, or government bureaus. Students read about social change, reflect on their experiences through writing, develop portfolios that record and document personal learning, and share that knowledge with others. They select areas to explore more deeply through independent study courses and community internships. For instance, someone interested in history may write for the local newspaper, while another extends science and mathematical competencies by assisting researchers at a nearby laboratory. Apprenticeships in diverse settings give students a way to connect coursework to productive activities and enable them to teach others about possible careers.

---

**Using words and pictures, design an ideal school for productive citizens. Outline a mission statement, and indicate some curriculum and key experiences offered to students in your school. How will you incorporate technology? Will it be non-tracked, gender-fair, multicultural and equitable?**

---

Institutions of higher education, together with public and private sector programs, can encourage lifelong networks that model learning communities. They offer opportunities for those engaged in upgrading job skills, changing careers, raising a family, enjoying recreational time, caring for one's health, planning for retirement, or pursuing baccalaureate and graduate degrees or certificates. Many colleges extend access to learning to underserved individuals and groups. Courses incorporate the diversity of society as the experiences and accomplishments of women and people of color are integrated into a liberal arts education. Ideas and research from laboratories improve businesses and government operations, while community involvement by college students and staff invigorates local schools and agencies.

### Making Work Meaningful

New organizational structures also reconstruct work experiences and their meaning. Many jobs today are repetitive, mindless and alienating, although customizing products and services to fit particular needs offers employees ample chances to think and innovate. Ideally, workers take charge of productive activities and improve company operations for employees, managers, owners, and customers. Firms such as American Saw, Channing Bete, and SAIC have pioneered structural adaptations to facilitate cooperative and flexible workplaces. Employees express their views about working conditions and organizational outcomes. Frontline staff apply information about quality, customer demands, and organizational strategies to respond quickly and appropriately. Moreover, useful communication depends on coworkers holding a general idea about what others do as well as the details of their own job.

Exciting examples of worker-owned plants, quality circles, collaborative agencies, and effective schools make the idea of workplace democracy attractive. Many organizations have adopted programs to give workers a greater stake in normal operations. Employee participation and stock plans are time-honored proposals to reduce alienation among those who work in large, multiunit corporations by rewarding everyone for successful operations. Quality circles invite workers at all levels to contribute toward efficient and pleasant interactions. Although public employees do not have profits to distribute, performance improves when they see connections between their job and broad civic purposes. In schools, needs-based staff development, active parent-community councils, and site-based school management can bring multiple stakeholders into small units so that everyone's view is heard.

A case for worker participation seems relatively straightforward. After studying over 1,000 firms, Simmons and Mares (1985, pp. 282–283) concluded, "when men and women take more responsibility for their work, they do a better job. Their involvement can affect alienation, mismanagement, and productivity." In firm after firm, absenteeism and complaints decline, product quality rises, and productivity gains are common. The Committee for Economic Development (1990, p. 82) argued that "as the advance of automation and the almost limitless applications of microchip-based technologies transform the workplace, they are creating demands for workers who can operate more autonomously, making decisions and innovations on the job." Employees who have some discretion predictably reduce current divisions between "painful" production and "pleasurable" consumption. Work environments become healthier, more sociable, supportive of self-esteem, and less marked by time clocks and intrusive accountability measures, while home activities support careers.

Cooperative organizations encourage employee participation as part of a larger framework of "direct, democratic control by the members" (Rothschild & Whitt, 1986, pp. 2, 51–60). They stand in contrast to bureaucratic organizations in at least eight ways:

- collective authority with consensus procedures;
- fewer rules and more worker discretion;
- common worldviews that form a basis for cooperative endeavors;
- striving for a holistic and value-rich community;
- recruitment and promotion based on shared values;
- work arranged to satisfy personal meanings and rewards;
- equality of roles, responsibilities, and pay; and
- open-ended jobs.

These developments in traditional and alternative organizations raise a puzzle about why there is less active participation by workers in corporations in the United States than in Japan or Sweden. Productivity gains follow from worker involvement. Effective participatory firms emphasize "profit sharing, long-term employment relations, narrow wage and status differentials, and guaranteed individual rights" (Levine & Tyson, 1990, pp. 235–236). Competitive markets discourage cooperation: "Despite the potential efficiency of such workplaces, product, labor, and capital markets can all make participation unprofitable for the individual firm. As a result, the economy can be trapped in a socially suboptimal position."

Achieving workplace democracy requires a cultural shift—different purposes that rearrange fundamental ways of understanding experience: "The contradiction is rooted in the fact that the traditional corporation is based on meritocratic principles that exploit human differences, while the democratic enterprise is premised, at least in part, on political and substantive equality" (Witte, 1980, pp. 156, 168). Imbued with individualistic ethics, Americans are fighting an uphill battle to fit democratic processes into schools and workplaces. The frustrations with participatory forums feed a distrust of all leaders. On the other hand, "the necessity of continuous interaction and integrated efforts provides the stimulus and lays the foundation for a sense of community within the work place."

Meaningful participation by organizational members also involves a radical shift of power and authority. Workplace democracy moves an organization from individualistic competition toward cooperation and fairness that supports personal dignity and self-respect. Members of the firm see that a key way to enhance learning, productivity and personal satisfaction is to engage in complementary activities that include companionship, self-expression, creativity, and periodic relaxation. They recognize that work need not be alienating, nor tiresome tasks endured, in order to earn a living. Competition to become the head of General Motors creates thousands of losers and only one winner. Worker participation also requires mutual trust in long-run employment within an organization that fosters change through education and accommodation to personal interests and goals.

Fostering dialog in an information age requires the "devolution of control and the active recognition of communal diversity." Communicating across boundaries of class, race and gender, however, often becomes "all-consuming (committees, negotiations, consultations) to the point of personal exhaustion and to the point of attrition where the blandest of commonsense must prevail. Teachers' control of their working environment shifts the burden of responsibility for curriculum onto them and increases workloads to the point of burn-out. The promise of the democratic rhetoric has not borne fruit either in the quality of teachers' lives or in significantly improved patterns of educational results" (Kalantzis et al., 1990, p. 249).

Without parallel developments in schools, households, and workplaces, it is difficult to see how attitudes of cooperation and democratic participation now present in limited cases can become institutionalized.

As long as some seek to advance their own interests over others, communication will be devoted to protecting one's position through resistance, defection, or misinformation. As long as citizens compete in a zero-sum game for rank-ordered status, people will seek to privilege their knowledge base and to deny some groups an equal chance for a decent education, job and community. As long as alienated adults seek distractions from issues that concern them, media will focus on mindless entertainment. A transformation requires dialog that starts with a fresh vision of learning and earning in democratic schools and workplaces.

## INSTITUTIONAL CONTEXTS FOR LIFELONG LEARNING

People readily learn as they intentionally act in widening circles of power—if they have time to reflect and anticipate a better future. That belief underlies our three key thresholds for productive citizenship— education that facilitates lifelong learning, a job with opportunities to acquire new competencies, and income for a comfortable and efficient household. We also recognize that many Americans feel alienated from power on the job and in civic affairs despite enjoying a decent income, a comfortable home, and favorable prospects. Training for subordination starts in schools, and many workers complain that they are made to feel like a child by their bosses.

Alienation and powerlessness are peculiarly acute for youth who are marginalized and discriminated against:

Inner-city youth feel lonely, isolated, and disconnected from larger society and its institutions: schools, churches, and workplace. In this context—in the fierce communion of the streets and the barren economic life of inner-city neighborhoods—the deep pessimism, low self-esteem, and destructive behavior that corresponds to this sense of personhood are not surprising. . . . The street becomes the refuge for youth who can no longer bear a sense of failure and invisibility in their family, school, economic life, or community. Passivity and fatalism become directives for self. (Heath & McLaughlin, 1993, p. 54)

Youth gain experience as autonomous individuals when they engage in group activities that meet needs, strengthen competencies, and support positive identities.

For seven in ten workers in 1994, the power of management seemed so overwhelming that they saw no way to bargain effectively, even with a union. According to the codirector of a study of employee attitudes, " workers want power and they know management cooperation is the key to having that power, but they don't know how to compel management to give that cooperation" (Uchitelle, 1994, p. D1). Three in five workers wished greater participation in decisionmaking, but they feared that it could happen only on management's terms. Without access to power either through unions or workplace democracy, most workers have no reason to stay engaged with issues affecting their productivity on the job or in civic affairs.

Current institutional frameworks do not encourage people to engage in behaviors that give meaning to their lives. Schools and workplaces generate resistance rather than engagement. Students disengage from the formal curriculum through apathy and truces negotiated with teachers for quiet and order in return for minimally challenging assignments. In workplaces, labor unions have institutionalized resentment and counterbalancing forces. Professional associations with their journals and conservative practices seek to enforce conformity while strengthening boundaries against rivals. Far from seeking liberation, these organizations reinforce a status quo. Key changes include adding meaningful experiences for youth, increasing options for formal training for adults, and infusing democratic purposes into nonformal learning.

## Rethinking Experiential Learning

Recently, community service learning (CSL) has reemerged as a popular measure to engage young people in activities that help others while involving them directly and usefully with social issues. Although experiential learning has a long history in apprentice training, it is honored in formal education more in philosophy than in practice. Current proposals for CSL projects emphasize the observed disengagement of youth from family and community responsibilities, as well as its instructional effectiveness. Service to others as a normal part of schooling raises awareness of individual and structural inequalities and asks for personal responses to actualize collective values.

A philosophy of helping others and addressing social problems distinguishes CSL from traditional cooperative education or internships with local businesses and agencies. As skills are developed and recognition earned, students feel more engaged and in control of their own future. According to a college student active in a tutoring project, youth leadership comes from *"the opportunity to help others, and taking initiative on your own. Leadership cannot exist without the leader being able to empower others so they too can become leaders."* Most crucially, *"youth leadership builds self-confidence and enables people to put plans/ideas into action."*

Community service is now required in many schools across the country and is supported by state and federal governments. One state calls for "making a difference through actions of caring for others, in the school or in the community, through direct service, indirect service and advocacy, with preparation and reflection" (Maryland Student Service Alliance, 1993, pp. 8, 3). Recognizing a loss of community, Maryland educators believed that CSL would promote "teamwork, leadership, problem-solving and communication skills" while helping to "build thoughtful, committed and educated citizens." After a decade of experience, educators have accumulated thousands of vignettes documenting the benefits of service learning for youth.

Combining service in academic courses loosens traditional patterns of texts, lectures and teacher-led discussions. In one urban middle school, youngsters connected with senior citizens at a nearby retirement home using Internet. Students who had distrusted the elderly learned to appreciate their humor and experiences; seniors felt useful while also learning how to use computers. At another school, adolescents built a tropical rain forest in their social studies room, complete with a netting across the ceiling donated by a local National Guard unit. Then, seventh graders demonstrated lessons about ecology and environmental pressures for first graders in their district. In a third school, a chemistry teacher arranged for students to document their eating habits as a way to develop nutritionally sound diets, which could be presented to the community at large.

> **List three things that involve you in learning outside of formal courses and assigned readings. For example, a job, volunteer service, a diary, or spirited discussions with friends.**
>
> **Contrast the experiences of mandatory and voluntary learning. From which do you learn most readily? Does learning from experience draw on different competencies than most classroom instruction?**

Experiential learning lends itself naturally to cooperative activities, team building, interdisciplinary approaches, cultural awareness, project-based learning, problem-solving skills, leadership development, antibias lessons, and values clarification. It can be incorporated in any curriculum area for all ages. When youth engage in activities with personal and social significance, they integrate academic knowledge with affective and volitional responses. When school programs build in reflection through discussions, journals and periodic reassessments, they open opportunities for critical thinking about the tension between America's democratic values and persistent inequities. Service learning reinvigorates public discourse about the meaning of justice and equal rights in light of social structures and cultural beliefs that segment society and sustain oppression.

CSL also introduces students to jobs in a service economy. The key lies in building effective teams around issues that concern youth, such as positive self-esteem and healthy lifestyle choices. For example, educational and human service agencies might use CSL volunteers in culturally diverse working groups with responsibility for educational or health projects in the community. Youth leaders might promote positive images through multicultural writing that facilitates self-expression by providing every child with access to materials, activities and occasions that support creative and imaginative communications. Other teams might offer peer counseling and role models to youths who face decisions about personal behaviors that affect their physical and mental health.

Youth engaged in CSL revise the job description of students. Student leaders build their skills through purposive activities in the schools and community. To implement CSL projects, they

- communicate with diverse people and organizations;
- resolve issues at service sites through meetings with staff and clients;
- build relationships with teachers, human service workers, and other community members;
- foster dialog rather than debate as they explain service-learning concepts to others;
- take responsibility for specific program activities;
- solve problems collaboratively;
- introduce a discourse of civic responsibility; and
- create new programs that involve youth in service.

### Recurring Education

Restoring productivity growth that will allow future generations a higher standard of living (or enable the United States to compete internationally without further reducing real wages) depends on recurring education. An investment in human capital ordinarily complements new plant and equipment. U.S. businesses spend well over $100 billion annually on formal staff development programs. High-tech firms estimate that as much as 40% of wages are paid for time spent learning new procedures or products. At the other extreme, some firms criticize low-skilled workers as lacking in basic skills required for filing forms or following simple directions.

Expenditures for formal training in conjunction with on-the-job learning have three notable weaknesses. First, unemployed and low-skill workers are denied learning experiences, particularly handicapping women and people of color. Second, companies want workers to learn site-specific skills and in-house procedures that augment top-down controls but do not enhance general employability. Third, declining industries seldom support retraining to prepare workers for other jobs, while rising industries lack resources for expanding both physical plant and a trained labor pool.

A comprehensive program supported by a special fund could spread the risks and create a convenient mechanism for shifting costs and savings over time. A public agency supported by a percentage of wages might pay jobholders (and potential workers) for adult education. Workers would be less constrained by company policies that encourage courses or workshops with immediate vocational applicability. Some senior workers might learn hobbies or crafts to engage their interests during retirement. General skills and new training would give workers flexibility and choices. In 1993, President Bill Clinton proposed a similar program as part of a comprehensive education reform that also includes apprenticeships and help for displaced workers.

The magnitude of existing programs is large but is neither systematic nor equitable. When France institutionalized adult-training opportunities, it set aside 1% of wages—a sum less than was then being spent and substantially less than the 3% typically budgeted by technologically advanced firms. Currently wages and salaries in the United States total over $2 trillion per year. An additional 1.5% contribution added to Social Security taxes would generate $30 billion for recurring education. In part, that sum might substitute for existing adult training programs, which cost the federal government approximately $16 billion annually. A new program might encourage collaborations with schools and colleges with workers contributing opportunity costs of their own time. Media and software packages facilitate low-cost, individual learning.

A pattern of 16 or more years of schooling followed by 30 or more years of work makes little sense for a knowledge-based economy. Projected career shifts suggest the value of a liberal arts education (that includes mathematics and science) and argue for combining practical experience with formal education. A comprehensive adult program could reduce the inequities currently plaguing on-the-job training. Entitlement would not depend on income or age but would be approximately equal for everyone—about $250 per year for adults. It might be accumulated for a period of time or "borrowed" against for later "repayment" when workers develop or enroll in a program. It would slightly equalize incomes because unemployed and low-wage workers have lower opportunity costs and their contributions of time might reduce differences.

A national program to facilitate a fairer system of recurring education should address the following probabilities:

- Typical workers will hold five to eight jobs in a lifetime; those who remain with one firm will undertake many different responsibilities.
- Past loyalties or hard work count for little. As firms grow in size (or dissolve) in order to compete internationally (or to fit into a

profitable niche), they close down branches and lay off workers (including white-collar staff).

- Technical, professional and managerial positions usually require and subsidize adult education, both on the job and through formal training.
- New informational technologies will reduce hierarchies and enhance workers' sense of control and flexibility only if schools and workplaces consistently encourage responsibility and decision-making.

Experiential learning in a context of socially valued activities throughout one's life span unites competencies with values. There is less fragmentation of facts and techniques—more connections to "real life." The importance of on-the-job training and recurring education may reduce the impact of grades and schooling as an occupational sorting machine, allowing for diverse learning styles and multiple chances to contribute to society. Learning through useful activities reduces alienation, supports personal identities, and stabilizes many interactive patterns. On the other hand, these approaches may discourage scientific discoveries and innovations that introduce radically new ways of looking at taken-for-granted phenomena.

Public policies that expand the range of competencies supported by schools together with opportunities for recurring education serve to encourage risk taking. Because investment in human capital is embodied in a single person, any miscalculation threatens one's income. The more uncertainty there is about the future, the higher are the risks for pursuing unconventional jobs or lifestyles. When confident that they will have later opportunities to change their mind, students may pursue a career that really interests them or that actualizes their values. A federal responsibility for recurring education and a local emphasis on service learning both foster interrelationships among people in communities and the nation. They may build empathy and group feelings that tie people together.

## Nonformal Education

Although formal training—in school, in adult classes, in job-related staff development—is the most visible aspect of learning, it resembles the tip of an iceberg. People learn through all their activities and interactions. Americans are surrounded by varied media and people with information to transmit. In a mobile, multicultural society, people from different background experiences, customs and values have much to teach each other. Radio, movies and television offer a rich fare of public affairs programs as well as dramas that reveal how others respond to diverse events. Print and electronic media available in libraries and over the Internet bring uncountable facts and ideas to anyone who can read. Indeed, it is puzzling how people living in a postmodern era stay in familiar ruts when faced with a juxtaposition of new and different viewpoints.

A partial answer to that puzzle comes from surveys indicating many dissatisfactions with, or disengagement from, modern life. Alcohol and drug abuse; tobacco consumption and overweight conditions that are known to shorten life; boredom, depression, and thoughts of suicide all stand in contrast to engaged workers and citizens. Families have disconnected: Young adults move away, couples divorce, retirees congregate in Florida and Arizona. At the same time, talk shows on radio and television attract large audiences, anonymous communication abounds on the Internet, and people often feel that their time is totally occupied. Sporting events and soap operas on television keep one from talking, thinking and acting. In a world surrounded by words and images, one has to seek out distractions to avoid learning.

Americans spend more on entertainment ($160 billion) than on higher education ($130 billion). Media has promoted a common national experience to support consumerism and mass markets—the Golden Arches or the admonition to Just Do It! are readily understood. Apparently, capitalists whose advertising dollars pay for most public media prefer active consumers and passive workers. Soap operas and comedies transform social and political issues into personal interactions. Newscasts focus on transient events without historical or social analyses. Entertainment and athletic displays seem to promote disengagement and vicarious thrills without personal consequences. Talk shows on radio and television allow people to vent frustrations or reveal their life stories but in ways that reinforce mainstream traditional customs. Understanding of others, when it happens, is personal and emotional rather than critical and reflective.

Most nonformal, educative groups respond to broad levels of interests. National magazines, radio and television depend on mass audiences to cover production costs. Advertisers seek large circulations to disseminate their messages. Proposals for computer-based, high-density videoscreens with high-quality audio connected to a cable offering 500 channels suggest that individual tastes and preferences can be satisfied through presenting legislatures in session, committee hearings, lectures by public figures, musical and theater performances, nature and geography, science and technology, as well as "entertainments." The advantage of low-cost informational technologies follows from customizing convenient access to meet diverse interests.

Business and civic groups, voluntary associations such as camera clubs or political parties, health and fitness centers, churches, and Girl Scouts organize nonformal learning but in ways that enhance conservative practices and ideologies. Organizational leadership ordinarily follows lengthy service, and these groups cling to established institutional ties. Indeed, networks of interest groups on E-mail suggests how limiting most forms of adult interaction have become. That assessment need not contradict the importance of informal activities in the interstices of society—pickup softball games, political associations, neighborhood block parties, family reunions, street entertainers, visitors to parks or wilderness areas, charity walkathons, and campus rallies—all create opportunities for learning about how others view their place in the world.

Ideally, most learning is complementary to other activities. Socializing with friends who share many values provides information about recreation, movies, and restaurants along with companionship. Middle-class readers of novels seek to discover how others interacted during times of crisis, where to travel, what to order for lunch or wear to the opera. Afterwork gatherings allow exchanges of gossip and facts that help one function on the job. Exercise contributes to one's physical health as well as providing a break from chronic tensions or worries. Informal political discussions offer a cross-check for one's interpretation of current events. For many commuters, driving time allows for news and weather reports, planning the day's activities, and perhaps a little music.

Paradoxically, most practical knowledge is not linked to instructional goals. Students who learn that writing is hard, that algebra is filled with unknowns, that Silas Marner is boring, and that the teacher does not expect much from them usually carry those lessons with them through life. Workers discover that they are expected to follow orders, to adjust their pace to that of machines, and to ignore insights from outsiders' knowledge. Citizens seldom understand the complexity of legislation and regulation in an industrial society, and democratic leaders seek votes through slogans, negative advertising, and patriotic appeals. Americans have learned a measure of cynicism about the motives of political and economic leaders.

Experiential learning requires purposive engagement in a wide variety of activities and interactions. Commenting on the qualities of a good society, Bellah, Madsen, Sullivan, Swidler, and Tipton (1991, p. 273) noted that democratic processes require that "people actively attend to what is significant." Too often "current politics seems designed to distract us from what is important and seduce us into fantasies that all is well." Workplace democracy and recurring education mean that people are continually engaged in creating not only products or services but also a sense of purpose. Bellah and colleagues added, "attending means to concern ourselves with the larger meaning of things in the longer run, rather than with short-term payoffs." Learning and working can be complementary activities, not separated into first schools, then jobs. Moreover, households and workplaces can combine useful and recreational activities.

## MULTIPLE FRAMEWORKS OF ORGANIZATIONS

Evolving schools and workplaces transform how people interact in organizations that coordinate activities over space and time. Learning communities for an information age can promote democratic settings with flexible, flatter structures. This does not mean that hierarchies or lines of authority have no place. Clearly defined responsibilities are important for seeing that certain things get done in a timely and efficient manner or in responding to emergencies. Moreover, useful information should command attention in any reasonable dialog. At the same time, it is essential to move beyond command systems. Instead of one view prevailing over another, depending on who is involved or where the organization is going at the moment, multiple goals and possibilities lead to the reconstruction of social meanings and to the implementation of new strategies and structures.

The power of cultural leadership is often underestimated by educators. Rigid tables of organization and staff development workshops are routinely proposed to induce change. Managing the culture of an organization can effectively coordinate curricular goals while allowing autonomy for each classroom. This approach supports the empowerment of both students and teachers far better than top-down demands for accountability or site-based management. Like other human constructions, organizations are continuously defining and redefining their actions and the ways people make sense of them. Open discussions draw strength from the multiple realities of all stakeholders, while information technologies reduce the time demands of oral dialog.

### Mapping Organizations

Strategies for educational improvement implicitly draw on a sense about how individuals interact with their world. Joyce, Weil, and Wald (1981, p. 127) identified four approaches:

(1) those oriented toward *social relations* and toward the relation between the person and the culture, and which draw upon social sources; (2) those which depended on *information-processing* systems and descriptions of human capacity for processing information; (3) those that emphasized *personality development*, the processes of personal construction of reality, and the capacity to function as an integrated personality; and (4) those developed from an analysis of the processes by which human *behavior* is shaped, reinforced, and modified.

People adapt various pieces of these frameworks in attempting to make sense of human development and educational reform, whether they seek a return to older ways, stability or innovation.

Institutions greatly simplify daily decisionmaking for both insiders and outsiders. Without rule-setting duties and responsibilities, one must ask what are the alternatives, what do I want, and how does it mesh with the alternatives? Within an organizational framework, one asks what is the situation and what action is appropriate, given my role:

Routines help avoid conflicts; they provide codes of meaning that facilitate interpretation of ambiguous words; they constrain bargaining within comprehensible terms and enforce agreements; they help mitigate the unpredictability created by open structures and garbage can processes by regulating access of participants, problems, and solutions to choice opportunities. Routines embody collective and individual identities, interests, values, and worldviews, thus constraining allocation of attention, standards of evaluation, priorities, perceptions, and resources. (March & Olsen, 1989, p. 24)

Depending on their roles and goals, people apply at least four frameworks when thinking about organizations—human resources, structural, political, and symbolic. From a human resources frame, improving a group's performance involves changing people through training, coaching, and personnel shifts. From a structural frame, innovation follows from a new chain of command with accountability to achieve a strategic goal. In political terms, reform entails redistributing power among shifting coalitions of groups formed by their self-interests and previous interactions. Within a symbolic frame, new behaviors follow as leaders refocus meanings, values and visions to reinspire an organizational ethos. Although one or another of these ways of making sense of an organization offers greater insights, at any given time, the others cannot be ignored.

At first, such multiple views of reality complicate thinking, breaking up linear cause-effect relations. With time, however, those categories provide dialog-building imagery. Multiple frames coalesce into organizational cultures that integrate patterns of thought and action. Innovations affect these assumptions and introduce ambiguities that threaten people's understandings and self-interests. As change occurs, "below the surface, the social tapestry begins to unravel, threatening the organization's collective unconscious and existential character" (Bolman & Deal, 1991, p. 375). Facing uncertain conditions, people in organizations need "opportunities for involvement" and "psychological support" (human resources), revised tables of organization and operating procedures (structural), open discussions of conflicts that may arise (political), and speeches and images to facilitate letting go of long-held attitudes (symbolic).

Members and leaders must think across frames and "see the same organization *simultaneously* as machine, family, jungle, and theater" (Bolman & Deal, 1991, p. 450). Schools have enough independence so that they cannot be reduced to any simple description—not simply a jungle in which the powerful rule or a family in which relationships matter or a machine whose output follows from its inputs or a theater where a staged narrative helps to make sense of community values. A teacher puzzled by resistance to innovations in schools might describe dynamics of change from several perspectives: The powerful cling to their position, hierarchies segment people, teachers' roles as classroom authorities shape familiar interactions, and powerful symbols of common schools muddy understandings of how segregated and unequal education has become.

Keeping multiple organizational formats in mind can unblock thinking about what might be possible in schools. Most stakeholders consider reform from a frame that makes sense to them but often cuts off dialog with others. Charisma, theater and widely shared symbols allow everyone to participate in discussions about purpose and strategy. Principals who stress rationalized decisionmaking and a competitive environment to downplay their arbitrary authority ignore the educational value of discussions about social justice. Students usually connect best with teachers who seem to care about them as a person, but those relationships may conceal the degree to which organizational demands reduce most teachers' roles to a desperate struggle to maintain order in their classrooms.

Schools do not fit well into market and hierarchical frameworks for understanding organizations. Hierarchical bureaucracies rely on rules, routines and rigid internal processes in order to defend functional roles. Market-oriented firms emphasize rational analyses of clear goals to be achieved through defined tasks and contracts. By contrast, agencies that are embedded in human relations build on tradition and experiential crafts to carry out group tasks. Those strategies served schools in the past. A transformation to a postmodern condition calls for a new strategy and structure. Professionals with flexible practices, open systems, and a prospector mentality need ad hoc structures that are congruent with high-uncertainty and high-intensity situations. Charismatic leaders can advance new cultural norms.

## Connecting Multiple Values

In a postmodernist world, no one can comprehend ordinary interactions from single framework, even when a dominant elite imposes views that facilitate predictions of likely outcomes. The consequence is not deformed or inadequate social science because its descriptions and conclusions are ambiguous. It is better science because its frameworks relate to purposes and perspectives based on historical developments and social structures. It opens plausible steps to shape more desirable futures by emphasizing alternative understandings and goals. It avoids a reductionist trap that opts for predictability (although based on dominant elites imposing their social frameworks on others) over volition and for material outcomes over democratic values.

Time and perspectives affect the importance of issues and concerns. For instance, effective schools might use cohesion and morale based on a commitment to teachers as professionals in order to reduce free riding and to uphold high standards. A district staff development coordinator might utilize planning and goal setting through a variety of needs assessment instruments in order to build support for human resource training. School administrators might seek flexible adaptability in order to stabilize school financing in an uncertain political environment. Alternatively, they might apply information gathering and publicity in order to secure external support for growth. In each case, there are value conflicts between ends and means and among organizational goals.

Low-cost information makes it possible to consider multiple realities and to include all significant stakeholders in decisionmaking in ways that facilitate feelings of autonomy and efficacy. A values map (Figure 9.1) prepared by Quinn and Hall (1983, p. 288) suggests ways to understand organizations. By relating means to ends in different perspectives, the diagram depicts cross-cutting conflicts that block understanding of organizations.

The purposes of organizations help set strategies and appropriate structures for their implementation. Public schools, like most political structures, represent the interplay of many interests and concerns. Internally, educators must give some attention to all those constituencies while coordinating varied and sequential learning opportunities for students. Because the payoffs to schooling are decades in the future, educators strive to maintain their system through staff development and an internal focus. Consequently, not only are schools loosely coupled to other parts of society, they also allow considerable leeway for individual classroom teachers. These complications are not flaws in organizational structures but reasonable adaptations to diversity among students, multiple goals, a complex environment, and an uncertain future.

What does this way of viewing organizations tell us about institutions and possibilities for change? A desire for certainty pushes toward simplifications and recipes for reform. To resist these pressures, ordinary dialog is important because "institutions create their own environment by the way they interpret and act in a confusing world" (March & Olsen, 1989, pp. 47, 94, 141). Governance or managing change is like gardening or building a coral reef: "long-run development of political institutions is less a product of intentions, plans, and consistent decisions, than incremental adaptation to changing problems with available solutions within gradually evolving structures of meaning." Final solutions are hazardous because they imply no need for ongoing dialog "among contending concerns, demands, and values."

**FIGURE 9.1**
**A Map of Competing Values**

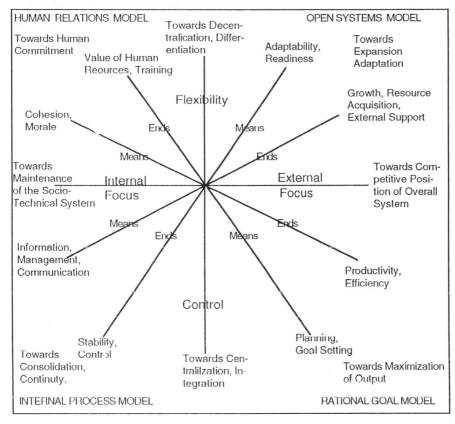

*Source*: R. H. Hall and R. E. Quinn (Eds.), *Organizational Theory and Public Policy* (pp. 281–298). Beverly Hills, CA: Sage Publications. Copyright © 1983 by Sage Publications. Reprinted by permission of Sage Publications.

Effective action depends on holding multiple views and applying the appropriate one to the issue at hand, much as Feynman suggested that physicists needed a half-dozen ways of viewing a new problem. A healthy organization attends to a variety of goals; each is best served by a different structure and mindset. Specialization between doers and thinkers is ineffective, sometimes dangerous. Members and clients who feel a part of the whole will inform the system of impending problems as they perform their designated tasks. Diverse frameworks open opportunities for discussion and guard against stability, control, or staff morale becoming ends in their own right. In a time of potential transformation, schools are well-served by open systems that emphasize public support and flexible adaptations.

## LEARNING AND WORKING COOPERATIVELY

Economic growth affects democratic politics both within organizations and the nation. Although labor productivity gains slowed in the United States and show little improvement when contrasted with previous recoveries, today's situation is puzzling, though not unprecedented. Over the past 30 years, workers have diverged from their European counterparts by toiling longer with fewer vacations and less income security, while many cannot find a job. Unions have weakened, and no party represents a clear working-class agenda. Swayed by Reagan's populist rhetoric, many blue-collar workers voted to shift some of their declining income to the wealthiest 10% of Americans in return for a promise that less of their taxes would go to needs-based programs for the poor. Reduced welfare and longer prison sentences aimed to punish those at the bottom of society, while the rich received tax breaks in the hope that they would save, invest and provide more jobs for "decent" working-class families.

During the 1980s, many U.S. firms acted to counter rising worker resistance by flattening hierarchies, involving workers in quality circles, and restructuring processes so that computers or robots handled most routine operations. Yet salary differentials for top management widened significantly during that decade. Moreover, many things cannot be done without broad public support and legal authorization for cooperative planning. For instance, society as a whole would benefit from reduced tobacco consumption, cleaner-burning fuels, packaging designed for recycling, effective and fair public schools, and safe streets and homes. Yet there are few satisfactory ways to achieve those ends without government programs, subsidies and sanctions that generate resentment.

Public discourse is formed (and deformed) by institutional patterns that treat hierarchical arrangements as natural and necessary. Some current problems arose because of past successes (e.g., a part of the current health-cost crisis reflects innovative technologies—previously, people died without expensive drugs and medical treatment). Those who invested effort in the Civil Rights Movement, in the War on Poverty, in equal rights for women, in disarmament and peace movements are understandably frustrated or alienated by recent reversals. Drug abuse, AIDS, teenage parents, and chronic unemployment among youth—especially African Americans and Latinos—diminish prospects and cannot be averted by blaming the victims for their lifestyles. Narrow public discussions block understanding of the needs and aspirations of democratic movements toward diverse learning communities.

## Social Fairness and Aspirations

The challenge remains one of maintaining flexibility and adaptability among organizations that compete not just on price and quality but also for worker satisfaction and customer loyalty. Just as individuals try new activities in order to learn, organizations or functional groups must take risks in order to respond quickly and innovatively. People who are close to the subsistence margin, however, are sensibly averse to risks. A chief executive officer who takes on a stagnant firm after being assured a $1 million salary and a golden parachute willingly bets the firm. A custodian or secretary whose salary pays the rent and grocery bill, whose job provides health-care and retirement benefits, and whose seniority offers job security may prefer the status quo. Without a broad substantive implementation of social justice, it is difficult to conceptualize a new kind of federalism that reframes institutional responsibilities to encourage risk-taking investments by firms and knowledge workers.

The United States has the productive capacity and organizational know-how today to provide everyone with a decent subsistence and still offer ample incentives to those who work harder, make unusual contributions, are creative, or introduce new products or processes. Americans also have a capacity to foster multiple communities that let everyone's identity be shaped by personal choices as well as ascriptive categories of family, religion and gender. Society offers multiple opportunities for useful activities so that each person's significant criteria can allow a measure of success. Individuals can be in the bottom half in some areas and the top half in others without any category dominating one's feeling of self-worth or ability to make sense out of daily experiences and to act purposefully.

If class, race and gender biases were magically eliminated and far greater equality prevailed, many people would still be affected by their history. One in five children live in poverty, and many schools serving them are truly dreadful—not because teachers want them that way but because they cannot overcome neighborhood effects and longstanding discrimination. Children of poverty and their parents lack skills or experience to fill positions in a high-tech, information-driven economy. Denied hope, children and adults lower their aspirations and their investment in education and health (physical and mental). Under those conditions, oppressed individuals and groups can neither catch up nor offer fresh perspectives to democratic organizations.

Equal educational opportunities for working-class children, students of color, and females would end the privileged position long enjoyed by male children of middle-class, White parents. In most states today, students attending schools in suburban districts will probably test well enough to attend college and have parents who can provide some assistance. They have a vested interest in opposing state equalization formulas that would allow low-income urban and rural districts to spend as much as suburban districts —not to mention compensating for their concentration of high-cost students in vocational, bilingual, and special education programs. Although promoting women and people of color into power positions substantially increases the pool of applicants, personnel departments worry about validating the competency of those who look "different," and many taxpayers manifestly resent programs that effectively equalize conditions for other people's children.

Currently, family income and wealth underlie so many opportunities for investment in human capital that class boundaries appear fixed and unequal, at least to those on the bottom. Because capitalist myths support schooling as a path toward more open society, an optimistic approach focuses on equity, information technologies, multiculturalism, and other large-scale changes. If public policies assured equality of basic rights and access to opportunities, diversity might flourish in other spheres. If everyone defines personal goals and achieves excellence in those arenas, then hierarchies need not block aspirations or distort individuals' self-esteem.

What does a multiframe approach imply for teacher involvement in decisionmaking as a way to revitalize educational organizations? Given diverse stakeholders with multiple values and interests, majority decisions are uncertain and unstable. Open dialog raises issues of race and gender as well as class. Public schools not only involve a mix of interests, values and generations but also mold future potential. Using all frames to envision future possibilities, teachers and students may embark on uncertain seas of learning—knowing more and questioning more, respecting the past while preparing for the future, balancing equity, efficiency and choice.

### Democratic Schools

When teachers place social justice at the center of their curriculum, they end up with a radically different classroom. According to a fifth-grade social studies teacher, democratic classrooms must include the following features:

- a curriculum grounded in the lives of our students,
- dialogue,
- a questioning/problem-posing approach,
- an emphasis on critiquing bias and attitudes, and
- the teaching of activism for social justice. (Peterson, 1994, p. 30)

That meant daily connections between text items and issues in students' lives. For example, violence in society leads to a discussion of fights on the playground, student negativism links to tracking and testing, and proposals for school improvement bring up the role of teacher unions.

There have been a number of experiments with justice as the foundation of alternative programs. They have proven memorable experiences for the staff and most students, both because of their openness to issues that affect the lives of children and because of the frustration over lengthy discussions and the difficulty of coming to resolutions. Drug use, racism, sexual orientation, and the degree of student responsibility raised both in-school and community issues that perplexed everyone. In most cases, issues could be compromised to everyone's satisfaction, but the experience revalidated the difficulties of achieving justice in a small segment of an inequitable society.

.As professionals with a tradition of collegial relationships, teachers seem naturals for establishing democratic participation in schools. They share similar experiences, have historically resisted efforts to distinguish master teachers or to offer "merit pay" awards, attend regular staff meetings, and exercise considerable autonomy within their classrooms. Nevertheless, endemic tensions and a multiplicity of goals diffuse and confuse discussions. Moreover, teachers, even in conjunction with parents and some community members, cannot make those decisions by themselves. Funds, curricular mandates, and competency standards come from the state. Although teachers "construct" a curriculum through daily interactions with students, they feel relatively powerless to discuss these public means and goals. The consequence is a distorted communication about what reasonable members of society want in the future.

Because educators depend on broad publics for support and necessarily prepare the young for adult roles, collaborative arrangements open participation to a range of experiences beyond those offered by schools. Interorganizational contacts reveal multiple perspectives and extend the dialog. Community service activities as well as apprenticeships offer ways for students to experience citizenship as well as productive labor, thereby substantively augmenting the capacity of schools to make relevant knowledge accessible to all students. As a result, school buildings should function as a node in an educational network that has permeable boundaries and is open to controversial issues.

A notion of fairness or justice evolves through dialog among relevant stakeholders. Classrooms can encourage debate while minimizing negative risks for those with the least self-esteem and family security. At the secondary level, schools or voluntary programs can make justice a part of ongoing discussions and decisions among students, thereby bringing issues of cheating, drugs, sex, and violence as well as a range of less controversial topics within the curriculum. Students practice being citizens by expressing their views, learn from peers and outside experts, and then arrive at agreements binding on the group. A diversity of classes, races, genders and ages among staff and students manifestly strengthens the value of democratic dialog.

Democratic classrooms, teacher empowerment, site-based management, local control, states as locations for federalist experiments, and court-ordered desegregation all define different sets of relevant stakeholders—and thus who comprises a potential majority. Depending on the problem and circumstances, any and all of these goals may be appropriate. Our sense is that the major stumbling block is the absence of settings for dialog that builds agreements on desirable futures. Too often, Americans have regarded it as futile to fight city hall, question the telephone company, boycott a firm, or change schools. They have stopped trying to communicate about things that deeply matter to them. When people have a sense of capacity to shape their own future, then there are things to discuss. If I want something and you want something, our discourse often reveals a shared cognition about an institutional framework for a good society.

This vision of multiple-purpose organizations raises consciousness that each has a functional mission but also serves as a locus for political organizing, human relations, and ongoing personal development. That recognition may make thinking about organizations more contingent *and* more value laden. To serve multiple goals, they must be more permeable to external environments and to the personal or social needs of their workers and customers. To gain coherence and build trust, they much explicate and demonstrate purposes and values. Communication of those views becomes the responsibility of everyone involved—not a public relations officer charged with putting the best face on events. Those ideas can facilitate a transforming consensus about educational purposes related to a better future, capable of inspiring students and workers.

Ideally, schools would exemplify an encompassing vision of justice. As publicly supported agencies charged with preparing the young for productive citizenship, they can no longer carry on as though unequal learning and unequal outcomes in life were necessary in practical terms. Information workers need a level of shared communication and trust inconsistent with currently segmented knowledge as patterns of class, race and gender discrimination. Because a capacity to learn efficiently is a key threshold for adult competence, schools must make those skills accessible to all students. Equality of outcomes for those minimal standards is feasible if students' identity is respected and their aspirations promoted by the curriculum and their mentors. That is a vision worth pursuing.

## RELATED READING

Bruce R. Joyce and Beverly Showers, *Student Achievement Through Staff Development* (New York: Longman, 1988) offer useful perspectives on meaningful change. Ann Bastian et al., *Choosing Equality: The Case for Democratic Schooling* (Philadelphia: Temple University Press, 1985); David A. Hamburg, *Today's Children: Creating a Future for a Generation in Crisis* (New York: Times Books, 1994); and Christopher Jencks, *Rethinking Social Policy: Race, Poverty, and the Underclass* (Cambridge: Harvard University Press, 1992) expand the range of alternatives for schools, workplaces and society.

On the values of multiple perspectives, see Nicholas C. Burbules, *Dialogue in Teaching: Theory and Practice* (New York: Teachers College Press, 1993) and Donald A. Schön, *The Reflective Practitioner: How Professionals Think in Action* (New York: Basic Books, 1983).

# 10

# Choosing Futures

We have presented evidence of a mindset that was shaped by 200 years of industrial growth and is now embedded in American institutions. Hierarchical command systems coordinated multiple activities over space and time, minimizing a need for communication. Students and most adults tolerated alienating tasks and subordinate roles in exchange for an implicit promise of greater income and leisure. Public education supported a modest social mobility, while a pluralist democracy enabled business interests to determine major political agendas with regard to income distribution. Periodic reforms regulated excesses of corporate power and established a welfare state to protect individuals from industrial fluctuations. Although falling short of equality, constitutional democracy and economic growth reduced the gap in income and social standing that prevailed in feudal Europe and that persists in most non-Western regions.

Since 1973, a stagnant economy has raised tensions between hierarchies and personal autonomy, fueling widespread resentment and resistance. Productive cooperation is inhibited by alienating jobs in segmented occupations by citizens who live anonymously within a bureaucratic state. Negotiating strategies are increasingly characterized by misinformation between principals and agents, buyers and sellers, political leaders and citizens. Fragmented cultural beliefs encourage selfishness and self-interested ideologies, leaving little foundation for rebuilding a sense of community. Meanwhile, power struggles within and among interest groups exacerbate ideological differences.

A first step toward making sense of events is to refocus on democratic schools that offer every child a fair chance to use their intelligence in creating a good society. Institutional trajectories are not easily redirected, especially widely dispersed, loosely coupled ones like schools. Popular reform proposals continue to fortify top-down controls over educators and students. Promising information technologies and a generally high level of literacy, however, allow efficient output and distribution of goods without mass production or mass marketing. Low-cost data collection, processing and transmittal enable people to work together within and among organizations as well as political units. Despite tentative steps toward cooperation, collaborative practices as yet characterize few schools or workplaces.

Ready or not, tomorrow's world is being shaped by our daily thoughts and actions toward competition or cooperation. Reconstruction entails a sorting out of which aspects to reinforce and which to recon-sider—or which features remain as context and which deserve consideration as a public text. Accumulations of scientific knowledge partially determine technological possibilities, but they too were shaped by class, race and gender discrimination, by hierarchical structures and pluralist democratic institutions, by cultural attitudes and moral creeds. Future well-being is limited less by our capacity to exploit natural resources through organizational structures than by the selfish actions and misperceptions of others. Long-run possibilities depend on cooperation among producers, consumers and learners—as well as greater coherence among these roles for individuals.

This chapter recapitulates central themes of the book in terms of their implications for how teachers prepare productive citizens for a future society. Previous assumptions that link material abundance to hierarchical structures no longer make sense. We begin by asking how students and teachers might make sense of learning if schools no longer rank ordered educational attainments in ways that produce, reproduce and legitimize class, race, gender, and other inequalities. Next, we propose including non-material goals as a part of productivity—in contrast to a singular focus on higher grades or income. Then, we explore relationships among equity and trust in rebuilding democratic communities. Finally, we summarize perspectives that foreshadow plausible and desirable transformations following from dialog about social justice.

## PURPOSIVE LEARNING

What are the purposes of education? For a half century, most edu-cators have focused on preparing students as productive citizens, as though job skills and voter readiness were known and fixed. Others have striven "to expand people's *horizon of possibilities,*" as John Friedmann (1987, p. 398) suggested about radical planning. In our interviews, we raised Ralph Tyler's question (1949, p. 35): "Should the schools develop young people to fit into present society as it is, or does the school have a revolutionary mission to develop young people who will seek to improve the society?" Although each person had partici-pated in, and valued, successful change, they described schools as stag-nant organizations. Their references to a stubborn status quo conveyed powerful messages about disengagement, disempowerment or disen-franchisement.

A veteran administrator compared preparing students to fit society with hitting a moving target: *"Basically society as it is today will not be society as it is five or ten years from now."* A special education teacher responded with a neat formula: *"To prepare them to be able to change the things that are bad, keep the things that are good, and to improve on them is what anyone would want for education for their children."* Recognizing that labor market forecasts offered little basis for planning one's education, she urged *"training students to be able to think for themselves, to be able to take care of themselves, to be able to make choices. And there are always choices!"* However, those opportunities depend on organizational and political contexts as well as individual preferences.

A young teacher insisted that most schools failed to prepare students even for current conditions: *"We're developing students to fit into schools and to fit into a society that existed 80 years ago, not now!"* Her indictment was specific: *"We're preparing students to follow orders, to sit in their seat when they're told to, to move when the bell rings and not until it rings, to fail to think for themselves, just to follow orders. And yet we want them to get out there and be able to work independently, to initiate and complete projects, to be motivators, go-getters, initiators."* An African American administrator commented that *"if we try to develop young people to fit into the mold as it is, society will not experience change."* After reciting society's failings, another educator insisted on *"our responsibility to prepare them* [students] *to make those changes and to encourage them to be diverse in their approach."*

A secondary science teacher in a vocational school serving many Latino students noted that *"if we want to put the kids into society as it exists now, then we are in for big trouble."* He worried about the natural environment as well as the violence in his city and on television. Cooperation offered an answer: *"Our economy is the root of all evil in this country. Greedy people and students are the worst and they grow up to be parents."* Too many problems—*"drugs, alcohol, sex, disease"*—threaten teenagers right now. If students are satisfied with the status quo, then they have little need for education: *"If they are not satisfied with it, then there are certain things we can teach them. And that is a respect for each other and the environment and learning to do with less or making more of what you have."*

A middle school principal emphasized a two-step process: Schools should *"develop skills in our young people that will help to make them productive and effective citizens."* Yet he recognized that educators invariably *"have a vision for the kind of world that we would like to see our society develop into; and given that, we certainly need them to develop the kinds of critical thinking, problem-solving, decisionmaking skills in our young people that may in fact help us to improve our society."* He foresaw *"new types of curriculums, new types of learning experiences, new approaches to teaching."* Noting public concern about health, environment and racism, an administrator concluded that *"more schooling and higher standards makes sense only if it prepares students for future responsibilities, not just for getting a higher score on a test."*

For a century, American teachers offered their students a narrow but positive message: Learn to read, write and compute—using texts that explain and legitimize capitalism, competition, democracy, and elite positions for White males—so that you can exceed your parents' level of material comfort. Now, that achievement ideology rings hollow for a majority of youth. Factually, real wage rates for most U.S. households have declined. Technologically, depletion of resources and environmental pollution threaten future output, health and ecological balances. Socially, inequalities motivate crimes against property and people, thereby jeopardizing everyone's safety. Logically, democratic and economic developments in the rest of the world simply cannot advance everyone to the material privileges enjoyed by educated males of European descent.

## Contested Terrain

People construct "accounts" of their experiences. Characteristically, they interpret events in ways that preserve a semblance of positive identity with purposeful actions—minimizing obvious conflicts. Individuals may intentionally slacken efforts if a teacher or supervisor appears unfairly negative or to have undeserved privileges. They may verbally condemn the motives or personal lives of powerful figures in order to reduce them to human scale or to focus attention on those aspects of productive activities or interpersonal relations where they can exercise positive or self-fulfilling control. None of these sense-making accounts offer much guidance if society's values and institutions embody deep contradictions.

Teachers today stand in the midst of conflicted terrain because economic growth no longer offers a reasonably convincing way to resolve contradictions between unequal futures and ideological commitments to equality, democracy and justice. Some educators instruct children whose prospects are bright and whose cultural heritage matches traditional school norms. A larger number teach in schools marked by poverty and racial or linguistic diversity; they often blame the students or their families for lacking motivation or ability to learn—as though ambition and competence were intrinsic, unrelated to one's life chances. Nearly all teachers experience conflicts between their desire to help others by making useful knowledge accessible and the organizational constraints of the school. They sense contradictions between fairness and competitive, rank-ordered grades, but they lack a framework to account for those disparate images of a good classroom.

As individual teachers struggle to make sense of the endemic tensions in their corrupted world of service, they usually focus on one or two aspects that stand for the larger contradiction of their situation. Many emphasize the mismatch between their mission and their resources. Would-be innovators who support alternative programs, curriculum or staffing patterns cite fears of change or organizational stasis. Currently, debates over process writing, cooperative learning, and multicultural curriculum generate anxiety about maintaining the teacher's authority. Focusing on one set of tensions, however, may keep one locked into a larger paradigm within which that aspect of conflict is embedded. Hence, we offer a visual representation of contested terrain as many educators experience it today (see Figure 10.1).

**FIGURE 10.1**
**Contested Terrain**

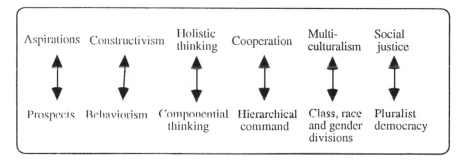

The items on the bottom line convey familiar ways to make sense of schools. Start with the students' prospects—what kind of jobs are projected that fit an individual's assessed skills and interests—then assign them to an appropriate track. Because people respond to rewards and punishments (among other things), teachers seek to motivate learning through competitive grades. Dividing knowledge into teachable facts makes testing simpler and prepares students for specialized roles in industrial-era organizations. Similarly, fragmented knowledge and norm-referenced grading scales prepare youth for a world of work that is competitive, hierarchical and bureaucratic. That curriculum and school culture help reproduce and order class, race and gender categories. Finally, individual choices about courses and careers ostensibly imitate pluralist democracies but also leave control of agendas to capitalists and legislators. The resulting opportunity structures tend to sustain categories and relationships.

Items across the top line offer a quite different reading of school experiences. Learning starts with students' aspirations, self-esteem, and goals for the future. It seeks to build a shared cognitive awareness through dialog and interactions. Although continually drawing on available facts and relationships, the emphasis remains on how puzzling new information fits into personal frameworks of interpretation. Rather than emphasizing the taken-for-granted cultural norms of modern industrial nations and the well-structured arrangements of knowledge in academic disciplines, students continually cross cultural and disciplinary boundaries. Political discourse around power and resource allocations within the group focus on social justice. Finally, public policies allow each person to strive to achieve their aspirations without crippling uncertainties.

## Dialog and Cognition

From a constructivist perspective, dialog is crucial for socially shared cognition in ways that are complex and rich in suggestions about the possibilities for systemic change in how we learn and live. As information is transmitted or, more accurately, as competencies are developed, knowledge becomes embedded in social structures and webs of relationships with other ideas and beliefs. The meaning of words, numbers and images depends in part on those familiar contexts. Discourse then conveys one's thoughts, partly shaping them and, likewise, being shaped by them. At the same time, it offers a window into our underlying frameworks; our words and those of others offer insights into what is practical, puzzling or unchallenged.

Established classroom roles shape how students perceive a teacher's questions, how much they want to answer them, and what cues they pick up to assist them. Symbols used in daily interactions influence how people interpret events: "Many signs, rules, notations rely on social consensus and cannot be invented or discovered by the individual alone. Like social norms and habits, they are made accessible to the individual by social transformation" (Peret-Clermont, Peret, & Bell, 1991, p. 48). According to Lave (1991, p. 67), cognition situated in practice "emphasizes the relational interdependency of agent and world, activity, meaning, cognition, learning, and knowing." Meanings are negotiated among specific persons with interests, roles and temperaments. Moreover, "learning, thinking, and knowing are relations among people engaged in activity *in, with, and arising from the socially and culturally structured world*. This world is itself socially constituted."

Ways of understanding create in-groups and outsiders whose boundaries interfere with future communication. When educators distinguish their frameworks from the backgrounds, languages, and aspirations of their students, they erect cultural boundaries that few students consider worth crossing. Without multiple dialogs that explore alternative dynamics and outcomes, however, those underlying social and cultural structures remain unexamined and subject to misinterpretation. The challenge for educators is 1) "to identify and characterize particular social languages"; 2) to ground those patterns in cultural settings; and 3) to "examine the processes of communicating whereby appropriating various social languages affects intrapsychological functioning" (Wertsch, 1991, pp. 97, 98). Specifically, students need opportunities to speak adult languages of competence and power; that process is easier if teachers acknowledge the legitimacy of their students' communication patterns.

A different image of learning emerges from situations where groups of students engage in dialog:

First, students often produce knowledge that can seldom be acquired without such interaction. Second, what a majority of them acquires varies from group to group, even when the interaction is induced by one and the same procedure. Third, knowledge differs considerably, even among those students who have been in the same group. Therefore, we must conclude that two processes are involved in the construction of knowledge through interaction: (a) individual invention of knowledge, motivated by group interaction; and (b) assimilation of information proposed by others in the preceding interaction, with some individual editing. (Hitano & Inagaki, 1991, pp. 344–345)

Significantly, students seemed more open to reconsideration after hearing contradictory views from peers than from adult authorities.

Building cognitive beliefs and patterns through interactions with others in specific situations does not readily translate into techniques for getting students to memorize discrete facts for standardized tests. Discussion is not simply a better way to transfer fragmented information into the minds of other persons. Instead, the issue is one of process, of trying out words in a realistic context, of varying roles from passive listening to active instruction. Speakers need feedback on what was heard and how closely it matched their intentions. The key is to use symbolic expressions to achieve something meaningful by sharing ideas, offering proposals or agreeing to those of others, and conceptualizing practical and coherent plans.

Youth who have a sense of self-identity that includes a viable future are motivated to acquire relevant skills, crafts, experiences, and formal knowledge. Grim prospects for too many children discourage thinking ahead or engaging in positive interactions. Accurate and relevant dialog both creates and is aided by shared values of democratic diversity and dignity. Only when goals are explicitly situated within a social context do ideals of freedom, happiness, tolerance, aesthetic creativity, and world peace become sufficiently concrete to permit agreement on collective steps in those directions. With material output as an important but no longer primary goal, emerging social purposes relate to how we interact with each other, to processes and values shaping interactions, to norms of fairness and freedom, to creativity and aesthetic appreciation.

## Self-identity and School Change

Exploring new roles requires students to have a sense of self-awareness and competence as well as personal security and well-being. Humans develop positive self-esteem by doing things and valuing goals that they are relatively good at or that are comparatively available in their environment. Yet educators use hierarchies of test scores, academic tracks, and urban-suburban differences to deny a sense of achievement to more than half of all students. Consequently, school rules and classroom directives foster student apathy or alienation, frustrating teachers who seek to assert tighter control. Young children naturally try activities and make mistakes, but students and adults risk their sense of self-competence when they venture into the unknown (Mecca, Smelser, & Vasconcellos, 1989).

In addition to one's competence, self-esteem depends on self-concept, or how one is viewed and treated by others. Ideally, children enjoy settings where healthy, functional and socially useful behaviors are valued and reinforced in a smooth transition to work and citizenship in an equitable, democratic society. Teachers often discover that giving special responsibility to students who "act out" transforms their behaviors. Students who see a positive future for themselves engage in those activities needed to perform well in school, opt for healthy lifestyles, cooperate with others, and participate in civic events. Each positive step builds toward the next in a natural sequence of expanding power and responsibility that in turn wins recognition and supports self-esteem.

Because oppression is often denied or internalized, it must be raised to consciousness in order for previously silenced groups to express their views. Hearing from oppressed groups may help other students understand how institutions have marginalized them, thereby inspiring those who despair and challenging the advantaged to rethink their beliefs. Authentic discourse around possible personal and community values encourages a desire to learn to function cooperatively in families or households, voluntary groups, workplaces, and democratic associations. Individuals need models and means to gain competence as students, wage earners, family members, and citizens so they focus on areas of relative proficiency that will stand them in good stead in future endeavors.

Teachers who feel relatively powerless—however dominant they appear in their classroom—face unpleasant dilemmas. Earlier, when it seemed that class structures were deeply embedded but that economic growth gradually expanded opportunities, they could simultaneously acculturate students to their status and prospects while promising enough chances for advancement to motivate academic achievement. Today, children whose family prospects have worsened can scarcely trust those teachers' promises about their future. Faced with a stagnant economy, teachers might improve their credibility by reversing their curricular stance. By describing barriers to class mobility and the advantages of a less hierarchical, nonracist, and gender-fair society, they might suggest how democratic learning communities improve conditions for everyone (except for currently powerful elites who relish their relative status).

One principal related deep reform to tracking and teachers' concerns: Some people view schools as *"the places that sort and determine who is going to do what in society."* Others, including herself, believe *"that schools should educate everyone to whatever their potential is."* She noted studies showing that homogeneous grouping brought much harm and no discernible benefits to kids. Nevertheless, *"school principals are unwilling to take on the job of changing it because they are threatening one of the most important values of our society. Our society is invested in and built upon the fact that there are some who have and some who have not."* Equitable school regularities *"threaten that balance of power."* Moreover, tracks, tests and grades give teachers a measure of control over students.

A transformation in embedded meanings cannot be conceived a subunit at a time, although most innovations are implemented that way. One of the puzzling responses to school reform is how it brings out different perceptions among the participants. Those differences generate miscommunication and may raise old conflicts into the open. Teachers question their own beliefs and find themselves changing their minds, often joining different coalitions. A successful paradigm shift must become part of a reflective dialog that involves students as well as faculty in a search for common ground from which to understand their multiple realities.

From a teacher's perspective, this analysis suggests a two-pronged approach to restoring dialog. First, within the classroom every student's identity and potential is respected. That includes positive expectations and high academic standards. Second, the everyday curriculum addresses the particular needs of students whose self-concept includes negatives because of their family life or ascribed characteristics. By treating cultural and linguistic diversity as positives while addressing issues of discrimination, teachers can facilitate learning by those who have been excluded historically. The resulting dialog allows educators to address their own identity and power in both personal and political terms. In turn, students can sense that society offers them some realistic options to act in accordance with their own values and aspirations.

## PRODUCTIVITY FOR WHAT?

Once an active role is established for self-identity and meaning-making dialog, the second step of considering what kind of society we want becomes possible. Efficient output makes sense only if it meets human needs rather than simply adding to material acquisitions. Obviously, lengthening one's time horizon and enlarging one's social framework brings more degrees of freedom to change things. Focusing on immediate labor markets and voting choices sustains a behaviorist framework in which individuals essentially have to adapt to existing conditions. By thinking ahead 30 years when today's high-school students will be mature leaders, we can envision quite different ways of arranging family, work and leisure that still preserve the material comfort made possible by industrial modes of production.

During a time of scarcity, what a typical worker could produce during an hour established an upper limit on collective well-being. When most people labored most of the year to raise and process food, fuel and fiber for household use, there was little surplus to invest in physical or human capital. Despite news reports and political rhetoric, there is no productivity problem in terms of meeting everyone's basic needs. The U.S. labor force is remarkably efficient, with ample capital stocks, low-cost energy, and plentiful natural resources to make and deliver familiar goods or services. What capitalist economies cannot do well is to resolve distributional issues, to keep everyone employed (and thus active as producers and consumers) while adapting to meet evolving demands for customized goods.

Raising social welfare through productivity gains has short-run, intermediate-run, and long-run aspects. First, manufacturing output per hour of labor could quickly increase if incomes were more equal. With one in four children living in poverty in the United States and millions of Africans, Asians and Latinos lacking food, clothing and shelter, no economy has satisfied everyone's basic human needs. People want decent housing, clean air, safe streets, and effective public schools, but many lack the means to pay for them. Americans who got richer over the past 15 years (mainly those making over $100,000 per year) already enjoy modern appliances, affordable housing, and adequate public schools. They spend to distinguish themselves from others by buying luxury items or positional goods (such as fine paintings or waterfront property that cannot be replicated).

Income inequality has many causes and requires multiple remedies. The United States taxes less progressively and is less supportive of needs-based programs than other industrial nations. Federal policies tilted away from equalizing incomes during the 1980s just when salary gaps between semiskilled workers and technicians, managers or professionals widened. Investing in people through better health care and schooling, as well as rebuilding an infrastructure of communication and transportation, creates jobs for ordinary workers (in contrast to a demand for engineers and managers generated by military spending). Progressive taxes on high salaries reduces demand for customized or rare goods and shifts it toward common items, where labor is efficient. Similar reasoning applies to foreign trade and lending to stimulate markets in the developing world.

From society's viewpoint, production and consumption make a circular flow with each sustaining the other. To maximize output, labor and management should work together while government assures full employment. Divided roles allow irrational conditions to prevail—surplus food and hungry people, deteriorating highways and idle construction workers, empty apartment complexes and homeless people. Firms laid off staff in an attempt to increase the dollar value of output per hour of the remaining employees. Idled workers—plus those fortunate enough to find another job, usually at a lower wage—cut back their buying, further reducing demand. Reported labor productivity may rise; but the unemployed contribute nothing to national output—except, perhaps, distrust and despair. Meanwhile, powerful groups who benefit from a conservative tilt in public policies naturally resist government programs to equalize schools, health care and incomes.

In an intermediate run of three to five years, productivity depends on redirecting an adaptive labor force in response to evolving consumers' demand. For many years, economies of scale gave the advantage to fixed assembly lines coordinated through tightly coupled structures, but rigid systems are inefficient at customizing technologically advanced goods and services. Now, informational technologies can facilitate short production runs with rapid changeovers based on timely assessments of consumer needs and accurate descriptions of possible options. They achieve efficiency without bureaucratic channels or hierarchical structures to coordinate specialized work roles.

Flatter organizational structures—with reduced differences in salaries, authority, security, and prestige between chief executive officers and custodians, between men and women, and among racial and ethnic groups—ease information flows essential for innovative organizations. Positive outcomes of job security and advancement diminish adversarial relationships between managers and workers (or consumers who were cajoled into buying). Information is filtered in light of its source and often reconfirmed, thereby building trust and cooperation around long-term benefits. Boundaries among occupations and groups weaken. Specialized roles are determined through mutual delegation of responsibilities. Everyone shares their ideas relevant to production, working conditions and innovations.

## Long-run Well-being

Basic questions about what humans want or need undercut a simplistic focus on productive efficiency. If output per worker in industrial nations continued to double every 30 years for the next 150 years, absurdities would abound unless paid employment fell to about 10 hours per week. How many "things" can a person use in a lifetime? Although people who are relatively better off than their neighbors typically indicate somewhat more satisfaction with their lives, there is no evidence that Americans were six times happier in 1975 than in 1900. Despite a higher standard of material things, America's poor appear less contented than China's middle classes. Relative status matters, yet only a few can win the race for income, power and prestige. Elites' efforts to sustain a privileged position through institutional practices in schools, businesses and governments as well as cultural beliefs in individualism and materialism, significantly reduce the collective sense of well-being.

As adults develop new interests and goals or seek fresh challenges, their job descriptions should expand. Persistent attitudes based on scarcity and competition—still strong among an older generation with memories of the 1930s depression—are replaced by new ones that highlight choices about values and quality of life. In so doing, they generate controversies over lifestyles and attitudes toward learning, working and civic virtues. Collaboration during a time of social transformation will prove increasingly difficult if schools and workplaces deny some groups access to information, constrain discretionary judgment, discourage group participation, and foster cultural misunderstanding. If the goal is human well-being, then work should bring personal satisfaction and autonomy, as well as an income sufficient to obtain goods and services.

What will productive efforts look like in 2010? We envision a number of plausible contrasts with today's conditions:

- Work will involve more human faculties and skill levels as people are involved from the creation of an idea through to the use of a product or service. Physical, aesthetic and mental aptitudes combine in normal routines.

- Divisions between paid work and home or community activities diminish as hobbies or personal avocations meld with on-the-job competencies and vice versa.

- Physical spaces serve multiple purposes and encourage interactions in pleasant and healthful surroundings.

- Schedules adapt to personal desires and production deadlines rather than fixed hours and arbitrary vacation times.

- Men and women as well as racial and language groups interact in business and neighborhoods with less obvious class or status differences.

- Everyone has access to information technologies related to internal and external data.

- People will engage in a variety of tasks and interactions without intrusive external supervision or control.

What household activities may look like in 2010 is more difficult to foretell. Households as settings for married couples to raise children and to participate in community affairs are under great pressure. Middle-class families typically do not reproduce themselves—apparently reluctant to pay the approximately $500,000 (costs plus foregone earnings) to prepare their children for as comfortable a life as their own. Working-class families and single parents lack resources to send their children to four-year colleges. As workplaces allow more opportunities for learning and autonomy, domestic production seems less crucial. Childless adults employed for wages and surrounded by convenient appliances establish households with few roots in local communities and fewer shared values and loyalties. Potentially, adults will gain greater choice of lifestyles and satisfactions over their lifetime—but many will invest less in the next generation.

What we want in the long run depends a lot on how democracy functions to implement social justice. Can information build trust across a segmented population? Suppose everyone prefers a peaceful, fair and equitable world that respects individual rights, creativity, and religious or cultural diversity—as long as others hold similar beliefs. To a considerable degree, that is achievable through democratic procedures when people share many values and experiences or have established ways to communicate cultural perspectives around issues that primarily affect personal and family values and behaviors. The alternative may be stronger measures of repression to keep people in traditional families, schools, workplaces, and political systems that make less and less sense to them.

Without equal and excellent education, decent housing in a neighborhood with public amenities, and a job with opportunities to learn, a goal of efficiency leads toward social control. Teachers have difficulty motivating children whose families have experienced a 20-year decline in their living standards and who have few reasons to identify with, or participate in, school activities. When tasks are repetitive and alienating, organizations closely supervise workers. When many citizens lack a stake in a capitalist economy, governments spend more to police and protect property. Stagnant economic growth turns competitive labor markets into a zero-sum game. Misinformation, angry threats, and occasional force become the norm, and communication proliferates in a futile search for certainty.

## Productive Schools

Ideally, education should facilitate—through schools and other mediating institutions—a sense of control over one's life. Persistent and powerful beliefs that allow us to act without conscious thought should enable one to cope with psychological pressures, to interact with peers, to function in the real world, and to express one's values. People need a capacity to plan and act, as well as an awareness of their limits. Information technologies make it possible to assess diverse learning approaches and achievements so that students practice making choices on a daily basis. A growing inequality of incomes affects households and makes the equalizing functions of public schools more important than ever.

As long as students' rank ordering serves as a primary determinant of their access to limited spaces in elite colleges or jobs, schools can scarcely increase their effective output. When low-achieving students improve their relative test scores, they perforce push others into the bottom half. Schooling is structured and corrupted by the fact that scores on standardized tests measure one's likelihood of higher education and a satisfying career. Under these conditions, multicultural approaches, cooperative learning, and transdisciplinary projects incorporating varied learning and teaching styles may make schools more meritocratic—that is, less influenced by parent's income, language or race—without upsetting a normal curve of As through Fs.

As long as hierarchies of grades, income and power are presumed natural and necessary as incentives for efficiency, educators will have difficulty moving toward equity. Successful individuals have a vested interest in preserving their status and authority. Those who liked school, earned good grades, received advanced degrees, and enjoy successful careers seldom advocate radical restructuring of education. Logically, the disaffected who received low grades or left school prior to graduation have a clearer sense of what did not work for them. Moreover, heeding those who have been educationally cheated strengthens a school's claim to fairness and may augment the nation's investment in human capital. By and large, subordinate groups and disaffected individuals do not differ in their goals but are denied access to the promise of American life.

A key part of our thesis is that mass education in the United States and around the world, if combined with information technologies, enables and facilitates a recognition of individual personalities within diverse cultures—without rank ordering them in terms of their value to a singular mode of production or mode of information. Modern production and governance make it possible for everyone to achieve a rough equality in primary goods—education, meaningful work, a pleasant household, and rights to participate in decisionmaking as well as freedom from coercion. By focusing on common grounds of human well-being, secondary choices of values and lifestyles provide an interesting diversity rather than a source of distrust and discord.

Making choices a part of the intended curriculum of schools reinforces current efforts to empower teachers as professionals with autonomy and responsibility. Teachers should model activities appropriate for a knowledge economy:

- accessing the widest possible array of information with time allowed for personal research;
- determining organizational and curricular strategies and structures collectively;
- supporting collaborative activities with outside parties to improve schools; and
- exploring options among instructional modes to achieve common purposes.

Dozens of ethnographic studies, as well as our interviews, show that teachers want to participate actively in those processes when they feel supported by administrators and public opinion.

In White, middle-class suburbs, schools face a tremendous task to foster cultural understanding of outsiders whose lifestyles are cramped by poverty and discrimination. As publicly supported witnesses, teachers can scarcely ignore the socially constructed boundaries that separate and order their students' prospects. Only if teaching liberates from oppressive cultural patterns can everyone join as a stakeholder in determining what each seeks to achieve and in what kind of society. In today's world, it will take time and commitment to communicate across disciplinary and cultural boundaries, to grasp some of their taken-for-granted assumptions, and to reflect on knowledge as socially constructed, historically contingent, and politically situated. It will take longer to build a democratic society, where schools are for everyone's hopes—not for one's self alone but for one's community, one's nation and the world.

## RECONSTRUCTING KNOWLEDGE

Low-cost transmittal of information opens unimagined possibilities for dialog so that people can establish identity and cooperate productively. Electronic databases facilitate comparing prices, obtaining facts, sending messages, or publishing one's views. Problems of verification are minimized in part because open systems allow others to check quickly and in part because interactive communities can effectively isolate those who intentionally mislead. Authors can publish in niche markets without sacrificing quality or production values. When significant information is perceived as an outcome of collaborative interactions, specific contexts allow a different kind of accuracy and relevancy than was possible for mass markets. Efficiency in an information age follows from trusting others not to lie, confuse or ego-trip.

In an interdependent global society, competition and military domination by industrialized nations are increasingly dysfunctional. During the 1980s, U.S. weapons manufacturers would have constituted the 13th largest economy in the world. In 1990, the United States spent over $300 billion a year for defense—about $2,000 per person, or $5,000 for every student enrolled from nursery school through doctoral programs. The federal research budget included $41 billion for military purposes, compared with $28 billion for health, energy, science, transportation, agriculture, space ecology, and so on. Little wonder that scientists and engineers investigate military applications or that educators link test scores to international competition when they lobby for increased funding.

Moreover, when knowledge is directly linked to power, elites may seek to curtail its dissemination. Science itself becomes a weapon that governments and large corporations use against each other, not to benefit humanity. Experts assert authority and demand secrecy because of perceived enemies abroad and within. State secrets required for military purposes justify limitations on trading items such as scarce metals or advanced computers; regulations restrict exchanges of research within universities; security clearances privilege mainstream ideas and an unreflective patriotism. Research and development of destructive weapons divert physics, chemistry and biology away from ecological considerations in developing nations. Educational resources focus on training workers.

For modern societies where knowledge is necessarily widely distributed and communication low cost, "democratic" governance is a practical necessity to encourage engagement, sharing, and nondestructive embedded meanings. As Representative David Obey (1986, p. 13) asserted, "inequality undermines the social consensus which is an essential prerequisite to growth." Democracy, nearly universal literacy, mass media, and worldwide industrialization increase our interdependence and the importance of mutual respect and trust. What is called for is not technical or professional advice but statements that build relationships and consensus by acknowledging historical developments and social structures that incorporated class, race and gender discrimination.

## Information and Trust

Given socially constructed realities, truth may be personal or widely shared by a group, yet regarded as a falsehood by others. For example, African Americans never understood the Declaration of Independence assertion that "all men are created equal and endowed by their creator with inalienable rights to life, liberty and the pursuit of happiness" in the same "self-evident" fashion as most European Americans. Feminists and many others no longer excuse sexual harassment or assault with a comment that "boys will be boys." Those who have experienced discrimination based on race or sex seldom view equality of opportunity in schools or society in the same unproblematic way as White males.

When trust in community values breaks down, exchanging information is uncertain and costly. Consider the following illustrations. Doctors believe as many as 30% of their patients ignore prescriptions or warnings about mixing them with alcohol or other drugs. Stores add up to 30% to their prices to cover losses because of theft, carelessness, or returns. Shoppers waste much time and money because sales personnel fail to offer accurate, timely and comprehensive descriptions of goods and services. People avoid the streets at night out of fear of criminals or angry people who may be influenced by alcohol or a gang psychology Frustrated by inattention and carelessness among otherwise able students, teachers focus on classroom control rather than on making useful knowledge accessible to others.

Many services entail a transfer of expertise. When we reasonably suspect the accuracy of communication, we "inefficiently" pay less attention, seek additional sources for confirmation or contradiction, and perpetuate adversarial relationships, even among the helping professions. What happens to a consumer's sense of security when General Motors, Dow Corning, and tobacco companies reveal—albeit reluctantly, when under oath—that they knew their products posed a danger while publicly proclaiming their safety? What happens to public trust when government officials blatantly mislead Congress about their actions and knowledge? Much of today's inefficiency is not a missing technique or knowledge on the part of the provider that can be remedied by higher academic standards for salespeople, officials or teachers. Confidence in the relevance and accuracy of media and experts has to be continually rebuilt through explanations that carry generally the same message to all audiences.

Seeking public support, scientists and engineers have depicted technology as a black box that yields startling results. For example, computer whizzes love to demonstrate flashy outcomes without addressing the costs of software or how students make sense of those activities. In general, experts exaggerate the importance of their empirically verified truths. Instead, people rely on "common sense, casual empiricism, or thoughtful speculation and analysis" (Lindblom &

Cohen, 1979, pp. 12, 16). Skill, craft and ordinary knowledge are acquired through one's experiences and exist as heterogeneous mixtures, unlike structured academic knowledge. In assessing the importance of organized research to social problems, Lindblom and Cohen described it as "tiny compared with the stock of propositions commonly employed in social problem solving," and empirical investigations add a "trickle" to the flow of new information.

Social science seems most amazing if its conclusions are counterintuitive. A relevant illustration may clarify the point: Is honesty the best policy? If everyone always expresses the truth or so close to it so that people trust others' words, any liar has an extraordinary advantage. On the other hand, a practice of usually telling the truth allows communication to proceed while alerting everyone to possibilities of lies. That logical explanation for an observed pattern of social interactions, however, fails to account for when and why people lie. After all, random misstatements could sustain vigilance against dubious propositions. A game theory "explanation" of the value of occasional lying may reduce a moralistic overtone of a commonsense preference for honesty, but it offers little guidance for how to act or what public policies should prevail.

Within a setting, people apply rules of thumb to assess how much to trust others. People ordinarily discount self-praise and self-exculpation, as well as persuasion where self-interests are at stake. A 1993 poll revealed that 60% of the public did not believe advertisers! How do youth find reliable advice about growing up today? Increasing numbers of adolescents receive little guidance from the institutional structures that supported their parents' transition from childhood to adulthood. Many parents feel uncertain about what advice to offer the young and lack resources to pay for four years of college. Too often, schools, churches, and health and human service agencies fail to address issues of identity, sexuality, relationships, and responsible choices in terms that match experiences on television, news reports, or observable adult behaviors. Facing the irrelevance of key institutions, adolescents turn to MTV, movies and peers to learn how other youth make sense of their uncertain futures.

Information that segments can also foster cooperation. For instance, many urban educators are reluctant to cite White racism as a constraint on students' prospects. They seldom address patterns of racial isolation among and within districts, the scarcity of elected officials living in poor neighborhoods, or Eurocentric biases in texts and tests. Instead, they blame inadequate funding, weak leaders, indifferent parents, and unmotivated students. After analyzing prisoners' dilemmas and ethnographic reports on endemic dilemmas of teaching, they begin to view themselves, their students and the community as hobbled by institutional forces and longstanding oppressions. In some cases, that recognition leads to a critical stance toward traditional curriculum; in others, toward an aggressively multicultural or Afrocentric approach.

Americans have much to learn from oppressed groups who practice a less destructive lifestyle or who keenly recognize the cost of war. Presumptions about the rightness of European American domination of income and status shape reactions to migration flows around the world. Although officials welcome newcomers as evidence of the United States' attractions, immigrant children from Africa, Asia and Latin America often are described as burdens to schools and society (although most studies show an overall benefit to the economy and community). Students from abroad who can pay tuition are accepted by U.S. colleges and universities with a hope that they will carry modern ideas and values back to their homelands. These responses conflict with the realities of international marketplaces for labor, goods, services, and ideas.

Not all communication effectively builds trust and agreement. Debaters, for instance, sharpen distinctions and seek to persuade through selective evidence and rhetorical devices. Advertisers use associations with sexual allure and power to sell their products. Politicians advocate popular notions without much concern for their feasibility. Scientists and teachers claim special authority for their views. For dialog to rebuild trust in shared cognitive frameworks, it should start with personal beliefs, explicate differences rather than concealing them, and seek common ground through questions and specifying underlying assumptions.

## Coordination without Control

In an information age, public discussion has another crucial role—as a means of arriving at consensus about social justice. This thesis can be stated in industrial-era terms of material well-being. Productivity requires coordination to apply specialized knowledge of artificially structured work roles and academic disciplines. That coordination through a system of competitive markets and hierarchical organizations functions less and less well in an affluent economy for two major reasons: First, educated workers both need and desire autonomy on the job, and second, segmented experts in a technologically advanced economy (especially with mass media) raise the likelihood of misinformation and mistrust across many transactions. Perhaps most salient has been a breakdown in implicit contracts in labor markets as seniority no long assures lifetime employment with health care and a pension.

Information technologies offer possible solutions for those miscommunications. Access to redundant data, which is already common for computer-controlled production and distribution systems, makes it possible to coordinate many activities within organizations without top-down control. In fact, knowledge producers scarcely can be supervised through traditional management techniques. Working together without bosses, however, requires agreements on organizational goals and practices. Thus, dialog—or open access to information as an alternative means to coordinate specialized roles and share segmented knowledge—is substantially strengthened by greater equality of roles and rewards within productive organizations.

> **Despite disagreements over priorities and strategies, most Americans want physical and mental health, individual autonomy and responsibility, a safe environment, a decent income and a safety net against the vicissitudes of industrial fluctuations, an education that includes literacy and technological competencies, world peace, use of personal property (that does not harm others), a right to vote, and freedom of expression.**
>
> **In two columns, list individual and collective strategies for achieving these goals. For instance, physical health may benefit from joining a health club or from public policies to clean the air and maintain parks.**

Management or decisionmaking within firms is only a part of today's lack of cooperation. The industrial era depended on mutual equivalence structures to achieve a great deal of coordination. As a major example, producers relied on consumers who depended on producers— mainly without contracts or even contacts. Capitalists built great factories, invested in machines and materials, and hired workers, all with an expectation that people would buy their output. Likewise, youth in school anticipated finding a job and a decent community in which to live. Prior to 1973, growth allowed those expectations to be fulfilled for most people. Today, global competition and rapid shifts in products and occupations generate uncertainties. Not even the largest information system can foresee future demands, and the resulting risks (together with economies of scale and external effects) make collective action desirable. That raises dilemmas of democracy and problems of government coercion.

Finally, many factors limiting American well-being today do not relate to technological capacities to produce goods or achieve coordination within and between mutual equivalence structures as they have historically developed. To promote general health, security and well-being requires national and international dialog to identify external costs (or benefits) and to devise ways to share costs for remedies. Competition will not conserve resources or preserve the environment. Prices for electricity in Ohio do not compensate for acid rain in Maine, and traditional market relationships offer no means to make that connection. Issues of personal health and safety (including security for one's property) are increasingly tied up in unknown or unpublicized health hazards from technological developments or unlawful behaviors flowing from social inequalities.

Many youth see little choice for themselves in industrial-era opportunity structures. For more than one in four, unhealthy lifestyles stem from low self-esteem along with lack of hope for themselves or their families. Social commentator Fred M. Hechinger (1992, pp. 24–25, 128, 121) graphically described the grim prospects of today's youth as "unemployment, poverty, and disintegrating families and communities. A significant number drop out of school, engage in violence or other criminal acts, become pregnant, suffer mental disorders, abuse drugs and/or alcohol, attempt suicide, are disabled by injuries, or die." Schools and other agencies must teach decisionmaking: "stop and think; get information; assess the information, always consider the consequences; weigh old options, or seek out new ones; get feedback from persons whose judgment and integrity can be trusted." Effective responses depend on "fostering pride, confidence, and genuine hope for the future."

Rather than focusing on signs of dysfunction, we also should look at the positive potential. All children deserve a hope factor for meaningful participation in families, schools and workplaces. Updating an African proverb, today it takes many communities to raise children. As Hechinger (1992, pp. 211, 213) noted, "all institutions serving young adolescents—family, neighborhood, school, community, youth organizations, churches and synagogues, news and entertainment media, and, of course, the private and public health services—must strive to provide trustworthy role models." Health care providers need to establish rapport with youth whose neighborhoods offer little support for healthy lifestyle choices. In urban settings, "safe areas must be cleared, not only of weapons, but also of the sale and use of drugs" while educators "must teach young people the skills and benefits of conflict resolution without the use of force."

Segmentation, isolation, alienation, and social inequities also add to the costs of violence and other crime—including efforts to protect persons and property, psychological feelings of security, the justice system, and incarceration. A thoughtful analysis of crime pointed to differences between the United States and other industrial nations with much lower crime rates: "These include a wider spread of inequality, greater extremes of poverty and insecurity, the relative absence of effective policies to deal with unemployment and subemployment, greater disruption of community and family ties through job destruction and migration, and fewer supports for families and individuals in the face of economic and technological change and material deprivation" (Currie, 1985, pp. 224–225). Inequities may not cause crime, but they provide a favorable climate for its growth and reveal hidden costs of a noncooperative, hostile society.

Major social issues of education, health care, crime, and environmental degradation can be solved through cooperative, public actions.
As long as those who are comfortable blame the victims for their ill
health, poor education, crime, violence, and other antisocial behaviors,
however, little will be done to change institutional patterns that
structure opportunities for youth and adults. Without economic growth,
few legislative majorities will coalesce because programs that help the
poor take something away from the well-to-do. Dissension and
divisions, in turn, make it harder to sustain current standards of living.
Multiple dialogs about a fair and good society build consensus by
including those who were educationally cheated, discriminated against
in labor markets, or denied equal protection of the laws.

## DEMOCRATIC CONSENSUS

Democracy requires procedures to sustain both diversity of opinion
and enough agreement for majorities to support collective actions that
institutionalize a framework of justice. For 200 years after the Constitution, social justice was defined in terms of civil rights for White males
and laissez faire capitalism to encourage economic growth. The greatest
good for the greatest number in a utilitarian framework was interpreted primarily in material terms and effectively relegated distributional issues to a secondary concern. In the 20th century, the United
States developed a welfare and military state in response to economic
interdependence, industrial fluctuations, and international disorders
that made equity or a fair distribution of resources central to public
policies.

A powerful government raises multiple issues in liberal democratic
theory and practice, giving a sharp bite to Rawls's (1993, p. 4) question
in political ethics: "how is it possible for there to exist over time a just
and stable society of free and equal citizens who remain profoundly
divided by reasonable religious, philosophical, and moral doctrines?"
Public policies toward education, health, conservation, criminal justice,
and income security shape each person's opportunities. Ordinarily,
those policies intrude into other ethical values. For instance, religious
beliefs clash with vaccination requirements, loyalty oaths, holiday
rituals, and sex education. Individual freedom is an important value,
but there remain questions about license becoming licentiousness,
liberty encouraging libertines, tolerance permitting intolerant groups,
and oppressed groups replacing their oppressors.

Equality and diversity often appear at odds. Rawls (1993, p. 6)
argued that a rational decision about political justice in modern societies requires three key features: "first, a specification of certain basic
rights, liberties, and opportunities (of a kind familiar from constitutional democratic regimes); second, an assignment of special priority
to those rights, liberties, and opportunities, especially with respect to

claims of the general good and of perfectionist values; and third, measures assuring to all citizens adequate all-purpose means to make effective use of their liberties and opportunities." We described those "all-purpose means" in terms of three thresholds of equal education, decent housing in a safe neighborhood, and work with advancement possibilities.

Political justice entails a continual questioning about what rights are primary or fundamental. The process of arriving at a minimum set of consistent and usable principles requires thoughtful attention to counterarguments in order to agree on what spheres should be equal and where diversity may flourish. By analogy, that process resembles a decision to standardize some items such as voltage and plug sizes in order to encourage a multiplicity of electrical appliances. Educators debate whether schools should standardize instruction with variations in scores or equalize achievements with diverse instructional inputs. We urge Americans to define equity for learning processes and adult capacities for work and citizenship while respecting everyone's personal and cultural experiences.

## Discourse and Power

A people's sense of what needs to be more (or less) equal evolves over time. What causes any particular conception of fairness to take hold? One answer is power—certain individuals or groups impose their conceptions on a larger collectivity. Yet, as political scientist Bruce Ackerman (1980, p. 4) observed: "power corrupts: the more power I have, the more I can lose by trying to answer the question of legitimacy; the more power I have, the greater the chance that my effort at suppression will succeed—at least for the time that remains before I die." He wondered, "what would our social world look like if no one ever suppressed another's question of legitimacy, where every questioner met with a conscientious attempt at an answer?"

A liberal democratic discourse requires a few major principles:

*Rationality*: Whenever anybody questions the legitimacy of an-other's power, the power holder must respond not by suppressing the questioner, but by giving a reason that explains why he is more entitled to the resource than the questioner is. . . .

*Consistency*. The reason advanced by a power wielder on one occa-sion must not be inconsistent with the reasons he advances to justify his other claims to power. . . .

*Neutrality*. No reason is a good reason if it requires the power holder to assert:

    (a) that his conception of the good is better than that asserted by any of his fellow citizens, or

(b) that, regardless of his conception of the good, he is intrinsically superior to one or more of his fellow citizens. (Ackerman, 1980, pp. 4, 7, 11)

These guidelines pass a simple Kantian test, that is, if everyone followed these norms, the outcome appears desirable, feasible and fair.

Based on sample dialogs, Ackerman demonstrated that his broad rules lead to a general equality of rights and condition among all citizens. Any claim to more than an equal share violates a consistent neutrality. As developing adults, children are both subject to greater control and treated as having a future right to ask their own questions. Specifically, adults must answer why the order of birth should determine a lesser holding of rights and things. Unable to justify that difference, each generation has a duty to conserve resources and to provide schools that offer an equivalent level of competence for the next generation. "Citizenship is not a sudden acquisition, grasped through the (metaphorical) signing of a social compact, but the product of a long and painful process by which we master conflict in the name of a common political culture" (Ackerman, 1980, p. 164).

This defense of reasoned dialog carries on a substantive tradition of Western liberal thought. It assumes that in addition to learning for utilitarian reasons, humans seek knowledge to build a sense of identity, to sustain self-esteem, and to establish consistency among beliefs. It assumes that the alternative to physical force is equal rights, that responsible autonomy is possible, and that acquired traits are more significant than ascribed ones. Given multiple personal satisfactions, everyone can succeed at things that foster personal self-worth without generating irreconcilable conflicts. Paraphrasing Isaiah Berlin: If being human is to act with purpose in light of one's chosen values, then nothing is worse than to treat others as though they lacked autonomy. To define others by one attribute, thereby denying other's a right to author their own values, is to deny their humanity, or, as Kant asserted, "paternalism . . . is an insult to my conception of myself as a human being" (see Gardels, 1991).

To a considerable extent, economic growth in Europe and the United States coincided with political liberalism—expressed in nation-states that developed constitutional democracies. Stable governmental institutions protected property rights and personal liberties (especially for the middle classes). In allowing individuals to develop their own identity and potential, society elevated the importance of education as well as a tolerance for different beliefs. A vision of responsible individualism and civic participation took hold during a period when literate yeoman farmers of European descent had positive hopes for democratic futures. That promise of America later included African Americans and women, protected workers against industrial fluctuations and poverty, and supported public education from nursery schools through doctoral programs.

New choices require mobilizing support for equitable policies and programs to serve a common good, which requires more dialog, not less. That educative function reasonably starts with voices from oppressed groups, who articulate alternative visions. Democratic workplaces in corporations and agencies encourage both employees and customers or clients to voice their concerns. Active citizens express their desires about possible candidates and policy choices, not just those offered through existing parties. That discourse should start in schools and predictably will enhance their public support faster than any accountability measures.

## Planning through Social Mobilization

Social and policy sciences lack reliable theories for predicting and thus for planning futures. During normal times, innovations occur step by step, with many small experiments and the gradual introduction of marginal improvements. However, isolated organizational or behavioral patterns may not foreshadow what would happen if changes were comprehensive and viewed as long-lasting. In most schools, hardworking teachers carry the burden of curriculum committees, extracurricular advising, and informal counseling of students—until they burn out. In effective schools, staff and students work together with high standards and expectations, despite organizational dilemmas that tempt some to become free riders. Because those educators take a perverse pride in being exceptions, efforts to mandate their successful behaviors for others are doomed—unless school cultures change.

Moreover, efforts to implement fairness within a subset of a society raises unexpected costs because of predictable organizational dynamics. School districts that have a reputation for meeting the needs of physically challenged students experience an increase in enrollment as parents seek what is best for children with handicaps. States that provide a decent level of welfare payments for dependent children may attract families in need. A company that encourages participation in decisionmaking and staff training within a salary framework that differentiates less between entry level positions and managers may lose its best workers to a competing firm that values their advanced initiative and skills. In all these cases, a simultaneous shift of general behaviors would avoid contradictory pressures from those who are denied justice in other settings.

Social learning draws from more traditional expert advice and from organizational programs to encourage human development but emphasizes loosening structures and encouraging a variety of charismatic voices. Prophets and carnival barkers inspire exploration, whereas a canon of traditional knowledge and technologically oriented experts reinforce old ways of thinking. Consciousness-raising experiences, liberation movements and utopian communities hold relevance for teachers who wish to encourage voice among previously silenced persons and groups. Perhaps the real democratic challenge is not to hammer out narrow majorities in representative legislatures but to establish a comprehensive framework of social justice within which multiple realities can enrich each other.

Dialog without some basis for agreement often increases feelings of separateness and hostility. An individualistic and diverse people, Americans sought a basis for consensus in a democratic ideology. Yet that political philosophy itself rested on personal independence and self-reliance. When mixed with capitalist competition, it served to conceal structural hierarchies behind myths about equal opportunities and the "self-made man." Based on extensive interviewing, Bellah and his coauthors (1985, p. 282) reported that competitive markets supported individualism (particularly in opposition to groups or governments), while Americans found community in traditional belief systems: Biblical and republican traditions "help us to know that it does make a difference who we are and how we treat one another." Despite earnest and attractive pleas for a renewed sense of community, however, there is little evidence that schools or society can build on those traditions.

Planning by experts has become problematic because formerly agreed-on beliefs are now questioned. John Friedmann (1987, p. 10) noted signs that "the system of industrial capitalism is so deeply mired in crisis that it may never fully recover." National governments appear weaker than huge corporations, unable to protect the environment when global firms move operations to impoverished nations with cheap labor and lax environmental standards. Moreover, international debts and continued cold war rivalries block cooperation among nations to resolve those issues. "Because it is invariably integrated into the state apparatus, planning for societal guidance is incapable of coping with the crisis of industrial capitalism." There is a renewed interest in "collective self-reliance in development and the recovery of political community."

Friedmann (1987, pp. 81, 348) identified social learning as a promising approach to planning: "Knowledge, in this view, emerges from an ongoing dialectical process in which the main emphasis is on new practical undertakings: existing understanding (theory) is enriched with lessons drawn from experience, and the 'new' understanding is then applied in the continuing process of action and change." In small political units, continuous dialog is feasible and likely to reach accord if built around certain principles:

In the final analysis, it is our instinct for collective survival that leads us to assert as our central guiding vision the recovery of political community from domination by the state and capital. As present contradictions mount, and as the crisis grows more severe, unprecedented opportunities present themselves for a broadly based social movement with inclusive aims.

- To equalize, through continuing struggle, people's access, both individually and collectively, to the bases of effective social power, among them, the time and space, knowledge and skills, social and political organization, instruments and tools of production, information, social networks, and financial resources that are needed for the collective self-production of life.

Altruistic teachers and charismatic leaders demonstrate new patterns for interactions, but they need to be encouraged by a sense of larger personal and social purposes and a rapid transition toward schools that emphasize equity of outcome over efficiency measured by achievement scores. Economic self-interests within an industrial framework lead to maximizing behaviors that resemble prisoner's dilemmas; local efforts to build open communication and trust, caring, cooperation, and collaboration simply enhance the short-term rewards for defection, lying or deceptive negotiations. As Jon Elster (1989, pp. 170–171) concluded, "the only thing that could motivate to suffer the transition costs would be perceiving the reform to be a matter of basic justice, not economic efficiency." Effective norms of social justice must pervade institutions and society.

## WHAT'S NEXT?

Postmodernism is marked by uneasy doubts about human progress, the singularity of truth, and the likelihood for compromise among conflicting interests. The affective domain—personal interactions involving emotional and volitional responses—are awkwardly handled in most classrooms. Critical theorists see contradictions and omissions in everyday explanations that support powerful institutions, and so they pay special attention to oppressed groups. They "read" meanings at several levels, emphasizing contingent conditions and intentions. By framing viewpoints in a context of historical development and social situations, they avoid the reductionism of linear cause and effect, although at a cost of diminished predictability.

We live in a complex world, and motivations or desires reflect people's personal experiences that are shaped by past and present social structures. Without claiming completeness of the list or the order of importance, we venture some plausible generalizations about the future:

- Material production is less important among those who have enjoyed abundance, growth and security—namely, most Americans and Europeans in the last half of the 20th century.

- Low-cost information and global communication make everyone aware of multiple perspectives and crucial inequalities within and among countries.

- Although affluent persons and nations care less about increasing wealth than their neighbors, they fear falling behind and feel threatened by others catching up through education, immigration or economic development.

- Agreements to cooperate are easier when contacts are repeated among parties who are alike in many ways. Those conditions were eroded by industrialism, although that perspective is potentially restored by a growing awareness of interdependence on a small planet.

- A sense of justice in a democracy depends on agreements about which aspects of life should be equalized, but technologically advanced economies require minimal thresholds of education, health and income for individuals to take advantage of opportunities and rights. Extending entitlements to basic economic equality challenges longstanding assumptions about individual motivations and justice embodied in antigovernment beliefs and utilitarian principles related to the greatest good for the greatest number.

- A transformation in ground rules of justice cannot really be explored or tested out in advance, but schools are a good place to start crossing cultural and disciplinary boundaries, fostering dialog about diversity and fairness, and equalizing achievements to support self-esteem. Schools are large, lasting, self-contained, and public institutions that directly affect future societies. They offer a reasonable place to test whether cooperation can flow from a communication of common interests rather than coordination of specialized roles through hierarchical command structures.

Given a history of class hierarchies, White racism, and patriarchal domination that are now embedded in institutional practices from families to legal rights, can ordinary Americans opt to be unselfish, empathetic, altruistic, sharing, peaceable, cooperative, and vulnerable? Current accumulations of knowledge offer powerful incentives to sustain established patterns. Innovations are risky for individuals and society. In the abstract, choices include all possible outputs in any imaginable social structure; in practice, options are constrained by history, organizational formats, governance practices, and received knowledge. Over long periods of time, choices are broader than usually imagined—especially when groups act together. Nevertheless, it matters a great deal what path we take to get from the present to any future situation.

Astute commentators working within mainstream traditions urge the creation of intermediate political communities such as worker participation in productive organizations as a way to restore a sense of personal efficacy. For example, Bell (1987), Lindblom (1990) and others propose a messy federalism covering major aspects of human life. Each group would assure rights to participate in decisionmaking appropriate for that level of endeavor. Large, powerful units would set broad contexts within which other organizations and individuals might function efficiently yet fairly. Presumably, reconstruction starts with family or household units, spreads to small groups who experience the benefits of working together, and then expands to democratic processes in communities and nations. Caring and concern about other people can rebuild consensus to guide policy decisions about public schools, economic justice, and political rights.

That vision is positive, forward looking, and generally feasible as a point of direction. It suggests that working together toward common goals is natural and fulfills personal and community interests. Among many middle-class adults and youth, sharing seems plausible. They believe they have something (mainly information) to offer the poor and working classes as well as something to gain from elites, who presumably would share their power with technicians, professionals and managers. A less divided electorate might agree on policies to preserve the environment, to overcome White racism and patriarchy, and to promote healthier lives—all within stable, peaceful and diverse communities. It suggests democratic reforms in the spirit of Progressivism, the New Deal, and the Great Society but not a transformation.

## Multiple Communities

Overlapping learning communities establish ways for sharing ideas across contested terrain, although it requires many stages of interpretation for a physicist to communicate with inner city youth. Knowledge clusters from plumbers to poets enable society as a whole to transmit expertise within groups and across disciplines and occupations. Each student needs to know something well in order to discover wonderful ideas about new concerns. For example, the experience of caring for an elderly relative may transfer into career skills or pride in the obstacles overcome by one's family. Once comfortable in several domains, teachers and students can scan across many data sources. Ideas and facts can be rearranged to guide activities or to gain fresh insights, rather like a kaleidoscope.

Teaching or sharing ideas is a good news–bad news kind of story. In phenomenological terms, people are locked into personal understandings that are incompletely conveyed to others. No matter how intimately others share their feelings and frameworks, we interpret them within established categories and cultural boundaries, accumulating "evidence" and "rational explanations" to support well-worn ways of making sense of phenomena. Consequently, people communicate efficiently in familiar surroundings where others attach similar meanings to common events and act in recognizable roles. For instance, when students behave like uninhibited youths and principals act like responsible supervisors, typical dynamics emerge despite differences in their interpretive frameworks. Such interactions, however, raise few puzzling juxtapositions that can transform insights.

If one wants certainty—objective "truth" to define proper actions and to clarify important knowledge—then phenomenological understandings are bad news. If one wants to engage with others in socially constructing a different future and in redefining freedom and equality to suit emerging possibilities, then the plasticity of socially shared cognition is essentially good news. It offers hope that unequal power and force—despite their prominence in recorded history—might give way to caring and cooperating as prevailing patterns in human interactions. After all, history offers many examples of love and altruism and justice along with war, disease, famine, and hatred. It suggests that new purposes lead quite pragmatically to restructuring knowledge to support new goals.

How do the multiple realities of postmodern life affect learning and teaching?

- It shifts awareness among educators away from what knowledge should be transmitted to the next generation toward what meanings are being made while reading, writing, computing, or discussing social relations and personal values. Students find diverse problems relevant in light of their experiences.
- Questions and answers are considered together, linked by a framework or paradigm for determining usable knowledge. Rather than focusing on a canon represented by standardized tests used to rank order classes, teachers and students explicitly discuss connections to desirable futures for individuals and communities.
- Engaged students develop a capacity to act with purpose in light of their personal goals and social situations.
- Principles of justice—appropriate to the age of students—serve as landmarks for orienting personal decisions.

Current debates over schooling remain focused on a goal of increasing material things when the question needs to be asked: What comes after abundance? We suggest an answer lies in fairness or social justice—defining minimum standards for major spheres of life. Low-cost access to information facilitates an awareness of the multiple realities of our postmodern age. Schools have taken many steps toward that end: cooperative learning, multicultural curricula, transdisciplinary discourse informed by values and critical thinking, site-based management, interorganizational arrangements that foster collaboration across cultural boundaries, and flexible structures that facilitate recurring education. A self-consciousness about how meanings are constructed may induce explicit attention to feasible futures and the contribution of schooling to those ends.

> **An argument in favor of conscious attention to multiple realities, as well as to multiculturalism, recalls reasons for preserving plant and animal species. Just as a fungus may have special properties for combating undiscovered viruses, unconventional ideas or frameworks for making sense of experiences may provide answers to tomorrow's "problems."**
>
> **How many different cultural groups can you identify among your friends, classmates, or neighbors? Recall instances where the juxtaposition of diverse viewpoints led to new insights or a change in your behavior.**

Interdependence prevails so that each person's options largely depend on what others think and do, thereby multiplying complexity and uncertainty. Economies of scale and external effects grow in importance. Institutional arrangements and dominant cultural values affect everyone's ability to express a satisfying identity. All this raises important questions: Can human minds attend to relevant inputs in a complex, interconnected, information-rich world while purposefully acting within local settings? Can democratic discourse arrive at common standards and norms of justice that allow diversity and preserve essential equalities without compulsion?

If the answers are no, then societies are subject to whim, to manipulation by elites, or to a "tyranny" of majority opinion. Working together under those conditions threatens disaster or careening from one extreme to another. Defensive learning and behaviors will prevail, rather like an audience remaining standing because those with front row seats will not sit down. If the answers are yes or probably, then liberating students and teachers from patterns of control and docility requires dialog about dominant and subordinate realities. That discourse has to move from awareness of difference to some consensus about an equitable society. Yet change is risky, especially for those who benefit least from current conditions because their margin for error is slenderest.

### Every Futurist an Educator

Everyone who teaches witnesses the excitement as students discover new ways to make sense of events and explorations that expand their repertoires. In our interviews, educators recalled personal and organizational experiences that gave them hope for improvements in schools and society. They had participated in caring, cooperative groups— family, athletic team, theater troupe, or on the job. Most people are motivated by feelings of common humanity—for example, in responding to pictures of hunger in Africa or devastation from natural disasters. As persistent, pervasive and powerful as White racism has been in the United States, millions of Whites as well as Blacks have resisted and fought for an inclusive multicultural respect. Values of social justice shape public discourse about taxes and welfare, even when private interests often win.

Public education has many successes and has helped sustain democratic values. Teacher preparation programs that start from consistently constructivist principles present innovations such as multiculturalism, whole language approaches, or computer literacy as ways to open discussion, not as technical applications for classrooms. When promising ideas are implemented as step-by-step recipes, then a practice of viewing technological solutions as a black box forestalls reflection about purposes. A self-consciousness about why one wants to teach and one's expectations for students helps activate dialectical reflections around their constructed beliefs and experiences. Those discussions should extend through student teaching and an induction period that continuously strives to connect learning to future societies.

Institutions of higher education that prepare teachers should expand discourse about their purposes and values. Faculty, staff and students need to demonstrate their capacity to establish personal relationships across class, race and gender boundaries. Courses should incorporate multicultural experiences that acknowledge oppression of many minorities and women as well as the privileged position of majorities and White males. Faculty can place natural and social sciences in historical and social frameworks so that students' knowledge is continuously reconstructed in their classrooms. Ideally, prospective teachers learn a vocabulary connecting positive self-identities to career goals with an awareness of organizational and political possiblities and constraints. Implicitly, that discourse relates to social ethics and the responsibility of persons and institutions for fostering justice.

For schools, the key lies in placing the needs of children front and center. A hope of getting ahead in a hierarchical society defined by material possession no longer motivates most students. The already affluent seek to actualize their values, while oppressed groups see little hope for themselves in a stagnant economy. Dialog around the nature of schools, personal aspirations, and institutional options is a place to start reconstructing new goals. Indeed, students, parents and teachers would welcome that discussion if it broke through the boundaries raised by class, race and gender as well as academic disciplines and occupational preoccupations. By addressing issues of personal and social identity, students and teachers may rediscover sufficient motivation for learning skills and competencies for an information age. By using information technologies, teachers and students may engage in mentor-apprentice relationships with everyone serving as a instructor while learning through intentional activities.

Perhaps, the symbolic role model for an age of information is not a powerful and errorless computer but a colleague who builds confidence by trusting others, by sharing in mistakes and learning from them, by acknowledging multiple realities, and by searching for common ground. It is the family member, friend, coworker, salesperson, professional, technician, manager, and policymaker who makes relevant knowledge accessible to others. Trust, fostered through dialog grounded in working together around shared processes or goals, both simplifies and enriches communication by allowing people to cooperate rather than compete. In order to keep pace with new goals and techniques, learning communities flourish in factories and agencies as well as in effective schools. By utilizing smart machines, people have time to build on knowledge within its social context that can be shared within and among groups to foster understanding, generosity and inspiration.

A plea for dialog evokes worthwhile tentative goals, but it will probably fail if its advocates unthinkingly presume that everyone "buys into" a middle-class mindset, that local communities can actualize cooperation and altruism without coercion, or that elites (including many who seek wealth and power) will give up their status, even if their well-being would improve as a result of sharing it with others. Prospects for subordinate groups are yet more daunting. They need adequate income for material needs and knowledge useful in a middle-class, affluent society. Over time, they have learned to distrust the promises of schools, welfare offices, legal systems, and businesses. Despair and anger discourage investment in technical skills as well as learning to accommodate to, or to assimilate within, a dominant culture that rejects them and excludes their realities.

Clearly everyone would be better off working together to envision a world in which reading, writing, computing, understanding how things work, thinking critically, appreciating aesthetics, and creating new art and science bring personal satisfactions in a more cooperative context. Human motivation is more than individualistic, self-interested, rational, pragmatic, and striving toward some goal. Sense-making interactions yield frameworks to account for a puzzling and difficult environment by incorporating empathy and other values. The question is how to shape patterns of social interactions so that cooperation and equality in teaching and learning gain ground on selfish individualism;

class, race and gender boundaries; mistrust based on zero-sum negotiations or prisoner's dilemmas; and fear based on threats as well as the use of force.

Two centuries of democratic experience have shown the power of discourse and the stability of equal rights. Industrialization has provided many of us with wealth and knowledge to seek more than material abundance. Our challenge is to explore fresh possibilities for a more humane, secure, and viable life on this planet. The transition will be difficult at best because force can be used to maintain injustice as well as justice; words can misinform and confuse as well as enlighten and liberate; loyalties can divide as well as unite. Yet the framework we have been building in this book offers a mission for American education that is achievable and necessary. It struggles to reconcile the contradictions of modern thought and to welcome, rather than resist, the strengths of postmodern understandings of the human dilemma. It does not prescribe a technique but seeks to validate a process of learning and living together.

A new way of thinking is not a prescription but an outcome of purposeful discourse. By exploring visions of a better future society, teachers and citizens will discover new meanings for equity, efficiency and choice that incorporate caring, concern, connection, commitment, cooperation, collaboration, and community. Those virtues are more commonly found today among the dispossessed and oppressed than among privileged elites. Fortunately, they are a majority. With greater communication and information, they may learn to work together to control democratic institutions. Only in learning communities will trust, engagement, and responsibility to self and others find institutional support. With every teacher a futurist and every futurist an educator, that is a possible reality.

**RELATED READING**

As the 20th century draws to an end, a flood of articles and books will interpret the past as a guide to the future. For examples, see O. B. Hardison, Jr., *Disappearing through the Skylight: Culture and Technology in the Twentieth Century* (New York: Viking, 1989); Paul Kennedy, *Preparing for the Twenty-first Century* (New York: Random House, 1993); Ray Marshall and Marc Tucker, *Thinking for a Living: Education and the Wealth of Nations* (New York: Basic Books, 1992); and Alvin Toffler, *Powershift: Knowledge, Wealth, and Violence at the Edge of the 21st Century* (New York: Bantam Books, 1990).

For youth and their concerns, see Michael Moffatt, *Coming of Age in New Jersey: College and American Culture* (New Brunswick: Rutgers University Press, 1989) and Francis A. J. Ianni, *The Search for Structure: A Report on American Youth Today* (New York: Free Press, 1989).

Amatai Etzioni eloquently appeals for cooperation in *The Spirit of Community: Rights, Responsibilities, and the Communitarian Agenda* (New York: Crown Publishing Group, 1993).

# References

Abbott, A. (1988). *The System of Professions: An Essay on the Division of Expert Labor*. Chicago: University of Chicago Press.

Abramson, E. (1987). Projections 2000. *Occupational Outlook Quarterly, 31*(3), 2–36.

Ackerman, B. A. (1980). *Social Justice in the Liberal State*. New Haven, CT: Yale University Press.

Adams, H. (1931). *The Education of Henry Adams*. New York: Modern Library.

Adas, M. (1989). *Machines as the Measure of Men: Science, Technology, and Ideologies of Western Dominance*. Ithaca, NY: Cornell University Press.

Allen, D. W. (1992). *Schools for a New Century: A Conservative Approach to Radical School Reform*. New York: Praeger.

Allport, G. W. (1958). *The Nature of Prejudice* (abridged ed.). Garden City, NY: Doubleday Anchor.

American Saw & Mfg. Company. (1990). *Our Corporate Principles*. East Longmeadow, MA: Author.

Arrow, K. J. (1974, November 2). Taxation and Democratic Values. *New Republic*, pp. 23–25.

Arrow, K. J. (1963). *Social Choice and Individual Values* (2nd ed.). New Haven, CT: Yale University Press.

Arrow, K. J. (1962). Economic Welfare and the Allocation of Resources for Invention. In *The Rate and Direction of Inventive Activity: Economic and Social Factors* (pp. 609–625). Princeton, NJ: Princeton University Press.

Barnes, H. (1989). Structuring Knowledge for Beginning Teaching. In M. C. Reynolds (Ed.), *Knowledge Base for the Beginning Teacher* (pp. 13–22). New York: Pergamon Press.

Bauman, Z. (1992). Life-world and Expertise: Social Production of Dependency. In N. Stehr & R. V. Ericson (Eds.), *The Culture and Power of Knowledge: Inquiries into Contemporary Societies* (pp. 81–106). Berlin: Walter de Gruyter.

Bell, D. (1987). The World and the United States in 2013. *Dædalus, 116*(3), 1–31.

Bell, D. (1973). *The Coming of Post-Industrial Society: A Venture in Social Forecasting*. New York: Basic Books.

Bell, D. (Ed.). (1968). *Toward the Year 2000: Work in Progress*. Boston: Houghton Mifflin.

Bellah, R. N., Madsen, R., Sullivan, W. M., Swidler, A., & Tipton, S. M. (1991). *The Good Society*. New York: Knopf.

Bellah, R. N., Sullivan, W. M., Swidler, A., & Tipton, S. M. (1985). *Habits of the Heart: Individualism and Commitment in American Life*. New York: Harper & Row.

Beniger, J. R. (1986). *The Control Revolution: Technological and Economic Origins of the Information Society*. Cambridge: Harvard University Press.

Benjamin, S. (1989). An Ideascape for Education: What Futurists Recommend. *Educational Leadership*, 47(1), 8–14.

Berger, P., Berger, B., & Kellner, H. (1973). *The Homeless Mind: Modernization and Consciousness*. New York: Random House.

Berliner, D. C. (1992). Educational Reform in an Era of Disinformation. Paper presented at the meeting of the American Association of Colleges for Teacher Education, San Antonio.

Bijker, W. E., & Law, J. (1992). General Introduction. In W. E. Bijker & J. Law (Eds.), *Shaping Technology/Building Society: Studies in Sociotechnical Change* (pp. 1–14). Cambridge: MIT Press.

Blauner, B. (1989). *Black Lives, White Lives: Three Decades of Race Relations in America*. Berkeley: University of California Press.

Bloom, B. S. (Ed.). (1985). *Developing Talent in Young People*. New York: Ballantine Books.

Blumberg, A., & Blumberg, P. (1985). *The School Superintendent: Living with Conflict*. New York: Teachers College Press.

Blumberg, A., & Greenfield, W. (1986). *The Effective Principal: Perspectives on School Leadership* (2nd ed.). Boston: Allyn and Bacon.

Bolman, L. G., & Deal, T. E. (1991). *Reframing Organizations: Artistry, Choice, and Leadership*. San Francisco: Jossey-Bass.

Bourque, S. C., & Warren, K. B. (1987). Technology, Gender, and Development. *Dædalus*, 116(4), 173–197.

Bowers, C. A. (1988). *The Cultural Dimensions of Educational Computing: Understanding the Non-Neutrality of Technology*. New York: Teachers College Press.

Bowles, S., & Gintis, H. (1976). *Schooling in Capitalist America: Educational Reform and the Contradictions of Economic Life*. New York: Basic Books.

Boyer, E. L. (1983). *High School: A Report on Secondary Education in America*. New York: Harper & Row.

Brand, S. (1988). *The Media Lab: Inventing the Future at MIT*. New York: Viking Penguin.

Bratiotis, D. (1982). *Implications of Teacher Coping Strategies for Staff Development in Urban Middle Schools*. Unpublished doctoral dissertation, University of Massachusetts at Amherst.

Bronfenbrenner, U. (1979). *The Ecology of Human Development: Experiments by Nature and Design*. Cambridge: Harvard University Press.

Brown, L. M. (1990). When Is a Moral Problem Not a Moral Problem? Morality, Identity, and Female Adolescents. In C. Gilligan, N. P. Lyons, & T. J. Hanmer (Eds.), *Making Connections: The Relational Worlds of Adolescent Girls at Emma Willard School* (pp. 88–109). Cambridge: Harvard University Press.

Bruder, I. (1990, January). Visions of the Future. *Electronic Learning*, pp. 24–30.

Bruner, J. S. (1977). *The Process of Education*. Cambridge: Harvard University Press.

Budin, H. R. (1991). Technology and the Teacher's Role. *Computers in the Schools*, 8(1/2/3), 15–26.

Burbules, N. C., & Rice, S. (1991). Dialogue across Differences: Continuing the Conversation. *Harvard Educational Review*, 61(4), 393–416.

Carlson, D. (1987). Teachers as Political Actors: From Reproductive Theory to the Crisis of Schooling. *Harvard Educational Review*, 57(3), 283–307.

Carnegie Council on Adolescent Development. (1989). *Turning Points: Preparing American Youth for the 21st Century*. Washington, DC: Author.

Carnegie Forum on Education and the Economy. (1986). *A Nation Prepared: Teachers for the 21st Century*. New York: Author.

Carnoy, M., & Levin, H. M. (1985). *Schooling and Work in the Democratic State*. Stanford, CA: Stanford University Press.

Carter, K. (1990). Teachers' Knowledge and Learning to Teach. In W. R. Houston (Ed.), *Handbook of Research on Teacher Education* (pp. 291–310). New York: Macmillan.

Castells, M. (1989). *The Informational City: Information Technology, Economic Restructuring, and the Urban-Regional Process*. Oxford, UK: Basil Blackwell.

Chandler, A. D., Jr. (1990). *Scale and Scope: The Dynamics of Industrial Capitalism*. Cambridge: Harvard University Press.

Chandler, A. D., Jr. (1977). *The Visible Hand: The Managerial Revolution in American Business*. Cambridge: Harvard University Press.

Chubb, J. E., & Moe, T. M. (1990). *Politics, Markets and America's Schools*. Washington, DC: Brookings Institution.

Churchill, W. (1991). *Fantasies of the Master Race: Literature, Cinema and the Colonization of American Indians*. Monroe, ME: Common Courage Press.

Clark, K. B. (1965). *Dark Ghetto: Dilemmas of Social Power*. New York: Harper & Row.

Cleveland, H. (1985). *The Knowledge Executive: Leadership in an Information Society*. New York: E. P. Dutton.

Cole, M. (1991). Conclusion. In L. B. Resnick, J. M. Levine, & S. D. Teasley (Eds.), *Perspectives on Socially Shared Cognition* (pp. 398–417). Washington, DC: American Psychological Association.

Coleman, J. S., with others. (1966). *Equality of Educational Opportunity*. Washington, DC: Government Printing Office.

Collins, H. M. (1990). *Artificial Experts: Social Knowledge and Intelligent Machines*. Cambridge: MIT Press.

Commission on the Skills of the American Workforce (1990). *America's Choice: High Skills or Low Wages!* Rochester, NY: National Center on Education and the Economy.

Committee for Economic Development. (1990). *An America That Works: The Life-Cycle Approach to a Competitive Work Force*. New York: Author.

Council on Environmental Quality and Department of State. (1982). *The Global 2000 Report to the President: Entering the Twenty-first Century*. New York: Penguin Books.

Cowan, R. S. (1985). How the Refrigerator Got Its Hum. In D. MacKenzie & J. Wajcman (Eds.), *The Social Shaping of Technology* (pp. 201–218). Milton Keynes, UK: Open University Press.

Cremin, L. A. (1988). *American Education: The Metropolitan Experience, 1876–1980*. New York: Harper & Row.

Cuban, L. (1993). Computers Meet Classroom: Classroom Wins. *Teachers College Record, 95*(2), 185–210.

Cubberley, E. P. (1947). *Public Education in the United States. A Study and Interpretation of American Educational History*. Cambridge: Houghton Mifflin.

Currie, E. (1985). *Confronting Crime: An American Challenge*. New York: Pantheon Books.

Dahl, R. A. (1982). *Dilemmas of Pluralist Democracy: Autonomy vs. Control*. New Haven, CT: Yale University Press.

Dede, C. J. (1990). Futures Research and Strategic Planning in Teacher Education. In W. R. Houston (Ed.), *Handbook of Research on Teacher Education* (pp. 83–97). New York: Macmillan.

Denison, E. (1985). *Trends in American Economic Growth, 1929–1982*. Washington, DC: Brookings Institution.

Dertouzos, M. L., Lester, R. K., & Solow, R. M. (1989). *Made in America: Regaining the Productive Edge*. Cambridge: MIT Press.

Dewey, J. (1956). *The Child and the Curriculum and The School and Society*. Chicago: University of Chicago Press.

Dewey, J. (1929). *The Quest for Certainty: A Study of the Relation of Knowledge and Action*. New York: G. P. Putnam's Sons.

Digest of Education Statistics. (1991). U.S. Department of Education. Washington, DC: Government Printing Office.

Dizard, J. E., & Gadlin, H. (1990). *The Minimal Family*. Amherst: University of Massachusetts Press.

Dollase, R. (1992). *Voices of Beginning Teachers: Visions and Realities*. New York: Teachers College Press.

Donahue, J. D. (1989). *The Privatization Decision: Public Ends, Private Means*. New York: Basic Books.

Dreyfus, H. L., & Dreyfus, S. E., with T. Athanasiou. (1986). *Mind Over Machine: The Power of Human Intuition and Expertise in the Era of the Computer*. New York: Free Press.

Drucker, P. F. (1973). *Management: Tasks, Responsibilities, Practices*. New York: Harper & Row.

Duckworth, E. (1987). *"The Having of Wonderful Ideas" & Other Essays on Teaching and Learning*. New York: Teachers College Press.

Edelman, M. W. (1992). *The Measure of Our Success: A Letter to My Children and Yours*. Boston: Beacon Press.

Edelman, M. W. (1987). *Families in Peril: An Agenda for Social Change*. Cambridge: Harvard University Press.

Edmonds, R. (1982, December). Programs of School Improvement: An Overview. *Educational Leadership*, pp. 4–11.

Edsall, T. B. (1984). *The New Politics of Inequality*. New York: W. W. Norton.

Edsall, T. B., & Edsall, M. D. (1991). *Chain Reaction: The Impact of Race, Rights, and Taxes on American Politics*. New York: W. W. Norton.

Elms, A. C. (1972). *Social Psychology and Social Relevance*. Boston: Little, Brown.

Elster, J. (1989). *Nuts and Bolts for the Social Sciences*. New York: Cambridge University Press.

Epenshade, T. J. (1984). *Investing in Children: New Estimates of Parental Expenditures*. Washington, DC: Urban Institute Press.

Erikson, K. (1990). On Work and Alienation. In K. Erikson & S. P. Vallas (Eds.), *The Nature of Work: Sociological Perspectives* (pp. 19–35). New Haven, CT: Yale University Press.

Evans, S. M. (1989). *Born for Liberty: A History of Women in America*. New York: Free Press.

Fantini, M. D. (1986). *Regaining Excellence in Education*. Columbus, OH: Merrrill Publishing.

Feynman, R. (1967). *The Character of Physical Law*. Cambridge: M.I.T. Press.

Fogel, R. W. (1964). *Railroads and American Economic Growth: Essays in Econometric History*. Baltimore, MD: Johns Hopkins University Press.

*Fortune*. (1990, March 26). 60th Anniversary Edition: Today's Leaders Talk about Tomorrow. *Fortune*

Freire, P. (1968). *Pedagogy of the Oppressed* (M. B. Ramos, Trans.). New York: Seabury Press.

Friedman, B. M. (1989). *Day of Reckoning: The Consequences of American Economic Policy*. New York: Random House.

Friedman, M. (1973, September 23). The Voucher Idea. *New York Times Magazine,* pp. 22–23, 65, 67, 69–72.

Friedmann, J. (1987). *Planning in the Public Domain: From Knowledge to Action.* Princeton, NJ: Princeton University Press.

Fuchs, L. H. (1990). *The American Kaleidoscope: Race, Ethnicity, and the Civic Culture.* Middletown, CT: Wesleyan University Press.

Gardels, N. (1991). Two Concepts of Nationalism: An Interview with Isaiah Berlin. *New York Review of Books, 38*(19), 19–23.

Gardner, H. (1983). *Frames of Mind: The Theory of Multiple Intelligences.* New York: Basic Books.

Gilligan, C. (1982). *In a Different Voice: Psychological Theory and Women's Development.* Cambridge: Harvard University Press.

Giroux, H. A. (1988). *Teachers as Intellectuals: Toward a Critical Pedagogy of Learning.* Granby, MA: Bergin & Garvey Publishers.

Goldberg, E. (1991, November). Teaching Quality: Schools and Business Forge Education Partnership. *BusinessWest,* pp. 4–5.

Goldin, C. (1990). *Understanding the Gender Gap: An Economic History of American Women.* New York: Oxford University Press/National Bureau of Economic Research.

Goodlad, J. I. (1984). *A Place Called School: Prospects for the Future.* New York: McGraw-Hill.

Gould, S. J. (1981). *The Mismeasure of Man.* New York: W. W. Norton.

Hampel, R. L. (1986). *The Last Little Citadel: American High Schools Since 1940.* Boston: Houghton Mifflin.

Handlin, O. (1951). *The Uprooted: The Epic Story of the Great Migrations That Made the American People.* Boston: Little, Brown.

Handlin, O. (Ed.). (1959). *Immigration as a Factor in American History.* Englewood Cliffs, NJ: Prentice-Hall.

Hannerz, U. (1992). *Cultural Complexity: Studies in the Social Organization of Meaning.* New York: Columbia University Press.

Harding, S. (1991). *Whose Science? Whose Knowledge? Thinking from Women's Lives.* Ithaca, NY: Cornell University Press.

Harding, V. (1970). The Afro-American Past and the American Present. In M. Goodman (Ed.), *The Movement Toward a New America: The Beginnings of a Long Revolution* (pp. 127–129). Philadelphia: Pilgrim Press.

Heath, S. B., & McLaughlin, M. W. (Eds.). (1993). *Identity and Inner-City Youth: Beyond Ethnicity and Gender.* New York: Teachers College Press.

Hechinger, F. (1992). *Fateful Choices: Healthy Youth for the 21st Century.* New York: Hill and Wang.

Heck, S. F., & Williams, C. R. (1984). *The Complex Roles of the Teacher: An Ecological Perspective.* New York: Teachers College Press.

Hirschhorn, L. (1984). *Beyond Mechanization: Work and Technology in a Postindustrial Age.* Cambridge: MIT Press.

Hitano, G., & Inagaki, K. (1991). Sharing Cognition through Collective Comprehension Activity. In L. B. Resnick, J. M. Levine, & S. D. Teasley (Eds.), *Perspectives on Socially Shared Cognition* (pp. 331–348). Washington, DC: American Psychological Association.

Hochschild, J. L. (1981). *What's Fair? American Beliefs about Distributive Justice.* Cambridge: Harvard University Press.

Hogan, D. (1982). Education and Class Formation: The Peculiarities of the Americans. In M. Apple (Ed.), *Cultural and Economic Reproduction in Education: Essays on Class, Ideology and the State* (pp. 32–78). Boston: Routledge & Kegan Paul.

Holmes Group. (1986). *Tomorrow's Teachers: A Report of the Holmes Group*. Lansing: Michigan State University.

Holusha, J. (1992, March 4). A Call for Kinder Managers at G. E. *New York Times,* pp. D1, D6.

Hughes, T. P. (1989). *American Genesis: A Century of Invention and Technological Enthusiasm*. New York: Viking Penguin.

Hughes, T. P. (1987). The Evolution of Large Technological Systems. In W. E. Bijker, T. P. Hughes, & T. J. Pinch (Eds.), *The Social Construction of Technological Systems: New Directions in the Sociology and History of Technology* (pp. 51–82). Cambridge: MIT Press.

Huntington, S. P. (1981). *American Politics: The Promise of Disharmony*. Cambridge: Harvard University Press.

Inglehart, R. (1990). *Culture Shift in Advanced Industrial Society*. Princeton, NJ: Princeton University Press.

Inkeles, A. (1983). *Exploring Individual Modernity*. New York: Columbia University Press.

Inkeles, A. (1966). A Note on Social Structure and the Socialization of Competency. *Harvard Educational Review, 36*(3), 265–283.

Institute for Education in Transformation. (1992). *Voices from the Inside: A Report on Schooling from Inside the Classroom*. Claremont, CA: Institute for Education in Transformation, Claremont Graduate School.

Jackson, P. W. (1968). *Life in Classrooms*. New York: Holt, Rinehart and Winston.

Jaynes, G. D., & Williams, R. M., Jr. (Eds.). (1989). *A Common Destiny: Blacks and American Society*. Washington, DC: National Academy Press.

Jencks, C. (1971). Testimony before Select Committee on Equal Educational Opportunity. In *Hearings before the Select Committee on Equal Educational Opportunity of the United States Senate, 92nd Cong., 1st Sess.* (pp. 10971–11018). Washington, DC: Government Printing Office.

Johnson, S. M. (1990). *Teachers at Work: Achieving Success in Our Schools*. New York: Basic Books.

Jones, B. L., & Maloy, R. W. (1993). Schools for an Information Age. *Journal of Curriculum Theorizing, 10*(1), 39–70.

Jones, B. L., & Maloy, R. W. (1988). *Partnerships for Improving Schools*. Westport, CT: Greenwood Press.

Jordon, W. D. (1969). *White Over Black: American Attitudes Toward the Negro, 1550–1812*. Baltimore, MD: Penguin Books.

Jorgenson, D. W., & Fraumeni, B. M. (1989). The Accumulation of Human and Nonhuman Capital, 1948–84. In R. E. Lipsey & H. S. Tice (Eds.), *The Measurement of Saving, Investment, and Wealth* (pp. 227–282). Chicago: University of Chicago Press.

Joyce, B. R., Weil, M., & Wald, R. (1981). A Structure for Pluralism in Teacher Education. In B. R. Joyce, C. C. Brown, & L. Peck (Eds.), *Flexibility in Teaching: An Excursion into the Nature of Teaching and Training* (pp. 119–140). New York: Longman.

Juster, F. T., & Stafford, F. P. (1991). The Allocation of Time: Empirical Findings, Behavioral Models, and Problems of Measurement. *Journal of Economic Literature, 29*(2), 471–522.

Kagan, J. (1989). *Unstable Ideas: Temperament, Cognition, and Self*. Cambridge: Harvard University Press.

Kalantzis, M. et al. (1990). *Cultures of Schooling: Pedagogies for Cultural Difference and Social Access*. London: Falmer Press.

Kamin, L. J. (1974). *The Science and Politics of IQ*. New York: Halstead Press.

Kanter, R. M. (1977). *Men and Women of the Corporation*. New York: Basic Books.

Katz, M. B., Doucet, M. J., & Stern, M. J. (1982). *The Social Organization of Early Industrial Capitalism*. Cambridge: Harvard University Press.

Katznelson, I., & Weir, M. (1985). *Schooling for All: Class, Race, and the Decline of the Democratic Ideal*. New York: Basic Books.

Kegan, R. (1994). *In Over Our Heads: The Mental Demands of Modern Life*. Cambridge: Harvard University Press.

Kegan, R. (1982). *The Evolving Self: Problem and Process in Human Development*. Cambridge: Harvard University Press.

Kevles, D. J. (1978). *The Physicists: The History of a Scientific Community in Modern America*. New York: Knopf.

Kohlberg, L., & Gilligan, C. (1972). The Adolescent as a Philosopher: The Discovery of the Self in a Postconventional World. In J. Kagan & R. Coles (Eds.), *Twelve to Sixteen: Early Adolescence* (pp. 144–179). New York: W. W. Norton.

Kohn, M. L. (1990). Unresolved Issues in the Relationship between Work and Personality. In K. Erikson & S. P. Vallas (Eds.), *The Nature of Work: Sociological Perspectives* (pp. 36–68). New Haven, CT: Yale University Press.

Kolata, G. (1992, October 13). Bacteria Are Found to Thrive on a Rich Social Life. *New York Times*, pp. C1, C9.

Kolb, D. (1986). *The Critique of Pure Modernity: Hegel, Heidegger and After*. Chicago: University of Chicago Press.

Kuhn, T. S. (1970a). *The Structure of Scientific Revolutions* (2nd ed.). Chicago: University of Chicago Press.

Kuhn, T. S. (1970b). Logic of Discovery or Psychology of Research? In I. Lakatos & A. Musgrave (Eds.), *Criticism and the Growth of Knowledge* (pp. 1–23). New York: Cambridge University Press.

Labaree, D. F. (1992). Power, Knowledge, and the Rationalization of Teaching: A Genealogy of the Movement to Professionalize Teaching. *Harvard Educational Review*, 62(2), 123–154.

Landow, G. P. (1992). *Hypertext: The Convergence of Contemporary Critical Theory and Technology*. Baltimore, MD: Johns Hopkins University Press.

Lasswell, H. D. (1958). *Politics: Who Gets What, When, How*. Cleveland, OH: World Publishing Co.

Latour, B. (1992). Where Are the Missing Masses? The Sociology of a Few Mundane Artifacts. In W. E. Bijker & J. Law (Eds.), *Shaping Technology/Building Society: Studies in Sociotechnical Change* (pp. 225–258). Cambridge: MIT Press.

Latour, B. (1987). *Science in Action: How to Follow Scientists and Engineers through Society*. Cambridge: Harvard University Press.

Lave, J. (1991). Situating Learning in Communities of Practice. In L. B. Resnick, J. M. Levine, & S. D. Teasley (Eds.), *Perspectives on Socially Shared Cognition* (pp. 63–82). Washington, DC: American Psychological Association.

Law, J., & Bijker, W. E. (1992). Postscript: Technology, Stability, and Social Theory. In W. E. Bijker & J. Law (Eds.), *Shaping Technology/Building Society: Studies in Sociotechnical Change* (pp. 290–308). Cambridge: MIT Press.

Lazerson, M. (1971). *Origins of the Urban School: Public Education in Massachusetts, 1870–1915*. Cambridge: Harvard University Press.

Lazerson, M., McLaughlin, J. B., McPherson, B., & Bailey, S. K. (1986). *An Education of Value: The Purposes and Practices of Schools*. New York: Cambridge University Press.

Leacock, E. B. (1969). *Teaching and Learning in City Schools*. New York: Basic Books.

Levine, D. I., & Tyson, L. D. (1990). Participation, Productivity, and the Firm's Environment. In A. S. Blinder (Ed.), *Paying for Productivity: A Look at the Evidence* (pp. 183–237). Washington, DC: Brookings Institution.

Levy, F. (1987). *Dollars and Dreams: The Changing American Income Distribution.* New York: W. W. Norton.

Lewis, A., & the *New York Times.* (1965). *Portrait of a Decade: The Second American Revolution.* New York: Bantam Books.

Lewontin, R. C., Rose, S., & Kamin, L. J. (1984). *Not in Our Genes.* New York: Pantheon Books.

Liebenstein, H. (1987). *Inside the Firm: The Inefficiencies of Hierarchy.* Cambridge: Harvard University Press.

Lieberman, A. (Ed.). (1994). *The Work of Restructuring Schools: Building from the Ground Up.* New York: Teachers College Press.

Lieberman, A. (Ed.). (1988). *Building a Professional Culture in Schools.* New York: Teachers College Press.

Lieberman, A., & Miller, A. (1992). *Teachers, Their World, and Their Work: Implications for School Improvement.* New York: Teachers College Press.

Lightfoot, S. L. (1983). *The Good High School: Portraits of Character and Culture.* New York: Basic Books.

Lindblom, C. E. (1990). *Inquiry and Change: The Troubled Attempt to Understand and Shape Society.* New Haven, CT: Yale University Press and Russell Sage Foundation.

Lindblom, C. E. (1977). *Politics and Markets: The World's Political-Economic Systems.* New York: Basic Books.

Lindblom, C. E., & Cohen, D. K. (1979). *Usable Knowledge: Social Science and Social Problem Solving.* New Haven, CT: Yale University Press.

Lipsky, M. (1980). *Street-Level Bureaucracy: Dilemmas of the Individual in Public Service.* New York: Basic Books.

Lortie, D. C. (1975). *Schoolteacher: A Sociological Study.* Chicago: University of Chicago Press.

Louie, S., & Rubeck, R. F. (1989). Hypertext Publishing and the Revitalization of Knowledge. *Academic Computing, 3*(9), 20–23, 30–31.

Lynn, L. E., Jr. (1981). *Managing the Public's Business: The Job of the Government Executive.* New York: Basic Books.

Macaulay, D. (1988). *The Way Things Work.* Boston: Houghton Mifflin.

Machlup, F. (1962). *The Production and Distribution of Knowledge in the United States.* Princeton, NJ: Princeton University Press.

MacLeod, J. (1987). *Ain't No Makin' It: Leveled Aspirations in a Low-Income Neighborhood.* Boulder, CO: Westview Press.

March, J. G. (1988). *Decisions and Organizations.* Oxford, UK: Basil Blackwell.

March, J. G., & Olsen, J. P. (1989). *Rediscovering Institutions: The Organizational Basis of Politics.* New York: Free Press.

Marvin, C. (1988). *When Old Technologies Were New: Thinking About Electric Communication in the Late Nineteenth Century.* New York: Oxford University Press.

Maryland Student Service Alliance. (1993). *High School Service-Learning Guide.* Baltimore, MD: Maryland State Department of Education.

Massachusetts Department of Education. (1994). *The Massachusetts Common Core of Learning.* Malden, MA: Author.

McLaughlin, M. W., & Marsh, D. D. (1978). Staff Development and School Change. *Teachers College Record, 80*(1), 69–94.

McNeil, L. M. (1986). *Contradictions of Control: School Structure and School Knowledge.* New York: Routledge & Kegan Paul.

Meadows, D. H., Meadows, D. L., Randers, J., & Behrens, W. W., III. (1972). *The Limits to Growth: A Report for the Club of Rome's Project on the Predicament of Mankind* (2nd rev. ed.). New York: New American Library.

Mecca, A. M., Smelser, N. J., & Vasconcellos, J. (Eds.). (1989). *The Social Importance of Self-Esteem*. Berkeley & Los Angeles: University of California Press.

Meier, K. J., Stewart, J., Jr., & England, R. E. (1989). *Race, Class, and Education: The Politics of Second-Generation Discrimination*. Madison: University of Wisconsin Press.

Merton, R. K. (1973a). The Normative Structure of Science. In N. W. Storer (Ed.), *The Sociology of Science: Theoretical and Empirical Investigations* (pp. 267–278). Chicago: University of Chicago Press.

Merton, R. K. (1973b). The Perspectives of Insiders and Outsiders. In N. W. Storer (Ed.), *The Sociology of Science: Theoretical and Empirical Investigations* (pp. 99–136). Chicago: University of Chicago Press.

Mishel, L., & Teixeira, R. A. (1990). *The Myth of the Coming Labor Shortage: Jobs, Skills, and Incomes of America's Workforce 2000*. Washington, DC: Economic Policy Institute.

Mitroff, I. I. (1983). Beyond Experimentation: New Methods for a New Age. In E. Seidman (Ed.), *Handbook of Social Intervention* (pp. 163–177). Beverly Hills, CA: Sage Publications.

Mosteller, F., & Moynihan, D. P. (Eds.). (1972). *On Equality of Educational Opportunity*. New York: Random House.

Myrdal, G. (1944). *An American Dilemma: The Negro Problem and Modern Democracy*. New York: Harper & Row.

Naisbitt, J., & Aburdene, P. (1989). *Megatrends 2000: Ten New Directions for the 1990's*. New York: William Morrow.

National Commission on Excellence in Education. (1983). *A Nation at Risk: The Imperative of Educational Reform*. Washington, DC: Government Printing Office.

National Council of Teachers of Mathematics. (1989). *Curriculum and Evaluation Standards for School Mathematics*. Reston, VA: National Council of Teachers of Mathematics.

Nieto, S. (1992). *Affirming Diversity: The Sociopolitical Context of Multicultural Education*. New York: Longman.

North, D. C. (1990). *Institutions, Institutional Change and Economic Performance*. New York: Cambridge University Press.

Oakes, J. (1985). *Keeping Track: How Schools Structure Inequality*. New Haven, CT: Yale University Press.

Obey, D. R. (1986). A Public Economics of Growth, Equity, and Opportunity. In D. Obey & P. Sarbanes (Eds.), *The Changing American Economy* (pp. 8–15). New York: Basil Blackwell.

Olson, M., Jr. (1968). *The Logic of Collective Behavior: Public Goods and the Theory of Groups*. New York: Schocken Books.

Orenstein, P., with American Association of University Women. (1994). *School Girls: Young Women, Self-Esteem, and the Confidence Gap*. New York: Doubleday.

Orfield, G., with Schley, S., Glass, D., & Reardon, S. (1993). *The Growth of Segregation in American Schools: Changing Patterns of Separation and Poverty Since 1968*. Washington, DC: National School Boards Association.

Organization for Economic Cooperation and Development. (1981). *Information Activities, Electronics and Telecommunications Activities, Impact on Employment, Growth, and Trade*. Paris: Author.

Pacey, A. (1983). *The Culture of Technology*. Cambridge: MIT Press.

Page, B. I. (1983). *Who Gets What From Government*. Berkeley and Los Angeles, CA: University of California Press.

Patterson, J. L., Purkey, S. C., & Parker, J. V. (1986). *Productive School Systems for a Nonrational World*. Alexandria, VA: Association for Supervision and

Curriculum Development.

Payne, C. M. (1984). *Getting What We Ask For: The Ambiguity of Success and Failure in Urban Education*. Westport, CT: Greenwood Press.

Pear, R. (1992, December 4). New Look at the U. S. in 2050: Bigger, Older and Less White. *New York Times,* pp. A1, D18.

Peret-Clermont, A.-N., Peret, J.-F., & Bell, N. (1991). The Social Construction of Meaning and Cognitive Activity in Elementary School Children. In L. B. Resnick, J. M. Levine, & S. D. Teasley (Eds.), *Perspectives on Socially Shared Cognition* (pp. 41–62). Washington, DC: American Psychological Association.

Peterson, B. (1994, July). Teaching for Social Justice: One Teacher's Journey. *Rethinking Schools,* pp. 30–33, 35–38.

Peterson, P. E. (1982). Federalism, Economic Development, Redistribution. In J. D. Greenstone (Ed.), *Public Values & Private Power in American Politics* (pp. 246–275). Chicago: University of Chicago Press.

Pettigrew, T. (1971). *Racially Separate or Together?* New York: McGraw-Hill.

Piaget, J. (1980). *Experiments in Contradiction* (D. Coltman, Trans.). Chicago: University of Chicago Press.

Pollack, A., Broad, W. J., Markoff, J., Feder, B. J., Wald, M. L., & Holusha, J. (1991, January 1). Transforming the Decade: 10 Critical Technologies. *New York Times,* pp. 35, 38–39.

Popper, K. R. (1962). *Conjectures and Refutations: The Growth of Scientific Knowledge*. New York: Basic Books.

Poster, M. (1990). *The Mode of Information: Poststructuralism and Social Context*. Chicago: University of Chicago Press.

Powell, A. G., Farrar, E., & Cohen, D. K. (1985). *The Shopping Mall High School: Winners and Losers in the Educational Marketplace*. Boston: Houghton Mifflin.

Prude, J. (1983). *The Coming of Industrial Order: Town and Factory Life in Rural Massachusetts, 1810–1860*. New York: Cambridge University Press.

Quinn, R. E., & Hall, R. H. (1983). Environments, Organizations, and Policymakers: Toward an Integrative Framework. In R. H. Hall & R. E. Quinn (Eds.), *Organizational Theory and Public Policy* (pp. 281–298). Beverly Hills, CA: Sage Publications.

Rasell, M. E., & Mishel, L. (1990). *Shortchanging Education: How U. S. Spending on Grades K–12 Lags Behind Other Industrial Nations*. Washington, DC: Economic Policy Institute.

Ravitch, D., & Finn, C. E., Jr. (1987). *What Do Our 17-Year-Olds Know? A Report on the First National Assessment of History and Literature*. New York: Harper & Row.

Rawls, J. (1993). *Political Liberalism*. New York: Columbia University Press.

Rawls, J. (1971). *A Theory of Justice*. Cambridge: Harvard University Press.

Reich, M. (1981). *Racial Inequality: A Political Economic Analysis*. Princeton, NJ: Princeton University Press.

Reich, R. B. (1991, January 20). Secession of the Successful. *New York Times Magazine,* pp. 16–17, 42–45.

Reich, R. B. (1990). *The Work of Nations: Preparing Ourselves for 21st Century Capitalism*. New York: Knopf.

Reich, R. B. (1988). *Education and the Next Economy*. Washington, DC: National Education Association, Professional and Organizational Development/Research Division.

Resnick, L. B. (1987). Learning In School and Out. *Educational Researcher, 16*(9), 13–20.

Resnick, L. B., & Klopfer, L. E. (1989). Toward the Thinking Curriculum: An Overview. In L. B. Resnick & L. E. Klopfer (Eds.), *Toward the Thinking*

*Curriculum: Current Cognitive Research* (pp. 1–18). Alexandria, VA: Association for Supervision and Curriculum Development.

Rice, R. E. (1990, Winter/Spring). Rethinking What It Means To Be a Scholar. *Teaching Excellence: Toward the Best in the Academy*, pp. 1–2.

Rist, R. C. (1978). *The Invisible Children—School Integration in American Society*. Cambridge: Harvard University Press.

Rothschild, J., & Whitt, J. A. (1986). *The Cooperative Workplace: Potentials and Dilemmas of Organizational Democracy and Participation*. New York: Cambridge University Press.

Rubin, L. B. (1976). *Worlds of Pain: Life in the Working-Class Family*. New York: Basic Books.

Rubin, M. R., & Huber, M. T. (1986). *The Knowledge Industry in the United States: 1960–1980*. Princeton, NJ: Princeton University Press.

Russett, C. E. (1989). *Sexual Science: The Victorian Construction of Womanhood*. Cambridge: Harvard University Press.

Sarason, S. B. (1983). *Schooling in America: Scapegoat and Salvation*. New York: Free Press.

Sarason, S. B. (1982). *The Culture of the School and the Problem of Change* (2nd ed.). Boston: Allyn and Bacon.

Schell, J. (1982). *The Fate of the Earth*. New York: Avon Books.

Schlesinger, A. M., Jr. (1977). The Evolution of the National Government as an Instrument for Attaining Social Rights. In D. C. Warner (Ed.), *Toward New Human Rights: The Social Policies of the Kennedy and Johnson Administration* (pp. 13–31). Austin, TX: Lyndon B. Johnson School of Public Affairs.

Schutz, A. (1971). *Collected Papers II: Studies in Social Theory*. The Hague, Netherlands: Martinus Nijhoff.

Schutz, A. (1962). *Collected Papers I: The Problem of Social Reality*. The Hague, Netherlands: Martinus Nijhoff.

Schutz, A., & Luckmann, T. (1973). *The Structures of the Life-World*. Evanston, IL: Northwestern University Press.

Schwarz, J. E. (1983). *America's Hidden Success: A Reassessment of Twenty Years of Public Policy*. New York: W. W. Norton.

Science Applications International Corporation. (1984). *Principles and Practices of SAIC*. Nashua, NH: Author.

Scribner, H. B., & Stevens, L. B. (1975). *Make Your Schools Work: Practical, Imaginative, and Cost-free Plans to Turn Public Education Around*. New York: Simon & Schuster.

Sen, A. (1990, December 29). More than 100 Million Women Are Missing. *New York Review*, pp. 61–66.

Shank, R. C. (1984). *The Cognitive Computer: On Language, Learning, and Artificial Intelligence*. Reading, MA: Addison-Wesley.

Shulman, L. S. (1987). Knowledge and Teaching: Foundations of the New Reform. *Harvard Educational Review*, 57(1), 1–22.

Silberman, C. E. (1970). *Crisis in the Classroom*. New York: Random House.

Simmons, J., & Mares, W. (1985). *Working Together: Employee Participation in Action*. New York: New York University Press.

Simon, H. A. (1981). *The Sciences of the Artificial* (2nd ed.). Cambridge: MIT Press.

Sims, R. (1982). *Shadow and Substance: Afro-American Experience in Contemporary Children's Fiction*. Urbana, IL: National Council of Teachers of English.

Slavin, R. E. (1985). Cooperative Learning: Applying Contact Theory in Desegregated Schools. *Journal of Social Issues*, 41(3), 45–62.

Sleeter, C. (1993). How White Teachers Construct Racism. In C. McCarthy & W. Crichlow (Eds.), *Race, Identity, Representation, and Education* (pp. 157–171).

New York: Routledge.

Solow, R. M. (1990). *The Labor Market as a Social Institution*. Cambridge, MA: Basil Blackwell.

Sternberg, R. J. (1988). *The Triarchic Mind: A New Theory of Human Intelligence*. New York: Penguin Books.

Toffler, A. (1970). *Future Shock*. New York: Bantam Books.

Touraine, A. (1992). A Critical View of Modernity. In N. Stehr & R. V. Ericson (Eds.), *The Culture and Power of Knowledge: Inquiries into Contemporary Societies* (pp. 29–38). Berlin: Walter de Gruyter.

Tyack, D. (1974). *The One Best System: A History of American Urban Education*. Cambridge: Harvard University Press.

Tyack, D., & Hansot, E. (1982). *Managers of Virtue: Public School Leadership in America, 1820–1980*. New York: Basic Books.

Tyler, R. W. (1949). *Basic Principles of Curriculum and Instruction*. Chicago: University of Chicago Press.

Uchitelle, L. (1994, December 5). "Workers Seek Executive Role, Study Says." *New York Times*, pp. D1, D10.

U.S. Congress, Committee of Ways and Means, 103rd Cong., 1st Sess. (1993). *1993 Green Book*. Washington, DC: Government Printing Office.

U.S. Department of Education. (annually). *Digest of Education Statistics*. Washington, DC: Government Printing Office.

U.S. Department of Education. (1991). *America 2000: An Education Strategy*. Washington, DC: Department of Education.

U.S. Department of Health, Education, and Welfare. (1973). *Work in America*. Cambridge: MIT Press.

U.S. Department of Health, Education, and Welfare. (1969). *Toward a Social Report*. Washington, DC: Government Printing Office.

U.S. Department of Labor, Bureau of Labor Statistics. (1992). *Occupational Outlook Handbook, 1992–93 Edition*. Washington, DC: Government Printing Office.

U.S. Department of Labor, Bureau of Labor Statistics. (1991). Outlook 1990–2005. *Occupational Outlook Quarterly, 35*(3).

*Update on State Legislation*. (1979, August 7). An Initiative For Family Choice in Education. *Update on State Legislation,* pp. 3–16.

Van Dijlk, T. A. (1987). *Communicating Racism: Ethnic Prejudice in Thought and Talk*. Beverly Hills, CA: Sage Publications.

Wallace, A.F.C. (1987). *St. Clair: A Nineteenth-Century Local Town's Experience with a Disaster-Prone Industry*. New York: Knopf.

Wallace, A.F.C. (1978). *Rockdale: The Growth of an American Village in the Early Industrial Revolution*. New York: Knopf.

Walzer, M. (1983). *Spheres of Justice: A Defense of Pluralism and Equality*. New York: Basic Books.

Weick, K. E. (1985). Sources of Order in Underorganized Systems: Themes in Recent Organizational Theory. In Y. S. Lincoln (Ed.), *Organizational Theory and Inquiry: The Paradigm Revolution* (pp. 106–136). Beverly Hills, CA: Sage Publications.

Weick, K. E. (1979). *The Social Psychology of Organizing* (2nd ed.). Reading, MA: Addison-Wesley.

Wertsch, J. V. (1991). A Sociocultural Approach to Socially Shared Cognition. In L. B. Resnick, J. M. Levine, & S. D. Teasley (Eds.), *Perspectives on Socially Shared Cognition* (pp. 85–100). Washington, DC: American Psychological Association.

Wiebe, R. H. (1975). *The Segmented Society: An Introduction to the Meaning of America*. New York: Oxford University Press.

Williams, R. M. (1964). *Strangers Next Door: Ethnic Relations in American Communities*. Englewood Cliffs, NJ: Prentice-Hall.

Wilson, W. J. (1987). *The Truly Disadvantaged: The Inner City, the Underclass, and Public Policy*. Chicago: University of Chicago Press.

Wilson, W. J. (1980). *The Declining Significance of Race* (2nd ed.). Chicago: University of Chicago Press.

Witte, J. F. (1980). *Democracy, Authority, and Alienation in Work: Workers' Participation in an American Corporation*. Chicago: University of Chicago Press.

Woodbury, R. L. (1993, March 23). Why Not Run a Business Like a Good University? *Christian Science Monitor*, Op. ed. page.

Young, M. I. (1990). *Justice and the Politics of Difference*. Princeton, NJ: Princeton University Press.

Zuboff, S. (1988). *In the Age of the Smart Machine: The Future of Work and Power*. New York: Basic Books.

# Index

## ABOUT THE AUTHORS

**Byrd L. Jones** is Professor of Education at the University of Massachusetts, Amherst. He teaches urban education, economics of education, staff development, and the impact of computers on schools and society as well as multicultural issues. He is currently coeditor of the journal *Equity and Excellence in Education* and codirector of the Eastern Regional Information Center on Community Service Learning in K–12 Schools. He is coauthor with Robert Maloy of *Partnerships for Improving Schools* (Greenwood, 1988).

**Robert W. Maloy** is a Lecturer in the School of Education at the University of Massachusetts, Amherst. He coordinates History and Social Studies Teacher Education and codirects the TEAMS Project, a tutoring program serving culturally diverse students in local elementary and secondary schools. He is coauthor with Sharon Edwards of *Kids Have All the Write Stuff: Inspiring Your Children to Put Pencil to Paper* (1992).

ISBN 0-275-95395-5

90000>

EAN

HARDCOVER BAR CODE